DIGITAL MARKETING

From Fundamentals to Future

SWAMINATHAN T. N.
Great Lakes Institute of Management, Chennai

KARTHIK KUMAR
Rage Communications, Chennai

CENGAGE

Australia • Brazil • India • Mexico • Singapore • United Kingdom • United States

CENGAGE

Digital Marketing: From Fundamentals to Future

Swaminathan T. N.
Karthik Kumar

Cover Image: ©Thinkstock

ISBN-13: 978-93-5350-153-2
ISBN-10: 93-5350-153-9

Cengage Learning India Private Limited
T-303, 3rd Floor
DAV Complex, Plot 3
Mayur Vihar Phase 1
Delhi 110091

Cengage Learning is a leading provider of customized learning solutions with office locations around the globe, including Australia, Brazil, India, Mexico, Singapore, United Kingdom, and United States. Locate your local office at:
www.cengage.com/global

Cengage Learning products are represented in Canada by Nelson Education, Ltd.

For product information, visit **www.cengage.co.in**

Printed by:
Rajiv Book Binding House
D-1518, DSIIDC Industrial Complex,
Narela, New Delhi 110040

Printed in India
Print Number: 05 Print Year: 2026

FOREWORD

As a digital immigrant and having been involved in marketing of products and services for well over five decades, the impact of convergence of technologies in our day-to-day lives continues to amaze me. In the 60s and 70s, we were ingrained in the concept of "Making available the right product at the right place at the right time". That was marketing then. Today, the classical marketing definition of "Time and Place Utilities" has been flipped by digital technologies and digital marketing.

The fitting opening of this book – *"When we wake up in the morning, chances are high that the first thing that most of us do would perhaps be checking our smartphones for overnight unread notifications. For the millennials, this could precede even brushing teeth or having a hot beverage"* strikes an instant chord with the reader.

Having known the author Dr. T. N. Swaminathan (aka Swami) for almost four decades now and having worked with him closely in the past, I see that his forty years of experience and expertise have been brought out in the form of an engrossing chronicle through this book. Due to his vast experience in both corporate and academics, Swami has been able to strike the right balance between sharing the domain expertise and providing an enhanced learning experience to the readers. The various concepts in digital marketing have been well laid out and sequenced for both students and digital marketing professionals in their early career phase.

Having seen it all in his thirty plus years of corporate experience as a marketer, Swami has been able to join the dots seamlessly—the book takes you through the evolution of marketing starting from the era of radios advertisements to the print ads, the dominance of TV ads and then the advent of Internet leading to the rise of digital technologies. Swami has tied Marketing 4.0 with evolution of Digital Transformation 2.0 and has comprehensively explained on how to provide an Integrated Customer Experience using this amalgamation, while stressing on the importance of profitability in any digital marketing objective.

The best part about the book to me is how Swami explains that any new technology/medium should augment the existing ones and no one technology can overthrow all the others. This is completely true. Despite being century old marketing medium, radio is still relevant in marketing; only the technology in it has changed. Such thoughts can come only from seasoned marketers who have witnessed the myriad changes in marketing over the decades. Swami has brought in his academic expertise by connecting many of the classical marketing concepts such as AIDA, IMC leading a new 3 D model, as a strategic tool for strategy development, planning and implementation that he has proposed in Chapter 3 of this book. The book concludes with an exposure to IoT and Industry 4.0 that exemplify digital transformation.

The book is aptly titled as "Digital Marketing – From Fundamentals to Future" and I am sure both the student community and professionals will gain significant insights and I strongly recommend this book as a companion to them.

R. Gopalakrishnan

CEO, The Mindworks,

(Former Executive Director

Tata Sons | Vice-Chairman Hindustan Lever)

Mumbai

FOREWORD

The question of whether or not to use digital marketing for your business has been put to rest. Digital marketing is like common sense that is needed to survive and has indeed become a "Strategic Advantage". You need to "Digitate", only now it is called "Digital Sense". Most marketers live in an illusion that investing in latest digital tools and technologies will help them succeed. That is far from reality. Businesses today are built over a digital minefield and digital marketers cannot afford a careless step.

With so much happening in the digital space presently, where businesses are focusing on reality technologies such as Artificial Intelligence, Machine Learning, Block Chain and so on, understanding the dynamics and the implication of each of these disruptive technologies is of great importance. Profound knowledge of Convergence of Technologies is mandatory in understanding the basics of digital marketing starting from web, social platforms, online campaigns, content optimization and most importantly, gaining insights from the metrics. This book does a terrific job of helping you attain these insights for both students and practitioners and leverage the same for "Competitive Advantage".

Having known the author Dr. T. N. Swaminathan for over a decade and a half now and having worked with him closely on the digital marketing initiatives in our own School, I am positive that his years of experience and expertise have been put into best use in bringing out an engaging narrative on digital marketing, that can be used by both aspiring and current digital marketers alike. Having seen it all in his forty years of experience as a marketer, Professor Swami has seamlessly related the evolution of traditional marketing, advent and rise of digital technologies starting from web to digital transformation 2.0 and why organizations are tying their digital marketing objectives to their profitability. The book concludes with an exposure to IoT and Industry 4.0 that exemplify digital transformation.

There are two strong reasons why I would recommend this book when there are several digital marketing books out there already. 1) The success of any digital effort is based on the RoI. If your digital marketing efforts are not translating into revenue, you might as well not do it. This book gives you a detailed perspective on that. It is not about doing, it is how well you measure your outcomes and calibrate. 2) Digital is a vast area and it works best when a marketer focuses on each platform individually and not in the aggregate. This book has a separate chapter dedicated to that with enough case studies and examples. Aptly the subtitle of the book is "From Fundamentals to Future". This alone is a reason why this is not just yet another book in digital marketing.

This book is a must have for leaders like you and me, people who believe in embracing digital technology that puts their customers and people first and weave every strategy around their supreme experience. Marketing is all about digital storytelling today and being the best at that. So, learn from this book to build a beautiful digital experience for your customers. If you want to go ahead, it is the only way to go!

I, most strongly and enthusiastically, recommend this book for your competitive strategic advantage.

Dr. Bala V. Balachandran

J L Kellogg Distinguished Professor (Emeritus in service) of Accounting & Information Management, Northwestern University, USA.

Founder, Dean & Chairman - Great Lakes Institute of Management, India.

Chancellor - Great Lakes International University, Sri City, Andhra Pradesh, India.

PREFACE

In writing this book, we were straddling and walking a tight rope considering both the authors graduated in 70s when digital marketing was not even a dream. Indeed there were hardly any computers in India in those years. That did not mean that marketing did not exist—marketing jobs were considered as dream jobs in India in 70s and 80s, thanks mainly to ITC, Unilever and a slew of other MNCs. Now marketing, on the whole, has undergone a sea change with every industry metamorphosing and offering various opportunities. As can be imagined, when digital marketing took roots, there were no digital marketing experts. The authors, perforce, had to learn the tools-of-the-trade as it were, sometimes even inventing processes and practices and thus have the hands-on experience and expertise in transcending traditional and digital marketing.

The book itself was triggered by two events, one was reviewing electives that is regularly done in the institution where one of us teaches and then a meeting with one of the acquisition editors of Cengage. While reviewing electives, based on inputs from recruiters, it was decided that there was a need to have an elective on digital marketing and the author developed a course outline for the same and offered the elective. Both the occurrences suggested a need for such a book in the Indian context not withstanding a host of other books available internationally.

Given the popularity and digital activities particularly with millennials, there is a school of thought that considers the end of traditional media or traditional brick and mortar models being replaced by digital marketing and brick and click model, respectively. However, the reality is that in India 91 percent is still traditional retailing and 84 percent is non-digital advertising. Also, recorded history from Ca 1400 AD indicates none of the technological advancements superseded advancement prior to them; on the contrary, they co-existed. The millennials seem to be overwhelmed with the term 'Digital Marketing'. Moreover, the principles of attracting consumers and establishing strong brands have not changed with the advent of digital technologies and media. What these have contributed to are a wider diversity of means by which brands can engage with consumers. Therefore, it is important not to be carried away by the buzz of going digital, but as an aspiring marketer, one needs to have a strong knowledge about the fundamentals before jumping into digital techniques. Thus, this book has been structured on these lines with 11 chapters.

The first two chapters provide the introduction and evolution of digital world with convergence of technologies, outline the digital consumers including natives and immigrants. Chapters 3 and 4 outline the theoretical framework of strategies highlighting some key factors differentiating digital marketing from a traditional one, pursuing social media and digital media as independent of each other and explaining when and how they can work inclusively and when otherwise besides outlining SMM process and management. Chapters 5 and 6 detail website planning, SEO, SERP and the analytics involved. The next three chapters—Chapters 7, 8 and 9 focus on digital operations in digital engagement, ORM, content marketing and B2B. The last two chapters focus on future viz. Marketing 4.0 and Industry 4.0—from traditional to digital as well as the impact of disruptive technologies in shaping future and career opportunities in marketing since marketing continues to be a popular career choice even today. Every chapter has two cases in both Indian and International contexts relevant to the topic with assignment questions drawn from authors' rich on the ground experiences. This book includes models and constructs, infographics and case examples which are amply supported by images and plates, tables and illustrations to ensure that the readers understand the concepts and constructs easily. It also provides chapter summary, key terms with definitions, discussion questions, activity based questions, glossary of terms and references that could help the readers as well as the instructor in learning/teaching this course and in evaluating the outcomes.

The title of the book itself "Digital Marketing: From Fundamentals to Future" has been chosen keeping in mind, the needs of students, academicians, corporates, entrepreneurs and individuals who would like to understand and explore digital marketing in their respective spheres. Though marketing has a high rate of interest with multiple prospects, it is also laden with risks while making managerial decisions, especially to those who skip the basics and begin with digital marketing directly. Thus, as we said earlier, this book aims to provide a foundation for using digital technologies and media based on the sound principles of marketing. We are sure the title itself will motivate and equip the readers to begin a career in digital marketing and use the concepts, illustrations, cases as a launchpad to venture into specific techniques, platforms and channels to unravel experiences in their digital marketing journey/career.

The authors and publisher wish the readers of this book "Happy Reading and Happier Learning".

Swaminathan T. N.
Karthik Kumar

ACKNOWLEDGEMENTS

The authors wish to thank all their colleagues and family members each one of whom have contributed in their own ways to this book, through discussion, examples, reviews and suggestions.

Dr. Swaminathan wishes to begin his acknowledgements with a big thank you to Ms. Susmita Das Gupta, an Alumna Great Lakes Institute of Management and Promoter of The Smart Ideas who was initially on board as a co-author at the book outline stage and subsequently had to withdraw on account of her other business commitments and travel. Nevertheless, a full chapter, Chapter 4 – Social Media Marketing, has been contributed by her. Thank you Sus!

It would not have been possible to complete this book without the help of Geetha Swaminathan, Dr. Swaminathan's wife who has been a constant source of inspiration right from the outline stage of the book by offering her valuable inputs as a digital immigrant consumer. Dr. Swaminathan wishes to place on record his sincere thanks to his former colleague, Ms. Sreelakshmi K., M.B.A., who has not only contributed a fair amount of content to this book, but also for going through every chapter carefully and editing at the first draft stage; his current colleagues, Rahul Ramachandran, for all the help in analytics, graphics and other suggestions from time to time, and Ms. Ramya K. in bringing in PR perspectives. Dr. Swaminathan wishes to specially thank Raj Narain, Founder Promoter Optima Response Management Pvt. Ltd., Chennai, for healthy suggestions and also contributing practical examples to the Analytics chapter. He also thanks all his students, present and past, who have not only been a source of inspiration but also have provided practical insights. Students have been a constant source of learning for him.

Karthik Kumar wishes to thank Ranjit Mokakshi, Sam Murthy and colleagues at Rage Communications who helped in putting together the case studies, data and graphics.

Both authors thank Cengage for their help and support.

Swaminathan T. N.
Karthik Kumar

ABOUT THE AUTHORS

T. N. Swaminathan Ph.D. retired in April 2019 from Great Lakes Institute of Management, Chennai as Professor of Marketing and Director, Branding, PR & Alumni Relations. He continues with Great Lakes as Strategic Advisor to the Dean and Adjunct Professor – Marketing. His career has spanned for 46+ years, both in industry and academics. Dr. Swaminathan has been teaching since 1992 - Marketing, Sales & Strategic Management courses & MDPs as visiting/guest faculty at IIMC, IIMB, IIM Ranchi, IFMR Chennai, IMT-Ghaziabad, IMI- Delhi, Fore school Delhi, BIM-Trichy, etc. His publications include papers, articles and case studies in leading Indian and International publications. Dr. Swaminathan received "100 Most Dedicated Professors" Award – A National Award at World Education Congress in July, 2018 and also "Best Marketing Professor Award" at ABP News National Education awards in July 2015. He was awarded Honorary Doctor of Letters by King's University, Hawaii, USA in 2017 for his contribution to educational services and entrepreneurship.

Karthik Kumar began his career in the trenches of marketing in 1976 with Indian Market Research Bureau. He was briefly posted to head Lanka Market Research Bureau in early 1983. In 1993, Karthik Kumar joined Rediffusion-DY&R, the storied advertising agency known for its breakthrough advertising for brands such as Lakme, Colgate, Eveready, Maruti, TI Cycles, etc. During his stint with Rediffusion-DY&R, he led teams across offices of the agency in different cities for award winning campaigns for several of its clients. In addition, Kumar also launched the Brand Asset Valuator™, a proprietary brand modelling process through the Asia Pacific region. Karthik Kumar embarked on an entrepreneurial journey in 2000. This led him to team up with friends who had started Rage Communication in 2003 to repurpose the business after the dot com bust. Rage is a pioneer of digital marketing in India and was among the first companies in India and the Asia Pacific region to offer comprehensive solutions covering Strategy, User Experience Design, Technology and Management as an integrated service for Digital Marketing and eCommerce.

Visual

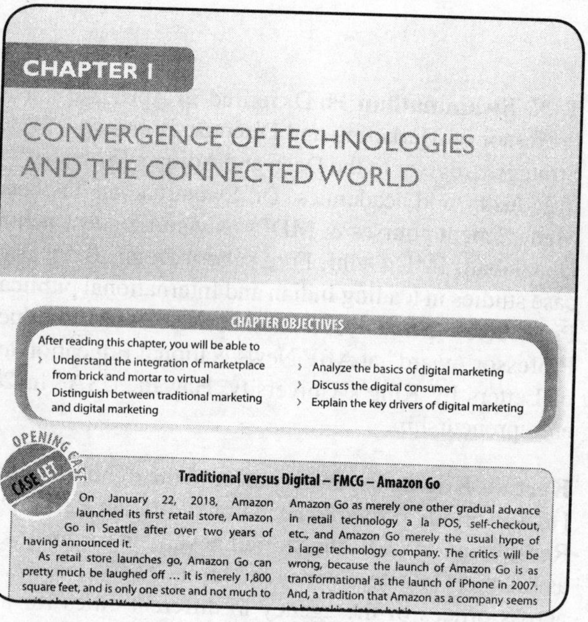
CHAPTER 1

CONVERGENCE OF TECHNOLOGIES AND THE CONNECTED WORLD

CHAPTER OBJECTIVES

After reading this chapter, you will be able to

- Understand the integration of marketplace from brick and mortar to virtual
- Distinguish between traditional marketing and digital marketing
- Analyze the basics of digital marketing
- Discuss the digital consumer
- Explain the key drivers of digital marketing

OPENING CASE LET

Traditional versus Digital – FMCG – Amazon Go

On January 22, 2018, Amazon launched its first retail store, Amazon Go in Seattle after over two years of having announced it.

As retail store launches go, Amazon Go can pretty much be laughed off … it is merely 1,800 square feet, and is only one store and not much to

Amazon Go as merely one other gradual advance in retail technology a la POS, self-checkout, etc., and Amazon Go merely the usual hype of a large technology company. The critics will be wrong, because the launch of Amazon Go is as transformational as the launch of iPhone in 2007. And, a tradition that Amazon as a company seems

Chapter Objectives: Chapters begin with chapter objectives which outline what each chapter aims at achieving and what the student/reader should know on its completion.

CHAPTER 2

DEMYSTIFYING DIGITAL MARKETING AND SOCIAL MEDIA

CHAPTER OBJECTIVES

After reading this chapter, you will be able to

- Understand evolution of marketing communication through ages
- Explain Web as an effective communication platform, from static Web 1.0 to Interactive 2.0
- Analyze the unfolding of consumerism and marketing in digital era
- Discuss from marketplace to marketspace – Brick & Mortar to Brick & Click
- Distinguish between digital marketing and social media marketing

OPENING CASE LET

From Brick and Mortar to Brick and Click – Travel Tickets

In the Indian context, IRCTC or Indian Railways demonstrated the disruptive power of the Internet and the speed with which the task of issuing tickets went from a cumbersome physical task to an activity that could be performed digitally in the presence of one's own space at any time of the day.

Earlier any manner of ticket to travel from one city to another required devoting nearly an entire day (sometimes sleeping overnight on railway

like the family jewels, for, without it one could not travel.

The first shot across the bow of this tyranny in India, was, surprisingly enough, fired by the Government owned public sector behemoth, Indian Railways. In 2002, the Indian Railway Catering and Tourism Corporation (IRCTC) launched railway tickets online. In its initial days, one would book the ticket online and the physical ticket would be couriered to the passenger. Since

Opening Case: All chapters open with a small case, based on the topics dealt with in the chapter. The purpose of these cases is to help the student/reader relate the concept to practical aspects as also to introduce the subject.

Walkthrough

CHAPTER SUMMARY

- Customers today are able to search for products, place and activities by image, voice, and gesture; automatically participate in others' transactions; and find new opportunities via devices that augment their reality (e.g. Google Glass).
- Majority of the decisions customers make are influenced by the quality of their experiences all along their journey.
- Digital marketing should be understood as online data-driven marketing. It is the marketing of products or services using digital technologies.
- **Inbound marketing** refers to marketing activities that bring visitors in, rather than marketers having to go out to get prospects' attention. In contrast, buying attention, cold-calling, direct paper mail, radio, TV advertisements, point of sale material, telemarketing and traditional advertising are considered "outbound marketing".
- Digital consumer spending in India is estimated to be $100 bn. opportunity and that online spender base is estimated to grow 2-3x across sectors led by women, new users from smaller cities and 35+ years shoppers will drive this growth".
- A 2017 Nielsen study in US indicates online for FMCG shopping is pervasive and all generations and income levels are shopping online. However, 61% are millennials and can be called Consumer 2.0.
- Customers 2.0 who are encountered online are the same people who walk into a store, call on the

Summary: These points will help students/readers review what all has been dealt with in the different topics covered.

Table and Figure: These amply support the concepts and ensure that the readers easily understand the concepts.

Table 1.1 Traditional Marketing Vs Digital Marketing

Area	Traditional Marketing	Digital Marketing
Segmenting and Targeting	Macro and mass	Micro and specific
Communication	Structured and clear	Unstructured; continuous updates
Direction	One way	Multi directional - Many to Many
Personalization	Low	High - can be customized
Imagery	Constrained by platform	Rich media tools
Privacy	Confidentiality can be maintained	Open and public
Period	Long term	Short term and dynamic
Agili		
Co		
Co		
Co		

Figure 1.1 Digital marketing vs traditional marketing

Key Terms: A list of important terms has been given at the end of each chapter. This will help student/reader recapitulate what all has been dealt with in the different topics covered.

KEY TERMS

Artificial intelligence (AI)
Campaign marketing
Content automation
Content marketing
Customer 1.0
Customer 2.0
Data-driven marketing
Digital consumer
Digital consumer spending
Digital immigrants
Digital marketing
Digital natives
Digital transformation
Display advertising
Ebooks
Ecommerce marketing
Email direct marketing
Inbound marketing
Influencer marketing
Marketing
Marketing mix
Outbound marketing
Pull digital marketing
Push digital marketing
Search engine marketing (SEM)
Search engine optimization (SEO)
Social media marketing
Social media optimization
4Cs of digital marketing
5 components of AI

Visual

Review Questions: These questions provided at the end of each chapter are intended to assess the student's/reader's understanding of concepts discussed.

REVIEW QUESTIONS

1. What is your understanding of digital marketing?
2. What are inbound marketing and outbound marketing? How are they related to digital marketing?
3. What is the estimated monetary impact of digital marketing in India?
4. Who are Consumers 2.0 and what role do they play in digital marketing?
5. Who are digital natives and digital immigrants?
6. What are the 5Cs of digital marketing? Explain.
7. What factors are driving digital transformation?
8. What are push and pull digital marketing strategies?
9. Name some tools in the digital world that you are exposed to.

ACTIVITY QUESTIONS

1. Using Kerpoof (https://lol.disney.com/kerpoof) create a short illustrated story.
2. Using befunky (https://www.befunky.com) create a collage of some funny emotions from your pictures library.

KEY TERMS

Artificial intelligence (AI)
Campaign marketing
Content automation
Content marketing
Customer 1.0
Customer 2.0
Data-driven marketing
Digital consumer
Digital consumer spending
Digital immigrants
Digital marketing
Digital natives
Digital transformation
Display advertising
Ebooks
Ecommerce marketing
Email direct marketing
Inbound marketing
Influencer marketing
Marketing
Marketing mix
Outbound marketing
Pull digital marketing
Push digital marketing
Search engine marketing (SEM)
Search engine optimization (SEO)
Social media marketing
Social media optimization
4Cs of digital marketing
5 components of AI

REFERENCES

1. Internet in India – 2017; IAMAI study.
2. Diffusion of Innovations, Everett Rogers
3. Rage Analytics
4. E. van Bommel, D. Edelman, and K. Ungerman, "Digitizing the Consumer Decision Journey", https://
7. Tunde Olanrewaju and Paul Willmott, "Finding your digital sweet spot", https://www.mckinsey.com/business-functions/digital-mckinsey/our-insights/finding-your-digital-sweet-spot. Accessed on February 7, 2019.

REVIEW QUESTIONS

1. What is your understanding of digital marketing?
2. What are inbound marketing and outbound marketing? How are they related to digital marketing?
3. What is the estimated monetary impact of digital marketing in India?
4. Who are Consumers 2.0 and what role do they play in digital marketing?
5. Who are digital natives and digital immigrants?
6. What are the 5Cs of digital marketing? Explain.
7. What factors are driving digital transformation?
8. What are push and pull digital marketing strategies?
9. Name some tools in the digital world that you are exposed to.

ACTIVITY QUESTIONS

1. Using Kerpoof (https://lol.disney.com/kerpoof) create a short illustrated story.
2. Using befunky (https://www.befunky.com) create a collage of some funny emotions from your pictures library.

KEY TERMS

Artificial intelligence (AI)
Campaign marketing
Content automation
Content marketing
Customer 1.0
Customer 2.0
Data-driven marketing
Digital consumer
Digital consumer spending
Digital immigrants
Digital marketing
Digital natives
Digital transformation
Display advertising
Ebooks
Ecommerce marketing
Email direct marketing
Inbound marketing
Influencer marketing
Marketing
Marketing mix
Outbound marketing
Pull digital marketing
Push digital marketing
Search engine marketing (SEM)
Search engine optimization (SEO)
Social media marketing
Social media optimization
4Cs of digital marketing
5 components of AI

REFERENCES

1. Internet in India – 2017; IAMAI study.
2. Diffusion of Innovations, Everett Rogers
3. Rage Analytics
4. E. van Bommel, D. Edelman, and K. Ungerman, "Digitizing the Consumer Decision Journey", https://
7. Tunde Olanrewaju and Paul Willmott, "Finding your digital sweet spot", https://www.mckinsey.com/business-functions/digital-mckinsey/our-insights/finding-your-digital-sweet-spot. Accessed on February 7, 2019.

Activity Questions: These exercises will encourage student/reader to acquire an understanding of the day-to-day applications of the concepts covered in the chapter. This knowledge is useful and application based.

Walkthrough

Closing Case: All the chapters have cases at the end which provide further insight into the topics discussed in the chapter. Questions following these cases will be helpful to the students/readers in testing and applying their knowledge.

CLOSING CASE
CASE LET

Digital Advertising – Foreign Bank

A leading foreign bank operating in India had a unique problem. The bank had a large consumer franchise for its core banking product through its zero-balance salary accounts (ZBSA). However, this large franchise was not yielding profitable business for the bank since, either, the salary account holders transferred the balance to other banks after receiving the salary transfer or the account holders were not taking up the bank's other product lines—credit cards, loans or mortgages.

Studies conducted by the bank showed that this group of account holders:

- did not perceive the ZBSA as a service to the account holders, but more as a service to the company they were employed by
- though the bank scored high on traditional banking parameters, the consumer's image of the bank was that it catered to a wealthier profile of consumers than themselves
- expected the other banking products provided by the bank to be more expensive, either in terms of user fees or interest rates, because the bank catered to a higher socio-economic class

Clearly the image of this bank among its ZBSA customers was that the bank was 'not-for-me'.

An integrated campaign that involved a digital campaign and on-ground events was conceived and launched. The digital campaign principally aimed at:

- Establishing a consumer connection with its account holders to ameliorate the lack of a relationship.
- Demonstrating how the zero-balance account helped them access other financial products based on the combination of the account relationship and the corporate connection
- Facilitating easy acquisition of the services of the bank through its digital platforms

The off-line events were aimed at putting a human face so that the account holders could tangibly experience the advertising campaign.

The digital campaign segmented the consumers based on their account behaviour and used a combination of:

- Display advertising, to give the context to the ZBSA as an account designed for the account holders that allowed them to access their accounts 24X7. A digital campaign was used, even though identity of specific account holders was known, since the account was not just for the individual but also for his family. A secondary benefit of the digital campaign was to give the feeling that the account holder belonged to a larger community, rather than being just a number for a bank.
- Organic search, was engineered with the insight that ZBSA holders would be curious to check out what was in for them after seeing the advertising. Specific key words that such account holders may use were targeted and the landing pages for those key words emphasized how the ZBSA provided unique value to the account holders.
- Social media was used to promote additional products that the bank provided ZBSA holders such as loans, mortgages and credit cards. The idea behind using social media was the specificity with which the account holders could be targeted and the fact that since the communication was informational, one could reach a larger universe for a smaller budget than any other digital opportunity.
- eMail campaigns were devised to promote the extensive range of online facilities that the bank offered such as zero-cost draft issuance, utility bill payments, standard instructions for regular payments such as school fees, maintenance bills, club bills, etc.
- A co-operative system was developed by which ZBSA holders could access the banks products like credit cards, personal loans, mortgages through their company's intranet and hence simplifying documentation requirements for such products.

INDEX

Index: An Index at the end will aid the readers in locating the entries in the right context in an accurate manner.

CONTENTS

CHAPTER I

CONVERGENCE OF TECHNOLOGIES AND THE CONNECTED WORLD

CHAPTER OBJECTIVES

After reading this chapter, you will be able to

- Understand the integration of marketplace from brick and mortar to virtual
- Distinguish between traditional marketing and digital marketing
- Analyze the basics of digital marketing
- Discuss the digital consumer
- Explain the key drivers of digital marketing

OPENING CASE

CASE LET

Traditional versus Digital – FMCG – Amazon Go

On January 22, 2018, Amazon launched its first retail store, Amazon Go in Seattle after over two years of having announced it.

As retail store launches go, Amazon Go can pretty much be laughed off ... it is merely 1,800 square feet, and is only one store and not much to write about, right? Wrong!

At first flush, the Amazon store is nothing great and seemingly nothing digital about it. However, consider that without the confluence of some pretty strong digital technology, the Amazon store would not be possible. But, without smart phones, sensor technologies, digital payments, copious bandwidth, Amazon Go would be pretty much impossible. These are the different technologies that make what seems possible — i.e. walking into a store, swiping your phone on entering, picking up your groceries and leaving . Critics may dismiss Amazon Go as merely one other gradual advance in retail technology a la POS, self-checkout, etc., and Amazon Go merely the usual hype of a large technology company. The critics will be wrong, because the launch of Amazon Go is as transformational as the launch of iPhone in 2007. And, a tradition that Amazon as a company seems to be making into a habit.

Think back to the early days of Amazon which merely started as an online book store. Pooh-poohed by brick and mortar enterprises and financial analysts in the wake of the dot.com bust in 2000, Amazon, not only survived, but thrived. The key to Amazon's success has not been as many would imagine, technological prowess, but a deep understanding of consumer behaviour and how to use technology to address that behaviour. It has used this approach and has ignored the 'brick and mortar' vs 'online' debate as a distraction and continued to reach out to consumers, at their homes (Alexa, Echo, et al), offices (AWS), on the commute (Amazon Video), pretty much ubiquitously.

It is often said that countries like India where Internet penetration is low are not great markets for digital technologies, particularly, in consumer product marketing. The reality is far from this. With Internet penetration at 35%[1], Internet adoption is mainstream. In urban India with a 64% penetration, only the laggards are left behind. In rural India too, Internet penetration is 20% well up in the early-majority phase of the adoption cycle of innovation[2]. Even with this penetration, usage of the Internet is probably much higher through, vicarious usage. There are anecdotal stories of how maids and handymen get their employers to order things for them on ecommerce channels or in smaller towns and villages micro entrepreneurs who use an Internet connection to offer services built around ecommerce, etravel, etc. Thus, notwithstanding, seeming room for the penetration to grow, one can safely say that usage adoption of Internet in India is pretty much universal, in some form or the other—directly or indirectly.

This is captured in the usage behaviour of ecommerce in India[3]:

- Average daily usage of three main ecommerce sites went from 12.81 million on January 1, 2017 to 22.79 million on January 1, 2018—a growth of 78% in just one year.
- While the big boys of the business grew, newcomers were not left behind—bigbasket.com, a home grown Indian grocery chain went from 4.67 million in January 2017 to 6.86 million visitors in January 2018.

Digital adoption is not only increasing in traditional consumer products and goods, but also creating new categories of services, such as ride share and food delivery.

On the obverse side though, traditional FMCG marketers continue to use the Internet as an advertising channel and are actually missing out on opportunities. Thus, while well-known brands are available on most ecommerce channels, the distributors of these brands are not the brand marketers, but distributors whose origins are not known. While this may be a sanguine solution for brand marketers who do not want to upset their traditional logistics chains, it does not augur well for them since they do not control what is being sold online in their name. All it takes is one bad experience to go viral and a brand reputation can be besmirched overnight with dramatic effects in the analog world too.

Case Questions

1. Why was the launch of Amazon Go transformational?
2. Why is the statement "that countries like India are not great markets for digital technologies, particularly, in consumer product marketing" untrue?

INTRODUCTION

When we wake up in the morning, chances are high that the first thing that most of us do would perhaps be checking our smartphones for overnight unread notifications. For the millennials, this could precede even brushing teeth or having a hot beverage. Such has been the power of convergence of technologies across platforms. In a classical marketing sense, digital technologies have provided an answer to time and place utilities.

Since digital marketing is a subset of marketing, let us begin by looking at the current definitions of marketing.

•AMA - 2013 – "Marketing is the activity, set of institutions, and processes for creating, communicating, delivering, and exchanging offerings that have value for customers, clients, partners, and society at large.

•Kotler 2013 – Shortest definition of marketing: "Meeting Customer Needs Profitability"- Create, Communicate, Deliver Value to a Target population at a Profit.

While the AMA definition looks at all the stakeholders, Kotler's is focussed on the customer. At the end of the day, marketing is all about value creation to customers and end users, may it be B2B, B2C or B2P (Business to People – Marty Homish, Global CMO, SAP). In this context, Kotler and Armstrong (2009) define digital marketing as "a form of direct **marketing** which links consumers with sellers electronically using interactive technologies like emails, websites, online forums and newsgroups, interactive television, mobile communications, etc." (Kotler and Armstrong, 2009).

Customers today are able to search for products, place and activities by image, voice, and gesture; automatically participate in others' transactions; and find new opportunities via devices that augment their reality (e.g. Google Glass). Therefore, it has become important for the companies to engage customers in these digital channels both from immediate opportunities (to convert interest to sales) and also on account of majority of the decisions customers make are influenced by the quality of their experiences all along their journey (McKinsey)[4].

DIGITAL MARKETING – THE BASICS

The Institute of Direct and Digital Marketing (IDM) defines[5] digital marketing as "Applying digital technologies which form online channels to market (web, email, databases plus mobile/wireless and digital TV) to contribute to marketing activities aimed at achieving profitable acquisition and retention of customers (with a multi-channel buying process and customer lifestyles) through developing a planned approach to improve customer knowledge (of their profiles, behaviour, value and loyalty drivers), then delivering integrated targeted communication and online services that match their individual needs". Thus, **digital marketing** should be understood as **data-driven online marketing**, the key operating words being **online and data driven**. It is the marketing of products or services using digital technologies, mainly the Internet, but also extends beyond the Internet to include other channels that may not require the use of Internet, mobile phones, display advertising, social media, search engine and any other digital medium.

> **Marketing:** The activity, set of institutions, and processes for creating, communicating, delivering, and exchanging offerings that have value for customers, clients, partners, and society at large
>
> **Digital marketing:** A form of direct marketing which links consumers with sellers electronically using interactive technologies like emails, websites, online forums and newsgroups, interactive television, mobile communications
>
> **Data-driven marketing:** Marketing of products or services using digital technologies

The Internet and the other channels mentioned above are way different from the traditional marketing communication channels. To clarify the terms, traditional and digital, the use of ads in newspapers, magazines and other print media are simple examples of **traditional marketing**. Other examples of traditional marketing include point of sale material distributed to homes or at point of purchase, commercials on TV, radio and billboards (hoardings). On the other hand, when a business invests on building a website, advertising the brand through different social media such as Facebook, Twitter and YouTube, it is called **digital marketing**. Though physical is more real to the brain[6] (Bangor University study, 2009), digital marketing essentially addresses specific targeting, interactive two-way communication and cost effectiveness which are the downsides of traditional marketing.

Inbound and Outbound Marketing

Inbound marketing is promoting through blogs, podcasts, videos, ebooks, enewsletters, white papers, SEO social media marketing, and other forms of content marketing which serve to attract customers.

In contrast, hard promotional materials, telemarketing and traditional advertising are considered "**outbound marketing**".

> **Inbound marketing:** A strategy that focuses on attracting customers, or leads, via company-created Internet content
>
> **Outbound marketing:** Any kind of marketing where a company initiates the conversation and sends its message out to an audience

Inbound marketing refers to marketing activities that bring visitors in, rather than marketers having to go out to get prospects' attention. Inbound marketing earns the attention of customers, makes the company/products easy to be found, and draws customers to the website by producing interesting content.

In other words, it flips **the sales funnel.**

John Wanamaker (1838-1922) is credited with a famous quote, "Half the money I spend on advertising is wasted; the trouble is I don't know which half". He opened one of the first and most successful department stores in the United States, which grew to 16 stores and eventually became part of Macy's. Today, almost a century later, he perhaps would have been happy that digital marketing is available and that digital marketing can overcome this limitation of traditional marketing.

Figure 1.1 Digital Marketing vs Traditional Marketing

As seen from the above, from the consumer perspective, digital marketing offers interactive engagement and ease of use though not necessarily touch and feel. Today's customer/consumer has the ability to sift through an abundance of information anytime anywhere any-which way he or she wants, thus making them better informed, better connected, more interactive and more in control, for, the digital world has come a long way from static adaptation of traditional print versions to interactive customer experience, thanks to web 2.0. Since the purpose of marketing is to provide value to the consumer, digital marketing focuses on consumer, their journey and delivering satisfaction.

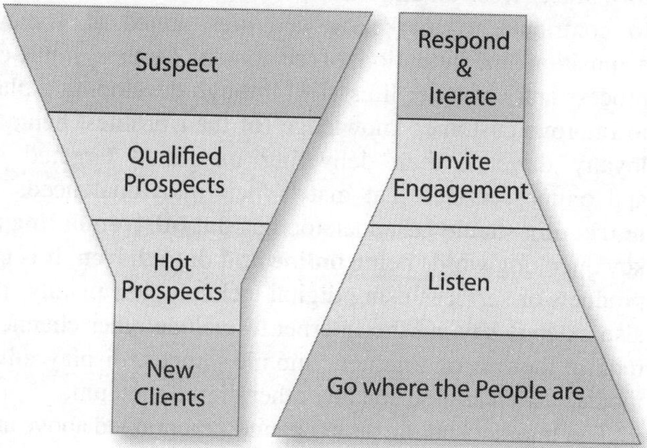

Figure 1.2 The Sales Funnel

Table 1.1 Traditional Marketing Vs Digital Marketing

Area	Traditional Marketing	Digital Marketing
Segmenting and Targeting	Macro and mass	Micro and specific
Communication	Structured and clear	Unstructured; continuous updates
Direction	One way	Multi directional - Many to Many
Personalization	Low	High - can be customized
Imagery	Constrained by platform	Rich media tools
Privacy	Confidentiality can be maintained	Open and public
Period	Long term	Short term and dynamic
Agility	Longer fulfilment time	Short, instant
Conversion	Lag	Short
Cost	Entry barrier	Small - Lends to scaling up
Cost of Failure	High	Low

Digital Transformation

Digital marketing can overcome the limitation of traditional marketing.
Does this mean the rules of the game (marketing) have changed? – No

- Marketing has not changed but the tools have
- Marketer needs to proactively help the customer in customer experience (CX) by
  - Empowering decision making
  - Be transparent and provide information
  - Provide expert's opinions
  - Not be a disruption during entertainment (zoo zoos refined this)
  - Using Web 2.0 tools and use user generated content to provide CX
  - Prioritize user reviews than testimonials

Exhibit 1.1 Digital Marketing: Overpowering Traditional Marketing

As seen earlier, **digital marketing** should be understood as **data-driven online marketing**, the key operating words being **online and data driven.** This involves a shift from the way data was obtained and stored in the traditional mode (analogue) to the manner in which it happens now (digital; binary). The implication of this transformation is not only for marketing but also for the business as a whole, impacting all verticals and stakeholders improving efficiency of operations at lower costs, key drivers being

- Automation of various functions
- Digitization of physical assets and processes on to a digital platform
- Collaboration integration and sharing across supply chain and a seamless customer experience (CX).

Basis expert interviews in 2013, McKinsey came up with a digital transformation model[7] of the potential impact of digital technology across industries, highlighting share of potential that can be captured by looking for impact across the whole value chain.

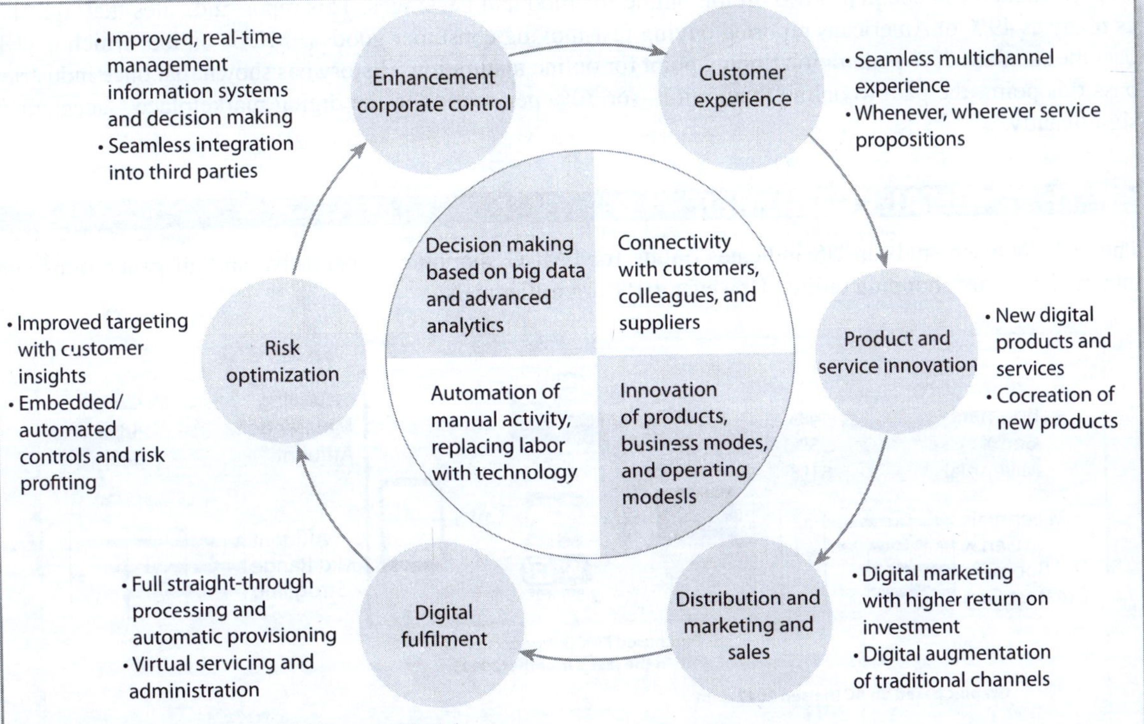

Source: Redrawn based on McKinsey's Model

Figure 1.3 Digital Transformation Model

Though digital transformation is across businesses and geographies, for the purposes of this book, we are focussing on consumption or customer perspective since finally it is the customer who is the king. A February 2018 Boston Consulting Group (BCG) and Google India's report estimates Digital Consumer Spending in India as a $100 bn Opportunity[8] and that online spender base is estimated to grow 2-3x across sectors led by women, new users from smaller cities. According to this report, "Capturing the growth of digital influence and key consumer insights that will drive the next phase of digital consumer spending in India. The report projects that the potential for digital spending is expected to grow 2.5 times from ~$40bn to ~$100bn by 2020 led by sectors such as eCommerce ($18-45bn), Travel and Hotel ($11-20bn), Financial Services ($12-30bn) and Digital media ($200-570mn). The report also finds that women, new users from non-tier 1 cities and 35+ years shoppers will drive this growth".

The report also states that "with deeper penetration of mobile phones and affordable data plans, the number of online spenders will not only increase over the next few years but there will be a dramatic change in the users' profile. With the improvement of infrastructure, online shopping will take off in India from cities beyond metros and together it is expected to comprise more than 50% of the total online shopper base by 2020".

Speaking about the key findings of this report, Partner & Director, The Boston Consulting Group, India said, "There is a clear evolution as consumers move from awareness of online platforms to their first purchase and further down to become more frequent buyers – triggers and barriers to online purchase evolve with each stage. Very different actions are needed to unlock growth and move consumers from one stage to the next."

At a global level, according to a 2017 report from Nielsen and the Food Marketing Institute (FMI), in the next 5 to 7 years, between 70% and 80% of food shoppers will buy online and estimate that by 2015, U.S. consumer will spend at $100 billion online for food and beverages. This report indicates that in 2017, as many as 49% of Americans reported buying fast-moving consumer goods (FMCG) online, which is well past the standard 20% penetration tipping point for online maturation. History has shown that once industries pass this point, the path to online maturation—or 70% penetration in the digital marketplace—accelerates significantly.

THE DIGITAL CONSUMER

The 2017 Nielsen study in US indicates online for FMCG shopping as pervasive and all generations and income levels are shopping online. However, 61% are millennials.

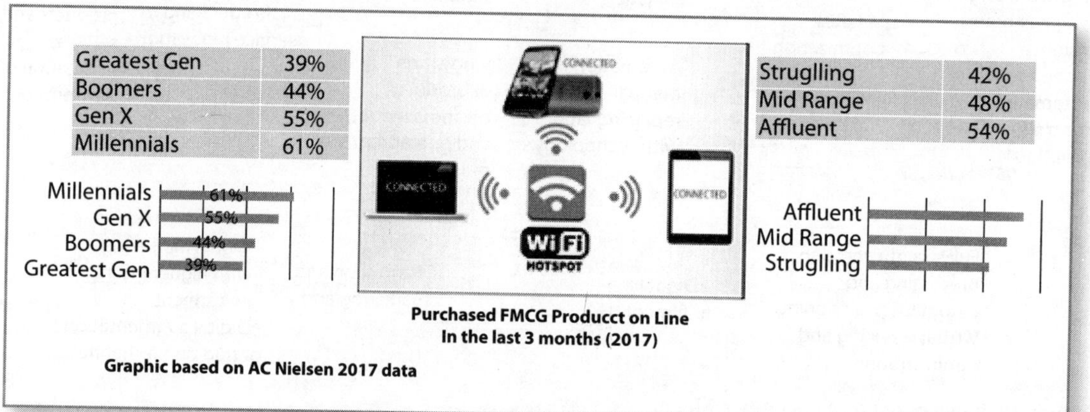

Figure 1.4 FMCG Online Purchases 2017

Given that online shopping is pervasive, it is important for us to understand who the digital consumer is. Like in all other spheres where updated editions are given progressive numerical numbers, current consumers can be called Consumer 2.0. The term Customer 2.0 came into being sometime in 2009 (Ryan & Jones, 2009[9]).

Consumer 2.0, who are encountered online, are the same people who walk into a store, call on the telephone, or order from mail order catalogue. They are doing exactly the same what people have been doing for many years—communicating with each other. The shift is that technology has enabled them to communicate faster, over distances, over mobile phones, and in non-grammatical texts and emojis. People talk to each other that they always have; however, they are not doing it in coffee shops or bistros talking to a few but doing it online with a few thousands, this is possible due to Web 2.0. as compared to static Web 1.0; Web 2.0 is an evolution in the way people are using technology.

Customer 1.0: Customers who are inclined to make brand choices based on traditional advertising

Customer 2.0: Tech Savvy consumer base who consume a lot of digital content and are more likely to make brand choices based on that

Before we look at Consumer 2.0, the following snapshots will explain how this technology evolution has impacted the industry dynamics and consumerism.

Customer 2.0 is essentially a reflection of the shift in consumer consciousness being experienced across Generation X and Y. Customers 1.0 love to read magazines and papers. They are inclined to make brand choices on the back of traditional advertising, and they do not quite understand what this digital is all about. To them, tweeting is what birds do, though 2000 years ago a saint poet from Tamil Nadu, Thiuvalluvar wrote 1330 couplets in Tamil, that were two liners on everyday virtues of an individual, approximating 160 word limit of Twitter (or the first recorded non digital Tweet)! Customers 1.0 expect to resolve product issues through the traditional avenues of phone and face-to-face customer support. Customers 1.0 tend to make decisions on word of mouth endorsements.

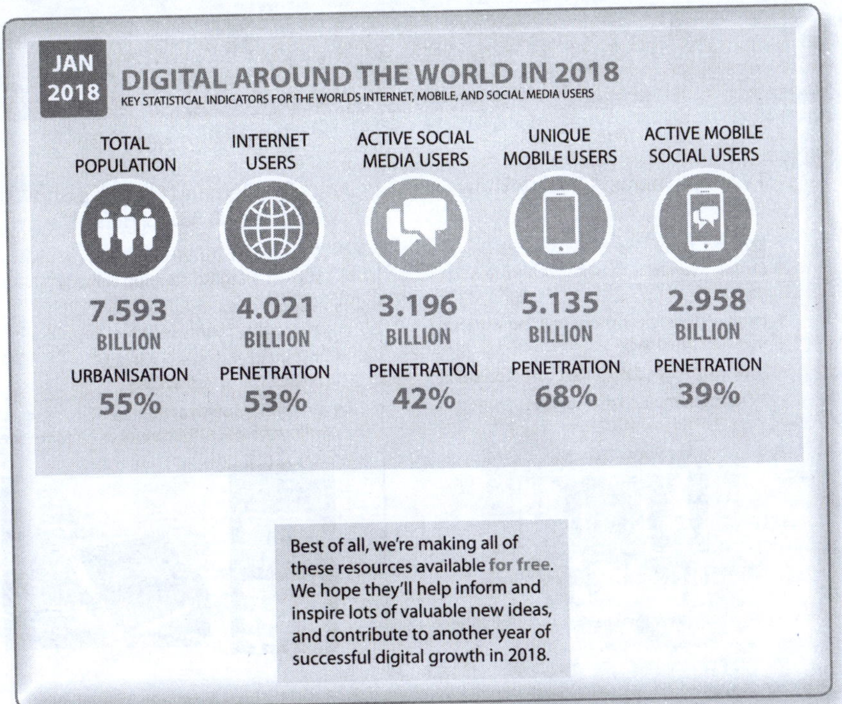

Exhibit 1.2 Digital Around the World - 2018

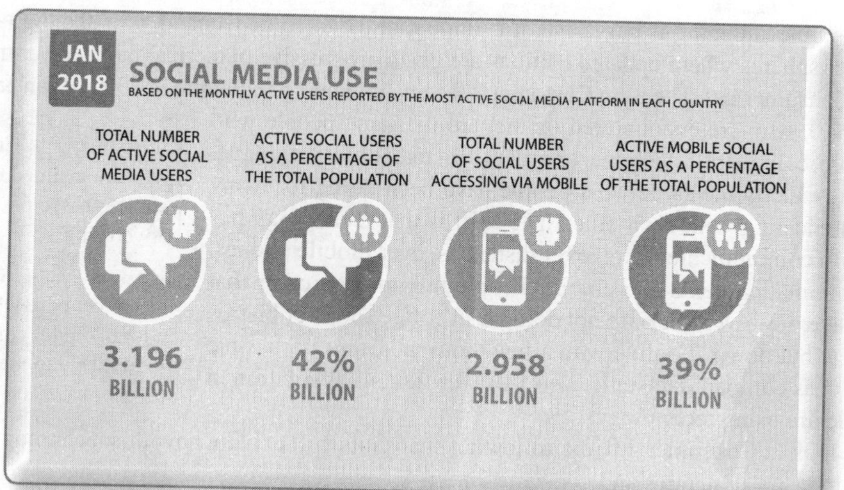

Exhibit 1.3 Social Media Use - January 2018

Customers 2.0 will tweet what they had for breakfast! Newspapers are growing ever-more defunct as the boom of online news and RSS functionality reaches epic proportions. They love viral content, and probably spend more time online than watching TV.

Customers 2.0 expect companies to have an online presence, they prefer to shop online (for majority of purchases), and they expect the e-commerce sites to be quick or they do not hesitate to migrate. Customers

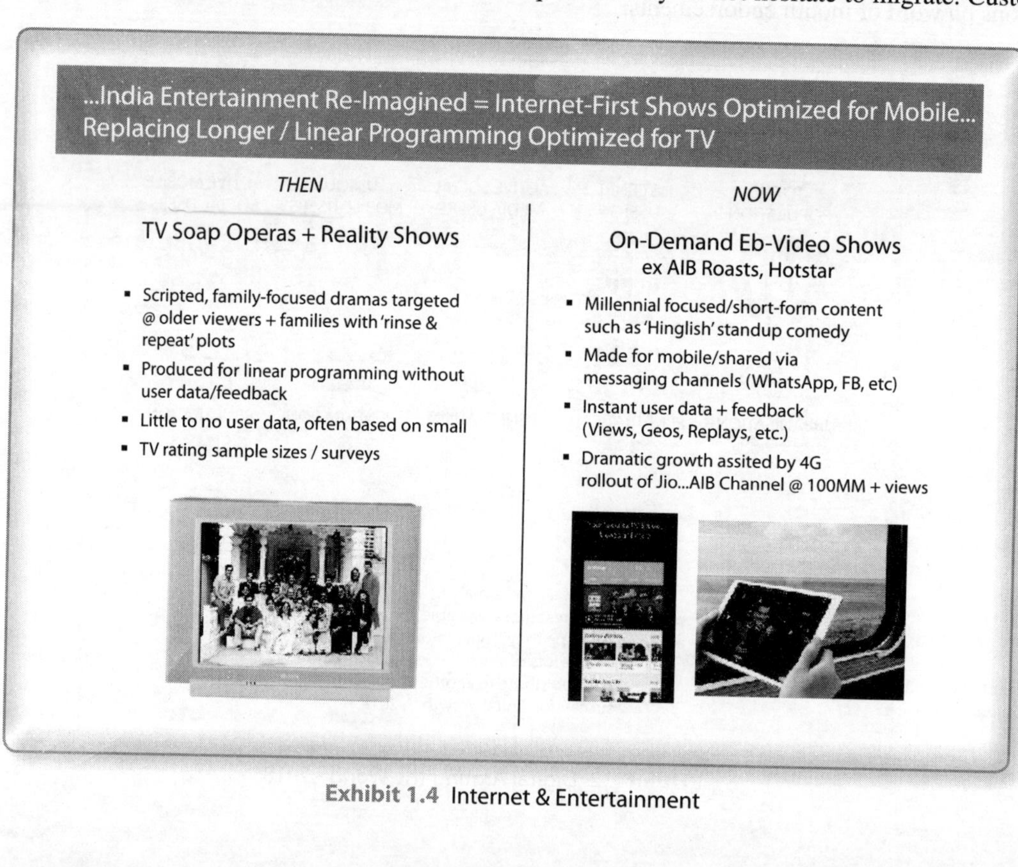

Exhibit 1.4 Internet & Entertainment

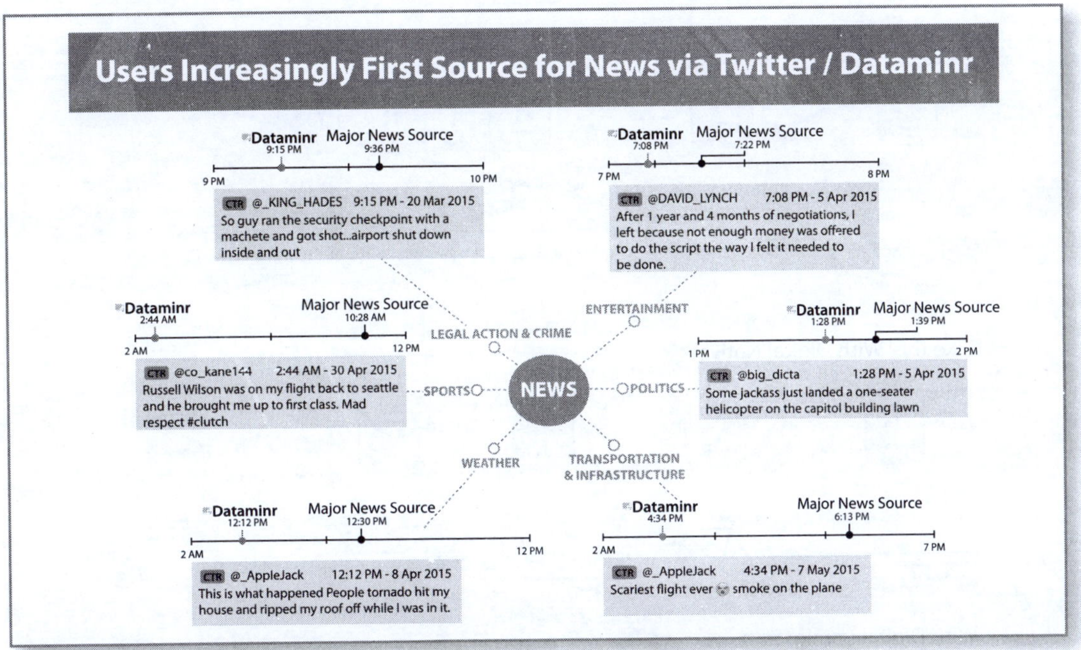

Figure 1.5 Users Increasingly First Source for News via Twitter/Dataminr

2.0 seek user-reviews to inform brand choices, and is likely to spend time into researching potential products and purchases. Customers 2.0 are starting to expect a social media presence, they love innovation and reward innovative brands. Customers 2.0 are moving from horizontal screen to vertical screen (monitor to phone). Customers 2.0 expect these technological advances to become a part of their consumer experience (CX). Technology is not treated as novel or new, they are just expected to be there. These consumers are called ***digital natives***, a word coined by Marc Prensky[10] in 2001. They have spent their entire lives surrounded by and using computers, videogames, digital music players, video cams, cell phones, and all the other toys and tools of the digital age.

Customers 2.0 are

- Wired and born with a keyboard
- Tech savvy, discerning and comfortable with different media and platforms
- Multi-tasking; Want it all and want it now and in control
- Flexible
- Of short attention span and fickle
- Vocal
- Dual personality and anonymity when they choose to be

Therefore, they expect

- Simplicity
- Interactivity
- Value
- Convenience
- Consistency

Exhibit 1.5 Customer 2.0

Digital immigrants, who are an older generation, not born into the digital world, but have, at some point in their lives, become fascinated by and adopted many or most aspects of the new technology. They co-exist with and will be, compared with digital natives. Since customers are getting harder to impress, digital native or digital immigrant, companies and products that have exposed customers to simple, streamlined user experiences designed from the ground for digital delivery, have succeeded in the recent past (e.g. Spotify, Uber). Established companies that build their offerings and processes on top of, or alongside, more traditional

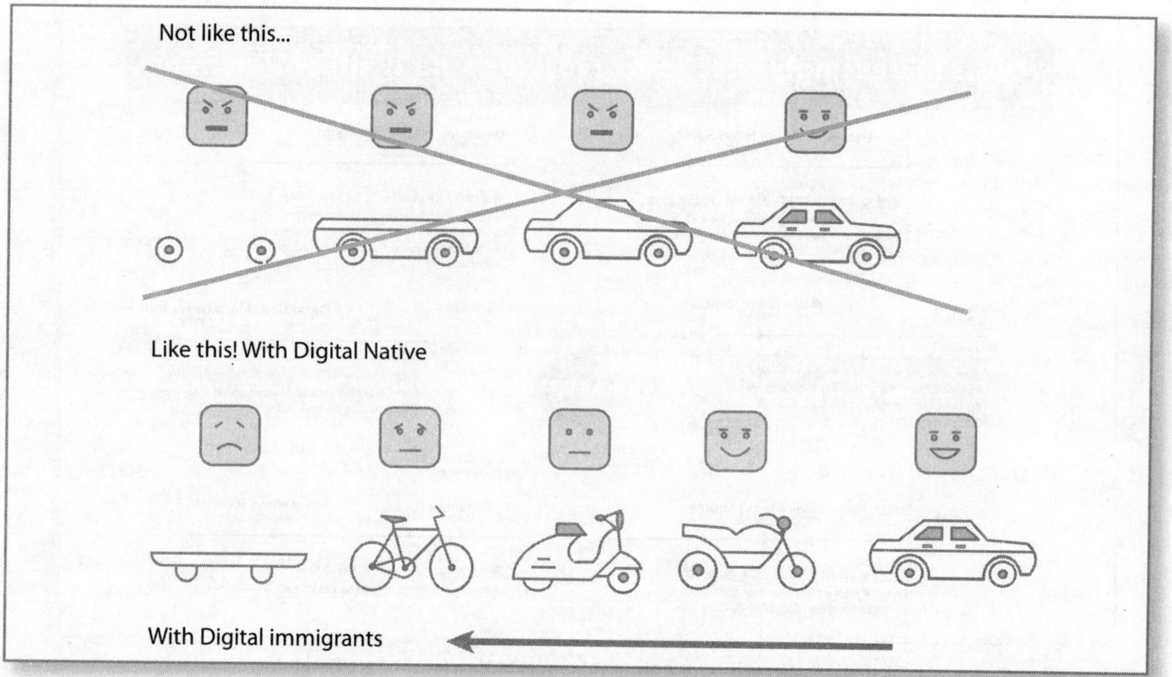

Figure 1.6 Digital Native Versus Digital Immigrants

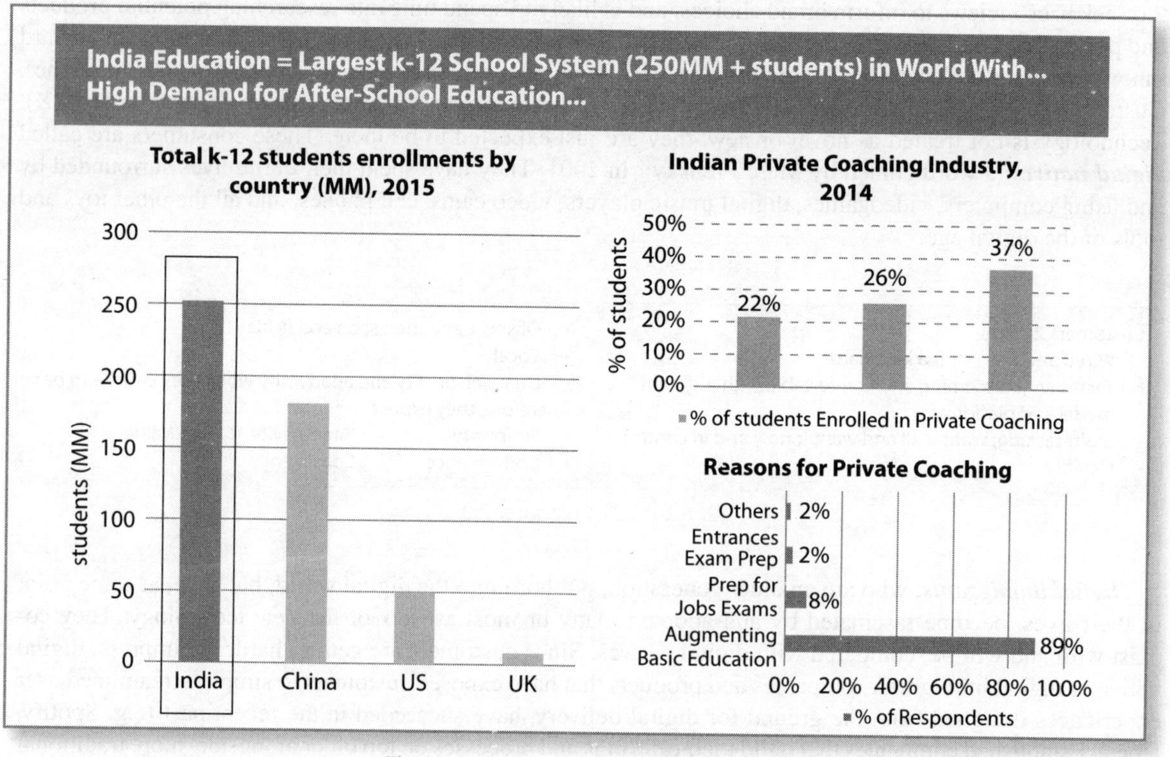

Figure 1.7 India Education - A Snapshot

channels often find it hard to meet the same standards. Fuelled by digital natives and digital immigrants, it is expected that[11]

- The Indian digital advertising industry to grow at a Compound Annual Growth Rate (CAGR) of 32% to reach ₹1,898.6 million (US$ 2.93 billion) by 2020.
- Online retail is estimated at $17.8 billion in 2017, to be at par with the physical stores in the next five years.
- Indian ecommerce sales to reach US$ 120 billion by 2020 from US$ 30 billion in 2016.
- There will be 530 million online shoppers by 2025, led by faster speed on reliable telecom networks, faster adoption of online services and better variety as well as convenience.

Success of Spotify with Digital Natives – catch them young for Digital delivery

In line with developments in ecommerce and FMCG sectors, education sector is also catching up rapidly as evidenced by the growth in K-12 enrolments and private coaching sector that today have included digital learning as a part of their curriculum (e.g. Byju's the Learning App).

Therefore, for any digital marketing strategy to be successful, it is imperative to understand both what digital marketing is and who the digital customer is right at the beginning. That is what has been attempted in this book.

KEY DRIVERS OF DIGITAL MARKETING

Marketers are familiar with the traditional 4Ps of marketing or the variables of the marketing mix. The **marketing mix** proposed in 1960[12] by McCarthy[13] is a foundation model in marketing and has been defined as the "*set of marketing tools that the firm uses to pursue its marketing objectives in the target*" (Kotler 12th Ed). The marketing mix refers to four broad levels of marketing decision, namely: *Product, Price, Promotion, and Place*. In the 1990s, a model of **4Cs** was proposed by Lauterborn as a more customer-driven equivalent of the 4Ps[14]. The 4Cs were *Consumer (Product)*, *Cost (Price)*, *Communication (Promotion)* and *Convenience (Place)*. Given that the digital consumer is wired, want it all and want it now in digital marketing, it makes sense to add a fifth "P" – "*Participation*" translating to a fifth C - *Collaboration*.

4Cs of Digital Marketing

Digital marketing's development since the 1990s and 2000s has changed the way brands and businesses use technology for marketing. As digital platforms are increasingly incorporated into marketing plans and everyday life, and as people use digital devices more and more, to accompany the 4Cs of classical marketing, Aditya Soni[15] of Flipkart proposed **Content, Cost, Channel and Creativity** as the 4Cs. A fifth C viz **Collaboration** be added since Consumer 2.0 is constantly communicating and collaborating with one another.

Thus, the key drivers are

- Content
- Channel – Platform
- Cost
- Creativity – Message
- Collaboration – Interactive Communication

Exhibit 1.6 Key Drivers of Digital Marketing - 4Cs

Digital Transformation

Figure 1.8 shows Digital transformation and user control of content is causing waves across the industry. This shift breaks into five inter-related insights.

1. Customer expectations continue to rise

A 2015 Forrester model[16] for the empowered customer, divides customers into five tiers, from Progressive Pioneers to Reserved Resisters that is similar to consumer adoption process wherein innovators (2.5%) and early adopters (13.5%) account for 16%. The empowered customer is increasingly savvy and expects a highly personalized experience, one that is consistent across channels.

> **Marketing Mix:** Set of marketing tools that the firm uses to pursue its marketing objectives in the target

According to a HBR paper[17] 73% of customer prefer to do business with brands that personalize their shopping experience and 80% of customers express frustration when their self-identity and current actions are lost while switching between channels.

2. SPEED is important

According to Eric Pearson, CIO of the InterContinental Hotel Group, "It's no longer the big beating the small, but the fast beating the slow." Technology change is occurring non-linearly as evidenced by principles such as Moore's Law and Metcalfe's Law, but businesses still "think linearly." In many cases, by the time marketers have devised a perspective on how to respond to an opportunity or threat, the world has changed by an order of magnitude that is a challenge for many legacy brands in that they struggle to move rapidly towards the future that digital disruptors have already commercialized.

3. Customer insight continues to be essential

Being able to rapidly respond to the expectations of today's empowered customer clearly starts with a strong focus on customer insight today and needs to be implemented at several levels—understanding your customer base overall, understanding the needs of individual segments and, increasingly understanding the needs of each individual consumer so that their experience can be personalized. Achieving this level of insight means not only developing customer intuition and gathering anecdotes and anecdotal evidence, but also leveraging data to continually feed organizations the pulse of our customers.

4. Artificial Intelligence (AI) is central

Success of interfaces such as Siri and Alexa indicates what practical AI really means today and how enterprises are and can be applying it now. AI systems are made of five key components:

1. **Sensing —** components which receive input such as text, voice, image, video or data triggers from systems.
2. **Comprehension** — components which discern what the data actually means (such as converting spoken language to not only text but also its underlying semantic meaning).
3. **Analysis** — components which leverage algorithms (rules) and data sets in order to arrive at either some kind of informational response, or to take some action.
4. **Guidance**, when needed, in which the system checks with human interface as to whether its certainty that it has the right answer is high enough or when an action requires confirmation.
5. **Action** which may simply mean communicating the "answer' (a solution) to the user or taking an automatic action such as adding something to the calendar, or paying a bill, etc.

5. Digital transformation means business transformation

"Digital transformation is a fundamental shift in how a firm delivers value and drives revenue." For example, Starbucks redesigning the layout of their stores to accommodate the logistics of "order ahead" customers, and Hilton wanting to allow customers to unlock doors through their app. Hilton faced not only a software development challenge, but also the challenge of changing tens of thousands of locks at their properties besides retraining facilities teams on how to properly repair and maintain the new locks.

Successful digital transformation requires three key personalities:

- Risk-taking digital executive who is ready and willing to try (and fail). To quote Mark Zuckerberg, Founder, Chairman and CEO Facebook, "The biggest risk is not taking risk. In a world that is changing really quickly, the only strategy that is guaranteed to fail is not taking risks."
- Technical competence to support through required hardware and software.
- An oversight function that supports risk and makes sure it is focused on the strategic objectives to deliver results.

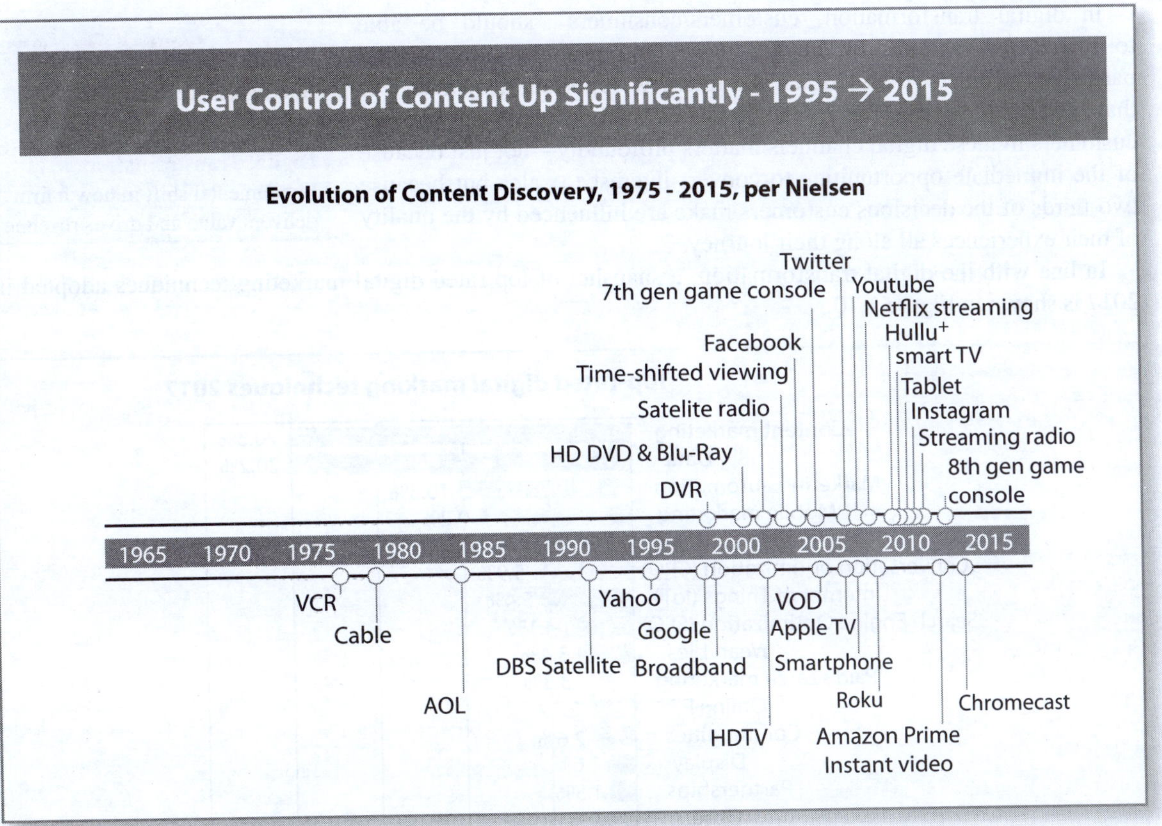

Figure 1.8 User Control of Content Up Significantly - 1995 - 2015

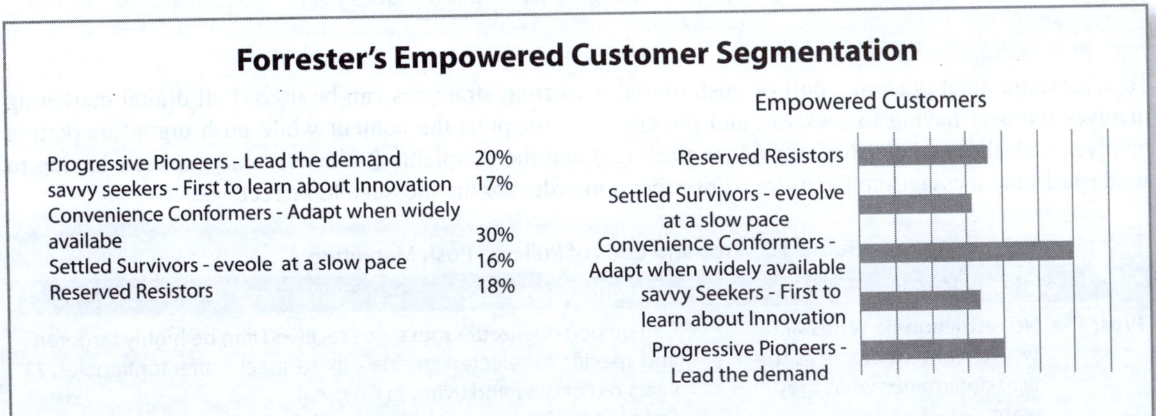

Source: Graphic based on The Data Digest: Introducing Forrester's Empowered Customer Segmentation, https://go.forrester.com/blogs/16-07-12-the_data_digest_introducing_forresters_empowered_customer_segmentation/.

Figure 1.9 Forrester's Empowered Customer Segmentation

In digital transformation, customers/consumers should be able to search for products by image, voice, and gesture; automatically participate in others' transactions; and find new opportunities via devices that augment their reality (e.g. Google Glass) and how companies engage customers in these digital channels matters profoundly—not just because of the immediate opportunities to convert interest to sales but because two-thirds of the decisions customers make are influenced by the quality of their experiences all along their journey.

> **Artificial Intelligence (AI):** Intelligence demonstrated by machines
>
> **Digital Transformation:** Fundamental shift in how a firm delivers value and drives revenue

In line with the digital transformation, a snapshot of top rated digital marketing techniques adopted in 2017 is shown in Figure 1.10.

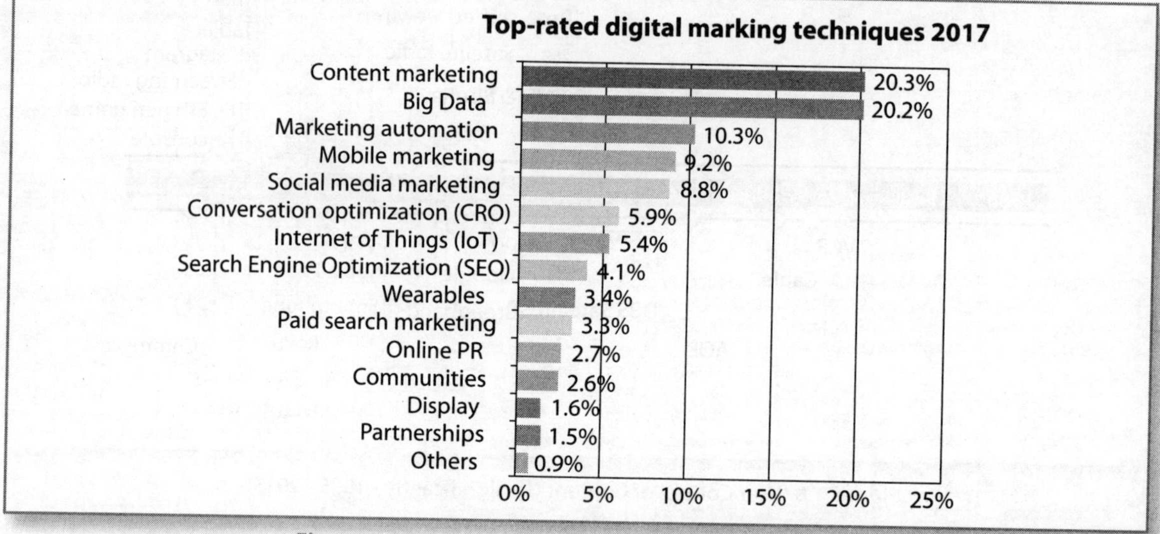

Figure 1.10 Top-rated Digital Marking Techniques 2017

Tools in the virtual world

To achieve the final outcome, pull or push digital marketing strategies can be used. Pull digital marketing involves the user having to seek out and directly grab (or pull) the content while push digital marketing involves both the marketer (creator of the message) and the recipients (the user)—the marketer having to send (push) the messages to the users (subscribers) in order for the message to be received.

Table 1.2 Pros and Cons of Pull and Push Marketing

	Pull digital marketing	Push digital marketing
Pros:	• No restrictions in terms of type of content or size as the user determines what they want. • No technology required to send the content, only to store/display it. • No regulations or opt-in process required.	• Can be personalized -- messages received can be highly targeted and specific to selected criteria – like a special offer for females, 21 years old or over and living in Chennai. • Detailed tracking and reporting – marketers can see not only how many people saw their message but also specific information about each user such as their name as well as demographic and psychographic data. • High Return on Investment (ROI) possible – if executed the right way, push messaging can help drive new revenue as well as brand reinforcement.

	Pull digital marketing	Push digital marketing
Cons:	• Considerable marketing effort required for users to find the message/content. • Limited tracking capabilities – only total downloads, page views, etc. • No personalization – content is received and viewed the same across all audiences.	• Compliance issue – each push messaging technology has its own set of regulations, from minor (RSS) to heavily controlled (email and text messaging). • Requires mechanism to deliver content – the marketer has to use an application to send the message, from an email marketing system to RSS feeders. • Delivery can be blocked – if the marketer does not follow the regulations set forth by each push message type, the content can be refused or rejected before getting to the intended recipient.

There are several digital marketing techniques and tools such as search engine optimization (SEO), search engine marketing (SEM), content marketing, influencer marketing, content automation, campaign marketing, data-driven marketing and ecommerce marketing, social media marketing, social media optimization, email direct marketing, display advertising, ebooks, and optical disks and games are becoming more common in our advancing technology. In fact, digital marketing now extends to non-Internet channels that provide digital media, such as mobile phones SMS and MMS, callback, and on-hold mobile ring tones.

In subsequent chapters, some of these techniques will be examined in greater detail.

In addition, we have today multiple and easy choices of digital tools to organize day-to-day functions. Some of them are given below:

- Dropbox – File sharing
- Asana- the project management tool
- Buffer – automizes posting to social media
- Canva – to create visual content
- Evernote – one stop organizer
- Picasa – Photo editor
- Reader – News snippets
- Navigators – Google Maps and Apple Maps

Exhibit 1.7 Some Digital Tools

CHAPTER SUMMARY

- Customers today are able to search for products, place and activities by image, voice, and gesture; automatically participate in others' transactions; and find new opportunities via devices that augment their reality (e.g. Google Glass).
- Majority of the decisions customers make are influenced by the quality of their experiences all along their journey.
- Digital marketing should be understood as online data-driven marketing. It is the marketing of products or services using digital technologies.
- **Inbound marketing** refers to marketing activities that bring visitors in, rather than marketers having to go out to get prospects' attention. In contrast, buying attention, cold-calling, direct paper mail, radio, TV advertisements, point of sale material, telemarketing and traditional advertising are considered "outbound marketing".
- Digital consumer spending in India is estimated to be $100 bn. opportunity and that online spender base is estimated to grow 2-3x across sectors led by women, new users from smaller cities and 35+ years shoppers will drive this growth".
- A 2017 Nielsen study in US indicates online for FMCG shopping is pervasive and all generations and income levels are shopping online. However, 61% are millennials and can be called Consumer 2.0.
- Customers 2.0 who are encountered online are the same people who walk into a store, call on the

telephone, or order from mail order catalogue. They are doing exactly the same what people have been doing for many years—communicating with each other. The shift is that technology has enabled them to communicate faster, over distances, over mobile phones, and in non-grammatical words and emojis. Customer 2.0 is essentially a reflection of the above shift in consumer consciousness being experienced across Generation X and Y.

- Customers 1.0 love to read magazines and papers and are inclined to make brand choices on traditional advertising. They do not quite understand what this digital is all about. Tweeting is what birds do! Customers 1.0 expect to resolve product issues through the traditional avenues of phone and face-to-face customer support. Customers 1.0 make decisions on the basis of word of mouth endorsements.
- Customers 2.0 expect these technological advances to become a part of their consumer experience. They are not treated as novel or new, they are just expected to be there and are digital natives. They have spent their entire lives surrounded by and using computers, videogames, digital music players, video cams, cell phones, and all the other toys and tools of the digital age.
- Digital Immigrants, who are the older generation not born into the digital world but have, at some later point in our lives, become fascinated by and adopted many or most aspects of the new technology.
- Digital marketing's development since the 1990s and 2000s has changed the way brands and businesses use technology for marketing. As digital platforms are increasingly incorporated into marketing plans and everyday life, and as people use digital devices more and more, to accompany the 4Cs of classical marketing, 4Cs of digital marketing have been proposed—Content, Cost, Channel and Creativity. A fifth C could be added viz. Collaboration.
- A 2015 Forrester model for the empowered customer, divides customers into five tiers, from Progressive Pioneers to Reserved Resisters that is similar to consumer adoption process wherein innovators (2.5%) and early adopters (13.5%) account for 16%. The empowered customer is increasingly savvy and expects a highly personalized experience, one that is consistent across channels.
- **Digital transformation and user control** of content is causing waves across the industry. This shift breaks into five inter-related insights.
  - Customer expectations continue to rise
  - SPEED is important
  - Customer insight continues to be essential
  - Artificial Intelligence (AI) is central through
    - Sensing
    - Comprehension
    - Analysis
    - Guidance
    - Action
  - Digital transformation means business transformation and requires three key personalities
    - Risk-taking digital executive who is ready and willing to try
    - Technical competence to support through required hardware and software
    - An oversight function that supports risk and makes sure it is focused on the strategic objectives to deliver results.

CLOSING CASE — CASE LET

Consumer 2.0 – Education

With a three-fold growth in average daily usage in 2018 over 2017, visitor growth in the education sector in India is twice as much as the broader web.

In January 2018, websites classified as 'education' websites received 440 million visits. Among categories that could be of potentially similar nature, education had the highest traffic[18].

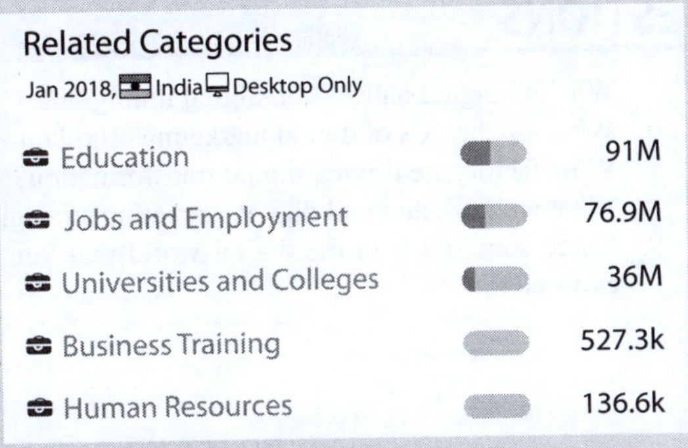

The education sector has a diverse range of online offerings ranging from websites that provide examination results to online training programmes.

What traditional analytics capture of traffic in the education sector is probably limited to the conventional end of the educational spectrum. This is likely only a part of the total universe of educational offering on the Internet, since there are many micro enterprises that offer a wide array of educational support and services using the Internet. Most of these are analogous to 'mom-and-pop' stores or cottage sector enterprises.

Khanacademy.org is probably the most famous of such organisations. Started from a bedroom and a Youtube channel, this site is now among the highest ranked sites of its type in the US with 250000 monthly unique visitors to the site in January 2018. Interestingly, though the site is most popular in the US, its next largest markets are India, Canada and Mexico. What is also interesting is that there are 40 other websites listed as similar to khanacademy.org. Two possibilities arise as a result—one, that the innate ability of digital capabilities allows individual educators to scale out without significant costs and, the second, that given the diversity of educational needs, it is possible to cater to small niches without the need to scale to Internet proportions.

It is this approach that has led to the spawning of sites that offer online tutorial help; homework help; music training among others. For example, buddyschool.com offers the services of tutors for lessons in subjects across the spectrum from humanities to sciences to applied knowledge. What is more, students can choose their tutors and set lesson timings.

These co-exist with the Massive Open Online Courses (MOOC) offered by some of the leading universities in the world who have put their curriculum online as well as spawned educational entrepreneurs like Udacity and Coursera.

Other such learning opportunities that digital technologies have spawned are the various certification programmes offered by the new breed of online enablers such as Google, Amazon, Microsoft, Salesforce among others.

Digital platforms also offer conventional education providers, schools, colleges, universities, to experiment and enhance their offerings by completing and supplementing education programmes as well as administrative processes.

The limits to which digital technologies can be used in education are only limited by one's imagination—the most recent application of digital technologies is a platform that offers a 360 degree view of the student across the students life. Through data capture across the student body, the application expects to be able to predict unconnected issues in personal and public health; social circumstances, etc.

Case Questions

1. Why are education portals important for Consumer 2.0?
2. What have been the recent developments in education sector on account of digital transformation?

REVIEW QUESTIONS

1. What is your understanding of digital marketing?
2. What are inbound marketing and outbound marketing? How are they related to digital marketing?
3. What is the estimated monetary impact of digital marketing in India?
4. Who are Consumers 2.0 and what role do they play in digital marketing?
5. Who are digital natives and digital immigrants?
6. What are the 5Cs of digital marketing? Explain.
7. What factors are driving digital transformation?
8. What are push and pull digital marketing strategies?
9. Name some tools in the digital world that you are exposed to.

ACTIVITY QUESTIONS

1. Using Kerpoof (https://lol.disney.com/kerpoof) create a short illustrated story.
2. Using befunky (https://www.befunky.com) create a collage of some funny emotions from your pictures library.

KEY TERMS

Artificial intelligence (AI)
Campaign marketing
Content automation
Content marketing
Customer 1.0
Customer 2.0
Data-driven marketing
Digital consumer
Digital consumer spending
Digital immigrants
Digital marketing
Digital natives
Digital transformation
Display advertising
Ebooks
eCommerce marketing
Email direct marketing
Inbound marketing
Influencer marketing
Marketing
Marketing mix
Outbound marketing
Pull digital marketing
Push digital marketing
Search engine marketing (SEM)
Search engine optimization (SEO)
Social media marketing
Social media optimization
4Cs of digital marketing
5 components of AI

REFERENCES

1. Internet in India – 2017; IAMAI study.
2. Diffusion of Innovations, Everett Rogers
3. Rage Analytics
4. E. van Bommel, D. Edelman, and K. Ungerman, "Digitizing the Consumer Decision Journey", https://www.mckinsey.com/business-functions/marketing-and-sales/our-insights/digitizing-the-consumer-decision-journey. Accessed on February 7, 2019.
5. https://www.theidm.com/getmedia/d12ca621-10e7-47c1-bd66-4d864a2e1d81/C-1-1.pdf.
6. "Digital Marketing Vs. Traditional Marketing: Which One Is Better"? https://www.digitaldoughnut.com/articles/2016/july/digital-marketing-vs-traditional-marketing. Accessed on February 7, 2019.
7. Tunde Olanrewaju and Paul Willmott, "Finding your digital sweet spot", https://www.mckinsey.com/business-functions/digital-mckinsey/our-insights/finding-your-digital-sweet-spot. Accessed on February 7, 2019.
8. "Digital Consumer Spending in India: A $100 Bn Opportunity",http://mediavataar.com/index.php/news/item/12375-digital-consumer-spending-in-india-a-100-bn-opportunity. Accessed on February 7, 2019.
9. Ryan, Damien and Jones Calvin (2009), *Understanding Digital Marketing,* Kogan Page, New Delhi.
10. Marc Prensky, (2001) "Digital Natives, Digital Immigrants Part 1", On the Horizon, Vol. 9 Issue: 5, pp.1-6. https://doi.org/10.1108/10748120110424816.

11. Retail Industry in India, IBEF, https://www.ibef.org/industry/retail-india.aspx.
12. Grönroos, Christian. "From marketing mix to relationship marketing: towards a paradigm shift in marketing." Management decision 32.2 (1994): 4-20.
13. McCarthy, Jerome E. (1964). *Basic Marketing. A Managerial Approach*. Homewood, IL: Irwin.
14. Needham, Dave (1996). *Business for Higher Awards*. Oxford, England: Heinemann.
15. A Soni, 4Ps of Marketing to 4Cs of Digital Marketing, https://www.linkedin.com/pulse/4ps-marketing-4cs-digital-aditya-soni/.
16. https://go.forrester.com/blogs/16-07-12-the_data_digest_introducing_forresters_empowered_customer_segmentation/.
17. A Sharma, "Online Retailers Should Care More About the Post-Purchase Experience," Harvard Business Review, https://hbr.org/2016/05/online-retailers-should-care-more-about-the-post-purchase-experience.
18. Rage Analytics

CHAPTER 2

DEMYSTIFYING DIGITAL MARKETING AND SOCIAL MEDIA

CHAPTER OBJECTIVES

After reading this chapter, you will be able to

- Understand evolution of marketing communication through ages
- Explain Web as an effective communication platform, from static Web 1.0 to Interactive 2.0
- Analyze the unfolding of consumerism and marketing in digital era
- Discuss from marketplace to marketspace – Brick & Mortar to Brick & Click
- Distinguish between digital marketing and social media marketing

OPENING CASE

CASE LET

From Brick and Mortar to Brick and Click – Travel Tickets

In the Indian context, IRCTC or Indian Railways demonstrated the disruptive power of the Internet and the speed with which the task of issuing tickets went from a cumbersome physical task to an activity that could be performed digitally in the presence of one's own space at any time of the day.

Earlier any manner of ticket to travel from one city to another required devoting nearly an entire day (sometimes sleeping overnight on railway platforms) standing in queues to buy a ticket, or, if one was not interested in standing in queues, being at the mercy of middlemen selling tickets at inflated prices. Even worse, the ticket, a precious slip of paper or cardboard had to be protected like the family jewels, for, without it one could not travel.

The first shot across the bow of this tyranny in India, was, surprisingly enough, fired by the Government owned public sector behemoth, Indian Railways. In 2002, the Indian Railway Catering and Tourism Corporation (IRCTC) launched railway tickets online. In its initial days, one would book the ticket online and the physical ticket would be couriered to the passenger. Since the ticket was issued without the presence of a railway staff, ticket holders of online tickets had to carry identification documents to show the railway staff for verification and to sate the suspicious railway bureaucracy that fraud did not take place.

The initial launch was circumspect with constraints placed on IRCTC. For instance, in its early days, the number of tickets that could be booked by IRCTC were restricted by the Railways. IRCTC though marched on, and wherever possible brought in digital functionalities as it could, within the constraints imposed on it. As a result, IRCTC has been launching enhancements with unfailing regularity and today, has moved from tickets being couriered to tickets being sent via SMS.

Somewhat similar to this was the move from physically handwritten/printed tickets from airlines to today's boarding passes on smart phones. In the case of the airlines though, the change was not voluntary, but induced by the airline ticketing systems like SABRE, Amadeus, Galileo, etc. With Redbus, pioneering bus tickets online, most of the public transport ticketing is now digital.

From 27 tickets in Day 1 when IRCTC launched online ticketing to nearly 6,00,000 tickets per day, accounting for 63% of the reservations on Indian Railways today, the transformation from brick to click is nearly complete. And, considering that there could be up to 67 variations in ticket pricing between two points in Indian Railways, this is no mean feat!

Case Question

How has digital transformation impacted ticketing in travel industry?

INTRODUCTION

Communication has been an essential component in marketing, and according to Kotler, the mantra of marketing is "CCDVTP or Create, Communicate and Deliver Value to a Target market at a Profit". Products create value, value is communicated through integrated marketing communication or IMC. IMC is one of the "Ps" of the marketing mix. As we saw in Chapter 1, the marketing mix refers to four broad levels of marketing decision, namely: *Product, Price, Promotion, and Place.* IMC was earlier referred to as advertising and sales promotion or ASP. This chapter will examine the importance and evolution of marketing communications .

> **CCDVTP:** Create, Communicate and Deliver Value to a Target market at a Profit (Definition by Philip Kotler)
> **Marketing Communication:** Use of different marketing channels and tools in combination

EVOLUTION OF DIGITAL: COMMUNICATION THROUGH THE AGES

Since the era of Adam and Eve, people have been trying to influence others, utilizing whatever means available to them at that point in time. Human voice was the first medium, which is now called word of mouth. In the Stone Age, pieces of sharp stone was used by natives, who etched images and markings on trees, on stones and in caves that may have appeared as random. However, these primitive images had stories to tell, communicated ideas and insights on life in that period. These have endured several ages and civilizations. These also demonstrated the power of images and messages in storytelling and propagation of ideas. These seem to be the first evidence of marketing and advertising, for, they influenced

Johannes Gutenberg invents Printing Press	1440
Emergence of Magazines	1730
First Print Ad in newspaper – France	1836
Earliest recorded use of Telegraph for mass transmission	1864
Earliest Recorded Bill board rentals	1867
Radio advertising	1922
Earliest computer	1940
First recorded use of Television advertising	1941
Telemarketing	1950

Exhibit 2.1 Evolution of Communication through Ages

the perception and behavior. Through millennia, advances in technology contributed to the evolution of communication, each altering the way business was carried out and the way businesses communicated with their customers.

None of these advancements, however, pathbreaking they may have been, superseded those which came before them. Rather they co-existed and augmented them, offering more variety and diversity. Even today, in these days of paid search placement, key word targeted pay per click advertising and social networking (digital marketing/inbound marketing), we still find earlier forms of communication (traditional/outbound marketing) co-existing. From China and New Zealand in the East to San Francisco in the West, human

Media Evolution – India	
1. Bombay Samachar in Gujarati	1822
2. Indian Broadcasting Company (IBC) , Bombay	1927
3. IBC turns All India Radio (AIR)	1936
4. PTI born	1947
5. ISI Calcutta acquires first 1 KB computer	1955
6. Vividh Bharati Kicks off	1957
7. ESSO installs IBM 1400	1961
8. IBM manufactures 1401 in India	1963
9. Hum Log DD's first soap opera	1984
10. Cable TV in Major Metros	1990
11. Launch of Mobile Phones	1995
12. VSNL Launches Internet	1995
13. Print circulation crosses 126 million	1998
14. KBC/Saas Bhi Bahu create histories	2000
15. Satellite communication through INSAT	2002
16. DTH Kicks off in Major Towns	2005

Exhibit 2.2 Media Evolution -India

Consumerism in India	
1. AI/IA launch	1953
2. H M starts manufacture of Ambassador cars	1957
3. Bajaj starts manufacturing scooters	1961
4. Colour television transmission commences	1982
5. Maruti 800 launch	1983
6. Minicomp launches first PC	1985
7. Entry of satellite TV during Gulf war & First ATM	1991
8. First private airline Damania	1992
9. Private FMs take slots on AIR	1993
10. Rediff.com & Indiainfoline launched	1995
11. McDonalds enter India at Delhi	1996
12. Import restrictions relaxed and sale legalized	2001
13. FlipKart Founded	2007
14. Amazon Entry through Junglee.com	2012

Exhibit 2.3 Consumerism in India

voice, the first communication medium in the history, still goes strong and can be heard, be it a bazaar in the East or a Mall in the West. In line with global developments, evolution in media and consumerism has been witnessed in India in the last two millennia.

Though many of the above were perceived to be pathbreaking and fueled consumer spending, India still was a traditional economy and was a seller's market. In most sectors, businesses sold what they produced sheerly on account of a huge and underserved domestic market. Consequent to first liberalization in 1991despite permitting entry of foreign players and FDI, license regime still persisted. Internet and mobile phones appeared only in 1995 but the infrastructure did not support the bandwidth. However, considering that the first web page globally went online in 1991, India was not far behind.

On the global scale, to understand the explosive growth of Internet, we need to look back at how early communications technology evolved into the global network of interconnected computers that we call today Internet. In his seminal book *The Victorian Internet,* Tom Standage looks at wired telegraph that was to be the first known electronic communication network. In April 1746, in an experiment conducted at a convent in Paris, 200 unsuspecting monks were wired to a battery that gave them an electric shock which conclusively demonstrated electricity could transmit a message from one location to another instantly. In 1842, Samuel Morse demonstrated a working telegraph between two committee rooms in Washington and sought USD 30,000 for an experimental telegraph line between Washington and Baltimore. Congress voted for the proposal, with a slim majority of 89 for and 83 against, with 70 abstentions. Despite the reservations, it was a huge success and by 1850, US had 12000 miles of telegraph. Gradually, the telegraph crossed Atlantic and transformed the way business was conducted across continents. For the first time, people could communicate almost instantly across continents and oceans. This paved the way for the next invention in 1877 when Graham Bell spoke with his assistant in the next room through his latest invention—The Telephone.

The birth of Internet can be traced to Advanced Research Project Agency (ARPA) in 1958. However, it was not till 1965 that researchers hooked up a computer at MIT with an US Airforce computer. ARPANET project was started in 1966 and in 1969 ARPANET was used to connect two computers one at UCLA and the other at Stanford Research Institute. This network grew quickly and by 1974 had 46 nodes including overseas locations of Norway and London. In 1971 Ray Tomlinson wrote the first program capable of sending mail from a user on one host computer to another user on another computer. This was the origin of email. The term Internet was first used in 1974 by Vinton Cerf (Father of Internet) who was working on standardizing the way different computers communicated and defined Transmission Control Program (TCP) which subsequently evolved as the TCP/IP protocol that was started using by ARPANET in 1983. This may be considered as the true birth of Internet. The same year the system of domain names such as .com, .net, etc. were invented. By 1984 the number of nodes in the fledgling network crossed 1000 and by 1989 crossed 100000 hosts.

Chronology

Fifteen years of the web	http://news.bbc.co.uk/2/hi/technology/5243862.stm
06-Aug-91	Tim Berners Lee releases web software.
12-Dec-91	First web server outside Europe goes online.
November, 1992	There are 26 web servers online.
22-Apr-93	Mosaic web browser for Windows is released.
30-Apr-93	Cern announces that the World Wide Web can be used for free by anyone.
May, 1993	The Tech published by students at the Massachusetts Institute of Technology becomes the first online newspaper.
June, 1993	HTML programming language used to create webpages is released.
November, 1993	First webcam goes online watching a coffee pot.
February, 1994	The precursor to Yahoo written by two US students goes online.
April, 1994	BBC launches its first website for TV programme The Net.
13-Oct-94	Bill Clinton puts whitehouse.gov on the web.
25-Oct-94	Banner adverts for network firm ATT and a drink called Zima appear on websites.
February, 1995	Radio HK becomes the first fulltime web radio station.
01-Jul-95	Online bookstore Amazon.com launched.
August, 1995	There are now 18957 websites online.
09-Aug-95	Dotcom boom begins on the stock markets.

Exhibit 2.4 First Fifteen Years of the Web

24-Aug-95	Microsofts Internet Explorer released as part of Windows 95.
04-Sep-95	Online auction site eBay founded as Auctionweb.
15-Dec-95	First multilingual search engine Alta Vista launched.
04-Jul-96	Hotmail is launched on Independence Day in the US.
August, 1996	There are now 342081 websites online.
March, 1997	BBC News launches a website to cover the 1997 election.
June, 1997	Domain name business.com sold for 150000 £80000.
17-Dec-97	Web commentator Jorn Barger coins the term weblog later shortened to blog.
01-Mar-98	Kozmo.com that promised free one-hour delivery of anything launches.
September, 1998	Google opens its first office in a garage in California.
16-Mar-99	Everquest a massively multiplayer online roleplaying game is released.
May, 1999	Shawn Fanning, a student in Boston founds Napster
19-Aug-99	Original MySpace website launched as a file sharing service.
November, 1999	Boo.com launches selling branded fashion wear.
10-Jan-00	AOL buy Time Warner for 162 bn, the largest corporate merger ever.
14-Jan-00	The dotcom bubble reaches its peak.
07-Feb-00	Eight websites including Yahoo, CNN and Amazon crippled by hacker.
August, 2000	Nearly 20 million websites online.
11-Jan-01	A Grateful Dead track demonstrates podcasting for the first time.
15-Jan-01	Online encyclopaedia Wikipedia is founded by Jimmy Wales.
04-Sep-01	Google awarded a patent for its PageRank algorithm used in its search engine.
22-Nov-01	Pope John Paul II sends the first papal email from a laptop in his office.
11-Dec-02	The FBI starts virtual wanted posts.
28-Apr-03	Apples iTunes music download service launched.
May, 2003	The first flash mob is organized in Manhattan over the web.
27-Jan-04	Amazon.com makes the first ever full year profit since its launch.
05-Feb-04	Janet Jackson's breast becomes the most searched for image in web history.
July, 2004	Tim Berners Lee receives a knighthood.
19-Aug-04	Google goes public. Shares are offered at 85. Fifteen months later they are worth over 400 each.
09-Nov-04	Mozilla Firefox web browser launched.
February, 2005	Video sharing site youtube.com goes online.
October, 2005	The web grows more in 2005 than during the whole dot-com boom. Seventeen million new sites go online.
12-Apr-06	Google launches a restricted service in China called Gu Ge.
2006	There are now 92615362 websites online.

Exhibit 2.4 (Continued)

WEB AS AN EFFECTIVE COMMUNICATOR

In 1989, Tim Berners-Lee built the first web page at CERN and went online on August 6, 1991. It contained information about World Wide Web (www), how to get a web browser and how to set up a web server. Over time this also became the first ever web directory, as Berners-Lee maintained a list of links to other websites on the page as they appeared. "Fifteen Years of the web, Internet time line", a report in bbc.co.uk reported, "In August 1995 there were 18957 websites on line; by August 1996 there were 342081."

In a subsequent interview,[1] Berners Lee explained on his first web page, "I wrote in 1990 the first GUI browser, and called it "WorldWideWeb". It ran on the NeXT computer. (I much later renamed the application Nexus to avoid confusion between the first client and the abstract space itself). The screenshot of WorldWideWeb in Figure 2.1 was taken for a CACM article. By this time it had colour and inline images. The original 1990 Version 1.0 would have looked identical except the book icon and the CERN icon would have been in separate windows - and the whole thing (like NeXT at the time) would have been in grey scale! The screen shot shows me making a link from "Atlas" in a list of experiments to some marked page. Look - no typing URLS, no <angle brackets>! WorldWideWeb was a graphical point-and-click browser with mode-free editing and link creation. It used style sheets, and multiple fonts, sizes, and justification styles. It would download and display linked images, diagrams, sounds animations and movies from anything in the large NeXTStep standard repertoire".

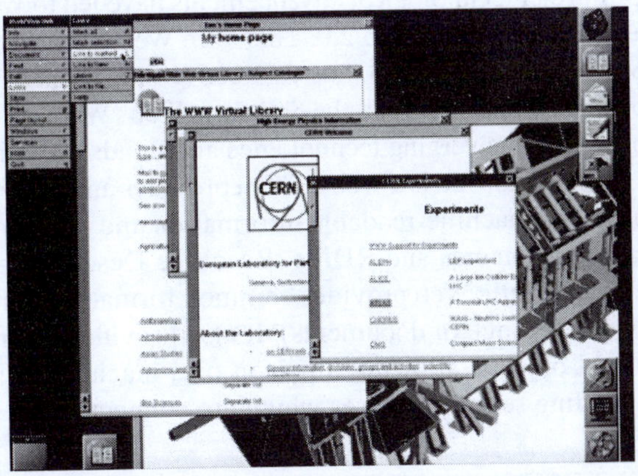

Image Credit: Wikipedia

Exhibit 2.5 Visual of the First Web Page

It soon became evident that webpage and browser could become a powerful medium of communication. In October 1994, Netscape launched Mosaic Netscape, successor to Nexus, a desktop application which became synonymous with Web 1.0. According to Cormode and Krishnamurthy (2008), "Web 1.0 is a retronym referring to the first stage of the World Wide Web's evolution. Content creators were few and Internet was used for very limited purposes, the emphasis used to be on providing information through overstuffing of web-pages consisting mainly of static pages hosted on ISP-run web servers, or on free web hosting services".

Web 2.0, Web 3.0 and Semantic Web

Web 2.0[2] refers to websites that emphasize user-generated content, usability (ease of use, even by non-experts), and interoperability (a website working well with other products, systems, and devices) for end users. Web 2.0 was introduced in 2003–04 to encompass various novel phenomena on the World Wide Web or "Web as Platform", where software applications were built on the Web as opposed to on the desktop and user-generated content (in the form of ideas, text, videos, or pictures) that could be "harnessed" to create value (O'Reilly, 2005). The term was popularized by Tim O'Reilly and Dale Dougherty at the O'Reilly Media Web 2.0 Conference in late 2004, though it was coined by Darcy DiNucci in 1999.

A Web 2.0 website allowed users to interact and collaborate with each other in a social media dialogue as creators of user-generated content in a virtual community, in contrast to the first generation of Web 1.0 websites where people were limited to the passive viewing of content. Web 2.0 features included social networking sites and social media sites like Facebook, blogs, wikis, tagging keywords on websites and links, video sharing sites, hosted services, apps, and collaborative consumption platforms.

Web 2.0: Websites that emphasize user-generated content, usability (ease of use, even by non-experts), and interoperability (a website working well with other products, systems, and devices) for end users
Web 3.0: Connective intelligence; connecting data, concepts, applications and ultimately people
Semantic Web: Web 2.0 that provides an easier way to find, share, reuse and combine information
Social Media: Websites and applications that enable users to create and share content or to participate in social networking

Further technological advancements have led to Web 3.0[3], a term used to describe the evolution of the Web as an extension of Web 2.0. This term Web 3.0 is the popular view held by Tim O'Reilly. In contrast, Nova Spivack defines Web 3.0 as connective intelligence; connecting data, concepts, applications and ultimately people. While some call the Semantic Web 'Web 3.0', Spivack's opinion is that the Semantic Web is just one of several converging technologies and trends that will define Web 3.0.

Semantic Web is a Web 2.0 that provides an easier way to find, share, reuse and combine information. It is based on machine-readable information and builds on XML technology's capability to define customized tagging schemes and RDF's (Resource Description Framework) flexible approach to representing data. The Semantic Web provides common formats for the interchange of data (where on the Web there is only an interchange of documents). It also provides a common language for recording how data relates to real world objects, allowing a person or a machine to start off in one database, and then move through an unending set of databases which are connected not by wires but by being about the same thing.

MARKETING IN DIGITAL ERA

Evolution through technology from static World Wide Web (www) or Web 1.0 through Web 2.0, Web 3.0 (semantic web) have fuelled the growth and emergence of various social media and the concept of ecommerce and ebusinesses. The infographic represented in Figure 2.1 captures the important timelines of the evolution of digital marketing.

Digital Era: The Information Age (also known as the Computer Age, Digital Age, or New Media Age) where the economy is based on information technology

Digital Marketing: Using of both Internet and non-Internet digital channels for marketing

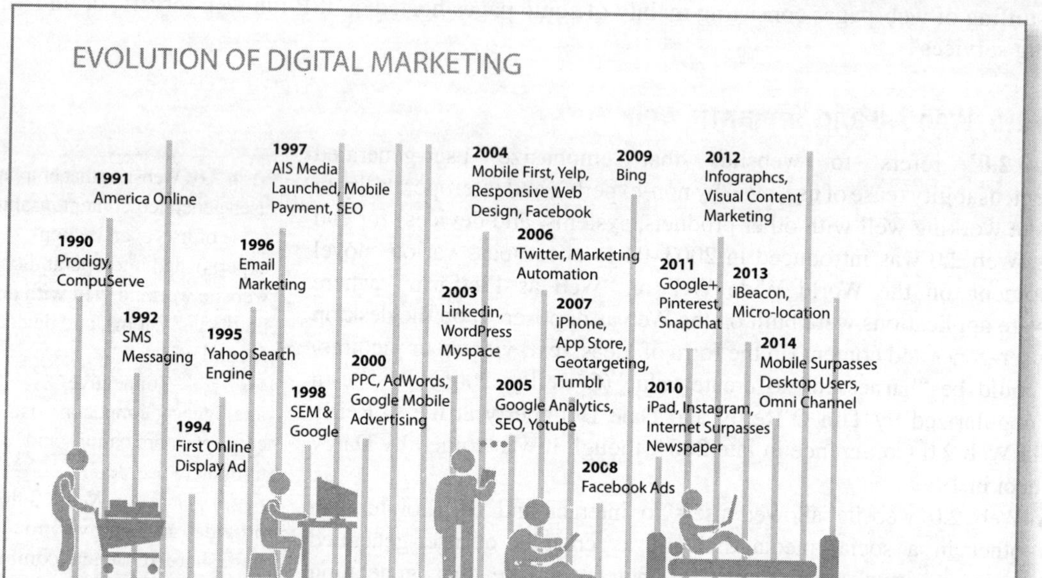

Figure 2.1 Evolution of Digital Marketing

Internet and Web - From Communicators to Marketplace to Marketspace

From Figure 2.1, it is clearly emerging that the Internet connected the world, and enabled by convergence of technologies evolved from a communicating platform to creating a digital marketplace. Rayport and Sviokla in 1994 called the digital marketplace "Market Space[4]"(HBR, Nov-Dec., 1994). A *marketplace* in a generic way is a regular gathering of people for purchase and sale of grocery, agricultural produce and other goods and merchandise. In other words, marketplace is the physical equivalent of what marketers term as the offline model where buyer and seller transactions occur in specific designated places without the use of any electronic communications or software.

The *marketspace* concept, on the other hand, is one which involves information and communication-based electronic exchange environment, where goods and services instead of being sold only physically are marketed through an online space that facilitates bi-directional commerce.

The three different dimension that define a marketspace transaction according to Rayport and Sviokla were:

- The *content* of the transaction being different: information about the product or service replaces the product or service themselves.
- The *context* in which the transaction occurs being different: an electronic, on-screen auction replaces a face-to-face auction.
- The *infrastructure* that enables the transaction to occur is also different: computers and communication lines replace product lots.

The integration and migration of the marketplace from traditional brick and mortar model to marketspace (a virtual or a combination thereof that we discussed in Chapter 1 under digital transformation model) provided the structure for the evolution of what we call digital marketing today.

Marketplace: Physical equivalent of what marketers term as the offline model where buyer and seller transactions occur in specific designated places without the use of any electronic communications or software

Marketspace: Involves information and communication-based electronic exchange environment, where goods and services instead of being sold only physically are marketed through an online space that facilitates bi-directional commerce

Marketspace transaction: Includes three dimensions—content of the transaction, context in which the transaction occurs and infrastructure that enables the transaction to occur

Brick and Click: Combination of offline (bricks) and online (clicks) and refers to digitization in part or full and their integration

Brick and Mortar: Refers to physical assets for operations

Digitization: The conversion of text, pictures, or sound into a digital form that can be processed by a computer

From Brick and Mortar to Brick and Click Model

Brick and mortar is a term that refers to physical assets for operations. On the other hand, a combination of offline (bricks) and online (clicks) refer to digitization in part or full and their integration. When physical components are high like agriculture produce or when customers can interact only offline like SMEs in small towns and most transactions are in cash, they are referred to as brick and mortar. In the brick and click model, companies start embracing on line components. The quantum or proportion of on line component vary. Some may have just begun their web journey with a basic website which may only have a bare bone structure and information. Next in the journey may be selling a small proportion of their products on line with a third party payment gateway integrated. They may still not have integrated the back end that can capture data and analytics. Some companies have adopted full digitization both as a part of value chain (including supply chain) and ecommerce. Apart from the companies, quantum of digitization varies across industries and countries.

Digitization Index

In a 2012 Booz & Company Digitization study on Digitization Index for Europe, financial services, automotive and computer electronics were the three top sectors with greater than 50% digitization whereas hotels, restaurants and construction companies were least digitized. This study used 4 parameters for digital presence—input, processes, infrastructure and output.

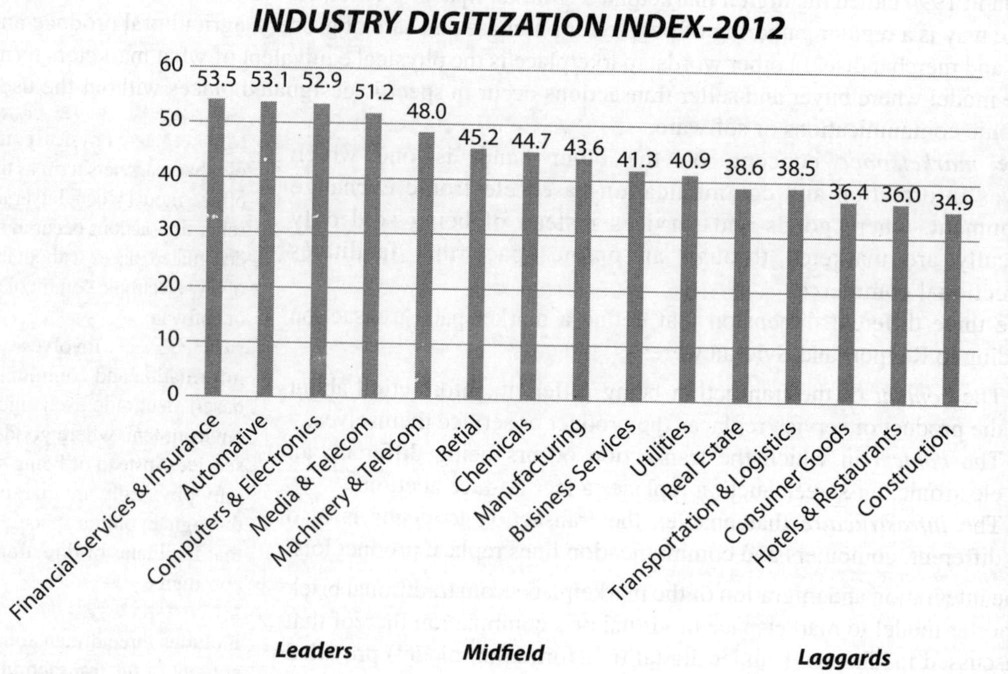

Source: Image created from Booz & Co Report data.

Figure 2.2 Industry Digitization Index - 2012

According to Strategy &[5] (Formerly Booz and Company) 2010 report, the following were the impact of digitization.

- Digitization contributes positively to job creation, with a 10 percent increase in digitization reducing the unemployment rate by 0.84 percent.
- Countries in the advanced digitization stage reap 20 percent more economic benefits than countries at the start of their digitization journeys.
- Policymakers need to acknowledge where their countries currently stand and set into motion programs and plans that focus on the widespread adoption and usage of digitization. That includes elevating digitization on the national agenda, evolving sector governance, adopting an ecosystem perspective, enabling sustainable competition, and stimulating demand.

In this report, India was placed among the 150 constrained countries with less than 30% digitization This would perhaps explain Government of India's digital India movement and demonetization. While digital transformation is important, beneficial and relevant, it is contextual and not necessary that a company operates only online and forgo traditional channels, particularly in India. A case in point will be Lenskart that commenced as purely an online retailer and has started physical store presence. USA Data indicate that even in the year 2040, both the formats will co-exist and have equal share of incremental sales.

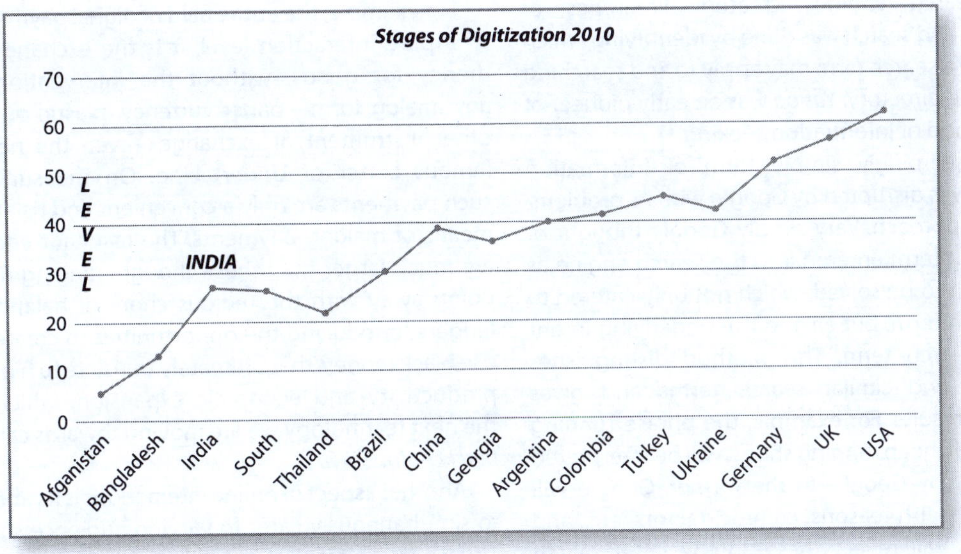

Figure 2.3 Stages of Digitization

As explained in Chapter 1, Table 1.1, comparing traditional and digital marketing as well as the forgoing, one of the main enablers of the migration from brick and mortar model to brick and click has been the growth of interactive platforms. These platforms facilitate a two-way interaction between a human and an electronic medium often in a conversational manner to obtain data or information and to give immediate results. Key types of interactions supported by interactive platforms are:

1. **Information Seeking Interactions –** matching query/search with products/services and guiding the user
2. **Problem-solving Interactions** – real time one on one discussion leading to a solution to problems/pain points
3. **Community Interactions** – utilizing the effects of networks with collaboration/group creation features
4. **Activity/promotions-based Interactions** - conduct online events and contests
5. **Expert Opinion Interactions** - showcasing knowledge and expertise going beyond general query based interactions
6. **Feedback Eliciting Interactions** - real time feedback forms and surveys

Information Seeking Interactions: Matching query/search with products/services and guiding the user
Problem-solving Interactions: Real time one on one discussion leading to a solution to problems/pain points
Community Interactions: Utilizing the effects of networks with collaboration/group creation features
Activity/promotions-based Interactions: Conducting online events and contests
Expert opinion Interactions: Showcasing knowledge and expertise going beyond general query based interactions
Feedback eliciting Interactions: Real time feedback forms and surveys

CASELET

Interactive Platforms – Search Engine

The classical example of a digital interaction is the search engine.

Even though *Google* is the most popular, early development in search engines was based on a completely different model. This model was built on the lines of an analog library. Libraries are typically structured by grouping topics together and creating an index of the items within the topic to make the task of locating a particular item of information. Similarly, early search engines created directories of websites and search was done by identifying which directory a search term may apply to and searching within the directory. *Yahoo* was an early pioneer of this method of information seeking.

This seemingly simple form of information seeking was disrupted by Google with its problem-solving approach. Very simply Google thought of the search term entered into the search engine as a problem to be solved, which not only catered to the search term, but also to the underlying intent of the search term. This method distinguishes between two similar search terms and gives different results. For example, the phrase 'running shoes' and 'cheap running shoes', will be interpreted differently by Google. In the former, Google will consider health reasons, comfort factors, etc., and its results will reflect these. In the latter search term, the operating search term will be the price of running shoes and the Google results will reflect stores ranked on their pricing of running shoes. In the early generation of search engines, a result for the two search terms would have been nearly identical.

Interactions in the digital world have become more sophisticated, fueled by the processing capacity, speed and sophistication in data processing algorithms. Thus, todays' online interactions are not merely the exchange of data, but more profound decision support and process systems.

For example, the entire field of digital payments. At a pure interaction level, it is the exchange of money for goods, without the intervention of any analog form—paper currency, plastic or any other instrument of exchange—even the newly famous Letter of Undertaking. On the surface, such payments are only a convenient and risk-free means of making payments. The resultant effects are much larger than these though, ranging from doing away with the tedious chore of balancing ledgers to reducing the opportunities to create or use black money, that ultimately translate to higher productivity and economic expansion, which is the next technology we are moving towards called *blockchain*.

Another aspect of online interactions is its ability to simultaneously cater to varying audience sizes. Thus, a music teacher in India is able to train and guide a student living in California and a university in California is able to teach a global student body with its Massive Online Open Courses!

Case Questions

1. Which are some of the online transactions you are familiar with?
2. How have search engines evolved to what they are today?
3. Why are online interactions considered disruptive?

THE DIGITAL MARKETSPACE – GLOBAL

Digital Economy: Refers to an economy that is based on digital computing technologies
Internet Economy: Another name for digital economy
New Economy: Another name for digital economy
Web Economy: Another name for digital economy

Electronic devices and the Internet have been the backbone of digital marketspace or digital marketing. In this section, we examine this digital marketspace in both the global and Indian context and how they have contributed to the overall economy in general and digital economy in particular. The term 'Digital Economy' was coined in Don Tapscott's 1995 book *The Digital Economy: Promise and Peril in the Age of Networked Intelligence*[6]. *The Digital Economy* was among the first books to consider how the Internet would change the way we did business. The digital economy is the worldwide network of economic activities, commercial transactions and professional interactions that are enabled by information and communications technologies[7] (ICT). The digital economy is also sometimes called the *Internet Economy*, the *New Economy*, or *Web Economy*. Increasingly, the "digital economy" is intertwined with the traditional economy making a clear delineation harder since both ICT goods and services are included under digital economy[8]. For the purposes of this book, we will consider digital marketing as a part of digital economy. In this section, we will examine the commercial impact.

Global Internet users in 2016 were estimated at 3.4 bn., with the usage growth at a steady 4%, which are credited to smartphones purchases and their installed base.

1. Global Internet Users = 3.4 bn. Flat Growth +10% vs. 10% Y/Y
2. Global Smartphone Shipments = Slowing +3% vs. +10% Y/Y
3. Global Smartphone Installed Base = Slowing +12% vs. +25% Y/Y
4. USA Internet Usage (Engagement) = Solid +4% Y/Y

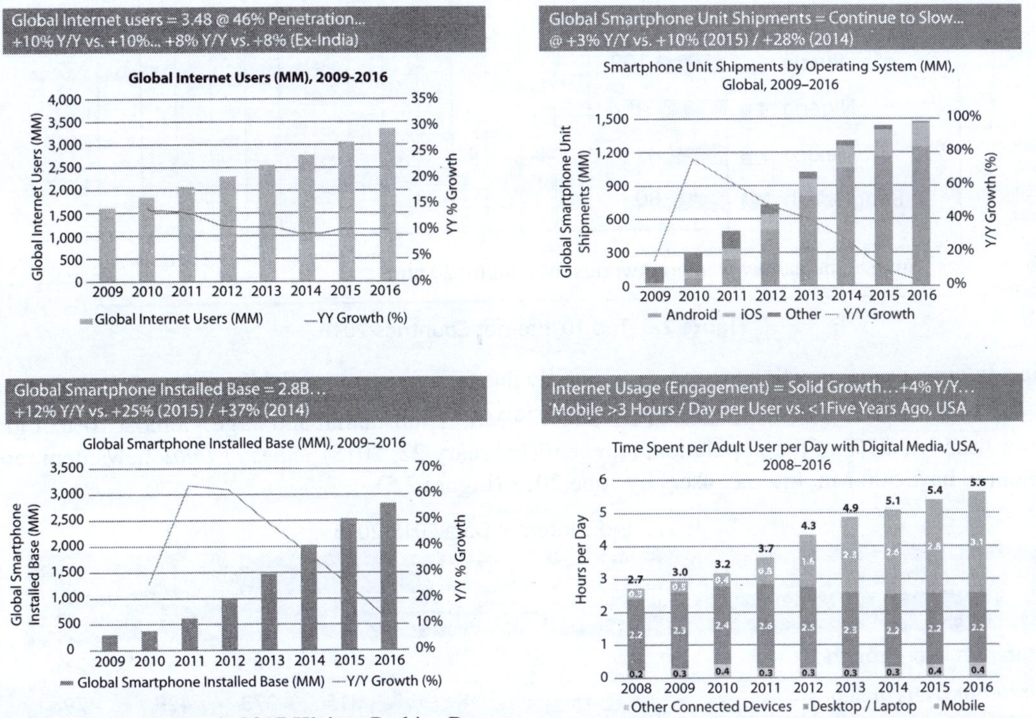

Source: Internet Trends 2017 Kleiner Perkins Report

Figure 2.4 Global Internet Users, Smartphone Users & Internet Usage

THE DIGITAL MARKETSPACE – INDIA

In line with global trends, India has also seen a robust growth in Internet usage. The key drivers for digital marketing environment in India have been

- Emergence of Internet
- Digital natives and digital immigrants
- Technology advancements in devices and user interface
- Liberalization, consumerism and stable economy

In a 2017 estimate, India tops the rank of Internet users next only to China and is significantly ahead of the USA.

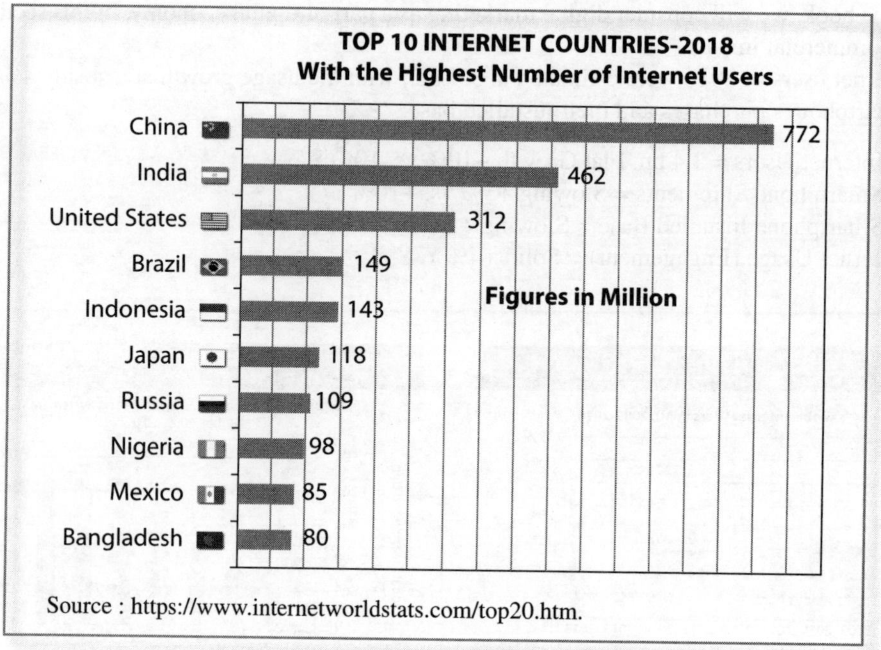

Figure 2.5 Top 10 Internet Countries-2018

India's Internet usage growth has been strong partly due to increasing availability of low cost data access.

- India Internet User Base estimated in 2018 at 479 Mn. is substantial and large - almost 10% of global user base and 27% of the population. A recent (February 22, 2018) *Times of India* news item reports India to have 500 Mn. Internet users by June 2018 (Figure 2.5).

Table 2.1 India Internet Data 2015-2018

India, 2015 – 2018	2015	2016	2017	2018
Internet User Growth	39%	18%	15%	12%
Internet Users (millions)	315	373	429	479
Internet Users (% of population)	25%	30%	34%	37%
Mobile Connections (millions)	986	1019	1047	1071
Mobile Connections (% of population)	79%	81%	82%	83%
Mobile Phone Messaging App Users (millions)	107	133	158	181
Mobile Phone Messaging App Users (% of mobile phone users)	17%	20%	22%	23%
Mobile Phone Messaging App Users (% of population)	9%	11%	12%	14%
Mobile Phone Users (millions)	638	684	731	776
Mobile Phone Users (% of population)	51%	54%	57%	60%

- Decline in data costs and smartphone prices will facilitate the addition of next 200 Mn users.

Source: e Marketer

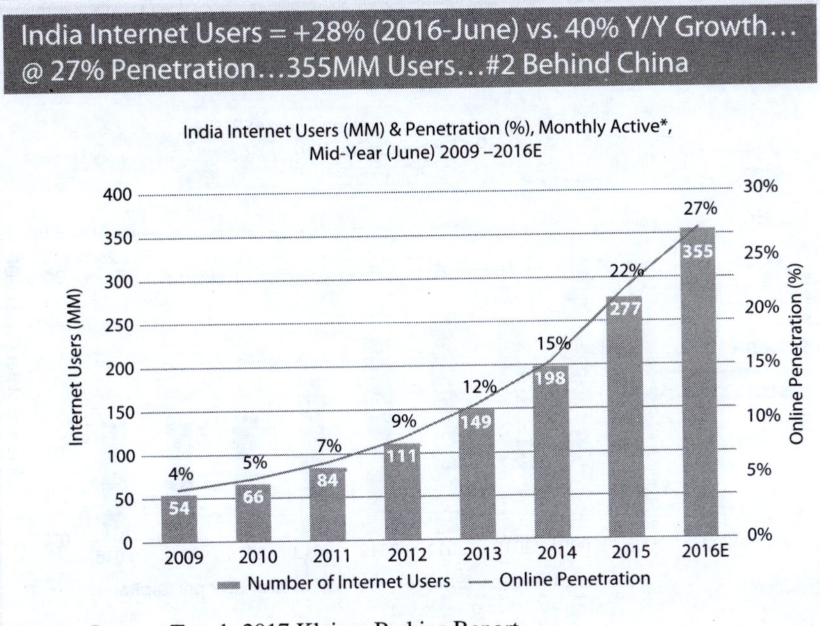

Source: Internet Trends 2017 Kleiner Perkins Report

Figure 2.6 Internet Users - India

- Consequent to the above, increasing time is being spent on smartphones and downloads industry and digital advertising

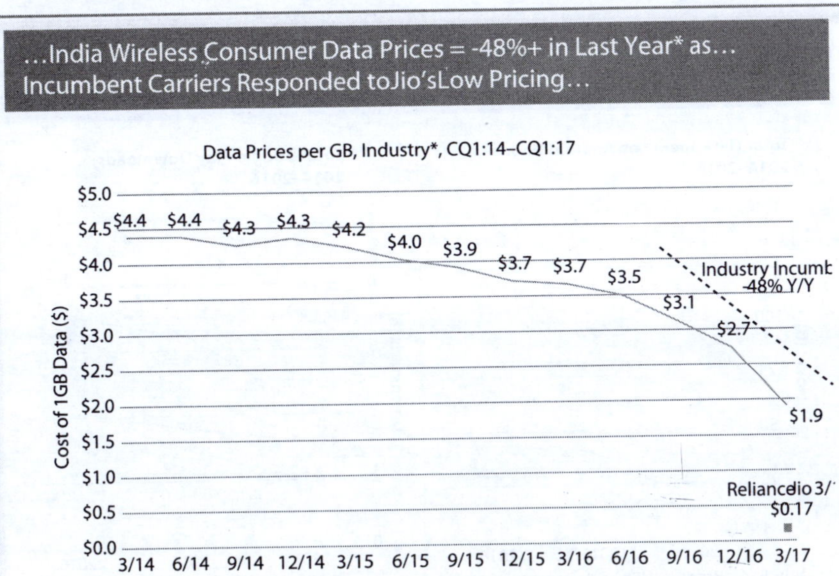

Source: Internet Trends 2017 Kleiner Perkins Report

Figure 2.7 Wireless Consumer Data Prices - India

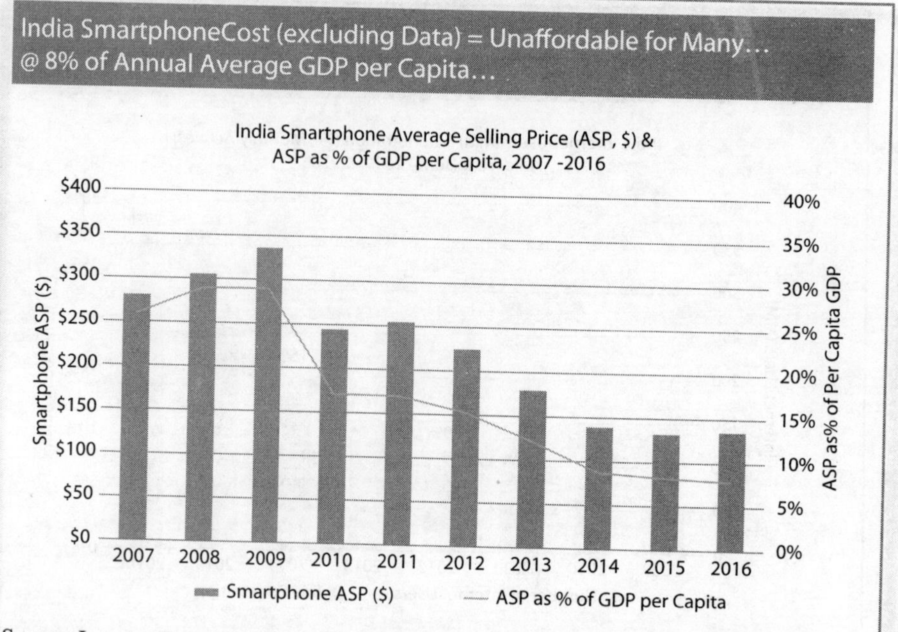

Source: Internet Trends 2017 Kleiner Perkins Report

Figure 2.8 Smartphone Cost - India

- Gen Z's (age 16 – 20) have a distinct preference for fun and streaming that is going to fuel entertainment industry and digital advertising

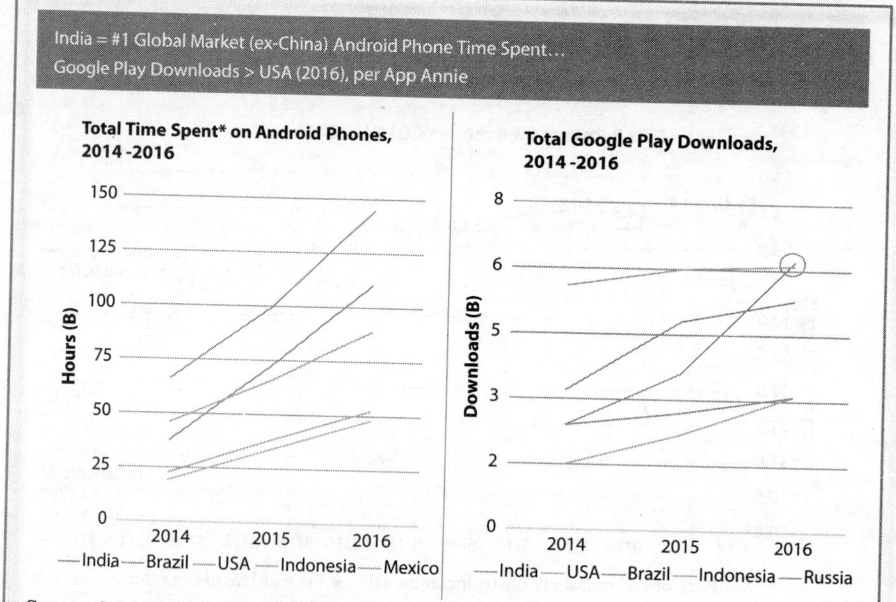

Source: Internet Trends 2017 Kleiner Perkins Report

Figure 2.9 Time Spent on Smartphones

% OF GEN Z WHO SAY THE FOLLOWING ARE THEIR MAIN REASONS FOR USING SOCIAL MEDIA

Gen z (Age - 20) Prefer Fun Content

		INDEX*
To fill up square time	48%	1.22
To find funny or entertaining content	45%	1.23
To stay in touch with what my friends are doing	41%	0.97
To stay up-to-date with news and current events	38%	0.92
To share photos or videos with others	35%	1.07
Because a lot of my friends are on them	34%	1.05
To meet new peoples	34%	1.26
General networking with other peoples	34%	1.00
To share my opinion	31%	1.04
To research/find products to buy	29%	0.98

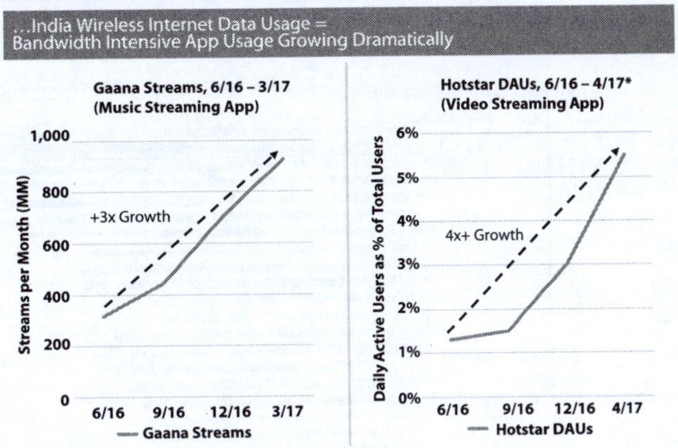

Source: Internet Trends 2017 Kleiner Perkins Report

Figure 2.10 Reasons for Using Social Media among Gen Z

- India is more mobilized than most countries with mobile contributing 65% of Internet traffic and 41% to e-commerce

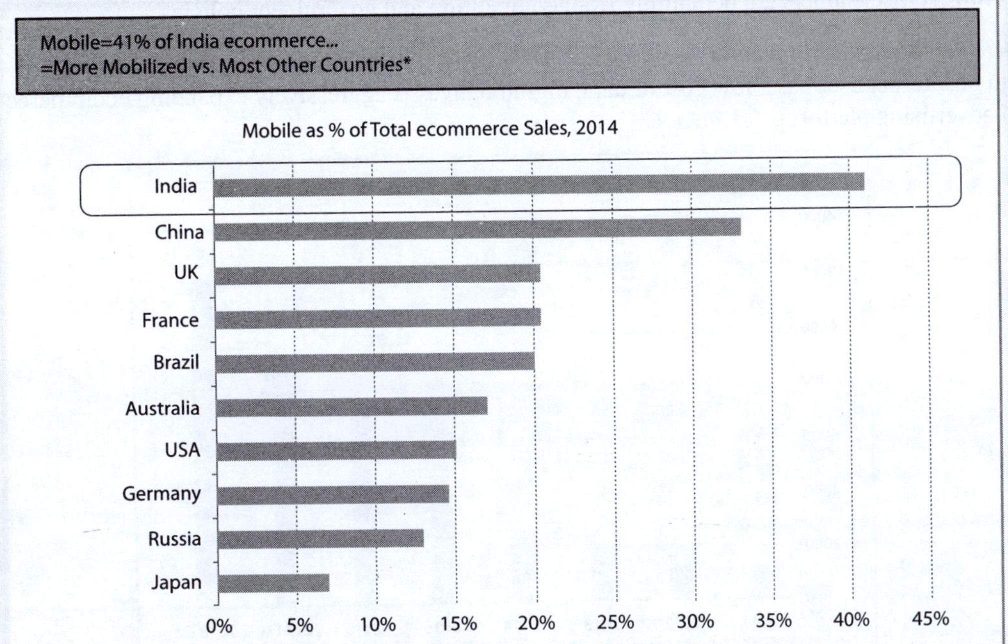

Source: Internet Trends 2017 Kleiner Perkins Report

Figure 2.11 India More Mobilized than Other Countries

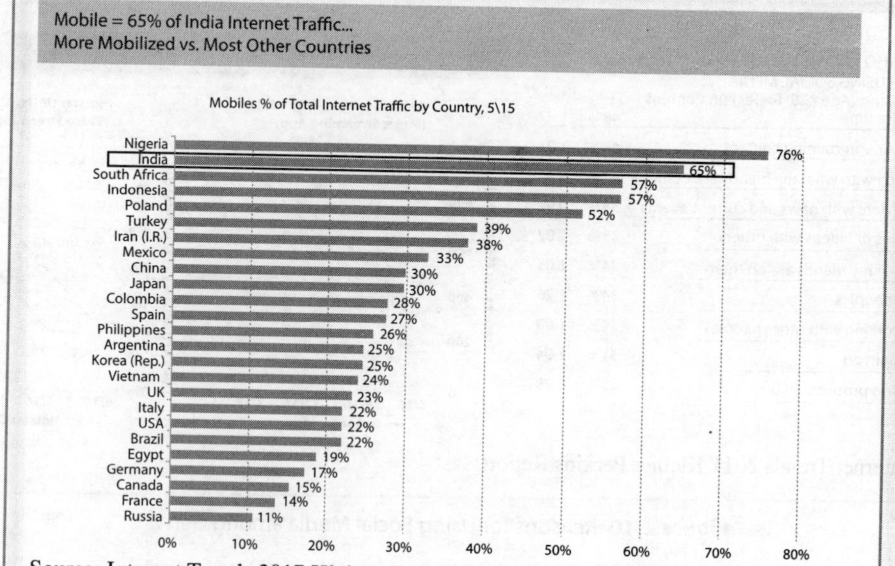

Source: Internet Trends 2017 Kleiner Perkins Report

Figure 2.12 Mobiles % of Internet Traffic

- Constraints of cash flow for many Internet businesses will be a challenge owing to fierce competition and will see a shake out of players. (Aircel winding up)
- However, consumers are benefitting from competition and government policies.

Digital Advertising and eCommerce

Growth of Internet user base, low cost of data, digital natives is aggressively expanding ecommerce and the digital advertising platforms.

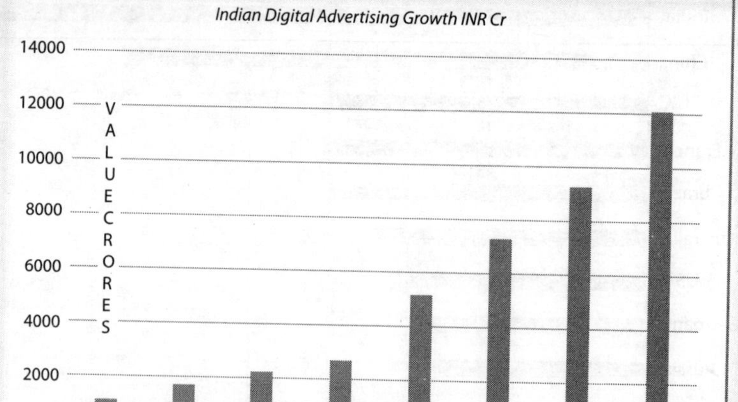

Source: Graphic recreated from mediavataar.com report, May 4 2018 accessed from http://mediavataar.com/index.php/news/item/12623-digital-ad-market-to-reach-inr-12-046-cr-by-dec-2018

Figure 2.13 Digital Advertising Growth - India

- In 2017, India's ad spending was expected to grow at 10% and reach INR 61000 crore or US$ 9.5 billion, of which
  - India's digital advertising is expected to touch ₹9300 crore or US$ 1.5 billion, that will be
  - Growth of 47% over 2016
  - would be Ca 15.5% of total advertising spending

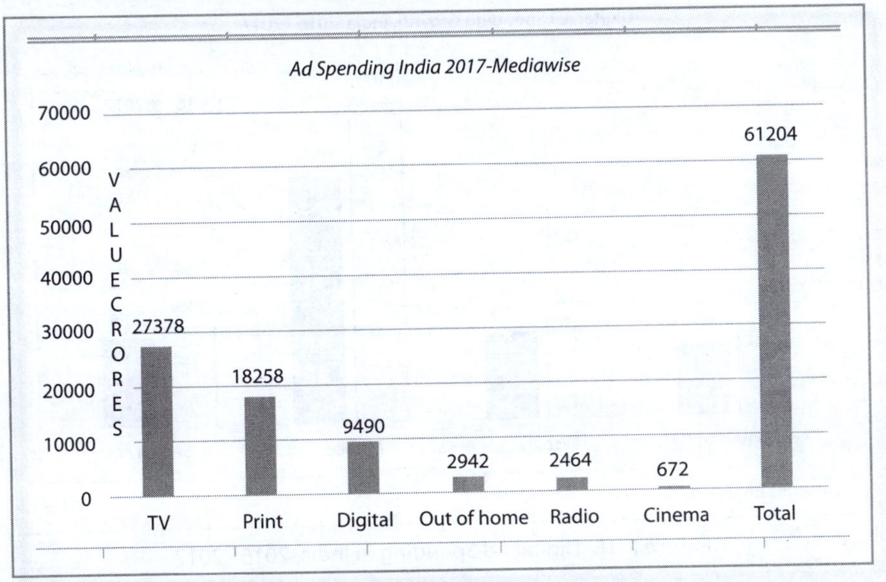

Figure 2.14 Ad Spending in India, 2017

Graph: Drawn basis Group M estimates (https://www.groupm.com/news/groupm-estimates-indias-advertising-expenditure-grow-10-2017)

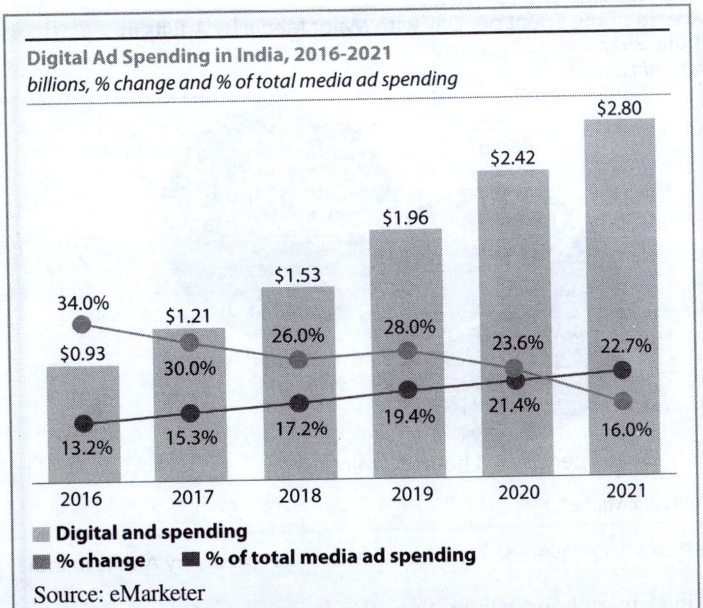

Figure 2.15 Digital Ad Spending in India, 2016-2021

- While the overall digital ad spending has grown by 47% in 2017, mobile ads have shown a robust growth of 110%, the trend mentioned in Chapter 1 that digital natives are on vertical screens than horizontal screens.

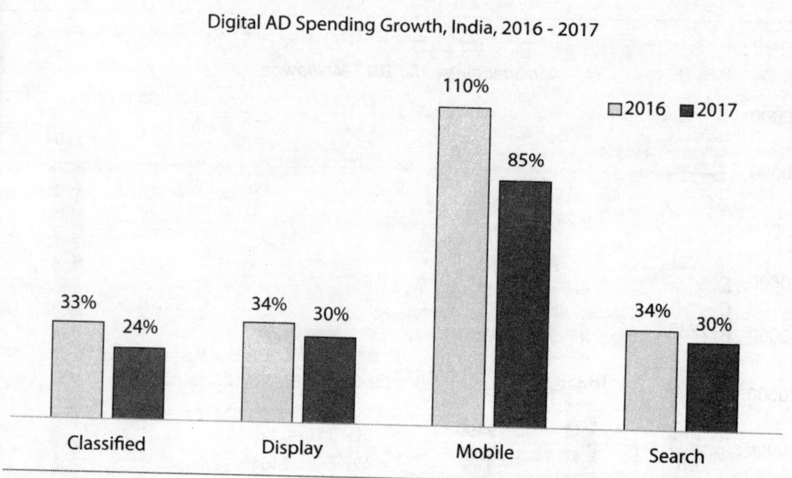

Source: eMarketer

Figure 2.16 Digital Ad Spending in India, 2016 - 2017

- The above has been on account of an average of 1.13 hours spent by an average Indian on digital media that has given a boost to online advertising, online shopping and ecommerce

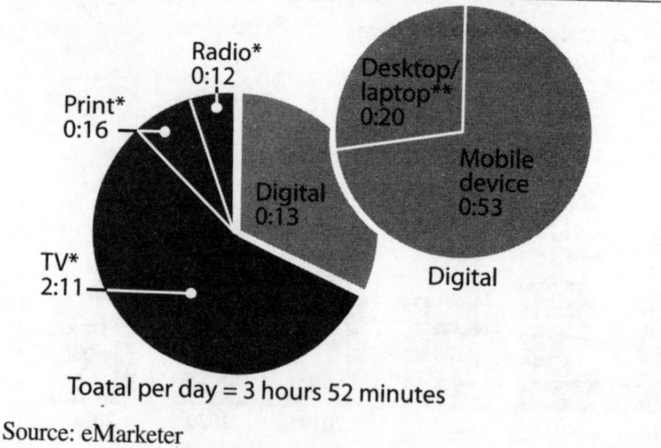

Source: eMarketer

Figure 2.17 Average Time Spent with Major Media by Adults in India

- Propelled by rising smartphone penetration, the launch of 4G networks and increasing consumer wealth, the Indian ecommerce market is expected to grow to US$ 188 billion by 2025. eCommerce is increasingly attracting customers from Tier 2 and 3 cities, where people have limited access to brands but have high aspirations.

- With the increase in awareness about the benefits of online trading, there has been a significant rise in investment in ecommerce business. Hand in hand with offline trading, many established businesses, e.g. Shoppers Stop or Lifestyle, have setup online transaction channels.
- Earlier food and grocery were never thought of as items for online trading. However, with the change of working habits, and consumers opting for adaptability and convenience, there are now innumerable small and large ecommerce companies selling provisions and food items like Grofers, BigBasket, etc.

Digital Marketing Versus Social Media Marketing

It is often assumed that engaging on social media is digital marketing. This is erroneous as there are many more components that make up a digital marketing campaign. Digital advertising fundamentally offers the promise of one-to-one advertising as opposed to the analogue model of one-to-many advertising. This means, **theoretically**, in digital media one can customize an ad to each individual viewer at an economic cost using digital technologies. The main advantage of social media, however, is in capturing the network capability (or, virality) of social media to spread advertising content principally using the sharing capability of social media and/or addressing the micro-communities that form up social media. Thus, at best, social media marketing is a means of digital marketing and not its essence.

- **Social media** is the latest buzzword in Internet marketing, on account of new generation of social media platforms, mainly Facebook and Twitter, that changed the way we socialize, interact and shop. This also brought new channels to digital marketing as well.
- Social media is the term we use to describe platforms that bring people together for the exchange of information. The most popular social media platforms are Facebook, Twitter, Google+, Pinterest, Instagram, Tumblr, LinkedIn, StumbleUpon and YouTube.
- **Digital marketing** goes beyond the Internet and tries to reach people in the off-line world using digital means while social media is limited to the boundaries of the Internet.
- A digital marketing campaign may include one or more components (Internet advertising, mobile ads, TV, SMS, etc.), while a social media strategy may include one or more social media platforms (Facebook, twitter etc.).
- Social media is strongly associated with a content strategy, i.e., you create content and use social media to promote it while a digital marketing can concentrate entirely on communication and visuals (either on the Internet, TV or billboards) for promotion.

> **Social Media Marketing:** The process of promoting a product or service through the various social media channels
> **Internet Marketing:** Includes Web, SEM (search engine marketing), smartphones, mobile markets, email marketing, online banner advertising and social media
> **Non-Internet Marketing:** Non-Internet digital channels include television, radio, SMS and digital billboards

Having examined the evolution and impact of the digital marketspace in this chapter, in subsequent chapters we will examine digital strategy development, planning and implementation, social media management and engagement, digital and business marketing (B2B) and other digital businesses.

CHAPTER SUMMARY

- Through millennia, advances in technology contributed to the evolution of communication, each altering the way business was carried out and the way businesses communicated with their customers.
- Telegraph in 1842 and Telephone in 1877 proved that instant electronic communication was possible and were the forerunners for the discovery of Internet. The birth of Internet can be traced to Advanced Research Project Agency (ARPA) in 1958.
- In 1989, Tim Berners-Lee built the first web page at CERN and went online on August 6, 1991. It contained information about World Wide Web (www), how to get

a web browser and how to set up a web server. Over time this also became the first ever web directory.

- In October 1994, Netscape launched Mosaic Netscape, successor to Nexus, a desktop application which became synonymous with Web 1.0. Web 2.0 was introduced in 2003–04 to encompass various novel phenomena on the World Wide Web or "Web as Platform", where software applications were built on the Web as opposed to on the desktop and users generated content (in the form of ideas, text, videos, or pictures) that could be "harnessed" to create value.
- Further technological advancements have led to Web 3.0, a term used to describe the evolution of the Web as an extension of Web 2.0. Web 3.0 is defined as connective intelligence; connecting data, concepts, applications and ultimately people.
- Evolution through technology from static World Wide Web (www) or Web 1.0 through Web 2.0, Web 3.0 (semantic web) have fuelled the growth and emergence of various social media and the concept of ecommerce and ebusinesses.
- None of these advancements, however, pathbreaking they may have been, superseded those which came before them. Rather they co-existed and augmented them, offering more variety and diversity. However, considering that the first web page globally went online in 1991, India was not far behind.
- Internet connected the world, and enabled by convergence of technologies evolved from a communicating platform to creating a digital marketplace. In 1994, digital marketplace was called "Marketspace".
- The *marketspace* concept is one which involves information and communication-based electronic exchange environment, where goods and services instead of being sold only physically are marketed through an online space that facilitates bi-directional commerce.
- One of the main enablers of the migration from brick and mortar model to brick and click has been the growth of interactive platforms. These platforms facilitate a two-way interaction. Key types of interactions supported by interactive platforms are:
  - Information Seeking Interactions
  - Problem-solving Interactions
  - Community Interactions
  - Activity/promotions-based Interactions
  - Expert Opinion Interactions
  - Feedback Eliciting Interactions
- Global Internet users in 2016 were estimated at 3.4 billion, with the usage growth at a steady 4%, which are credited to smartphones purchases and their installed base.
- In line with global trends, India has also seen a robust growth in Internet usage. The key drivers for digital marketing environment in India have been
  - Emergence of Internet
  - Digital natives and digital immigrants
  - Technology advancements in devices and user interface
  - Liberalization, consumerism and stable economy
- In a 2017 estimate, India tops the country rank of Internet users next only to China and is significantly ahead of the USA.
  - India Internet User Base estimated in 2018 at 479 million is substantial and large, almost 10% of global user base and 27% of the population. A recent (February 22, 2018) Times of India news item reports India to have 500 million Internet users by June 2018.
  - Gen Z's (age 16 – 20) have a distinct preference for fun and streaming that is going to fuel entertainment industry and digital advertising.
  - The above has been on account of an average of 1.13 hours spent by an average Indian on digital media that has given a boost to online advertising, online shopping and e-commerce.
  - India is more mobilized than most countries with mobile contributing 65% of Internet traffic and 41% to ecommerce.
- While the overall digital ad spending has grown by 47% in 2017, mobile ads have shown a robust growth of 110%.
- Propelled by rising smartphone penetration, the launch of 4G networks and increasing consumer wealth, the Indian e-commerce market is expected to grow to US$ 188 billion by 2025. eCommerce is increasingly attracting customers from Tier 2 and 3 cities, where people have limited access to brands but have high aspirations.
- The difference between digital marketing and social media is that social media is just one of the available channels of digital marketing. Many people believe that by engaging on social media they are doing digital marketing but this is not 100% true as there are many more components that make up a digital marketing campaign.
- Digital marketing goes beyond the Internet and tries to reach people in the off-line world using digital means while social media is limited to the boundaries of the Internet.

CLOSING CASE

CASE LET

Digital Advertising – Foreign Bank

A leading foreign bank operating in India had a unique problem. The bank had a large consumer franchise for its core banking product through its zero-balance salary accounts (ZBSA). However, this large franchise was not yielding profitable business for the bank since, either, the salary account holders transferred the balance to other banks after receiving the salary transfer or the account holders were not taking up the bank's other product lines—credit cards, loans or mortgages.

Studies conducted by the bank showed that this group of account holders:

- did not perceive the ZBSA as a service to the account holders, but more as a service to the company they were employed by
- though the bank scored high on traditional banking parameters, the consumer's image of the bank was that it catered to a wealthier profile of consumers than themselves
- expected the other banking products provided by the bank to be more expensive, either in terms of user fees or interest rates, because the bank catered to a higher socio-economic class

Clearly the image of this bank among its ZBSA customers was that the bank was 'not-for-me'.

An integrated campaign that involved a digital campaign and on-ground events was conceived and launched. The digital campaign principally aimed at:

- Establishing a consumer connection with its account holders to ameliorate the lack of a relationship.
- Demonstrating how the zero-balance account helped them access other financial products based on the combination of the account relationship and the corporate connection
- Facilitating easy acquisition of the services of the bank through its digital platforms

The off-line events were aimed at putting a human face so that the account holders could tangibly experience the advertising campaign.

The digital campaign segmented the consumers based on their account behaviour and used a combination of:

- Display advertising, to give the context to the ZBSA as an account designed for the account holders that allowed them to access their accounts 24X7. A digital campaign was used, even though identity of specific account holders was known, since the account was not just for the individual but also for his family. A secondary benefit of the digital campaign was to give the feeling that the account holder belonged to a larger community, rather than being just a number for a bank.
- Organic search, was engineered with the insight that ZBSA holders would be curious to check out what was in for them after seeing the advertising. Specific key words that such account holders may use were targeted and the landing pages for those key words emphasized how the ZBSA provided unique value to the account holders.
- Social media was used to promote additional products that the bank provided ZBSA holders such as loans, mortgages and credit cards. The idea behind using social media was the specificity with which the account holders could be targeted and the fact that since the communication was informational, one could reach a larger universe for a smaller budget than any other digital opportunity.
- Email campaigns were devised to promote the extensive range of online facilities that the bank offered such as zero-cost draft issuance, utility bill payments, standard instructions for regular payments such as school fees, maintenance bills, club bills, etc.
- A co-operative system was developed by which ZBSA holders could access the banks products like credit cards, personal loans, mortgages through their company's intranet and hence simplifying documentation requirements for such products.

Prior to the campaign, appropriate measurement systems were set up for each campaign element to capture the relevant metric and track performance so the campaign could be optimized on a continual basis.

Needless to say, the overall impact of the campaign were met and the bank's relationship with the ZBSA holders widened with the transferring out reduced and, deepened, with more usage of the bank's products.

Case Questions

1. What was the aim of the digital campaign for this foreign bank?
2. How did the digital campaign help the bank?

REVIEW QUESTIONS

1. What factors are responsible for the transition of traditional marketing to digital marketing?
2. How does digital marketing score over traditional marketing?
3. What has been the role of technology in communication that transformed traditional marketing to digital marketing?
4. What is the difference between the brick and mortar and brick and click models?
5. How is marketspace different from marketplace?
6. How did Internet and Web transform marketing from communicators to marketplace to marketspace?
7. What are the three different dimension that define a marketspace transaction?
8. What is the impact of digitization? Comment on digital India and Make in India.
9. What are the key types of interactions supported by interactive platforms?
10. What is digital economy and what is the impact of digital economy globally and in India?
11. What have been the key drivers for digital marketing environment in India?
12. What has been the commercial impact of India Internet usage growth?
13. How have digital natives and gen z impacted digital marketspace in India?
14. Compare the growth of traditional and digital advertising in India?
15. Is digital marketspace ecommerce only or going beyond ecommerce?
16. What is the difference between digital marketing and social media marketing?

ACTIVITY QUESTIONS

1. Book on line a movie ticket or order food on line and explore if the promised cashback is for real or notional.
2. Search on the web for any of the references in this chapter, read the article or the paper and explore what additional information or knowledge that can be derived.

KEY TERMS

Activity/promotions-based Interactions
Brick and click
Brick and mortar
CCDVTP
Community interactions
Digital economy
Digital era
Digital marketing
Digitization
Expert opinion interactions
Feedback eliciting interactions
Information Seeking interactions
Internet economy
Internet marketing
Marketplace
Marketspace
Marketing communication
Marketspace transaction
New economy
Non-Internet marketing
Problem-solving interactions
Semantic web
Social media
Social media marketing
Web 2.0
Web 3.0
Web economy

REFERENCES

1. https://www.w3.org/People/Berners-Lee/FAQ.html - browser.
2. https://en.wikipedia.org/wiki/Web_2.0 - cite_note-8
3. https://www.webopedia.com/TERM/W/Web_3_point_0.html.
4. https://hbr.org/1994/11/managing-in-the-marketspace
5. https://www.strategyand.pwc.com/media/file/Strategyand_Maximizing-the-Impact-of-Digitization.pdf.
6. Tapscott, Don (1997). *The Digital Economy: Promise and Peril in the Age of Networked Intelligence*. New York: McGraw-Hill. ISBN 0-07-063342-8.
7. http://searchcio.techtarget.com/definition/digital-economy.
8. https://www.indianeconomy.net/splclassroom/what-is-digital-economy/.

CHAPTER 3

DIGITAL STRATEGY DEVELOPMENT AND PLANNING

CHAPTER OBJECTIVES

After reading this chapter, you will be able to

- Understand business interaction model going beyond B2C and B2B
- Define consumer behaviour models of marketing/sales funnel
- Explain 3D model of customer engagement through their marketing journey
- Discuss integrated communications and SMART goal setting and impact measures
- Describe digital channels – types and revenue models
- Enable choosing appropriate channels or channel mix at different stages

OPENING CASE

CASE LET

IMC – Creating Awareness – Digital – An Established Supermarket

ABC Company is primarily in the business of selling and delivering fresh fruits and vegetables to the people. However, it has a special Department X as well that is dedicated to delivering products from nearby stores to the people within 90 minutes, which not many people were aware of. Department X hired an intern for pointers to making consumers aware of this department as well and thus enabling the department to contribute more towards revenue pool of the organization as a whole.

In a meeting with the city head of Department X, the intern was given a communication task that makes the customers aware of the kind of services the company offers under the name of Department X leading to an increase in traction of its business. Department X was doing sufficiently well in terms of sales and was clocking reasonable orders on a weekly basis. However, on account of a lack of marketing budget and other constraints the awareness for various services of Department was very low.

The intern proposed an idea of exploring **'email marketing' as a tool of engagement and creating awareness** and created an email template that incorporated the highest revenue generating categories of Department X. Various links were incorporated strategically in the design to ensure that when a customer clicks on a particular category, the right landing page opens up. The design incorporated a direct link to Department X section in the official website of the company as well so that the customer can view all the categories and products that are deliverable by the company through the services of Department X. The design also had a prominent CTA (Call-to-Action) button that prompted the reader of the email to take action, i.e. make a purchase through the app or the website of the company. Refer visual below.

The design also incorporated links to social plugins of the company to ensure that the overall message of the company is not distorted and is in tandem with the industry standards and design. After rolling out a dummy campaign with the team members of Department X and getting the go ahead from the department head, the intern was ready to roll out the campaign city wide – which meant reaching out to almost 1 million existing customers of the company.

However, due to insufficient funds and conflicting company policy about regional marketing, no paid versions of email marketing platforms were made available to the intern. Only a list of 2000 subscriber base was allowed to be made with a free account. The intern circumvented the problem by creating multiple accounts at various platforms to reach out to all the contact base provided for the campaign.

Once the campaign went live, the results were analyzed. The statistics showed an open rate of 6.7% and a click through rate of 0.4% compared to industry standards of ecommerce which are 8% and 1%, respectively.

Case Questions

1. What was the objective of the store for this campaign?
2. What were the salient features of the campaign suggested by the intern?

INTRODUCTION

Traditional marketing or outbound marketing focusses on finding customers and pushing products or services to them for consumption. Outbound techniques were one way communications, standardized and broad targeting measures that often interrupted the consumer. Cold-calling, print advertising, TV advertising, outdoor media were some of the channels of communication used. Technology is making these techniques less effective and more expensive. Inbound marketing is marketing focussed on getting found by customers. That is it is all about attracting potential customers with high-quality and targeted content, engaging and nurturing them into action till they are ready to buy/consume your product or service. Inbound marketing thus has flipped outbound marketing on its head.

CONSUMER BEHAVIOUR AND MARKETING STRATEGY

Central to inbound marketing is the focus on consumer and their behaviour. This theme of consumer being central to any business was well articulated by Mahatma Gandhi as "Customer is the most important visitor". This was way back and prior to Indian Independence.

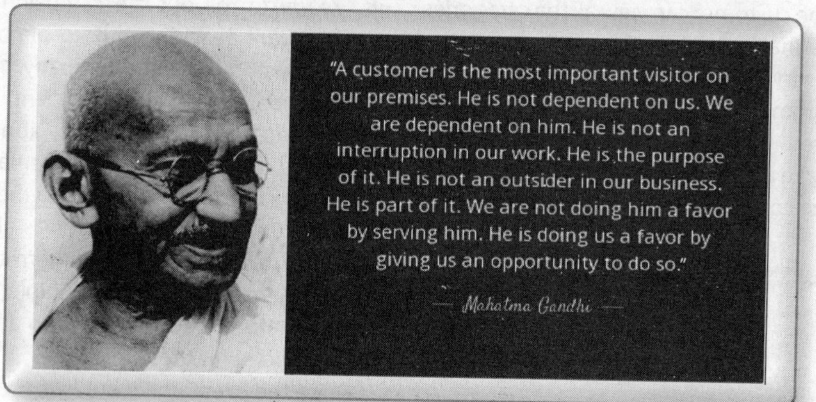

Exhibit 3.1 Customer is the King - Mahatma Gandh

BUSINESS INTERACTIONS

For long we have been used to two familiar buckets B2C (Business to Consumer - FMCG) and B2B (Business to Business). As we move forward and embrace digital world and its multiple channel of interaction, this landscape is fast changing. As businesses grow, they are also becoming multi-faceted through homogeneity and heterogeneity. We now have the following multiple scenarios that are both for profit and not for profit. Figure 3.1 captures digital business interaction model between individuals, MSMEs, large businesses, government and NGOs.

> **FMCG:** Fast-moving consumer goods (FMCG) or consumer packaged goods (CPG) are products that are sold quickly and at relatively low cost

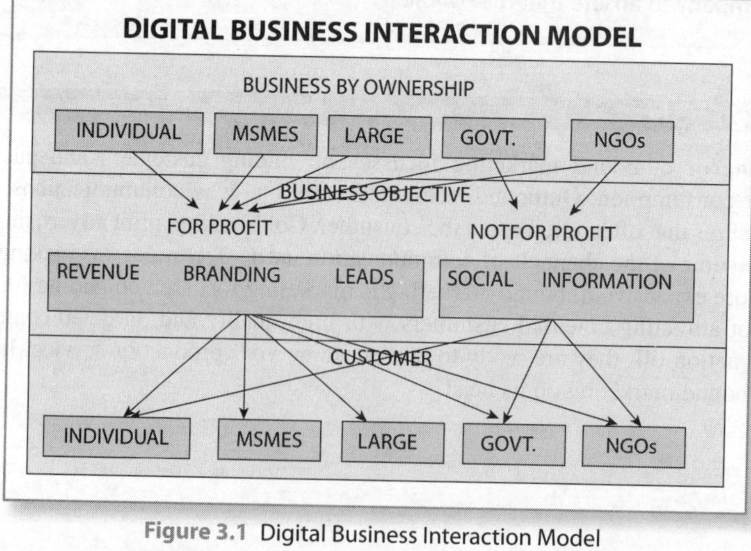

Figure 3.1 Digital Business Interaction Model

- Individual to Individual – one to one commerce and data sharing on digital platforms. P2P (Peer to Peer or People to People)
- Individual to MSMEs – Traditional home made products to MSMEs for resale to large Businesses (C2B)
- MSMEs to Individuals – Many services using social media marketing to individuals
- MSMEs to MSMEs – Transactions amongst MSMEs for value additions, services
- Businesses to Consumer (B2C) – Large businesses and brands using digital and e-commerce through retargeting
- Business to Government (B2G) – DGS &D, CSD , Defence, etc.
- Businesses to Social Enterprises – Supporting social causes in line with their products
- Individuals to NGOs and Social Enterprises – Professional services by individuals such as accountants and doctors and value addition
- NGO s to Consumers – Products like handicrafts and services
- Government to Government (G2G) – Domestic and international

Irrespective of the business models, successful companies have realized that the boundaries between products, services, and environments have blurred. Today's consumers do not buy just products or services. More and more, their purchase decisions revolve around buying into an experience. Therefore, marketers need to provide an integrated view and design end-to-end experiences that are truly valuable to consumers to be successful in the market. Given these complexities, the shift also requires an innovative approach to business models and a new look at how companies provide value to customers. It's not just about designing the best product or service but rather about striking the right combination

B2B: Business-to-business (B2B or, in some countries, BtoB) refers to a situation where one business makes a commercial transaction with another. This typically occurs when: A business is sourcing materials for their production process (e.g. a food manufacturer purchasing salt).

B2C: Business-to-customer (B2C) marketing refers to the tactics and best practices used to promote products and services among consumers.

NGO: Non-governmental organization are usually non-profit and sometimes international organizations independent of governments and international governmental organizations that are active in humanitarian, educational, health care, public policy, social, human rights, environmental, and other areas to effect changes according to their objectives.

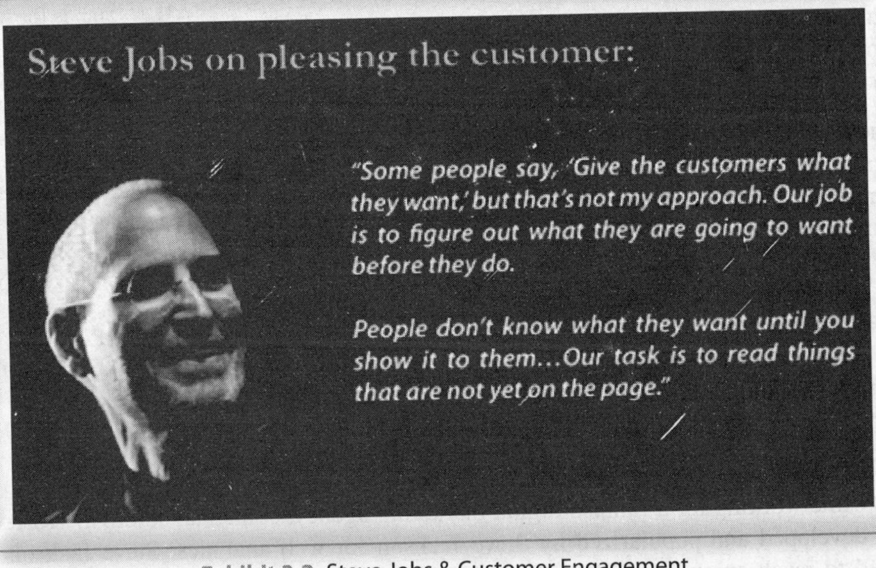

Exhibit 3.2 Steve Jobs & Customer Engagement

and making sure the integrated customer experience is compelling. This kind of successful, convergence-designed strategy can deliver a durable competitive advantage. To quote Steve Jobs, "Our Job is to read things that are not yet on the page."

THE SALES OR MARKETING FUNNEL

For understanding business strategies, digital or otherwise, we first need to understand consumer behaviour and the standard sales funnel that is also referred to as the marketing/customer funnel. At the core of the funnel concept is one of the earliest marketing models that is still valid and prevalent and referred to as AIDA model.

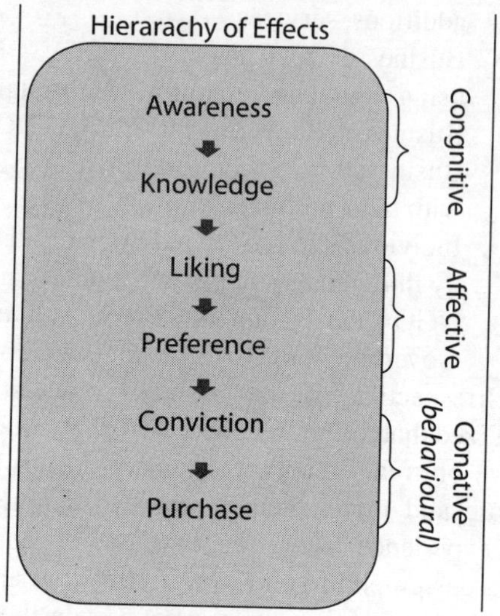

Source : Wikipedia

Figure 3.2 Hierarchy of effects

What is the AIDA Model?

AIDA is an acronym that stands for Attention, Interest, Desire and Action. The term, AIDA and the overall approach are commonly attributed to an American advertising and sales advocate E. St. Elmo Lewis[1] (1872-1948). The AIDA model is just one of a class of models known as hierarchy of effects models or hierarchical models, all of which imply that consumers move through a series of steps or stages when they make purchase decisions. These models are linear, sequential models built on an assumption that consumers move through a series of cognitive (thinking) and affective (feeling) stages culminating in a behavioural stage (doing, e.g. purchase or trial).

AIDA to AIDAR[2]

Over a period of time marketers have added "Retention" to AIDA as an outcome a marketer would like to retain and convert a customer to a loyal customer from a mere customer. Thus, AIDAR helps structure some key points in the customer journey.

> **AIDA:** Stands for Attention, Interest, Desire and Action. The AIDA model is widely used in marketing and advertising to describe the steps or stages that occur from the time when a consumer first becomes aware of a product or brand through to when the consumer trials a product or makes a purchase decision.

1. **A**wareness: To make potential buyers aware of products or services; the outreach strategy; the brand awareness campaign; tools or platforms to be used; and what will the messages be?
2. **I**nterest: To gain their interest - the content and communication strategy; how to make relevant information available and where?
3. **D**esire: What makes our product or service desirable? How do we engage and interact to make an emotional connect?
4. **A**ction: What are the call to actions? Is it easy for consumers to connect and where would they expect to find it? Which marketing channel/platform are we using and how to engage?
5. **R**etention: What is the proposition to retain loyalty? How do we engage?

The marketing funnel needs to be converted to marketing cycle to retain the customer. In this context, Xavier Blanc, while working for a Finnish digital marketing agency, coined an acronym "REAN" in 2006. It was further developed and popularized by Steve Jackson for web analytics. Steve Jackson realized all businesses need to reach an audience. In order to achieve this, businesses utilize a variety of methods—

inbound or outbound. But that's only the first part. After reaching to them, they need to be assisted in accomplishing the desired outcome which is creating an intent or further search to purchase a product. The REAN framework provides a model on how to go about to measure and make adjustments for more of these conversions or activations.

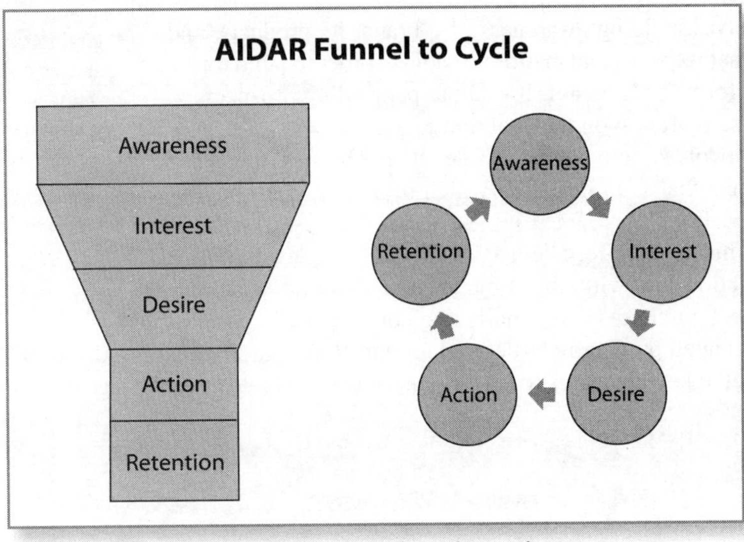

Figure 3.3 AIDAR funnel to cycle

What is REAN and What does it Stand For ?

REAN is a marketing acronym. It is a simple yet powerful framework to plan ahead and/or analyze the often complex sequence of interrelated, multichannel, marketing activities that are needed to build and nurture a customer relationship. It stands for:

R – Reach: The set of activities needed to raise prospects' attention for your brand, product or service.

E – Engage: The gradual, typically multi-channel, often recursive set of activities needed to engage the prospects you just won.

A – Activate: The activities needed for your prospects to take, eventually, the actions you wanted them to take.

N – Nurture: The activities needed to nurture the customer relationship you just managed to create.

But how you interpret these categories can yield different results. Which interpretation you use depends on which question you need answering.

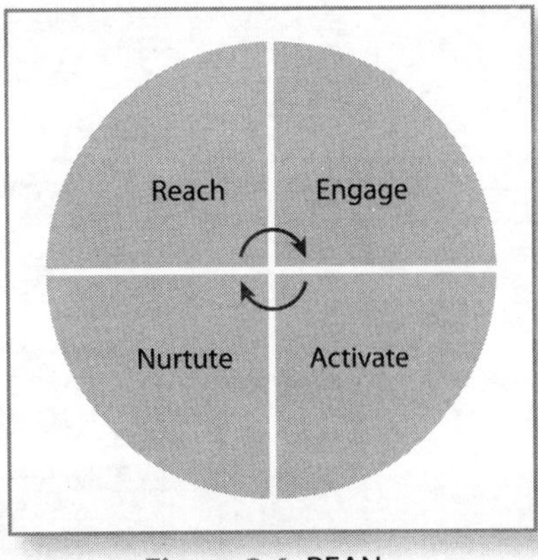

Figure 3.4 REAN

From REAN to (P)RACE

In the digital context, REAN framework was adapted to create (P)RACE framework by Dave Chaffey to help (digital) marketers plan and manage their activities in a more structured way on finding that many companies, at least initially do not have a well-formed (digital) marketing strategy. The RACE acronym summarizes the key online marketing activities that need to be managed as part of digital marketing. RACE covers the full customer lifecycle or marketing funnel from:

REAN: The REAN model was popularized by Steve Jackson in Cult of Analytics: Driving Online Marketing Strategies using Web Analytics (2009) and originally developed by Xavier Blanc in 2006. REAN stands for Reach, Engage, Activate and Nurture

(Plan) > Reach > Act > Convert > Engage

(P)RACE consists of five steps or online marketing activities designed to help brands engage their customers throughout the customer lifecycle.

- **PLAN** involves creating the overall digital strategy, objective setting and plan
- **REACH** involves building awareness of a brand, its products, and services on other websites and in offline media in order to build traffic
- **ACT** is short form for **Interact**. It is about persuading prospects to take the next step, *Action* on their journey.
- **CONVERT** involves conversion to sale. It involves getting your audience to take that vital next step which turns them into paying customers.
- **ENGAGE**. This is long-term engagement that is, developing a long-term relationship with first-time buyers to build customer loyalty as repeat purchases using marketing communications.

> **RACE:** A planning framework that you can apply to your digital marketing practices that uses critical thinking to develop a customized, agile, and strategic approach to your business' unique needs. It stands for Reach, Act, Convert and Engage
> **(P) RACE:** Nothing but RACE with P (Plan) > Reach > Act > Convert > Engage

An infographic created by Chaffe structured around RACE in 2012 and updated in 2015 is as shown in Figure 3.5. It shows the key measures to set targets for and evaluate at each stage of the funnel.

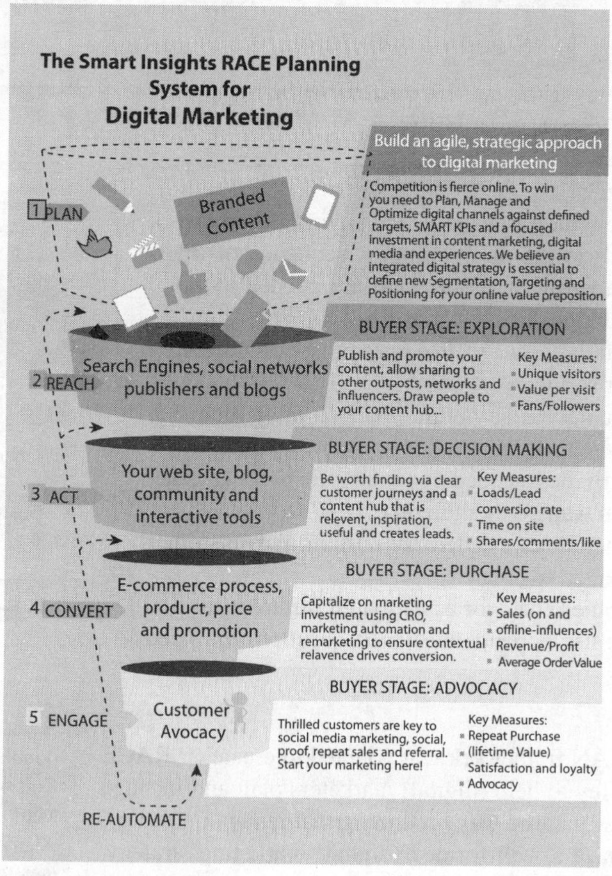

Source: Smart Insights

Figure 3.5 RACE Planning System

Integration of AIDA and (P)RACE

In conjunction, AIDA and (P)RACE would lead to KPI, (Key Performance Indicators) and five points of interaction:

Interaction Point "A" – Awareness - Plan – Involves integration of premarketing activities including consumer activities, outbound and physical placement towards products and services.

Interaction Point "B" – Interest – Reach – Basis the overall plan structure targeted communication that may include Search Engine Marketing, Search Engine Optimization, Display, etc.

Interaction Point "C" – Desire – Act - Customized communication pushing the product or service in consideration set as a precursor.

Interaction Point "C" – Action – Convert - Selling/closure/calls, etc.

Interaction Point "D" – Retention – Engage - Post purchase engagement to repeat buy or loyalty

Figure 3.6 shows the integration process.

> **SEM:** Search engine marketing (SEM) is a type of Internet-based marketing associated with the researching, submitting and positioning of a website within search engines to achieve maximum visibility and increase your share of paid and/or organic traffic referrals from search engines.
> **SEO:** Search engine optimization (SEO) is the process of affecting the online visibility of a website or a web page in a web search engine's unpaid results—often referred to as "natural", "organic", or "earned" results.

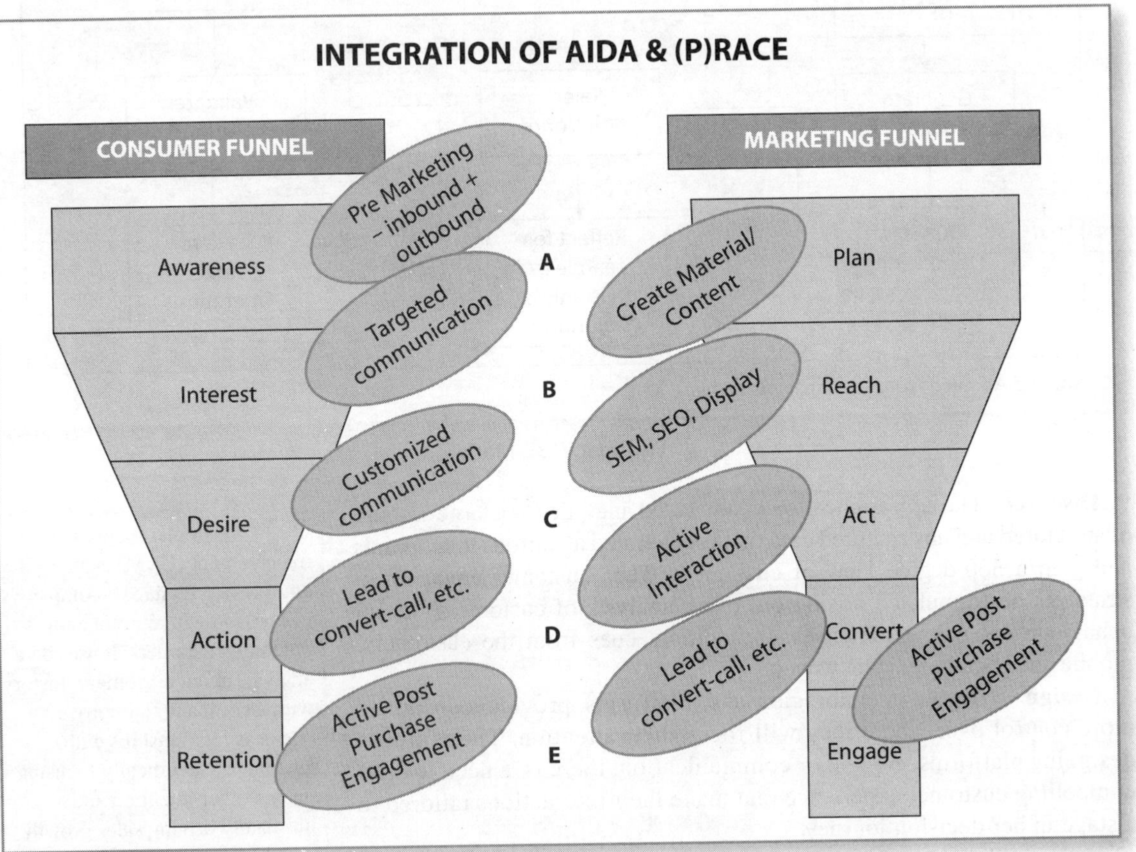

Figure 3.6 Integration of AIDA and (P)RACE

Digital marketing (as different from traditional marketing) and the 3D model come into play at this point. 3D model provides insights into changing and disrupting digital technologies from a consumer decision journey perspective. It suggests multiplatform approach to marketing efforts considering the consumer is no more on one channel through her journey. For example, she may find a product during window shopping but order it online and *vice versa* that requires focus and capabilities in three areas. 3D model facilitates understanding rapid technology cycles to improve multiplatform marketing efforts and takes a different approach in managing the consumer decision journey—one that embraces the speed that digitization brings and focusses on capabilities in three areas:

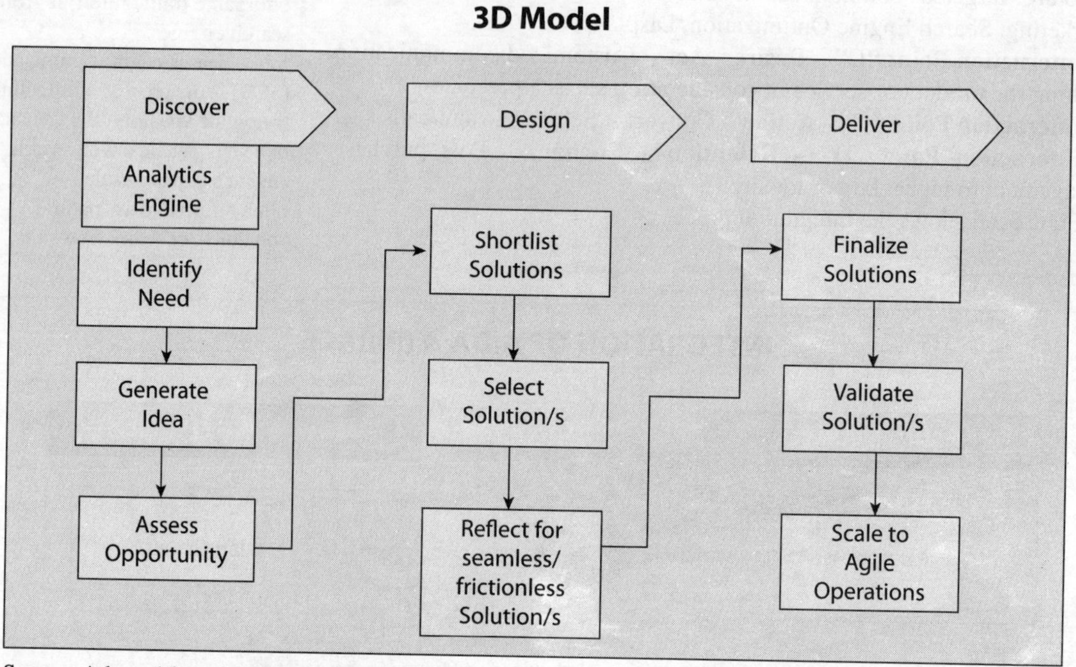

Source: Adapted from McKinsey Insights

Figure 3.7 3D Model

> **CRM:** Customer relationship management (CRM) is an approach to manage a company's interaction with current and potential customers. It uses data analysis about customers' history with a company to improve business relationships with customers, specifically focusing on customer retention and ultimately driving sales growth.

Discover - Through application of advanced analytics to a large amount of structured and unstructured data that is generated at various touchpoints and gain a 360-degree view of customers. The customer engagement strategies be formulated arising out of an analysis of customers' recent behaviour and past experiences. In addition, cues from the customers' mobile and social media be woven.

Design - Digital technologies and platforms provide consumers more control over where they will focus their attention. Therefore, in designing platforms, content or communication, there is a need to craft compelling customer experience that make their interactions tailored to a stage in her decision journey.

Deliver - Today 24 x 7 is the buzzword in CRM. Marketing programs, therefore, be on an "Always on" mode in which the engagement is exactly right at any contact point along the journey. It is not only do it right, but do it right first time and time after time through cross functional agile teams to optimize customer journeys and not just touch points since individual touchpoints may perform well though the overall experience may be below par.

Let's consider what an optimized cross-channel experience could look like when companies target improved capabilities in these three areas.

Integration of (P)RACE with 3D Model

The 3D model integrates into the (P)RACE model as shown in Figure 3.8.

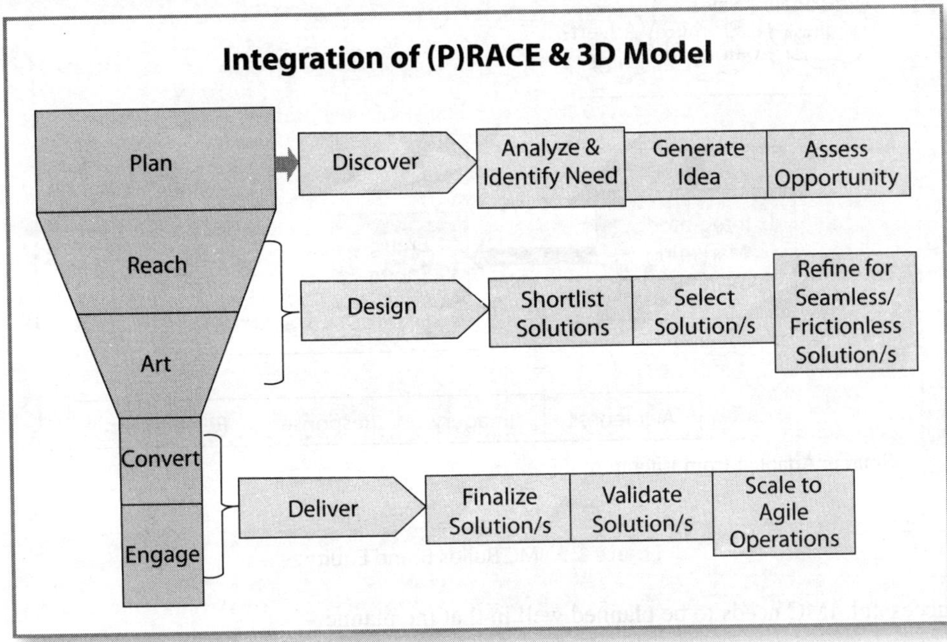

Figure 3.8 Integration of (P)RACE and 3D Model

Having looked at consumer behaviour, AIDA and (P)RACE and their integration, let us now understand the importance of integrated marketing communication (IMC) in marketing.

Integrated Marketing Communication (IMC)

Integrated marketing communication or **IMC** ensures that all forms of communications are carefully linked together integrating all the communication and promotional activities, namely advertising, public relations, personal selling, sales promotion, etc., so that they work together to convey a consistent message to the company's internal and external stakeholders. According to Philip Kotler (2014), IMC plays a very important role in establishing brand equity, should be media neutral. He describes an **Integrated Marketing Communications** approach as

> **IMC / IDC:**
> Integrated marketing communications (IMC) is the use of marketing strategies to optimize the communication of a consistent message of the company's brands to stakeholders. And if the same is carried out digitally, it is integrated digital marketing.

"the concept under which a company carefully integrates and co-ordinates its many communications channels to deliver a clear, consistent message about the organisation and its products".

The characteristics of integrated marketing communications have been summarized by Pickton and Broderick[3] as the 4Cs of:

- *Coherence* – different communications are logically connected.
- *Consistency* – multiple messages support and reinforce, and are not contradictory.
- *Continuity* – communications are connected and consistent through time.
- *Complementary* – synergistic, or the sum of the parts is greater than the whole!

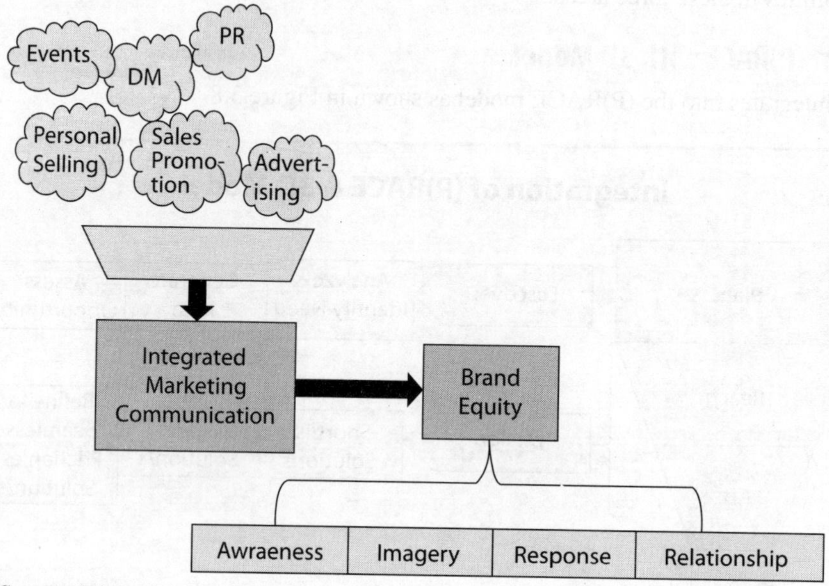

Source: Adapted from Literature

Figure 3.9 IMC Builds Brand Equity

To be successful, IMC needs to be planned well in that the planner—

*"Needs to understand the customer and the brand to unearth a key **insight** for the communication/solution [Relevance].*

*As media channels have mushroomed and communication channels have multiplied, it has become increasingly important for communication to cut through the cynicism and **connect** with its audience [Distinctiveness].*

*...the planner can provide the edge needed to ensure the solution reaches out through the clutter to its **intended audience** [Targeted reach].*

*...needs to **demonstrate** how and why the communication has performed [Effectiveness]"*

As seen above, effective communication is delivering the right message to the right audience at the right time. Business interaction model in Figure 3.1 means, since interactivity is multiple it calls for multi-channel marketing that is more complex as we are trying to integrate traditional channels with other channels.

*A **Multi-channel Communications Strategy Customized** for **Individual Prospects** and Customers forming **different segments** across a **defined customer lifecycle** which delivers the **Right Message** featuring the **Right Value Proposition** (product, service or experience) across **different platforms** with the **Right Tone** at the **Right Time** with the **Right Frequency in Right Media/Communications channels** to achieve **Right balance of value** between consumer and brand.*

Digital marketing supports and supplements traditional outbound marketing at this stage. Done well, this strategy will also make implementation more fruitful for the company and more seamless for the customers who engage with the product or service. In this evolving environment, maintaining an integrated customer-experience perspective is necessary right from the beginning of any customer journey. Therefore, there is a need to look at key aspects of the customer's experience to understand and resolve pain points by answering a few questions as given in Exhibit 3.3.

- What do customers really need, desire, and aspire to?
- What are they trying to achieve by consuming a product or service?
- What kinds of behaviour are connected to the experience, natural or constructed?
- What do customers think about the product, the service, and the experience? And why do they think the way they do?

Exhibit 3.3 Key Drivers - Digital Strategy Planning

The answers to the above questions will lead to optimizing customer journeys and not just touch points since individual touchpoints may perform well though the overall experience may be below par.

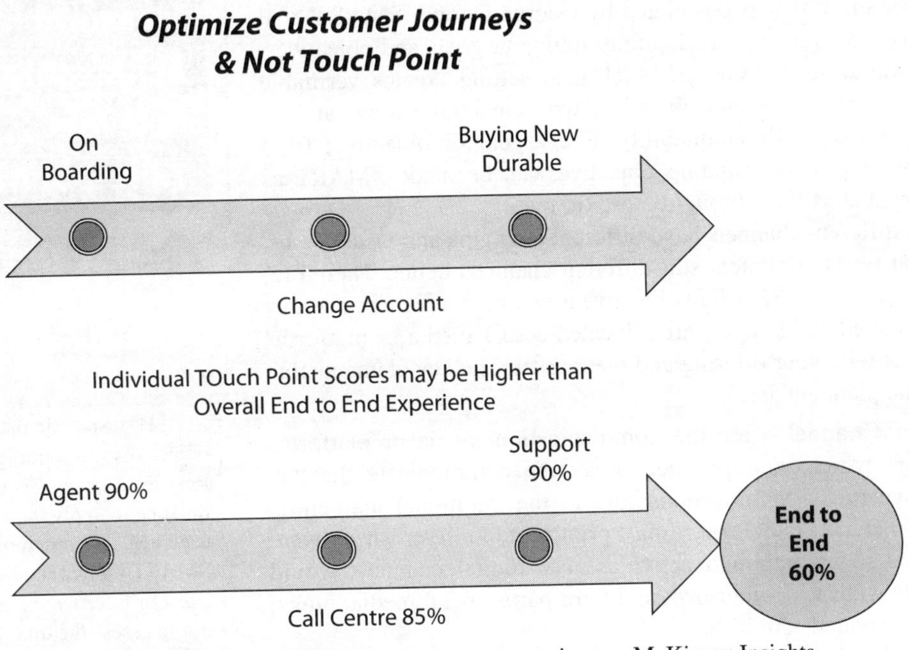

Source: Adapted from The CEO guide to customer experience – McKinsey Insights

Figure 3.10 Optimize Customer Journeys and Not Touch Points

Benefits and Advantages of Digital Marketing

Integration of AIDA and (P)RACE brings to focus the advantages of digital marketing that are

- Easy consumer reach and shop online
- Direct advertising
- Global and cost-effective reach
- Real-time customer advertising and feedback
- Real-time social sharing and exposing of promotional or other media content
- Complimenting existing digital infrastructure like websites, etc. through social media
- Targeted exposure in the networks you choose
- Increased likelihood of free advertising (word of mouth, verbally and digitally)
- Increased traffic to a targeted page by easy navigation and sharing of the link to said page

- More accurate tracking and monitoring of your efforts and campaigns
- Potential for business in previously non-explored communities and target markets
- Demographically targeted exposure in new and existing target markets
- Compliment your traditional marketing efforts with your digital
- Broadening of overall business potential and increase in exposure
- Better PR and business relations
- Better market research and analysis leading to better transparency and accountability
- Career opportunities

Planning or media planning, therefore, becomes paramount in IMC. A good model to follow will be the SMART model of goal setting. SMART is a mnemonic acronym, giving criteria to guide in the setting of objectives and was first postulated by George Doran[4]. SMART goal setting brings structure and track ability into your goals and objectives. Instead of vague resolutions, SMART goal setting creates verifiable trajectories towards a certain objective, with clear milestones and an estimation of the goal's attainability. Every goal or objective, from intermediary step to overarching objective, can be made SMART as shown below and as such, brought closer to reality.

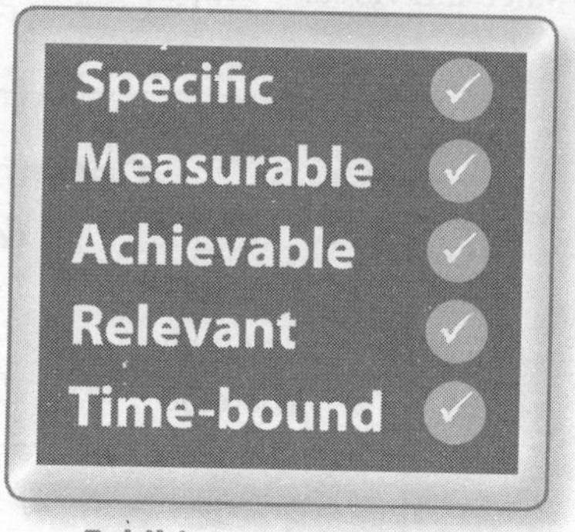

Exhibit 3.4 SMART Goals

Besides, different channels have different strengths and weaknesses, and different types of content suit different channels better. Therefore, once the specific (S of SMART) objective is set, media planning is how content is created and budgets are allocated across media or platforms that is in sync with your offering and the market. The key elements that impact media planning are:

> SMART: Specific marketing objectives to support your long-term goals, it is common practice to apply the widely used SMART mnemonic. The SMART mnemonic helps as a test or filter which one can use to assess the quality of measures. SMART stands for specific, measurable, actionable, relevant, time-bound.

- **Media Channel** – are the communication media or platforms through which your product or service communicate the key message or the value proposition. In the traditional marketing, these included television, radio, print, outdoor, etc. These were referred to as outbound activities. The digital channels would include websites – your own and third party, social media, blogs, etc. or inbound activities.
- **Media Vehicle** – refers to the specific medium used such as a particular program on television (IPL matches) or radio (music or news programs). In digital, it could be a sponsored post in FB, Twitter or in personalized emails.
- **Media Audience** – are the TG consumers who consume the communication. In case of television or radio, it will be the viewers or listeners of that particular program. In online, it will be the audience that is exposed to your communication may it be your website, third party website or the social media.
- **Media Schedule** – refers to the specific time slots or period of specific insertions.
- **Media Budget** –allocation of the spend or revenue on defined channel
- **Media Delivery** – reach, frequency, opportunity to see (OTS), impressions, etc.

Let us now look at Measurable, Attainable, Relevant and Time (MART of SMART) part of media planning. They are:

- **Reach -** refers to the total number of potential audience (from among the universe) exposed during the plan period at least once.

- **Response –** actual audience who read, viewed, heard or visited the web and performed an action which is related to the campaign
- **Relevance –** of the vehicle chosen as described in the previous section
- **Timing and Scheduling –** Time period for the proposed campaign and how to schedule for maximum impact. Scheduling could be one of
  - **Continuous –** even exposure during the period
  - **Concentration –** a specific period of the year and spending the entire budget
  - **Burst –** Alternate periods of high and low communication
  - **Pulsing –** Low round the year and heavy during certain periods
- **Frequency –** Number of times the target audience is exposed to a particular communication. Frequency can be a number of exposures in the same medium or single exposure in multiple media

Having looked at the channels and SMART goals, the next is to understand the basis for measurement of the impact to arrive at the effectiveness and RoI (Return on Investment). Some of the measures are:

- **Web visits -** A visit refers to a visitor's session on all the firm's product sites within a particular period of time. During the session, the visitor may view multiple pages but still the session is counted as one overall.
- **Page visits –** refers to the number of people visiting a particular page of the website that could be the home page or a landing page specifically designed for the campaign to pre-defined channel for specific consumer action.
- **Unique visitors –** refers to number of unique individuals visiting a website or a page during a specified time frame that is tracked through cookies or unique IP addresses.
- **Impressions –** relate particularly to display advertisements placed on multiple webpages and is the sum total of responses from a web server to a page request from the user's browser. This is calculated as *Reach*Frequency (number of people reached X number of times they saw the advertisement across all media vehicles)*. This is measured automatically by designated servers and therefore if a user lands on a particular page twice in the same session, it would be counted as two.
- **Page views –** total number of pages viewed by an user in a particular session.
- **Clicks –** when a visitor downloads another file by clicking an advertisement. This is recorded by the server. ***Impressions and clicks are important metrics in the conversion funnel.***
- **Click through –** the action following a link within an advertisement or editorial to another website or another page or frame within the website.
- **CPM (Cost per thousand) –** refers to the cost incurred for every 1000 impressions. **M in CPM** denotes Roman Numeral M for thousand. Most digital media buys are based on this metric.
- **CPC (Cost per click) –** refers to cost of advertising based on the number of clicks.
- **CPA (Cost per action) –** also known as ***Cost per acquisition*** where the advertiser pays for a specified acquisition – for example, a sale, click, or form submit

Integrated Digital Communications (IDC) and the Channel Mix

Earlier in the chapter, we examined how **IMC** ensures that all forms of communications are carefully linked together integrating all the communication and promotional activities, namely advertising, public relations, personal selling, sales promotion, etc., so that they work together to convey a consistent message to the company's internal and external stakeholders.

Let us now look at an Integrated Digital Communication (IDC) that is the digital adaptation of IMC and a key aspect of digital marketing. Revisiting the IMC construct, Kliatchko (2005)[5] proposed four pillars of IMC to provide a better understanding of this construct to an applied process.

The four pillars of IMC as given in Exhibit 3.5 can be adapted to IDC as channels, affiliates, content creator and influencers.

The four pillars he postulated were—

- Stakeholders : all relevant people and markets – external and internal
- Content : flowing from deep understanding of multiple markets
- Channels : relevance and preference than carpet bombing all touch points
- Results : including behavioural responses such as actual purchase and financial outcomes

Exhibit 3.5 Four Pillars of IMC

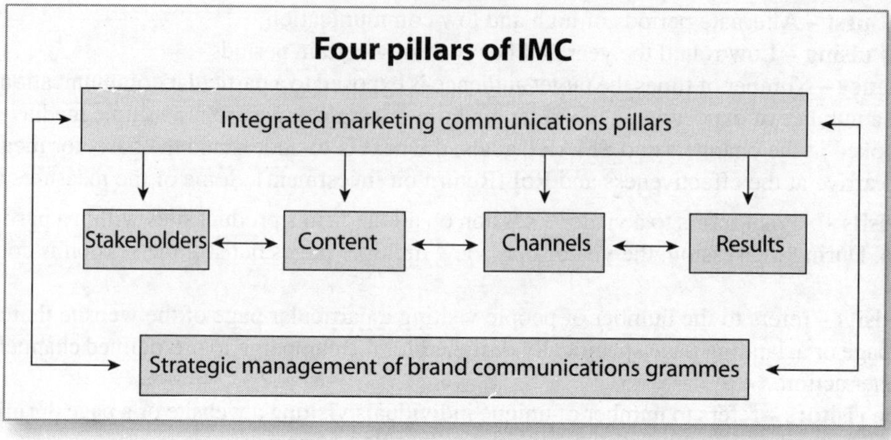

Figure 3.11 Four Pillars of IMC

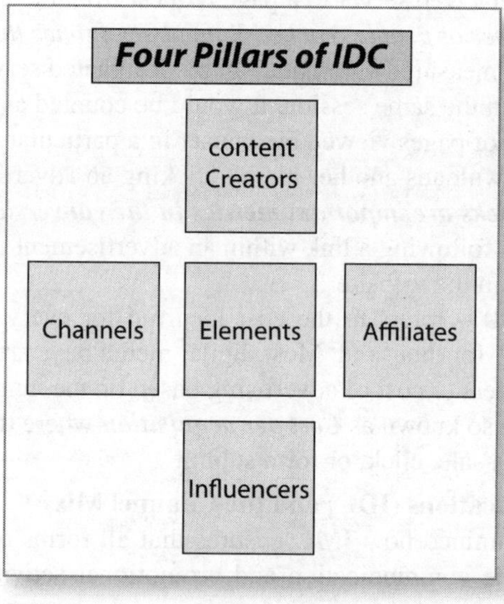

The four elements of IDC:

- **Channels** - like search engines, display sites, social media communities and other platforms like mobiles, video sites
- **Affiliates** – partner network in the same business such as price comparison portals, aggregators, vertical sites, rewards and loyalty sites, etc.
- **Content Creators** – third parties or crowd sourced to create compelling content and curated
- **Influencers** - inducing advocacy and incentivising for reviews , feedback, etc.

Figure 3.12 Four Pillars of IDC

THE CHANNEL MIX[6]

With an understanding of different marketing and customer models *viz.* AIDA, (P)RACE, 3D, IMC and IDC and some of the key terminologies and metrics, let us now look at the various digital channel options that are available to arrive at the most optimal channel mix for your product or service. The digital channel mix decisions are a function of

- Type of digital marketing
- Revenue based business model
- Product life cycle (PLC)
- Impact

> **PLC:** Product life-cycle management (PLM) is the succession of strategies by business management as a product goes through its life-cycle. The conditions in which a product is sold (advertising, saturation) changes over time and must be managed as it moves through its succession of stages.
> **PPC:** PPC stands for pay-per-click, a model of Internet marketing in which advertisers pay a fee each time one of their ads is clicked.

Types of Digital Marketing and Channels

Basis IDC, we can broadly classify digital marketing into seven key types that form the underlying basis. They are

1. Intent (Internet) based marketing – through messages based on data from search queries
2. Brand based marketing (Display Marketing) – Advertising across digital media formats and websites
3. Content marketing – through messages in story based format
4. Community base marketing – use of social platforms, communities and networks
5. Partner marketing – PR, involving affiliates, third party sites and sponsorships
6. Communication channel marketing – Direct marketing
7. Platform based marketing – Integrating digitized traditional and new platforms in devices and media

Intent Based Marketing

One of the earliest forms in which marketers used Internet for digital activities, prior to Web 2.0, mostly static information on the websites besides blogs and random listings. Search technology and Google revolutionized marketing and marketers could for the first time know the intent of customers (in a mass market) through key words and hence called ***Intent Marketing***. This enabled search marketing and target customers in their buying cycle and lead to the development of **Search Engine Optimization** (SEO), **Pay per Click (PPC)**, etc. Considering the importance of intent marketing in digital, in this book, a separate chapter (Chapter 4) is dedicated to this topic.

Brand Based Marketing (Display Marketing)

Graphical digital images *a la* hoardings, print, TV ads are executed across web, mobile and other platforms. The displays will be rich in visual and imagery and include videos, animation, sounds, etc. and lend themselves to be dynamic and interactive. Thus they differentiate themselves from text based **SEM**. US retailer Sears in collaboration with IBM is credited with display marketing in the 80s. The underlying assumption for display ads is a revenue stream for a portal that attracts a significant traffic by offering a section of the page for commercial advertising like print media. The area that is let out is called inventory and there are some standard specifications followed as presented in Exhibit 3.6.

- **Banner** – 480 X 60 pixel horizontal bar at the top
- **Sky Scraper** – 120 X 600 pixel vertical on either side
- **Leader Board** – 728 X 90 pixel at the bottom
- **Others** – Host of smaller ones like 300 X 250; 120 X 60; 180 X 150, etc.

Exhibit 3.6 Display Inventory Terminology

For us to understand and appreciate how display ads are placed, we need to understand the following terms:

- **Ad Network** – helps publishers sell extra inventory that they are not able to sell through their sales force – basically an aggregator
- **Ad Exchange** – tools that facilitate buying and selling of aggregated ad inventory from multiple ad networks
- **DSP (Demand Side Platform)** – tools that advertisers use to control access impressions from multiple sources
- **SSP (Supply Side Platforms)** – tools that publishers use to control access impressions from multiple sources

How DSP, SSP and DMP Work Demand side platforms (DSP), supply side platforms (SSP) and data management platforms (DMP) are all integral to the digital advertising process. They operate together to enable the automated buying and selling of advertising, but perform very different functions.

DSP: To purchase inventories, a software called demand side platform (DSP) is used by marketers or their agencies since DSPs act as aggregators (like MakeMyTrip). Ad exchanges pool inventories from publishers and make them available and this software aggregates various exchanges and facilitates an automated buying process of inventory that is appropriate basis buyers' requirements. Thus based on individual user behaviour, action, demographic, location, or previous online activity, it facilitates advertisers to buy inventory across publishers. This helps advertisers optimize campaigns.

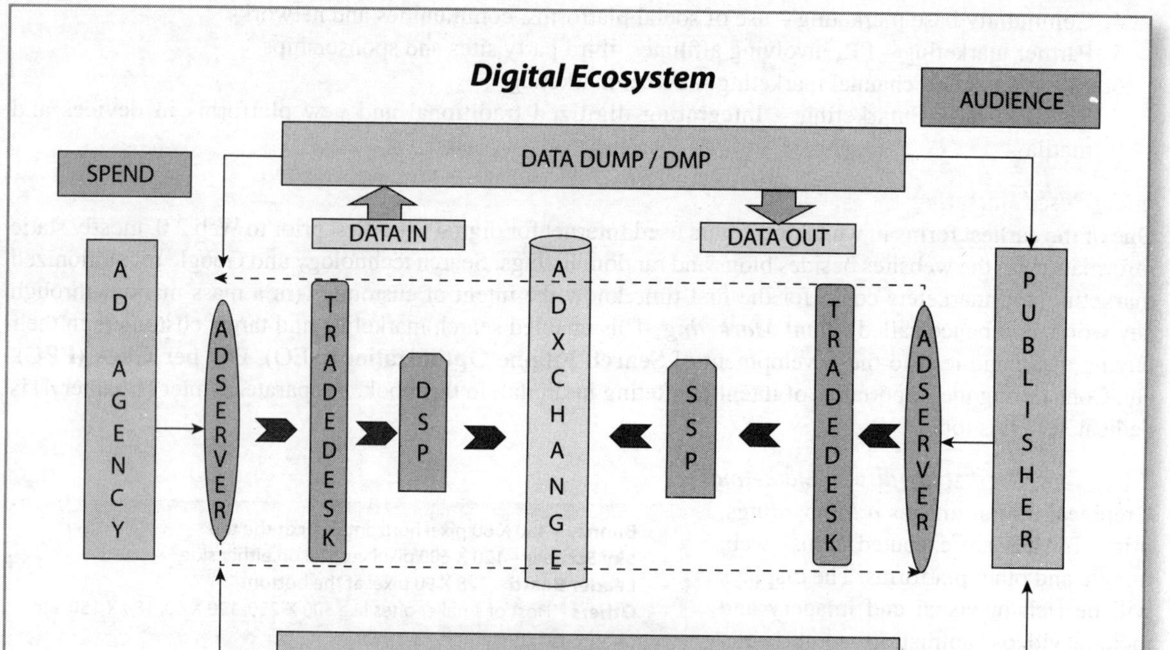

Figure 3.13 Digital Ecosystem

DMP: To segment audiences and enable targeting and improving results, a software is used that is called data management platform or DMP. This mines primary, secondary and third party data, and organizes the same. Essentially, this software is used to collect and organize select cookies from browsers basis the requirement of the marketer such as demographics, browsing behaviour, etc. This information is then used by the advertising platforms to deliver inventory when the selected cookies appear. A DSP buys advertising based on information provided by a DMP.

SSP: A supply-side platform (SSP) is another software that publishers use to sell digital inventories via automated auctions. Since publishers or content generators need an electronic platform (like the newspapers or magazines providing hard copy space advertisements) for their inventories, it is called 'supply-side'.

SSP is the publisher's version of DSP which allows publishers to connect to a large number of potential buyers through ad exchanges, thus enabling publishers to manage inventory and revenue by realizing the highest cost (or CPM) for their ads.

Like the stock exchange, the software permits publishers to set floor price (the minimum price a publisher will accept for an impression), create guaranteed deals and define a range of rules around which advertisers or buyers can and cannot purchase their inventory.

Integrated Inventory Buying

1. DMP provides the audience data for the product or service.
2. Once the product or service decides its target audience with a particular ad campaign, DSP is fed with this information.
3. DSP connects to an SSP.
4. SSP offers various options to reach the desired audience at different prices, and the DSP will automatically determine what is the most appropriate purchase to reach the intended audience (based on the information for the campaign contained in the DMP) at the best price.
5. If advertiser (via the DSP) is satisfied with the price and inventory on offer by the publisher (via the SSP), an exchange takes place and the ad is purchased and delivered.

Content Marketing - POEM

POEM is an acronym for Paid, Owned and Earned Media. POEM is emerging as an important channel of marketing particularly in B_2B, high end products and services where content plays a crucial part in end of the funnel activities leading to purchase and include blogs, white papers, webinars, demo videos, etc. The strength of content lies in its relevance and a possibility to be non-intrusive (like zoo-zoos). It creates traffic through a desire to consume quality content. These can be

> POEM: POEM is an acronym for Paid, Owned and Earned Media and refers to the different means for a brand to gain visibility on the Internet and beyond.

- **Paid content (Native content) –** placement in a format native to the online channel or publisher (very similar to advertorials in print)
- **Owned content -** Websites, blogs, white papers and webinars
- **Earned (Viral) content –** Essentially viral marketing with rich media content – Videos, cartoons, caricatures, etc.

Community based Marketing (Social Media Marketing)

Sociological theories indicate "Humans are social animals". Using this concept of human need of community interaction which was also the birth of communication (Chapter 1), social media marketing has made rapid strides. Word-of-mouth, networking, referrals, personal communication are effectively leveraged. Since this activity is a very large chunk of digital marketing and also often confused with digital marketing itself (refer Chapter 1), a separate chapter has been included on SMM (Chapter -).

Partner Marketing Partner marketing is involving partnership with other potential influencers in the same domain or area of operation. These could be affiliates such as review sites, e-commerce sites, comparison sites; PR sites sharing news and events and editorial partnerships wherein paid articles specifically written are placed. Partner marketing is helpful to leverage strong influence some of the above have developed with a specific segment or a specific audience in each part of the sales funnel.

Direct Marketing Direct marketing involves channels that directly reach out to the customers through push such as email/SMS or pull such as customer service calls and toll free numbers. These are considered very cost effective and have the highest RoI in relation to other channels. However, the data for this activity would need to come from other types of marketing. In this category, there is also response marketing wherein a customer's response to a brand interaction in any of the touch points (social media, comment, chat, etc.) are responded in such a manner that reflects the concern and care, typically service recovery.

Platform Marketing Platform marketing is the use of newly emerging vehicles and platforms such as wearables, gaming platforms or even kiosks in a retail store. Digital messages and ads could be placed in these platforms that are checked multiple times a day by the consumer.

Table 3.1 summarizes the various media types and their activities.

Table 3.1 Various media types and their activities

Media Type	Owned Media	Paid Media	Earned Media
Activity			
Intent Marketing		*Search Marketing*	
Brand Marketing		*Advertising*	
Content Marketing	*Website, Blogs Videos, Webinars*	*Native Content*	
Community Marketing (SMM)	*Community Platforms*	*Social Media Ads*	*Social Media Posts*
Partner Marketing		*Affiliate, PR, Editorial*	
Direct Marketing	*Direct Response, Chat*	*Email, SMS*	*Inbound calls, Comments*
Platform Marketing	*Mobile Apps*	*Wearables, In-game, Retail Kiosks*	

Revenue based Digital Marketing model[7]

Having looked at key types of digital marketing, the focus is now on major business models deployed by marketers to earn revenue from investments across digital media types described earlier.

When talked about Internet companies and their services that are used on a daily basis, Google, Facebook, Twitter, LinkedIn, Quora, Wikipedia, etc. come to minds. These provide various types of information, almost instantly. Apart from access to this information, a website can be set for free at Wordpress or blogger, download free mobile apps on iTunes and Google Play Store, watch videos for free on YouTube, and post free classified ads on sites like Quikr.

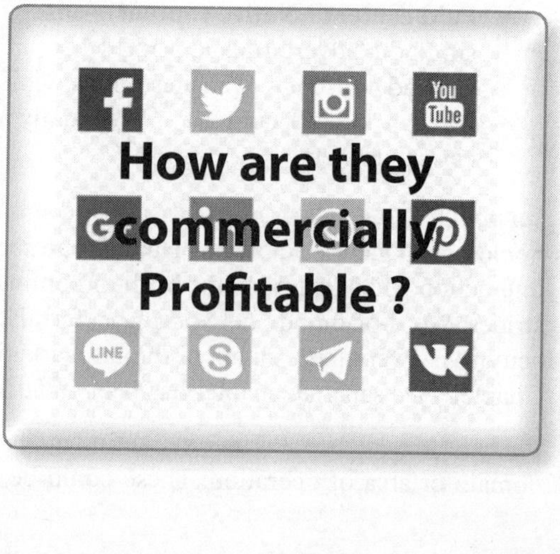

While many of these come for free and most of them are also profitable, the question arises where the revenue comes from. Advertising is the first thing that comes to mind when thought of revenue models. While advertising is the major revenue source for many of them, there are several other revenue models. Following are some of the revenue models that are in practice:

1. Advertising
2. Freemium
3. eCommerce
4. Affiliate marketing
5. Subscription
6. Licensing
7. Sale of Data
8. Sponsorship/Donations
9. Build to sell (to Google, Facebook and others)
10. Mobile and gaming

1. Advertising

Advertising, which is any form of paid communication, has been the oldest platforms – traditional or digital. However, in the digital space this platform is under constant evolution and refinement with customers having access to ad-blocking tools. Today, complex tools are employed to stay relevant. Some selected examples are given below.

- Display/Search/Text Ads - Google, Yahoo!, Facebook
- Video/Audio Ads –YouTube, Gaana, Wynk
- Promoted Content - FB, Twitter
- Recruitment Ads – LinkedIn, Naukri, Rediff
- B2B - Classifieds – Indiamart, JustDial
- Higher Education Admissions – PaGalGuy, MBA Universe
- Featured listings - e.g. Zomato, CommonFloor
- Email Ads – Google, Yahoo!
- Location-based offers – Google, Foursquare

2. Freemium model

Based on Loss Leader pricing in traditional marketing, this model is used by Web services in particular SaaS (Software as a Service) products. It may be noted that there is nothing free in freemium. This model uses the axiom to sell a basic free product to as many customers as possible to drive the traffic, and other features are kept premium exclusively for paying customers. A good example will be Smart Insights that share basic blogs and newsletters for free, but if advanced tools are needed, they are subscription basis.

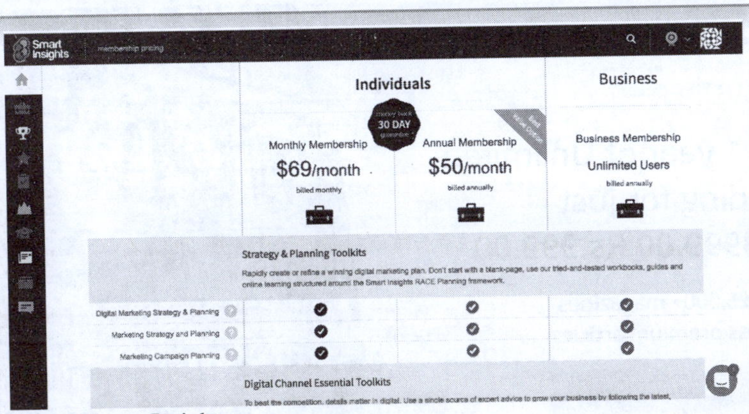

Source: Smart Insights

Other noteworthy examples include Google Docs/Drive, LinkedIn, Prezi, Slideshare, Skype, Wordpress, etc.

3. eCommerce

The traditional Indian retailing started changing this millennium with what was then called supermarket, high street stores and malls. Soon eretailers such as Flipkart, Amazon entered the Indian scene to change the landscape forever since these etailers could save on expensive real estate costs. As we discussed in Chapter 1, a recent report projects that the potential for digital spending is expected to grow 2.5 times from ~$40bn to ~$100bn by 2020 led by sectors such as ecommerce ($18-45bn), travel and hotel ($11-20bn), financial services ($12-30bn) and digital media ($200-570mn).

Selling through e-commerce can include:

- Retailing – Flipkart
- Marketplace – India Mart
- Sharing Economy - OYO
- Aggregators – Redbus
- Music/Video - iTunes
- Training – Hubspot, Google, Coursera
- Auction commerce – OLX, eBay

4. Affiliate Marketing

Mostly followed by high-traffic blogs, in this model, the publisher signs up for affiliate programs related to their service/content and convert their users to customers of their affiliates/advertisers. An example would be promoting culinary food ingredients through Chef. Sanjeev Kapoor's recipes, in his website or food blogging columns across digital channels.

The revenue model involves a publisher earning a commission when a user follows a link on their blog to another site and this converts into the user buying something at the affiliate site.

5. Subscription Model

This model is used a lot by magazines, newspapers, facilities and other such services. Most of us have been familiar with software that were once licensed, but with cloud platforms becoming popular, they are migrating toward a subscription model. Similarly, ISPs and broadband providers are another example of subscription based model that comes with options, unlimited usage is offered or a specified cap above which a higher rate is charged. Amazon Prime offers free deliveries and unlimited movies in their subscription model. Subscription model is common among SaaS, content services (news and magazines), infrastructure platforms such as Azure of Microsoft, maintenance services and many others.

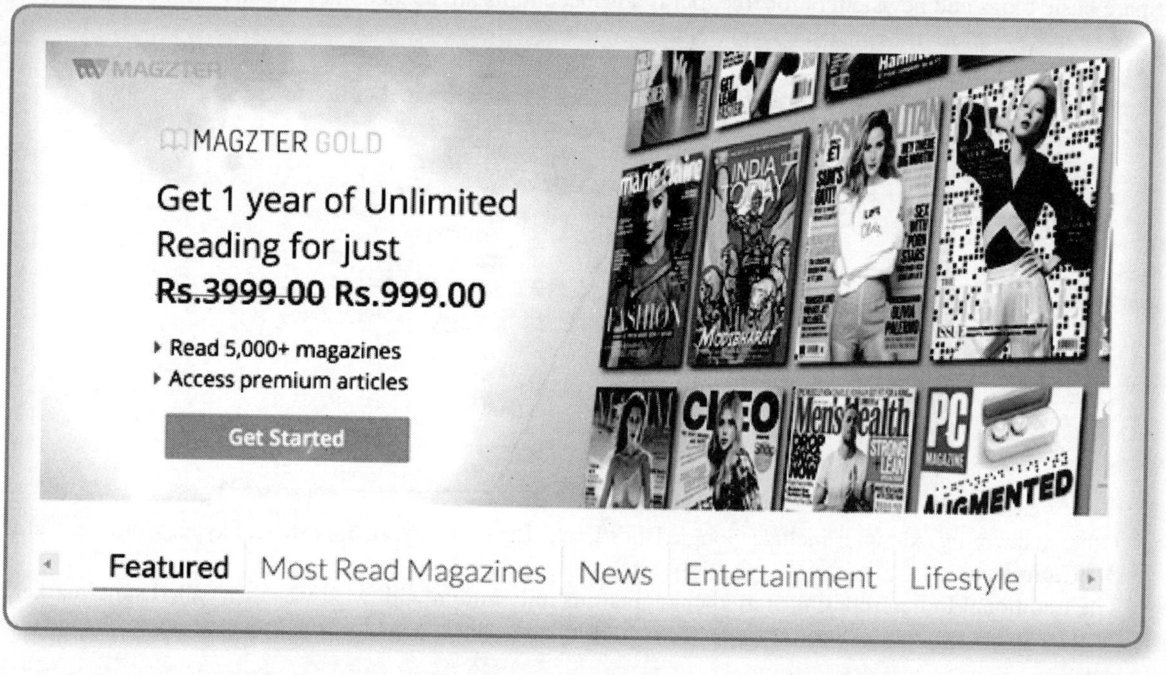

MSME: The Ministry of Micro Small and Medium Enterprises (MSME) is a branch of the Government of India, the apex body for the formulation and administration of rules, regulations and laws relating to micro, small and medium enterprises in India.

6. Licensing

This model was very common among software companies. With emerging SaaS, subscription is slowly being replaced. Licensing is generally for usage and limited by volume, device, time, type of service. Licensing could also be for certification that could be franchised (typically in education sector).

7. Selling Data

Many players like Google, Facebook and others do not charge for their service, but have access to and aggregate user data and monetize the same. All of us have heard of Cambridge Analytica having used Facebook data in multiple geographies and for multiple purposes. There is a famous quote by Scott Gordon, "If you are not paying for the product, you become the product[8]."

8. Sponsorship/Donations

Bill Gates Foundation and Google sponsor and fund projects that directly or indirectly help them or make the world at large better. As we saw in Chapter 2, Internet may not have been borne but for the US defense budget support. Several government and government agencies also similarly fund projects many of which could be for social causes. Wikipedia appealed to users to willingly donate to help support the initiative. Many browser extensions and Wordpress plugins, etc. also follow this route.

In summation, some of the major business models deployed by marketers to earn revenue from investments across digital media types described earlier, have been outlined above. We must remember that this is not an exhaustive or a comprehensive list, the digital world and engagement is continuously evolving.

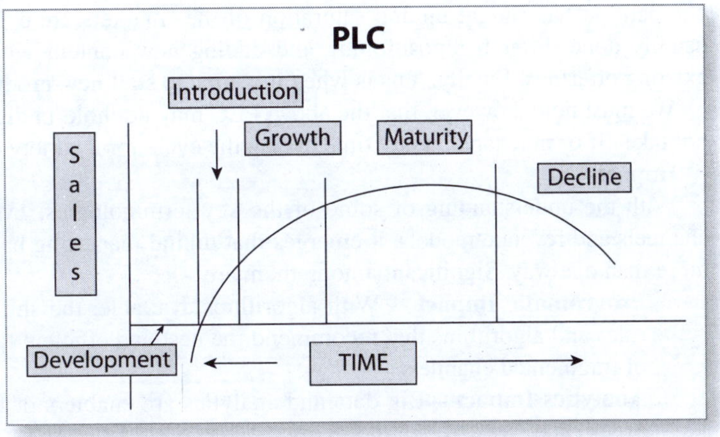

Figure 3.14 Source Author basis Literature

Product Life Cycle (PLC)

"Product Life Cycle" (PLC) refers to the stages a product goes through, from beginning to end. Sales and profits rise and fall and will lead to cumulative of profit before the journey is over. Let's take a closer look at the different stages of the cycle to uncover the lessons for content marketers.

Stage 1: Introduction

The first stage in PLC is "introduction." Prior to the introduction stage, a lot of money has been spent in product development. Therefore, it is assumed that the returns will be negative at this stage. Now more investment needs to be made to garner product awareness since merely posting on social network is unlikely to work. Therefore, investing and spending on deriving awareness and pushing visibility through digital and offline channel becomes important and the spend goes up impacting returns.

Brand Equity: Brand equity refers to a value premium that a company generates from a product with a recognizable name, when compared to a generic equivalent. Companies can create brand equity for their products by making them memorable, easily recognizable, and superior in quality and reliability

CEO: A chief executive officer or a chief marketing officer is responsible for marketing activities in an organization.

PR: Public relations (PR)is the practice of managing the spread of information between an individual or an organization and the public.

Stage 2: Growth

The growth stage is critical in the life cycle of all successful products. At this point, evaluate whether the content is gaining traction. "Early adopters" (or educated opinion leaders) will start sharing the content with their networks. When it is seen that the tweet promoting your content retweeted, you know the growth stage has started and that it's time to focus on earned media and invest in distribution by running display ads on websites that specialize in social media advertising or running sponsored stories.

Notwithstanding the returns will likely still be negative at this stage, the spending continues because now you can see that downloads from your site begin to happen. Sales are also starting to give you some positive feedback on your leads.

Stage 3: Maturity

Maturity is when the firm starts seeing the revenue accruals happening from the leads generated by the content, for, the content has been consumed and shared by "early and late majority" adopters. Besides, at this stage, the ad spend has been reduced taking advantage of a steady flow of downloads or CTA that happens and when how many visitors/downloads can be predicted because mainstream customers are seeing and sharing your content. At this point, a likely breakeven on the investments is also reported.

Stage 4: Decline

Strategically, decline becomes a critical phase from the decision making perspective since by now the competition has caught up and saturation of the markets are evident. Delaying the process of decline is usually done through repositioning and adding new content with new information and new features to existing offerings. Finally, this is when it is time to start new product development as replacement.

We must note, however, that the above PLC may not hold in digital marketing since your campaign may not take off or may taper at any time during the cycle for a variety of reasons.

Impact

With the understanding of some of the key terminologies, IMC, IDC, types of digital marketing and channels and revenue models, it emerges that digital marketing has impacted traditional media planning in more than one way. Significant among them are –

- **Programatic Impact** - With algorithms available, the shift is from manual to automated business rules and algorithms that recommend the best and efficient targeting of prospects particularly in view of fragmented channels.
- **Analytics Impact** – Big data and analytics are enablers of following the data rather than instinct or experience.
- **Pricing Impact** – Both the above (algorithm and analytics) enable cost effective planning of the inventory with a mix of premium and low cost options.

CHAPTER SUMMARY

- For long two familiar buckets B2C (Business to Consumer - FMCG) and B2B (Business to Business) have been in use. While moving forward and embracing the digital world and its multiple channel of interaction between individuals, MSMEs, large businesses, Government and NGOs, this traditional landscape is fast changing.
- Besides multiple channels of interaction, boundaries between products, services and platforms have blurred, leading to consumers' purchase decisions revolving around a buying experience that needs an integrated view and an end-to-end experience design that are truly valuable to consumers.
- For understanding business strategies, understanding consumer behaviour and the standard Sales Funnel is crucial. At the core of the funnel concept is the AIDA model.
- AIDA is an acronym that stands for Attention, Interest, Desire and Action. The AIDA model is just one of a class of models known as hierarchy of effects models and are linear, sequential models built on an assumption that consumers move through a series of cognitive (thinking) and affective (feeling) stages culminating in a behavioural stage (doing e.g. purchase or trial).
- Marketers have now added "Retention" to AIDA since as an outcome a marketer would like to retain and convert a customer to a loyal customer from a mere customer. AIDAR helps structure some key points in the customer journey.
- REAN is a marketing acronym. It is a framework to plan ahead and/or analyze the often complex sequence of inter-related, multichannel, marketing activities that are needed to build and nurture a customer relationship. It stands for Reach, Engage, Activate and Nurture.
- In the digital context, REAN framework was adapted to create (P)RACE framework to help (digital) marketers plan and manage their activities in a more structured way throughout the customer lifecycle and stands for *- (Plan) > Reach > Act > Convert > Engage.*
- 3D model facilitates understanding rapid technology cycles to improve multiplatform marketing efforts and take a different approach to managing the consumer decision journey—one that embraces the speed that digitization brings and focuses on capabilities in three areas—Discover > Design > Deliver.
- The 3D model when integrated with (P)RACE shows what an optimized cross-channel experience could look like when companies target improved capabilities in these three areas.
- Integrated marketing communication or **IMC** ensures that all forms of communications are carefully linked together integrating all the communication and promotional activities so that they work together to convey a consistent message to the company's internal and external stakeholders.
- Planning or media planning, therefore, becomes paramount in IMC. A good model to follow will be the SMART model of goal setting. SMART is a mnemonic acronym and stands for Specific, Measurable, Achievable, Relevant and Time bound goal setting.
- Media planning is how content is created and budgets are allocated across media or platforms that is in sync with your offering and the market and includes media channel, media vehicle, media audience, media schedule, media budget, media delivery, reach, response, relevance, scheduling and frequency.
- Integrated digital communication (IDC) that is the digital adapt of IMC and a key aspect of digital marketing and consists of four pillars *viz.* content creators, channels, affiliates and influencers.
- The digital channel mix decisions are a function of type of digital marketing, revenue based business model, product life cycle (PLC) and impact.
- Digital marketing can be broadly classified into digital marketing into 7 key types that form the underlying basis. They are intent (Internet based marketing), brand based marketing (display marketing), content marketing, community based marketing, partner marketing, communication channel marketing and platform based marketing.
- Digital marketing operates on several revenue models. Some of the revenue models that are in practice are advertising, freemium, ecommerce, affiliate marketing, subscription, licensing, sale of data, sponsorship/donations, build to sell (to Google, Facebook and others) and mobile and gaming.
- Digital strategies differ based on the stage of the product life cycle (PLC) that the offering is in.
- With the understanding of some of the key terminologies and models in this chapter, it emerges that digital marketing has impacted traditional media planning in more than one way. Significant among them are programmatic impact, analytics impact and pricing impact.

Data Knox

Paritosh Gupta was busy preparing for a meeting with his CEO that would determine if his company took its next step successfully or faltered. He had to put together a digital communications plan based on the concept of POEM (Paid, Owned and Earned Media) that would deliver growth without spending too much money. Knowing this was next to impossible, he looked at putting together a combination of media that would be both effective and efficient.

Data Knox was a pioneer in the field of data security. While other service providers offered security for its own sake, Data Knox understood the business-critical nature of data. The concept of data lifecycle — data capture, storage, usage and disposal — was the cornerstone of its business approach; and this helped build credibility with its clients.

The data security product itself was highly customizable, with built-in controls. It was already in use in a variety of industries. Leading global companies, academic institutions, and the big four accounting firms were Data Knox's clients. Using them as references to generate new leads was a tempting thought but Paritosh wondered if sharing such information went against the very thought of data security. He wasn't too sure about this, and decided not to risk it.

Data Knox enjoyed the advantage of being an early mover. That, coupled with its approach to data security, had contributed to its early success. Intuitively, it made sense to replicate that strategy on a larger scale. However, Paritosh recognized the inherent risk in making the company's business strategy widely known. He was hesitant.

Hoping to get clarity on all this, Paritosh listed out the communications objectives as he saw it:

1. Announce data security services based on a thorough understanding business-critical issue
2. Build immediate preference for Data Knox.
3. Generate serious enquiries.

It was clear to him that in order to retain its early mover advantage, Data Knox would have to move through these three stages rapidly. It would also have to highlight the immense business relevance of its approach to data security, in an unimpeachably credible way.

Given below was Paritosh's outline plan:

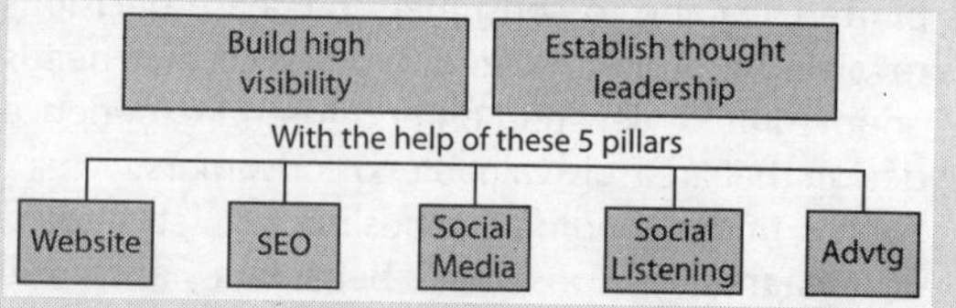

Additionally, Paritosh detailed how he would use each of the five pillars in developing and delivering the key messages. He viewed them as distinct activities that he would combine in a meaningful way to deliver a more powerful punch.

This is how he defined the efforts of each of these five pillars:

Website	Build and convey thought leadership through a variety of tools e.g. white papers, research, case-studies, blogs, Q&A, etc.
SEO	Ensure immediate website visibility to relevant high value prospects.
Social Media	Co-ordinate a social media presence with focus on the business community.
Social Listening	Monitor chatter and lead or intervene as necessary.
Advertising	Develop targeted advertising in support of all these efforts.

It was all suddenly coming together very well. Paritosh could see distinct elements delivering a pre-determined set of messages that would all work together in concert to move the prospect from awareness (of the issue and Data Knox) to preference, to enquiry. He also recognized that he would not have complete control over all these pillars, some he could pay for and some actually belonged to Data Knox.

While Paritosh felt he had the basis of a strong communications support, he wasn't very sure how it would all come together. What should he do?

Case Questions

1. Has Paritosh identified all the pillars and assigned tasks appropriately?
2. How should he plan and sequence the use of these pillars to get maximum impact?

REVIEW QUESTIONS

1. How has the digital world changed channels of interaction between businesses and consumer?
2. What is AIDA model? What does it stand for and why is it called hierarchy of effects model?
3. Trace the evolution of (P)RACE model from AIDA model and what is the significance of this evolution?
4. What is 3D model and what does it facilitate?
5. What is media planning in digital context?
6. What is integrated digital communication (IDC) and how is it different from IMC (Integrated Marketing Communication)?
7. What are the components of digital channel mix and explain them briefly?
8. Name the key types of digital marketing and explain them briefly.
9. What are the revenue models that operate in digital marketing?
10. Given the above, how has digital marketing flipped the traditional marketing on its head?

ACTIVITY QUESTIONS

1. Design a mailer for an event or activity using a free Mailchimp template and do a pilot test with your friends using a free trial version of bul mailing software
2. Refer Activity Quest 1 and get metrics and analyze using any free tool on the web.

KEY TERMS

AIDA
REAN
RACE
(P) RACE
IMC / IDC
SMART
B2B
B2C
FMCG
NGO
MSME
SEM
SEO
CRM
Brand Equity
CEO
PR
PLC
PPC
POEM

REFERENCES

1. https://en.wikipedia.org/wiki/AIDA_(marketing).
2. AIDA to AIDAR.
   https://www.searchenginejournal.com/applying-aida-digital-marketing/67755/.
   https://4cm.co.uk/aida-is-dead-long-live-aaaaa/.
3. D. Pickton, A. Broderick, (2001) "Integrated Marketing Communications", Corporate Communications: An International Journal, Vol. 6 Issue: 1, pp.53-54, https://doi.org/10.1108/ccij.2001.6.1.53.2.

4. Doran, G. T. (1981). "There's a S.M.A.R.T. way to write management's goals and objectives". Management Review. AMA FORUM. **70** (11): 35–36.
5. Jerry Kliatchko (2015) Revisiting the IMC construct, International Journal of Advertising, 27:1, 133-160, DOI: 10.1080/02650487.2008.11073043.
6. http://www.marketingteacher.com/digital-marketing-mix/
   https://www.7boats.com/services/internet-marketing/the-right-digital-marketing-mix-and-profit-channels-for-your-online-business/
   https://www.strategyand.pwc.com/media/file/Strategyand_Create-your-own-buzz.pdf
   https://www.digitaldoughnut.com/articles/2016/november/finding-the-right-channel-mix-the-first-step-towa
   https://www.capgemini.com/wp-content/uploads/2017/07/digital_marketing25-06.pdf
7. https://www.strategy-business.com/article/00241?gko=20aae
   https://digitalintelligencetoday.com/the-10-business-models-of-digital-disruption-and-how-to-respond-to-them/.
8. https://www.forbes.com/sites/marketshare/2012/03/05/if-youre-not-paying-for-it-you-become-the-product/#5487f2955d6e.

CHAPTER 4

SOCIAL MEDIA MARKETING: PROCESS AND MANAGEMENT

CHAPTER OBJECTIVES

After reading this chapter, you will be able to

- Understand how social media and traditional media differ
- Identify social and digital media and where to use them
- Analyze why the myths around social media can hamper a SMM program
- Estimate how to build a plan for an effective social media marketing program
- Define social engagement, why it is crucial and how to improve it
- Discuss how to categorize your customers and how to engage with them constantly
- Explain how SMM program is linked to the SMM objective setting and RoI

OPENING CASE CASELET

La Appeal

La Appeal was a reputed and recognized international brand of hair styling products and looked at India with a lot of optimism. The young population, with their increasing openness for new experiences presented a fantastic opportunity. Indira Mukherjee was part of the creative team of Sigma Digi, one of the Digital Agencies of *La Appeal*. Sigma Digi received a communications brief to work on an activation campaign for La Appeal and Indira Mukherjee was very excited when she was assigned to it.

An international campaign, adapted to India, would precede the brand launch. Focused on mass media, that campaign would make the Indian consumer more familiar with the brand and its Indian line-up, while kindling desire for hair styling. Although an important piece of the communications mix, mass media would not directly lead to consumer enquiries at stylists and brand sales. The client acknowledged that fact and so briefed Indira's agency on an activation campaign.

One part of that activation campaign would include engagement with hair stylists. Having worked with stylists around the world, *La Appeal* had years of data on how they felt about their profession, the brand they used, their purchase and usage habits, etc.

Most of that behaviour would apply to hair stylists in India as well. The brief provided the following:

- While working within accepted hair styles and looks, stylists liked to put their own interpretation of it on their work.

- Style is ever-evolving, and stylists spent a lot of time understanding and keeping up with the latest trends.
- Peer appreciation is important to them. They liked being acknowledged for their work, in as wide and visible a circle of fellow hairstylists as possible.
- Equally, developing and retaining a loyal customer base is important to them. They know that once a customer has confidence with a particular stylist, they almost never try someone new. So stylists work hard at keeping customers.
- Stylists felt the need to keep their skills and techniques up-to-date and in step with what the newest technology, appliances and products made possible.
- They had a natural preference for working with reputed brands, as this almost always led to good results and once used to a particular brand, they are unlikely to switch to a new one.

Although this information gave Indira some great ideas on how *La Appeal* could engage with hairstylists, Indira wasn't sure how well *La Appeal* understood Indian women. There was little information available about Indian women's preferences in the public domain. To put herself in the consumer's shoes, she decided to get her hair styled, making notes of her thoughts, feelings and experiences as she went along. This is what she discovered:

Concern type	Concern verbalised
Rational	Choosing a hairstylist is not as easy as it seems. It's not the same as choosing one when I want my hair cut. Styling is a far more serious decision.
Rational	Going to a reputed stylist is all very well, but my hair is not the same as everyone's. It's unique and needs to be treated accordingly. There should be some way to know how experienced a stylist is with different types of hair.
Non-rational	My friends and others I trust could recommend a good stylist. That's always a safe bet. But if I wanted to experiment and try something new, where do I start?
Rational	I need advice from an impartial expert. What would look good on me? What would suit my face type, my skin tone, height, personality, etc? Who could I ask?
Non-rational	Hair colouring was the new trend, and several of my friends have tried it. I am not sure how I would look. Some of my friends use colouring to touch-up premature greying. I am haunted by images of Meena aunty with henna in her hair.
Non-rational	Styling was still an international concept. I don't want to try something and appear a 'wannabe'. So I must go to someone skilled and experienced with styling Indian women's hair. Should I take one of my friends along and help me choose?
Non-rational	How my hair looks impacts my confidence and feeling of well-being. I have to be absolutely sure at each step.
Unknown	Indian hair and grooming regimens are different from international norms. Would an international company know these differences? Can it 'force-fit' international practices for Indian women?

With this experience and the information on hair stylists, Indira felt better able to develop a campaign to address the three objectives specified:

1. Build a strong relationship with stylists.

2. Use women who currently style their hair to convert those who do not.
3. Be seen as the only international brand most suited for Indian women.

Given the above, she understood that the underlying need for any campaign should be to make two-way communications possible. Consumers had to be able to discuss, share ideas, get recommendations, see styling possibilities and feel confident enough to try styling their hair. Therefore Indira understood social media will be the best way to do this.

She handpicked the social media that she wanted to be in, instead of making a presence in all social media. She believed too many social media will dilute the efficacy of communications. She followed a hub and spikes model and built a central hub of content derived from pain points using key topics, her own experience and target key words. The content hub was a free ebook and a tip sheet. Primary content spokes were blogs, emails and the secondary content spokes were social media posts concentrating on local stakeholders since preferences and influencers were not uniform throughout and needed a customized approach at each target group. The creation of such supportive secondary handles uniquely concentrating on regions allowed her to make a better connect.

This also made communications on regional sales strategies easier. She understood that the customers would not engage with the brand directly and focussed on content marketing that facilitated her social media interactions genuine with real solutions with subtle branded content. Indira reached out to influencers at the regional and national level and partnered with them to create and share content about the brand. She invited influencers to write in their media and also in their representive media to reach out to followers of similar interest groups. She created a brand persona that represents the brand image and personified it in social media, i.e what if *La Appeal* were to be a person and what would he say on such situations? She used this to engage with the customer whenever there was a mention or an appeal in the social media. The personification of the brand resonated well with the customers.

Indira regularly posted open ended questions on real time problems of the customer and solutions without endorsing their products directly. This helped her build trust of the followers and increased the engagement even further. Whilst the engagement was growing, she also started noticing a lot of negative engagement. There were online trolls and miscreants who regularly posted negative comments and disturbed the flow of engagement. But then, these were expected and the community took care of itself. Overall *La Appeal* was satisfied with the campaign.

Case Questions

1. What are the questions Indira should be asking before creating a brand persona?
2. Is Indira right in restricting herself to certain social media? Why?

INTRODUCTION

Social media marketing has become an integral part of many companies' marketing strategies with an estimated 2.5 billion people worldwide being active on social media. Thus when it comes to purchasing products and services, social media influences consumers almost as much as television ads and continues to trend upward. Social media is the latest buzzword in Internet marketing, on account of new generation of social media platforms, mainly Facebook and Twitter, that changed the way we socialize, interact and shop. This has also brought new channels to

> **App:** An application or a program designed to run on a digital device such as a computer/phone/tablet or watch

digital marketing. Social media is the term we use to describe platforms that bring people together for the exchange of information. The most popular social media platforms are Facebook, Twitter, Google+, Pinterest, Instagram, Tumblr, LinkedIn, StumbleUpon and YouTube. Earlier in Chapter 2, it was noted that engaging on social media is digital marketing and that this is erroneous. This chapter explains the main advantage of social media in capturing the network capability (or virality) of social media to spread advertising content principally using the sharing capability of social media and/or addressing the micro-communities that form up social media.

SOCIAL NETWORKING AND SOCIAL MEDIA MARKETING

It is important to understand the basic concept of social network before delving into social media marketing.

Social networking is the practice of expanding the number of one's business and/or social contacts by making connections through individuals. Social networking is based on the six degrees of separation[1] concept that any two people on the planet could make contact through a chain of no more than five intermediaries. Social networking establishes interconnected communities (sometimes known as social graphs) that help people make contacts that would be good for them to know, but that they would unlikely have met otherwise. Traditional offline examples are clubs, associations and the like. Today it is easy to do so using online and depending on the social media platform, members may be able to contact any other member. In other cases, members can contact anyone they have a connection with, and subsequently anyone that contact has a connection with, and so on. Some services require members to have a preexisting connection to contact other members. While social networking has gone on almost as long as societies themselves have existed, Internet and Web have facilitated social networking leading to an exponential and ongoing expansion of social networking.

Social Media Marketing (SMM) is a form of Internet marketing that utilizes social networking[2] websites as a marketing tool. The goal of SMM is to produce content that users will share with their social network to help a company increase brand exposure and broaden customer reach. *Social media marketing is the process of creating content that you have tailored to the context of each individual social media platform in order to drive user engagement and sharing.*

In addition to social media platforms, the capacity for social interaction and collaboration is increasingly built into business applications.

Some of the prominent social media are:

- **Facebook** is a popular free social networking website that allows registered users to create profiles, upload photos and video, send messages and keep in touch with friends, family and colleagues.
- **Twitter** is a free microblogging service that allows registered members to broadcast short posts called tweets. Twitter members can broadcast tweets and follow other users' tweets by using multiple platforms and devices.

Social media: Term we use to describe platforms that bring people together for the exchange of information
Social media marketing: Form of Internet marketing that utilizes social networking websites as a marketing tool
Social networking : The practice of expanding the number of one's business and/ or social contacts by making connections through individuals

Facebook: A popular free social networking website.
Google Ads: An online advertising service developed by Google, where advertisers pay to display brief advertisements, service offerings, product listings, and video content within the Google ad network to web users
LinkedIn: A social networking site designed specifically for the business community
Pinterest: A social curation website for sharing and categorizing images found online
Reddit: A social news website and forum where stories are socially curated and promoted by site members.

- **Wikipedia** is a free, open content online encyclopedia created through the collaborative effort of a community of users known as Wikipedians. Anyone registered on the site can create an article for publication; registration is not required to edit articles.
- **LinkedIn** is a social networking site designed specifically for the business community. The goal of the site is to allow registered members to establish and document networks of people they know and trust professionally.
- **Reddit** is a social news website and forum where stories are socially curated and promoted by site members. The site is composed of hundreds of sub-communities, known as "subreddits." Each subreddit has a specific topic such as technology, politics or music. Reddit site members, also known as, "redditors," submit content which is then voted upon by other members. The goal is to send well-regarded stories to the top of the site's main thread page.

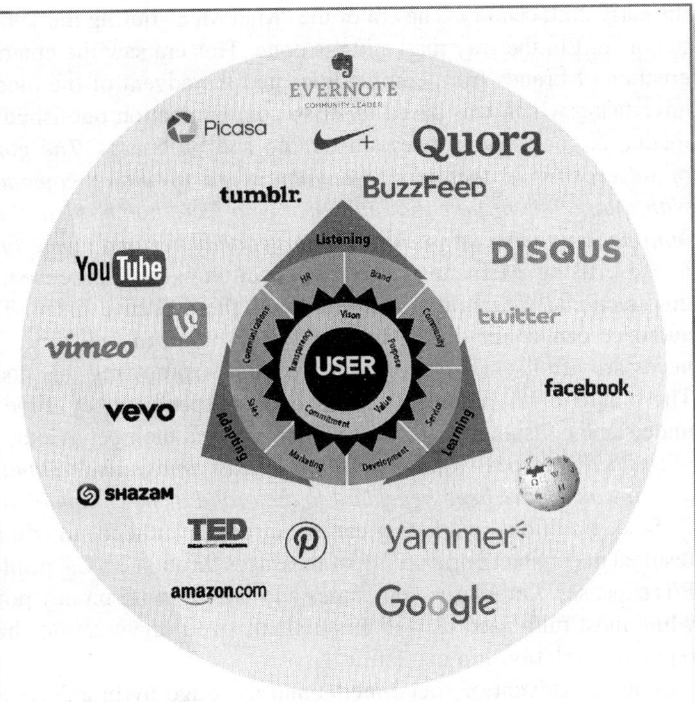

Source : Adapted from Brian Solis' Conversation Prism

Figure 4.1 Conversation Prism

- **Pinterest** is a social curation website for sharing and categorizing images found online. Pinterest requires brief descriptions but the main focus of the site is visual. Clicking on an image will take you to the original source, so, for example, if you click on a picture of a pair of shoes, you might be taken to a site where you can purchase them. An image of blueberry pancakes might take you to the recipe; a picture of a whimsical birdhouse might take you to the instructions.

Social media is becoming an integral part of life online as social websites and applications proliferate. In business, social media is used to market products, promote brands, connect to current customers and foster new business. Social media marketing (SMM) takes advantage of social networking to help a company increase brand exposure and broaden customer reach. The goal is usually to create content compelling enough for users to share it with their social networks. SMM is based on the principle of ***Listening, Adapting and Learning.*** Brian Solis[3] created the following social media chart, known as the conversation prism, to categorize social sites and services into various types of social media.

> **Twitter** : A free microblogging service.
> **Wikipedia** : A free, open content online encyclopedia.

WHY SOCIAL MEDIA MARKETING OVER TRADITIONAL MARKETING

Marketing as a practice is known to mankind since the earliest days of human civilization; however, "marketing" as a term has been in use since the late 19th century, while "marketing" as a field of study began only during

B2B Product: Business to business product or commonly referred to as industrial product.
B2C Product: Business to consumer product or commonly referred to as consumer goods.

the early 20th century. The era of the "Mad Men" during the 1960s saw a major shift in the way marketing is done. This era saw the emergence or creation of brands from commodities and the advent of the modern day advertising which was based on crisp communication published through media like newspaper, television, radio and billboards. *The golden era of advertising is therefore, the golden era of direct communication with a large set of potential audience who were bombarded with brand information aiming at reaching the target audience and converting them as buyer.*

Advertising as means of communication is still practised, without much changes and is typically unidirectional. The brand communicates, the audience listen. There are no means or ways by which the audience can communicate back with the brand in real time. The objective also here is to say and not necessarily to listen. The consumer feeling is something that does not get reflected in this communication. The brands or the companies subsequently spend money, time and effort to conduct market research to understand consumer sentiments and understand their behaviour. *The most important thing that emerges out of this is that in traditional marketing it takes time to understand consumer reaction; sometimes much later than it would have been beneficial to the brand or its communication or marketing strategy.*

Since traditional marketing can not target an audience to communicate a customized message, it usually resulted in constant bombarding of messages through TVCs, print ads, billboards, etc. which ends up as huge P/L expenses. Only large companies and brands, with money power can undertake such massive activities, while most mid-sized as well as all small sized organizations had to survive on plain word of mouth and reputation/relationship marketing.

With the advent of social media and its usage by brands as a communication and marketing platform, it gave brands and organizations of all sizes a level playing ground. Not only social media is a more cost effective platform as compared to traditional marketing, it now gave the brand and the brand users an opportunity to directly talk to each other in real time. This effectively means, that a brand with a good social media marketing program in place, can now not only understand, in real time, how its customers are reacting to it but also to its competition.

Such insights are of tremendous value to any brand/company as these used to cost them a lot of money earlier and they were never on real time basis. With social media, now they are not only communicating directly everyday with their target audience, but also measuring their actions, reactions and sentiments right at that time.

These insights are helping the brands to:

1. align their communication strategy
2. align brand promise
3. be customer centric
4. take quick actions as and when required

These are particularly helpful for new product launches, new market entry, start-up businesses, and also for larger brands who are now becoming more outward focus in terms of the business strategy as compared to inward focus as they used to be even just half a decade ago.

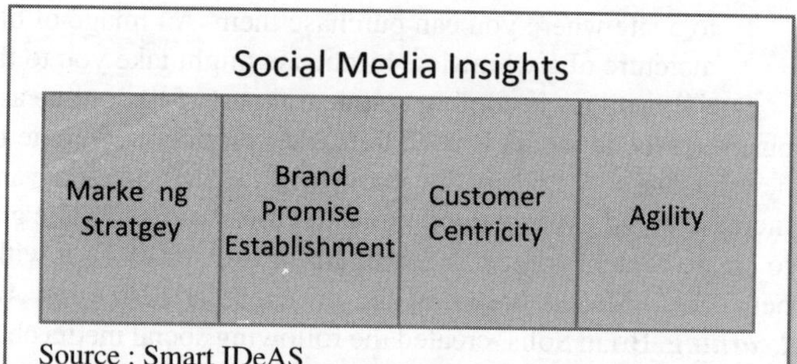

Source : Smart IDeAS

Figure 4. 2 SM Insights Model

The good news, however, is that all these are now being achieved at fraction of a cost of that of the traditional approach, saving the brands huge amount of money which ultimately improves their gross margin.

According to a survey of 344 social media marketers from around the world by Clutch[4] partnered with Smart Insights in 2017, social media positively influences most companies' revenue and sales. More than half (52%) of social media marketers said social media has helped increase their company's[5] revenue and sales, while 48% said it has had a limited impact but still needs to be managed.

Some findings of survey of 344 social media marketers from around the world by Clutch[5] partnered with Smart Insights in 2017 were:
- The most valuable social media platforms for businesses are Facebook (89%), LinkedIn (83%), YouTube (81%), and Twitter (80%).
- Written articles (27%), videos (26%), and images (24%) are the three most engaging types of content on social media.
- Nearly 80% of companies share mostly original content on social media.
- The most important metrics for tracking the success of social media are engagement (36%) and conversion rates (35%).
- More B2C companies (58%) consider investing time and money in social media than B2B companies (46%).
- The major challenges companies face with social media are not having enough human and financial resources (26%), lacking a formal strategy (24%), and building a community of followers and influencers (24%).

Exhibit 4.1 Clutch Insights - Social Media Marketing

Value of Social Media

Social media marketing program:
1. helps in two-way communication between brands and brand users or target customers.
2. is real time.
3. helps in immediate consumer insight rather than a post market research.
4. is cost effective, thus improving profitability.

Myths about Social Media

> **BPOA (Brad Plan of Action):** Identifying who your customer is and building a customer strategy accordingly to suit the customer.

Before proceeding further, let us first look into some of the myths associated with social media marketing. It is true that the social media has become, perhaps, the most important strategic marketing platform in recent years; however, there are still many misconceptions around it that create hindrances in making a successful social media marketing program. While an experienced social media marketer will know how to plan and strategize a great social media program, there are many brands, big and small, who are repeating the same mistake over and over again because of such misunderstandings. Sometimes, even a so called social media 'agency' also ends up committing these mistakes because they themselves are not thorough in understanding of its process and are simply part of the quick money-making racket that has churned up recently around social media.

While the list of social media myths can run a few pages, let us talk about a few important ones here:

1. **Social media means being on Facebook**
   Many organizations and brand believe that just being on Facebook would be sufficient. While Facebook is indeed a strong social medium platform, (and it is suggested to be on this platform for all most all kinds of organizations and brands), it will be immature to think that only Facebook can meet all your brand or marketing objectives. The brand must select a medium or a combination of media based on their target customers, market they serve and the product/services they are offering. For example, Instagram is a visual medium therefore, a food brand or a fashion brand would do well to be on Instagram to connect with their customers in a visual and attractive way, and they can also select Facebook or YouTube or Twitter or a combination of these for better engagements, brand building, influencer marketing and lead generation.
2. **Putting pretty pictures make it an awesome social media program**
   Yes they can, provided they are part of your marketing communication and content strategy. If content is the king, then visual content would be a more powerful king, only if they are being used in the

right context and for communicating a consistent story that connects your customers to your products, without being promotional or pushy.

3. **It's all about promoting your products**
   That's a very big NO. It is social media *marketing*, right? Not social media promotion. Besides, only promoting the brand pushes the customer away from you, since no one wants to be sold so much on their face. The best approach is to showcase how the brand adds value to the customers' lives.
4. **Can I make some quick sales?/Social media is solely for increasing sales**
   Social media is all about relationship building with your customers. If pushing sales is the primary motif, then the SMM program will fail and not give the desired results. The primary goal should always be to increase engagement with the audience; and as mentioned earlier to add value to their lives. Once a committed community of customers is built, sales will automatically increase.
5. **Social media marketing is my technology team's responsibility**
   Your technology team would be a great enabler in running the social media marketing program. But the main responsibility lies with the corporate as well as the marketing and sales team. However, having said that, the social media is the responsibility of all employees in an organization. How an employee behaves anywhere in social media, whether in the corporate platform or in personal capacity, reflects on the brand value of the company. Hence, it is a must to have social media training program as well as guidelines for all employees.
6. **Only young people are on social media**
   Take a look at the two charts in Figures 4.3 and 4.4:

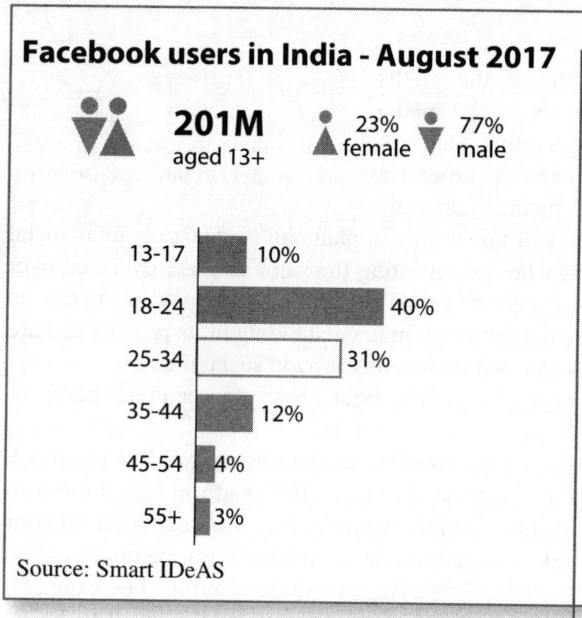

Figure 4.3 FB Users India - August 2017

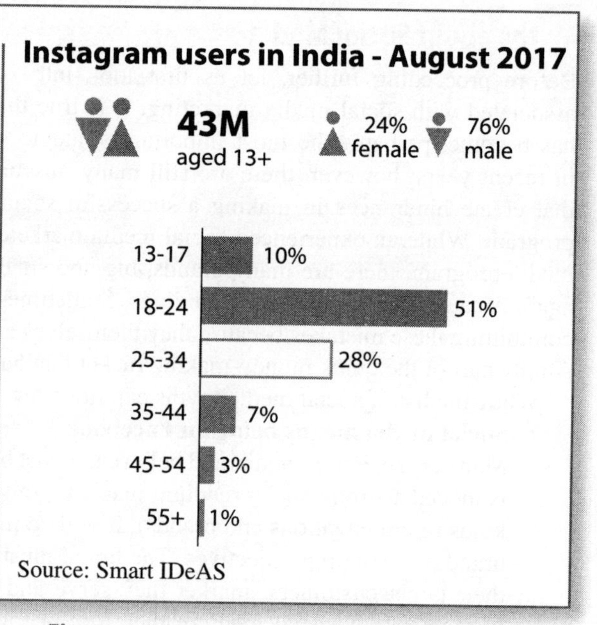

Figure 4.4 Instagram Users India - August 2017

While it seems like it is usually people below 30 years who are on social media in India, it has been observed that the highest growing demography is for the age of 40 years and more.

In the USA, with more Americans adopting social media, the social media user base has grown more representative of the broader population over the year. Young adults were among the earliest social media adopters and continue to use these sites at high levels, but usage by older adults has increased in recent years as represented in Figure 4.5:

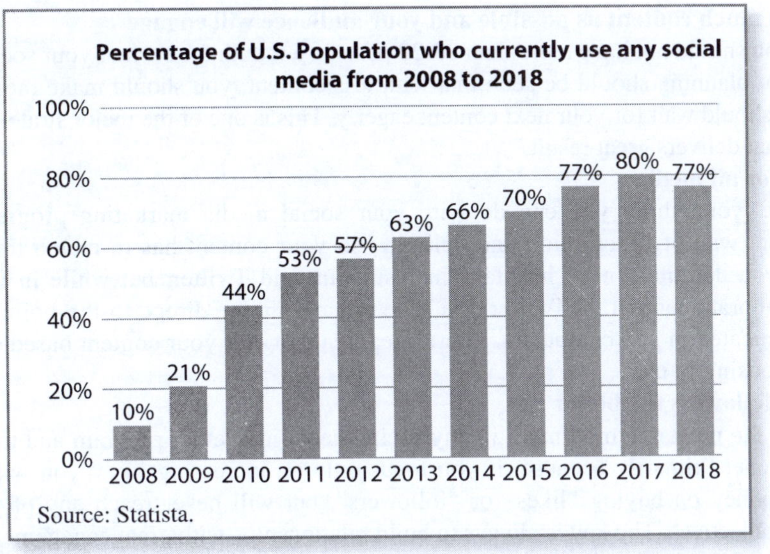

Figure 4.5 Percentage of Population on SM -2008-18 -USA

But the most important question to ask is "who is your customer?" If it is only young adults, then choose social platforms where they participate. If your customer base involves a mixed age group, choose social media accordingly.

7. **Let's be on every social network**
   As explained earlier, choose social media based on the target customers, the market being operated and the product or services being offered. So, if you are in the business of selling solar energy technologies, you should be on LinkedIn as well as have a blog. A YouTube channel with interesting videos is another option.
8. **If my friends and family 'Like' every update, my social presence will rock**
   Only if they are your customers and will be paying for your brand purchases consistently over years. Identifying the customers is the top activity in any social media marketing program. This needs thorough research and detailed targeting.
9. **Social media gives people a venue to publicly bash my company**
   People post negative comments about a brand in social media for two reasons:
   i. Your brand did not deliver as it promised and was actually disappointing.
   ii. They care about your brand.

   In either case, it is an opportunity to re-build a stronger relationship by solving their problems and taking note of their complaints. This process is called reputation management, and any good brand should have a solid reputation management plan in place.
10. **Anyone can do it!**
    Social media marketing is a specialized service and only those who are trained or comes with extensive experience should be given the responsibility of managing the program.
11. **You can make a big splash in a short time**
    If you don't have patience, stay away from social media marketing. Social media marketing takes time to show results, simply because it takes time to build trust and relationship. So, you cannot hurry up that process. Once the relationship is built solid, you will start seeing results immediately.
12. **You cannot measure social media marketing results**
    Most certainly you can. Social media marketing results are based on the social media marketing objectives.

13. **Publish as much content as possible and your audience will engage**
Usually, you should not have more than 20-22 posts in a month for each of your social media platform. The content planning should be such that with less content, you should make more impact and your customers should wait for your next content eagerly. This is one of the major strategies in social media planning that delivers great result.
14. **One post for all media**
That is the worst thing you can do with your social media marketing program. Each medium has different way of functioning and delivery; so your content has to match that completely. For example, you definitely need hashtags in Instagram and Twitter, but while in Instagram you can have an elaborate content, in Twitter you have to have a more direct, to-the-point approach that can be communicated in 280 characters. Therefore, create or edit your content based on which platform you are choosing to use.
15. **The more followers the better**
Yes, this is the most common myth in any social media marketing program and the most potentially dangerous one. Primarily because, if you focus only on increasing likes, you will not only end up spending money on buying "likes" or "followers", but will never reach any of your social media marketing objectives. The key is always to build relationships with great engagement.

SOCIAL MEDIA VS. DIGITAL MEDIA

Many people casually use digital media to mean both social and digital media. This is not correct. Primarily because they are different things altogether even though they are both online activities. ***Simply put social and digital marketing are online marketing but they work differently, achieving different objectives and delivering different results.*** Some brands may need to use both social and digital media, while others may use either one.

> **Digital media:** Those online platform, which are not two way but that help the brands to gather useful information about their clients or communicate directly to a set of their customers without engaging in any kind of communication.

Social media, as explained in the first chapter, helps the brands to communicate directly with their target customers and vice versa. In social media either party, i.e. the brand or the customer can initiate such communication; and they can converse on real time not only between two of them, but also with the customers' network of people.

Social media, therefore, are those platforms which help two-way, and at time, multi-way communication between the brand and its customers on a real time basis. As we saw earlier in the chapter, Facebook, Twitter, Instagram, Pinterest, Snapchat, YouTube, etc. are some of the social media platforms because in each one of them the above mentioned two-way and multi-way communication are the fundamental basis of their activities or core offering. A brand uses a social media like Facebook or Snapchat to directly talk to their customers because almost all their customers are already present in these platforms, thereby facilitating the communications.

Digital media, on the other hand, are those online platform, which are not two way. These are the platforms that help the brands to gather useful information about their clients or communicate directly to a set of their customers without engaging in any kind of communication. Google Ads, Websites, Apps, etc. are such digital media. While, these platforms help the brands to reach targeted customers with customized or general messaging, they are not useful for two-way or multi-way communications.

Many website, these days, have chat support. Does that make them social media? The answer is no. This is because such chats are only with a particular customer on a specific issue. This is simply a replacement of customer emails/letters/phone calls to the brands, but just at a quicker speed.

ESSENTIALS OF SOCIAL MEDIA MARKETING

The ***myths about social media marketing*** reflects one major problem that most current social media marketing programs are suffering from. Instead of being social media marketing, they have become **unsocial media promotions**, which unfortunately is counterproductive to social media marketing potential for a brand as explained below:

An unsocial program is one where the brand does not allow any two-way communication, thereby being contrary to the very essence of 'social' in social media marketing. In such a case, the brand is the only one talking through content which either restricts customers to interact or repels them away from the brand. A social scenario is one where everyone is allowed to communicate and opinions are listened to and shared. When that doesn't happen, it becomes one-way, dull, self-professing and UNSOCIAL. ***Therefore, the first essential element of social media marketing is to be 'Social' – that is allowing communications from the customers.***

> **Engagement:** Key measure such as visits, likes, posts, etc. in any social media marketing.

When only the brand talks, it is self-promotion. That is the brand keeps on talking about and promoting itself. As mentioned earlier in the chapter, that this is not social media promotion that we are talking about, but social media marketing. While promotion is an important part of marketing, it is not the only component of it. The classical definition of marketing has 4Ps and 3Cs: So you need the product (or the service), the price, place and then promotion. But most importantly you also need (to understand your) customer, (analyze) competition and (create and establish your) competencies. Thus as mentioned earlier in this chapter, social media marketing is very different from social media promotion.

Therefore, to be a successful social media marketing program, it should:

1. Be *Social* – that is allow two-way/multiway communication
2. Select the right *medium* to be in (based on target customer, market, objectives and offering), Facebook, Twitter, LinkedIn, Instagram, Snapchat, Blog, etc.
3. Communicate about the product (or service), delivery (place), price, and promotion, *after* understanding the customers thoroughly through in-depth market research, with continuous monitoring of the competitions and creating value for the customers through competencies.

A typical social media marketing program is represented in Figure 4.6.

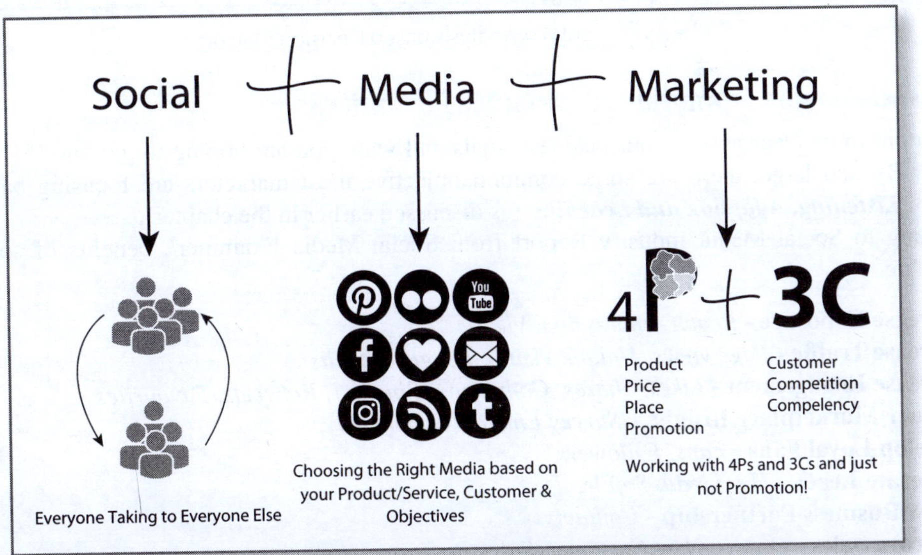

Figure 4.6 SMM = Social + Media + Marketing

The value of following this process is not just that it helps in creating a successful social media marketing program, it also becomes an in-built platform for collecting and analyzing valuable customer and market insights, and a decision making process, as shown in Figure 4.7:

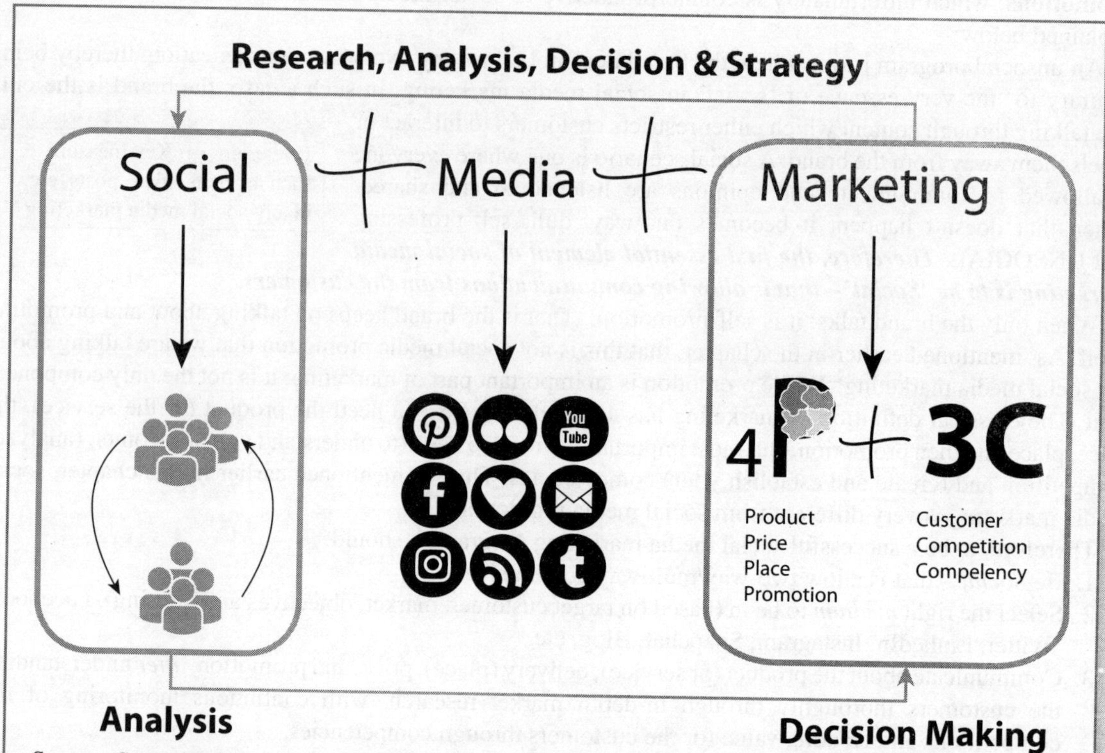

Source : Smart IDeAS

Figure 4.7 SMM = Analysis based Decision Making

From Unsocial Media Promotion to Social Media Marketing[6 (T)]

It is important to be clear about your business goals and what you are hoping to get out of social media marketing. By and large, there are some common objective most marketers are focusing based on the principle of ***Listening, Adapting and Learning*** (as discussed earlier in the chapter).

According to Social Media Industry Report from Social Media Examiner[7], benefits of social media marketing are

1. **Increase Exposure** - *Reach, Impression, View*
2. **Increase Traffic** - *Page views, Unique Visitor, Length of visits*
3. **Increase Engagement** - *Likes, Shares, Comments, Pins, +1, Retweets, Favourites*
4. **Garner Marketplace Insight** - *Survey Entries, Comments*
5. **Develop Loyal Fans** - *Fans, Followers*
6. **Generate Leads** - *Hard lead, Soft lead*
7. **Grow Business Partnership** - *Contacts*
8. **Improve Sales** - *Orders, New Customer, Sales Revenue*

Let us now examine how a plan moves away from being unsocial and promotional to being social and marketing by following the steps given below:

a. **Objective Setting** – This is where the brand defines what it wants to achieve through the social media marketing program. This is the first and most important part of any social media marketing plan. If the objective is not set clearly, there will be no measurements of the activities. Some of the objectives could be:
   i. Reaching a set of customers in a given market
   ii. Build brand awareness
   iii. Connect with influencers
   iv. Generate leads
   v. Bring customers to the ecom website

b. **Research** – After objective setting, the research becomes easy because it is now simpler to understand the customer, market, the competition, etc. The customer research is the most important in this case, and a detailed analysis of the customer is important. For example, if it is a premium brand, understanding the customers through their habits, lifestyle, interests, other brands they follow, etc. becomes critical.

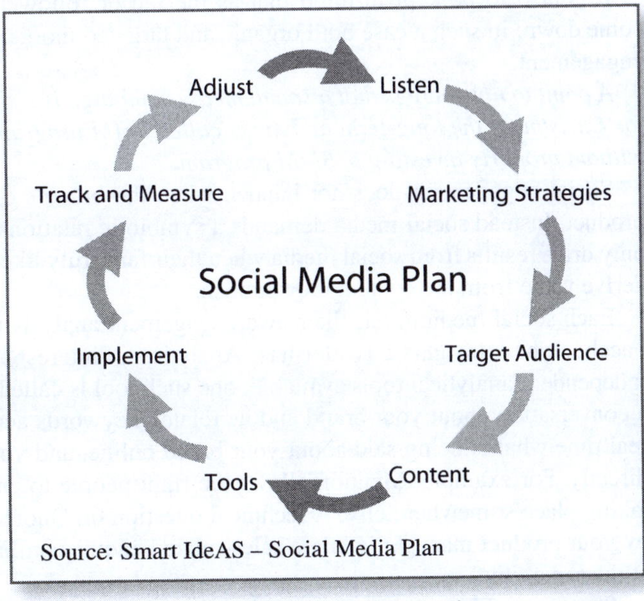

Figure 4.8 Social Media Plan

c. **Plan** – Planning and strategy is the third step and is the roadmap for any social media marketing program. This is where the media planning is done – and the content strategy and content calendar is created. This plan must be re-looked after at least every 3 months to see if the desired results are being achieved; and if not, to once again align it with the set objectives.

The ideation and strategy for 'social' and 'marketing' part of social media marketing in a SMM program is a result of in-depth research and thorough planning.

If the brand already has social media presence and a new program is being planned, a social media audit becomes imperative at this stage. An audit will identify the gaps in the previous social media marketing plan and implementation, and shall help in re-aligning the current program to its desired objective/s.

A social media audit is a very critical task and just a handful of companies in India are capable of offering this service.

d. **Stories You Tell** – The stories are the most important part of the content strategy. Identifying the stories, linking it to the brand communication objective and the customer's lifestyle/interest, modifying it for different media and finally presenting in a way that is visually appealing and easy to understand – are the major parts.

e. **Implementation** – Implementation is the last step where you follow all the social media roadmap completely, until it's time to analyze the results and if needed, changes are made to the plan. Implementation becomes the easiest task once all the above are done right.

Summary: Social Media Marketing Plan is a continuous process.

Social Engagements

Engagement is the key measure in any social media marketing. Simply put engagement is the interaction that a brand's customers do with the brand in social media like, share, comment, re-tweet, tag, mention, etc. Most brands find it difficult to engage with their customers and thousands of rupees are spent on this. From "*UnSocial Media Promotion to Social Media Marketing*" process, as explained above, helps in building the right engagement.

Globally, it has been found that engagement rate varies between 1 and 29%; there is a large gap because it depends on industry, market and product (or service). ***A B2C product like a fashion accessory shall have a higher engagement than another B2C product like real estate, while having even higher engagement rate as compared to a B2B product like specialty chemicals.***

It is also to be kept in mind that as the fan or follower base will increase, the engagement rate may come down; in such a case both organic and targeted inorganic campaigns should be undertaken to increase engagement.

A point to note here is that a social media campaign is a short-term tactical activity, e.g. a paid promotion for Christmas; the long-term activity is called SMM program. No brand should ever undertake a campaign without properly investing in SMM program.

Social engagement does not happen when the brand's only objective is to either promote or sell their product. Instead social media demands a symbiotic relationship between brands and their fans. Brands can only drive results from social media when their fans truly like them, identify with the values they project, and derive value from the content they publish.

Each social medium has their own engagement analysis tools and are quite simple to understand them. Facebook has 'Insights'; Twitter has "Analytics", Pinterest also has "Analytics", etc. There are many other independent analytical tools available; one such tool is called *Mention* which offers the ability to listen in to a conversation about your brand and its related keywords across the web. With Mention, you get to hear in real time what is being said about your brand online, and you also get to participate in these conversations directly. For example, Mention allows the right people to engage with an audience in discussions that are taking place somewhere else. A technical question on Quora can be answered directly from within the tool by your product manager, while a sales-related enquiry on Facebook can be tackled by your sales manager at the same time.

Summary: The measurement in social media marketing is engagement.

Who is Your Customer?

In marketing, social media or otherwise, it is important to understand who your customer is. There are, in fact, 3 types of customers –

- The Buyers – those who pay for your product or services either regularly or at least once
- The Brand Ambassador - who is loyal to your brand and will always talk about it or flaunt about it within her community (but may not inspire others to like you or buy from you)
- The Influencer - who influences and inspires others to buy your product

The point to keep in mind is that the last two categories of customers – The Brand Ambassadors and The Influencers began their relationships with you as The Buyer. It is needless to say that it is the brand ambassadors and the influencers who shall help you in finding, keeping and engaging with your future customers.

It is noteworthy to understand that many of your online customers may not return to you for a repeat purchase and/or may choose not to talk about their experience in dealing with you over social media.

The idea in social media marketing is to not only bring repeat customers but also convert as many of them as possible into your brand ambassadors. If handled well, some of these brand ambassadors also turn into your brand influencers.

This simply means that each of these three categories of your customer needs to be addressed and handled differently.

It is also possible that many of your offline customers never come online and be active in your social media activities. The challenge here is to understand if it makes sense to bring these offline customers online, and if yes who and how.

So how do you do all these?

Through a Brand Plan of Action (BPoA[8]) that is identifying who your customer is and building the customer strategy are two important aspects of this BPOA. This means:

1. You need to have a clear cut process of continuous customer research to understand your customers—their lifestyle, social behaviour (offline as well as online), buying patterns (offline and online), their life values (important psychological aspect of customer research and customer strategy) and then connecting these lifestyles, behaviours, values, etc. to your communication strategy for your products or services. This is typically done in two ways:
   a. Through thorough study of the market by talking directly with the customers (primary research)
   b. By sentiment analysis of your customers by using various sentiment analysis tools available in the market. Some of these sentiment analysis tools are free like Facebook Insights, TweetStats, etc., and there are others that come with a fee like Google Analytics, Hootsuite, Meltwater, etc.
2. To create a character and voice of the brand for your social media marketing (in line with your current brand positioning in the market). To simplify, it means you must decide as a brand if you want to position yourself as an authoritative brand, youthful brand, fun and funky brand, a knowledge brand, a happy brand, etc. You should choose only ONE personality for your brand and stay with that personality. Once you have decided on your brand personality, you must now decide on the brand voice; and this brand voice should absolutely match your brand personality. That means if you are an authoritative brand, your brand voice cannot be fun or youthful. *In most cases, this personality of the brand is completely mixed up and you end up talking in a voice which gives unclear messages to the customers in all your social media activities.*

As mentioned in the other sections of this chapter, social media programs cannot be successful when you constantly try to promote or sell your products. A successful social media program only happens when you create a brand strategy and a brand storytelling format which communicates clearly how your product or service is going to *positively affect* the life of your customers. At the end of the day, a customer is only interested in buying your product or service only if they derive some value that is unique and different from others who are offering a similar product or service. That unique value is what she understands as something that would improve her life (give her better options, make her life easy, help her decide quickly, take actions without complications, etc). If your product or service cannot improve your customers' life and if you fail to communicate this aspect through your social media activities, your social media activity will never be successful. The moment you start selling your product or pushing or promoting your services, you start losing engagement, which simply means losing the interest of your customers (all three).

Therefore, the key in any social media marketing strategy as part of the Brand Plan of Action, are

- understanding your customers
- segregate them as buyers, brand ambassadors and influencers
- design content customized for each of these three categories of customers
- create content that clearly communicate how your customers' lives shall be improved by using your product or services

Summary: If you do not understand your customers, your social media activities are likely to be without any direction and no results.

SOCIAL MEDIA AND ROI

At the end of the day, social media marketing is also like any other business where companies look for return on their investment (RoI). Understanding RoI is a critical aspect of SMM program because it indicates how their marketing effort is working. RoI is not only a misunderstood subject, it also carries lot of misconceptions around it. However, every brand manager, marketing manager and the CEO should be interested in social media RoI and how it is measured.

RoI: Return on Investment usually expressed as a percentage.

Since social media is different from the traditional media (already explained in the beginning of the chapter), the RoI calculation in social media is also different from traditional RoI calculation. Many brand managers or marketing managers fail to understand this simple concept. They end up chasing money spent on SMM program rather than implementing it in the right way. ***RoI is Return on Investment, therefore, the money spent in SMM program should be considered as an investment, that is an asset, and not as an expense.*** Once this concept is clear, measuring ROI becomes easy.

Social Media ROI Process

Step 1 Set the SMM objectives

The first step in SMM program is to set the SMM objectives or goals. There are a whole lot of possibilities when it comes to setting SMM objectives. Let's use the list mentioned above and add a few more to it:

i. Reaching a set of customers in a given market
ii. Build brand awareness
iii. Connect with influencers
iv. Generate leads
v. Bring customers to the ecom website
vi. New followers
vii. Clicks on links
viii. Online purchases
ix. Filling in contact forms
x. Revenue generated / New customers

Step 2 Set up a process to track and monitor your objectives

Once you have identified your set of objectives (which can be any of the above or anything else), set up a process to track and monitor it. As mentioned earlier, each social medium has its own in-built analytical tool. One can also use Buffer as a one-stop tracking platform for all social media activities.

Step 3 Track the objectives

If you wanted to generate 500 leads in 6 months through Facebook, have you achieved that?

If you wanted to enter a new market and wanted to engage with 1200 customers from this market over a period of 3 months, have you achieved this?

If you wanted to increase your ecom website visit to another 15% over 3 months, did you reach that goal?

If you have successfully achieved all your objectives within the stipulated period, then you have achieved 100% RoI. If you could achieve only 50% of your objectives within the stipulated period, then your RoI is only 50%.

However, since understanding RoI in real monetary terms is important for business decisions, the brands assign monetary values to each of their met objectives and then compare them to the amount spent, to arrive at the RoI. They use the SMM program cost (if outsourced), cost per click, ad spent, man hour cost for time spent (if in-house), etc. for calculating the total cost. This is then compared against the monetary value of each of the objectives achieved –

I. 500 leads, 20% conversion, revenue in INR

II. Lifetime value of new customers acquired in a new market

III. 15% increase to the ecom site visit resulting in increase in INR sales revenue

Some of the ROI measurement tools that are in use at the moment include Hootsuite, Cyfe, Google Analytics, Kissmetrics, etc.

Step 4 Re-adjust and re-align SMM activities

The RoI measurement is an opportunity to understand how the SMM program is running, achieving objectives and delivering results. Therefore, ROI measurement shows what worked for the SMM program and what did not; and it is a chance to take a re-look at the plan and re-align the strategy.

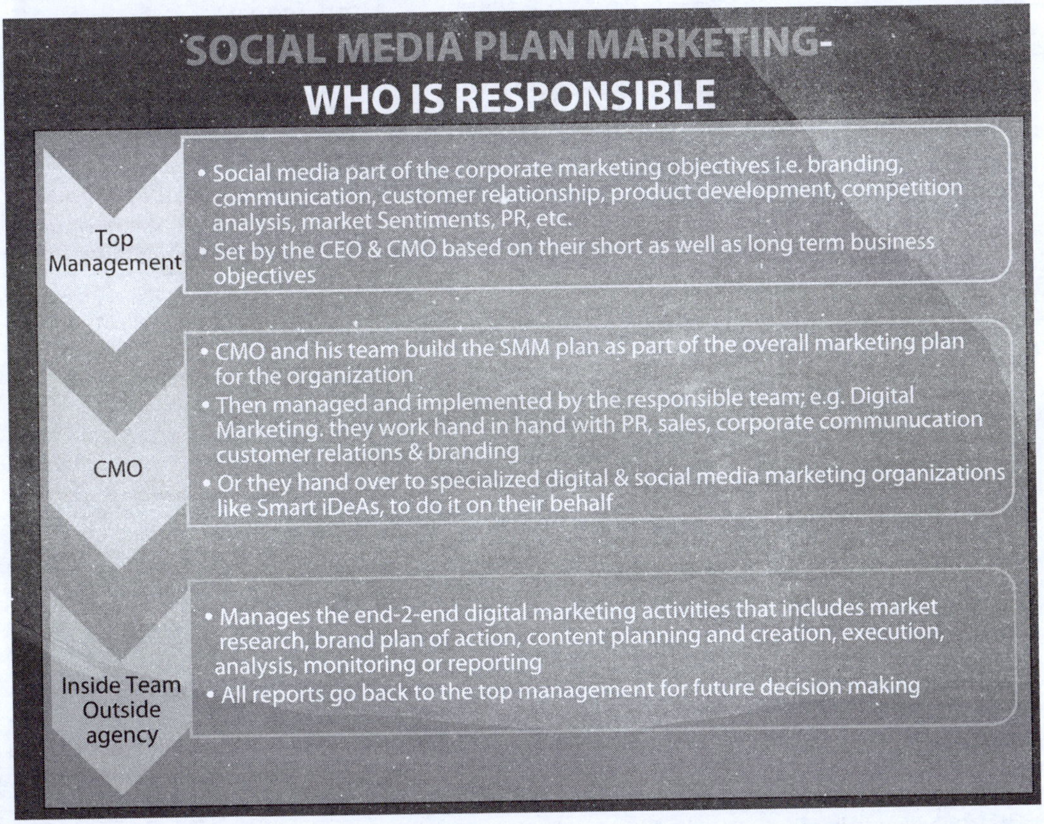

Source : Smart IdeAS

Exhibit 4.2 SMM - Ownership

Summary : Social Media RoI is the measurement of Social Media Objectives.

This chapter explains the main advantage of social media in capturing the network capability (or, virality) of social media to spread advertising content principally using the sharing capability of social media and/or addressing the micro-communities that form up social media. In subsequent chapters, we will look at some more social media tools such as search engine, content, email.

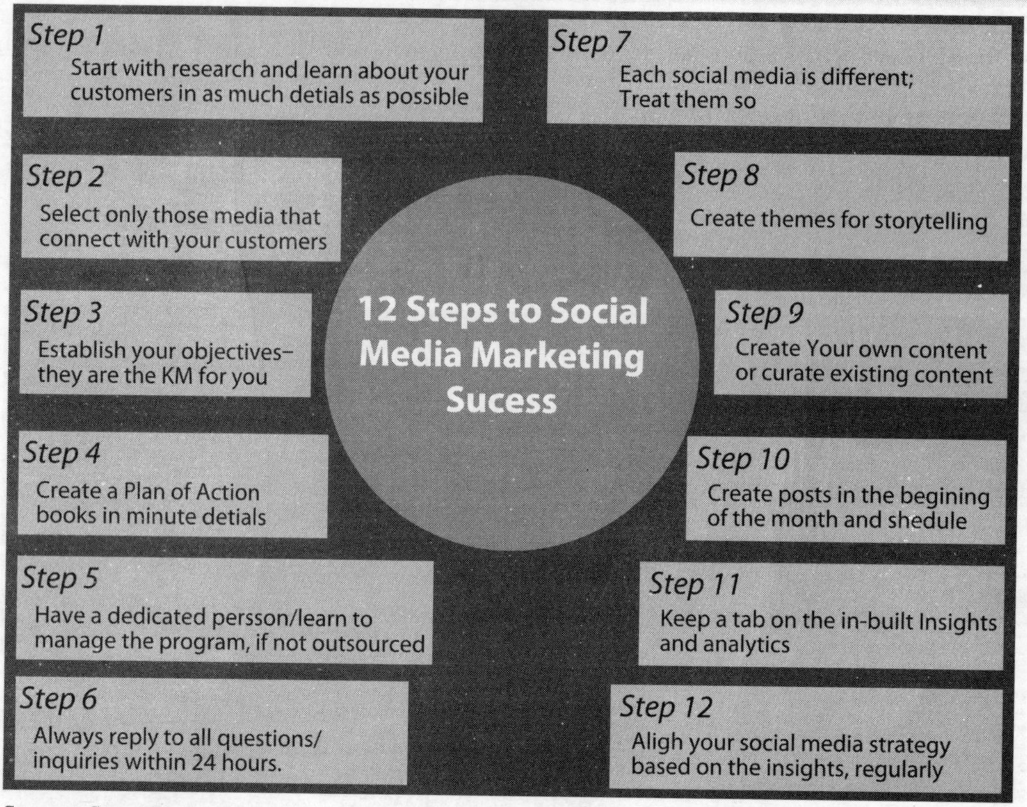

Source : Smart IdeAS

Exhibit 4.3 12 steps to SMM success

CHAPTER SUMMARY

- Social networking is the practice of expanding the number of one's business and/or social contacts by making connections through individuals. Social networking is based on the six degrees of separation concept that any two people on the planet could make contact through a chain of no more than five intermediaries.
- Social media marketing is the process of creating content that you have tailored to the context of each individual social media platform in order to drive user engagement and sharing. Social media marketing is based on the principle of *Listening, Adapting and Learning.*
- Some examples of the prominent social media are Facebook, Twitter, Wikipedia, LinkedIn, Reddit and Pinterest.
- Social media are a more cost-effective platform as compared to traditional marketing and give the brand and the brand users an opportunity to directly talk to each other in real time. This effectively facilitates in real time, how the customers are reacting to SMM.
- According to a survey of 344 social media marketers from around the world by Clutch partnered with Smart Insights in 2017, social media positively influences most companies' revenue and sales.
- SMM helps in two-way communication between brands and brand users or target customers in real

time, helps in immediate consumer insight rather than a post market research and is cost effective, thus improving profitability.

- While the list of social media myths can run a few pages, the following are not true:
  - Social media means being on Facebook.
  - Putting pretty pictures make it an awesome social media program.
  - It's all about promoting your products.
  - Can I make some quick sales?
  - Social media is solely for increasing sales.
  - Social media marketing is my technology team's responsibility.
  - Only young people are on social media.
  - Let's be on every social network
  - If my friends and family 'Like' every update, my social presence will rock.
  - Social media gives people a venue to publicly bash my company.
  - Anyone can do it!
  - You can make a big splash in a short time.
  - You can't measure social media marketing results.
  - Publish as much content as possible and your audience will engage.
  - One post for all media.
  - The more followers the better.
- Although social and digital marketing are online marketing but they work differently, achieving different objectives and delivering different results.
- An unsocial program is one where the brand does not allow any two-way communication, thereby being contrary to the very essence of 'Social' in social media marketing. The first essential element of social media marketing is to be 'Social' – that is allowing communications from the customers.
- A successful social media marketing program will be *Social* – that is allow two-way/multiway communication, in the right *Medium* and communicate about the product (or service), delivery (place), price, and promotion, *after* understanding the customers thoroughly through in-depth market research, with continuous monitoring of the competitions and creating value for the customers through competencies.
- According to Social Media Industry Report from Social Media Examiner, benefits of social media marketing are
  - Increase Exposure - *Reach, impression, view*
  - Increase Traffic - *Page views, unique visitor, length of visits*
  - Increase Engagement - *Likes, shares, comments, pins, +1, retweets, favourites*
  - Garner Marketplace Insight - *Survey entries, comments*
  - Develop Loyal Fans - *Fans, followers*
  - Generate Leads - *Hard lead, soft lead*
  - Grow Business Partnership - *Contacts*
  - Improve Sales - *Orders, new customer, sales revenue*
- Social engagement is the key measure in any social media marketing. Simply put engagement is the interaction that a brand's customers do with the brand in social media – like, share, comment, retweet, tag, mention, etc. The measurement in social media marketing is engagement.
- In marketing, social media or otherwise, it is important to understand who your customer is. There are 3 types of customers: The Buyers, the Brand Ambassador, and the Influencer. A Brand Plan of Action (BPoA) identifies who your customer is and accordingly helps build a customer strategy.
- Social media programs cannot be successful when you constantly try to promote or sell your products. A successful social media program only happens when you create a brand strategy and a brand storytelling format which communicates clearly how your product or service is going to *positively affect* the life of your customers.
- At the end of the day, social media marketing is also like any other business where companies look for return on their investment. Understanding RoI is a critical aspect of SMM program because it indicates how their marketing effort is working.

CLOSING CASE

CASE LET

Designing SMM for A Premium Jewellery House

Introduction - A forty year old, leading jeweller in Calcutta known for their design capabilities and excellent customer service.

Social Media Objective

Following were the social media objectives that were set by us for The Client:

- Build Brand Equity based on its Positioning as "Bespoke Handcrafted Bengal Jewellery" Designer.
- To reach every Indian anywhere in the globe
- To be known as "The Place" of bespoke gold jewellery designer for all people passionate about gold jewellery

The Social Media Marketing mix chosen were Facebook, Twitter and Pinterest.

Facebook

- Brand building, brand awareness. Establish the brand positioning.
- Targeting the right customer across globe.
- Building engagement with target audience.
- Achieving result-oriented multi-way communication between the brand and its target audience.

Twitter

- For personal one-on-one communication with the target audience.
- Platform for personal branding for the owner and their design mentor.
- Pinterest
- One-stop location for showcasing all designs and products.

Strategy

Social media marketing requires a strategic approach with continuous market research and a step-by-step implementation plan:

- Since the Client was well established and known in Kolkata, initially the approach was to connect to Bengalis in India, thereafter engaging with them globally. Interacting and talking to them was easy in the first phase as they were exposed to the brand name. Showcasing different designs started driving engagement and generating inquiries.
- The next step was to connect to Indians around the world who could be potential customers. With specific targeting (mostly organic), we could connect to potential customers.
- The next strategic step was talking to non-Indians who were interested in jewellery designs from India.

During this process, the social media content is maintained and organized in a way which keeps the fans, followers and customers continuously curious about new designs and products.

- A storytelling approach to communicate the provenance of each design was adopted.
- A set of interactive content was decided to drive user engagement at all times keeping in mind the diverse geographical locations of the customer base.
- All such content are created and story themes are chosen after a thorough research on the lifestyle and interests of our target customer – the HNIs.

Twitter is used more as a personal one-to-one communication platform to talk to customers. It is used to talk to customers directly so that it gives the customers a faith and belief that they are talking to an individual in the company.

Pinterest is used to showcase all the great designs and artworks, to demonstrate variety and capability.

Brand Plan of Action (BPoA)

The BPoA, the Annual Master Plan of Action, is built based on our own research on the brand, market, TG, competition as well as a thorough interview with key people in the organization.

The BPoA has the stories and themes to be told, the social media mix that is to be used for this storytelling and their respective daily/weekly frequency.

This strategic plan is further broken down into monthly activity sheets and daily content management plans.

This gives a clear, systemized and planned structure and approach to social media marketing.

Success Story

They are the social media marketing partner for The Client for the last 48 months and the brand has grown from strength to strength:

Facebook

- The Facebook page has a fan base of 11000+ people, 90% of which have been acquired organically (that means – hardly any money spent on ads for customer acquisition), making it one of the most popular jewellery brands on Facebook (The brand does not require millions of fans on FB, but only those who matter; the nearest competition has half the fan base).
- The engagement rate, on an average, is maintained at 50% (way above the global average of 1%-29%).
- Post reach is again 50% on an average on a daily basis.
- We generate at least 70-80 inquiries every month, each inquiry is worth at least ₹150,000.0 and conversion rate is almost 70% (in the 4th month itself, our social media efforts generated 10 inquiries).
- The inquiries come from all across the globe—particularly from Australia and the US. And in India, the largest markets after Kolkata are Kerala, Delhi, and Bangalore.
- Have established a set of dedicated Brand Ambassadors and Brand Influencers who have helped in increasing engagement in social media profiles, as well as in bringing in new customers both online and offline.

Twitter – A Personal handle for the in-house Design Mentor, it is one of the most popular media in the jewellery world. On an average, her tweets get ~ 55K impressions every month.

Pinterest – Enjoys ~280K monthly views with ~15k daily viewers resulting in ~30K monthly engagement. Inquiry and orders are placed through Pinterest too.

Twitter and Pinterest are also used to bring people to Facebook where all the activities happen.

If you note, the social media objectives did not put inquiry generation as an objective; but the objectives that were set resulted in bringing a large number of inquiries that resulted in 70% conversion.

Case Questions

1. What were the social Media objectives set by the client?
2. What was the social media strategy that was adopted?

Sources:

NapoleonCat - https://napoleoncat.com/blog/en/facebook-and-instagram-user-demographics-in-india-august-2017/

(2) Source: Surveys conducted 2005-2018.

REVIEW QUESTIONS

1. What is social networking and explain the six degrees of separation concept?
2. What is social media marketing and what are the principles it is based on?
3. Name some examples of prominent social media. Why are they called social media and what benefits do they provide for a marketer or a product?
4. Why are social media known to be more cost-effective platforms as compared to traditional marketing?
5. "SMM helps in two-way communication between brands and brand users or target customers in real time, helps in immediate consumer insight" — From your personal or professional experience, give some examples in support of this statement.
6. List top 5 myths about social media.
7. "Although social and digital marketing are online marketing but they work differently, achieving different objectives and delivering different results" — From your personal or professional experience, give some examples in support of this statement.
8. List any 5 benefits of social media marketing according to Social Media Industry Report from Social Media Examiner.

9. What is social engagement in any social media marketing? What does it indicate and list some examples of social engagement from your personal or professional experience?
10. Why is understanding your customer important and give a brief typology of different customers?

ACTIVITY QUESTIONS

1. Create a Social Group and give it a suitable name (like B WEL for fitness or Xplor for trekking) and create a Facebook campaign using https://www.facebook.com/adsmanager/creation?act=210640589
2. For the group thus created, do a sentiment analysis using free tools like Facebook Insights, TweetStats, Google Analytics, etc.

KEY TERMS

App
B2B product
B2C product
BPOA (Brad Plan of Action)
Digital media
Engagement
Facebook
Google Ads
LinkedIn
Pinterest
Reddit
RoI
Social media
Social media marketing
Social networking
Twitter
Wikipedia

REFERENCES

1. Six Degrees of Separation - https://whatis.techtarget.com/definition/six-degrees-of-separation. Accessed on February 17, 2019.
2. Definition Social Networking - https://whatis.techtarget.com/definition/social-networking. Accessed on February 17, 2019.
3. https://conversationprism.com/. Accessed on February 17, 2019.
4. https://clutch.co/agencies/social-media-marketing/resources/social-media-survey-2017. Accessed on February 17, 2019.
5. https://clutch.co/agencies/social-media-marketing/resources/social-media-survey-2017. Accessed on Febraury 17, 2019.
6. Unsocial Media Promotion or Social Media Marketing (T) - proprietary to Smart iDeAS.
7. https://www.linkedin.com/pulse/20140624131845-105117131-8-social-media-marketing-objectives-and-metrics-that-matter/. Accessed on February 17, 2019.
8. BPoA is a tool used by Smart iDeAS.

CHAPTER 5

WEBSITE PLANNING, SEO & SERP

CHAPTER OBJECTIVES

After reading this chapter, you will be able to

- Understand website planning, importance, and benchmarking
- Explain what POEM (Paid, Owned & Earned Media) is
- Discuss what SEO is and why SEO is important
- Evaluate how search engines rank pages
- Examine SEO/content creation strategy
- Design the page for indexation–SERP
- Describe search engine marketing
- Discuss SERM–search engine reputation management

OPENING CASE

CASE LET

GREAT LAKES|AIMLA

Great Lakes Institute of Management Chennai introduced a new MBA program—MBA in Technopreurship and AIMLA as well as an elective AIMLA in 2018. AIMLA is an acronym that stood for Artificial Intelligence, Machine Learning and Analytics. This new program and elective were started to emphasize and prepare prospective graduate students and entrepreneurs in disruptive technologies that had come to stay. Besides they were opportunities for current professionals to reskill themselves in disruptive technologies. Since they were new and unique, a lot of content in terms of blogs, white papers were generated to aid SEO/SERP. Considering AI & ML were popular and competitive keywords and AIMLA combines these keyword, Long Tail keywords of AI & ML were targeted to ramp the ranking. Given below are screenshots of current search results.

A search for AIMLA (Artificial Intelligence Machine Learning and Analytics returned a screenshot as below. The search returned 172000 results in 0.53 seconds and MBA in Technopreneurship and AIMLA|Great Lakes Institute of Management not only topped the list at # 1 but also produced images and related links for Great Lakes Institute of Management, thus illustrating importance of SEO/SERP activities.

AIMLA: An acronym for Artificial Intelligence, Machine Learning and Analytics.

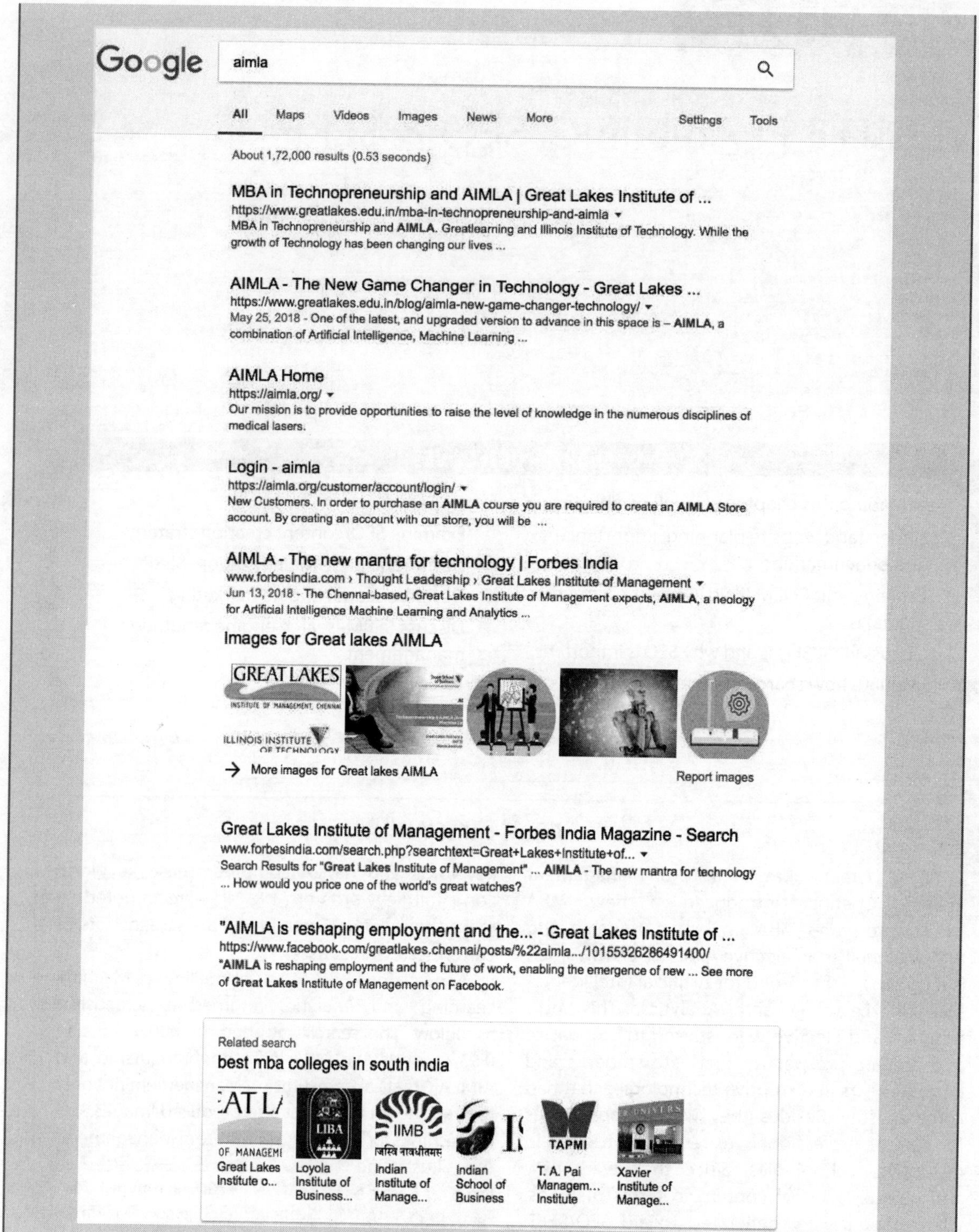
Google
aimla
All
Maps
Videos
Images
News
More
Settings
Tools
About 1,72,000 results (0.53 seconds)
MBA in Technopreneurship and AIMLA | Great Lakes Institute of ...
https://www.greatlakes.edu.in/mba-in-technopreneurship-and-aimla
MBA in Technopreneurship and AIMLA. Greatlearning and Illinois Institute of Technology. While the growth of Technology has been changing our lives ...
AIMLA - The New Game Changer in Technology - Great Lakes ...
https://www.greatlakes.edu.in/blog/aimla-new-game-changer-technology/
May 25, 2018 - One of the latest, and upgraded version to advance in this space is – AIMLA, a combination of Artificial Intelligence, Machine Learning ...
AIMLA Home
https://aimla.org/
Our mission is to provide opportunities to raise the level of knowledge in the numerous disciplines of medical lasers.
Login - aimla
https://aimla.org/customer/account/login/
New Customers. In order to purchase an AIMLA course you are required to create an AIMLA Store account. By creating an account with our store, you will be ...
AIMLA - The new mantra for technology | Forbes India
www.forbesindia.com › Thought Leadership › Great Lakes Institute of Management
Jun 13, 2018 - The Chennai-based, Great Lakes Institute of Management expects, AIMLA, a neology for Artificial Intelligence Machine Learning and Analytics ...
Images for Great lakes AIMLA
GREAT LAKES
INSTITUTE OF MANAGEMENT, CHENNAI
ILLINOIS INSTITUTE OF TECHNOLOGY
More images for Great lakes AIMLA
Report images
Great Lakes Institute of Management - Forbes India Magazine - Search
www.forbesindia.com/search.php?searchtext=Great+Lakes+Institute+of...
Search Results for "Great Lakes Institute of Management" ... AIMLA - The new mantra for technology ... How would you price one of the world's great watches?
"AIMLA is reshaping employment and the... - Great Lakes Institute of ...
https://www.facebook.com/greatlakes.chennai/posts/%22aimla.../10155326286491400/
"AIMLA is reshaping employment and the future of work, enabling the emergence of new ... See more of Great Lakes Institute of Management on Facebook.
Related search
best mba colleges in south india
Great Lakes Institute o...
Loyola Institute of Business...
Indian Institute of Manage...
Indian School of Business
T. A. Pai Managem... Institute
Xavier Institute of Manage...

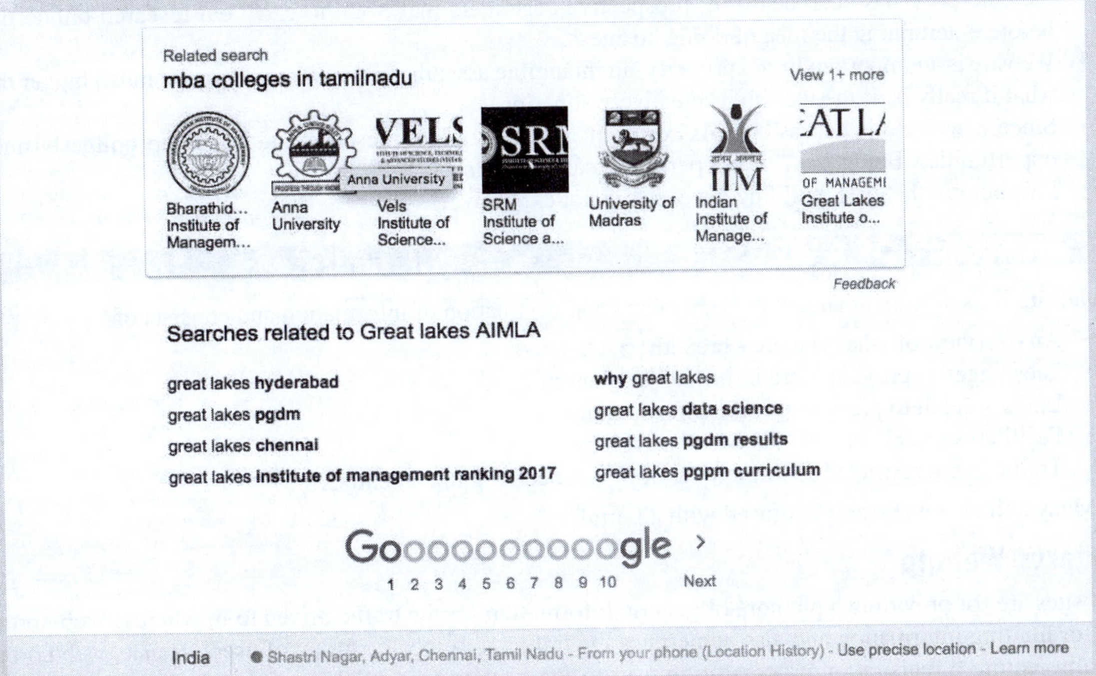

Case Questions

1. What should Great Lakes do to continue returning #1 in search results?
2. What should Great Lakes do to ensure AIMLA is not usurped by competition?

INTRODUCTION

In Chapter 1, inbound marketing was discussed as different from traditional or outbound marketing. Inbound marketing is marketing focused on being found by customers. That is, it is all about attracting potential customers with high-quality and targeted content, engaging and nurturing them into action till they are ready to buy. Anything that needs to be found needs an address and that address in inbound marketing is the website. Websites usually provide a map and directions to the premises of the enterprise, so that visitors are less likely to have trouble finding your location.

Inbound and Importance of Website

A website in itself can be used to accomplish many different marketing strategies to help a business grow. A website is important on account of the following factors:

- The web has a far wider reach than any other form of advertising.
- Website is like a business card that everybody assumes you have!
- It is the face of an organization or a product and is almost the first contact point with your prospective customer/user.

- A good website helps in increasing the visibility and establishing credibility for the business. Even if the enterprise has been heard of, prospective customers may want to carry out research online first, before entertaining the idea of doing business.
- Website is an important brand property, an intangible asset that projects an enterprise much bigger than what it really is, if the website is creatively superior.
- Since a website is accessible 24x7x365, it gives an online presence and opens up online business opportunities. Being 24x7, it is a perpetual salesman on call.
- Last but not the least, building a website is not expensive!

ANATOMY OF A WEBSITE

A website is usually an amalgam of both source and destination of information and consists of

- An overview of what you are - breadth
- Tabs/pages to provide more information – length
- Links – depth to provide specific information
- Facilitates visual content
- Traffic is not restricted or limited (i.e. may not need log in credentials)

Many a time, a website is confused with a portal.

Portal vs. Website

Websites are for providing a plethora of generic information for the traffic driven to it, whereas web portals are for limiting information and also sometimes the traffic, to a specific group of users. Hence, web portals usually require a registration process of an user to log in with credentials or authentication that facilitate the site to deliver a more specific content based on the user profile. Websites are usually destinations that everyone can get to, and therefore are generally designed for a broader audience.

However, with technology available today, there is an overlapping of functionality between portals and websites. Today websites use a fair amount of content targeting or other tools to create a personalized user experience (UX). Similarly, portals develop pages that do not need credentials. With the help of technology platforms, portals are created that have anonymous public pages as well as personalized access.

Platform vs. Page

One difference between portals and websites is that of ownership. Typically, the ownership of company portals and websites will vest with different teams that have different vision of how they should work. The marketing team may own the public website and prefer software built for blogging, measuring user engagement and enabling a strong visual design of web pages. The marketing team therefore will want a solution that can build and edit pages quickly that are either connected or independent, with complete control within the overall structure of the site. However, the support team may own the customer self-service portal and need a solution that integrates their other applications. They need a solution that is focused on building a platform, complete with multiple types of users and systems that are all connected. Portal is usually related to web. Platform is about the device and the required hardware/software support.

> **Platform:** The underlying hardware or software for a system. The **platform** defines a standard around which a system can be developed.
> **Portal:** A web portal is a specially designed website that brings information from diverse sources, like emails, online forums and search engines, together in a uniform way.
> **Page link:** A list that takes you to another page, URL, page owner or source.

Portal or a Website?

The decision to build either a website or a portal is based on the company's needs. With the amount of overlapping functionality between platforms, most projects can be built with either of the options. Table 5.1 gives some suggested guidelines for when to use each.

Table 5.1 Guidelines – Portal or Website

Website if …..	Portal if ….
Create a public website focused on delivering and managing content	Create specific audience experience
Operates separately and independently of internal site/systems	Need advanced control over what users see
Draw traffic from a broad and anonymous audience	Have multiple designs to be integrated into one visual design
	Need advanced user management and permission features

Website Musts

While planning or designing a website, it is advisable to pay attention to details and it is imperative that the following be built in a website.

- **Sitemap** - It is basically an XML file that contains URLs of all individual webpages. It's like an archive of every webpage in a website. This file should be made easily discoverable in a website so that search engine crawlers can find them.
- **Primary navigation** -A navigation strip at the top of every page that stays the same, with links to the major sections of the site, to facilitate visitors to navigate quickly.
- **Ease of Navigation** - Uncluttered, simple and avoiding unnecessary links.
- **Load time** – The time it takes to download and display the entire content of a web page in the browser window and is measured in seconds.
- **Content Management system** - It manages the creation and modification of digital content that supports multiple users in a collaborative environment.
- **User Interface (UI)** – It displays screens, calls to actions and overall appearance.
- **User Experience (UX)** – It is the overall satisfaction in search by getting the right answer or solution to the problem that involves a search.
- **Interactivity** - Content that facilitates the participants' active engagement beyond a simple reading.

Crawler: A program that systematically browses the World Wide Web in order to create an index of data.
Load Time: Time it takes to download and display the entire content of a web page in the browser window (measured in seconds).
Snippets: A small piece or brief extract.
UI: The means by which the user and a computer system interact, in particular, the use of input devices and software.
UX: The overall experience of a person using a product such as a website or computer application, especially in terms of how easy or pleasing it is to use.

It may be worthwhile to point out that it is not necessary to have web development skills to develop a website for business. Website development can be outsourced to a designer/developer. However, as a professional, it should be ensured that the developer is briefed on the above as musts for a proposed website.

Website Benchmarking

Benchmarking is essentially to gauge a website that gives a measure of where a website stands in relation to other websites—direct competition, category or general. It can throw a light on competitive advantages and show the most effective ways to improve a website performance. It also provides information on respective current levels of elevation as compared to that of your competition.

Some typical benchmarking parameters are:

- Site performance
- Search performance
- Usability

Exhibit 5.1 Examples of Benchmarks from GT Metrix

Many different tools are available that can help determine how effective a website is; but for beginners, it is best to start with a free analytics tool. Google Analytics tool is recommended to start with, for, it has many features and is easy to integrate with most sites and add-ons.

Some Examples of Website Benchmarks

- Page load time is a critical factor. Some studies indicate that after two seconds lag visitors begin getting impatient if webpage fails to load.
- Bounce rate measures number of visitors going deeper than the page they enter on.
- Bounce rate from email campaigns looks at the traffic you get from email marketing.
- Website visitor metrics show you how effective your site is at drawing traffic.
- Acquisition source metrics indicate where your visitors are coming from.
- Conversion rates (CR) indicate the effectiveness of your strategy and tactics by gauging everything from how many people opt-in to your mailing list to the number of people who come to your site as visitors and leave as customers.
- Cart abandonment rate tells you how many prospective buyers select one or more items to buy, begin the checkout process, but drop off before completing the purchase.
- Products per transaction is an excellent benchmark to consider in tandem with cart abandonment.

Examples of Benchmarks from GT Metrix – Identity of website masked for confidentiality

Exhibit 5.2 Examples of Benchmarks from GT Metrix

While Exhibit 5.2 is one example of website benchmarking, there are many more analyses available, since anything that can be measured can be benchmarked. A specific chapter on Analytics in this book covers more analytics and tools. It should also be borne in mind that there is nothing right or wrong about building a website. Although currently a lot of free website building templates are available, they lack the ability to integrate with SEO tools and hence an investment in a domain is recommended that will facilitate Optimization (SEO).

Also, most beginners are tempted to imitate competition and brief the developer to design a website *a la* XYZ or ABC corporation. This is best avoided and the focus must be on trying to be unique and with respect to own product or service on offer since, as mentioned in the beginning of the chapter, website = business card. A few other points to be kept in view while developing a website are—

- Focus on User Experience (UX)
- Capability to benchmark social proof since social proof is very powerful
- Considering products or services that get the most reviews for benchmarking

It must be kept in mind that benchmarking is labour intensive that requires setup time, monitoring time, evaluation time, and planning time. Therefore, an appropriate budget should be provided for treating the website development as an investment.

Paid Owned and Earned Media (POEM) and Website

POEM: Paid, owned and earned media.

This chapter began with inbound marketing and importance of website. Inbound marketing is marketing focused on getting found by customers. Therefore, it is all about attracting potential customers with high-quality and targeted content, engaging and nurturing them into action which is that they are ready to buy. This brings us to an important communication framework called POEM. POEM stands for paid, owned and earned media. A website is central to POEM framework.

The POEM framework is explained as below:

- Paid media are those when a paid third-party channel is leveraged, such as advertising on third-party sites and sponsorships.
- Owned media are those channels that are created and controlled by the owner. This could be a company blog, YouTube channel, own website, or even own Facebook page. Although your YouTube channel or your Facebook page are not 'strictly' owned by you , they can be directly controlled and are free for basic usage.
- Earned media are those wherein customers, the press and the public share your content, speak about your brand via word of mouth, and otherwise discuss your brand. In other words, the mentions are "earned," since they are voluntarily given by others.

Table 5.2 POEM Framework Benefits and Challenges

Media Type	Definition	Example	Role	Benefit	Challenges
Paid Media	Paid to Leverage a channel	• Advertising in any medium • Paid search • Sponsorship	• To feed owned media • To stimulate earned media	• On demand and immediacy • Scale and con-trol of message	Clutter and credibility
Owned Media	Own and control the channel	• Website • Blog • Brochures • Collaterals	Long-term relationship building	• Control • Cost efficient • Longevity • Versatility • Reach Niche Audience	• Trust • Time to scale
Earned Media	Third party channels	• PR in traditional media • Social media–mentions and likes • Word of mouth and viral	• 2-way communication • Listen and respond • Power of like and viral	• Credible • Transparent • Cost efficient • Versatile • Humane and responsible	• No control • May be negative • Time to scale • Measurement difficult

It is a common misconception that own and earned media must be maximized than paid media. However, every part of the activity for lead-generation is important and should contribute to the bottom line success of the business. Thus, every page , irrespective of paid, owned or earned should have a specific job to do along the prospect's journey to becoming a customer and justify RoI. Also, over years, the boundaries between paid-owned-earned media have blurred, resulting in convergence as shown in Figure 5.1.

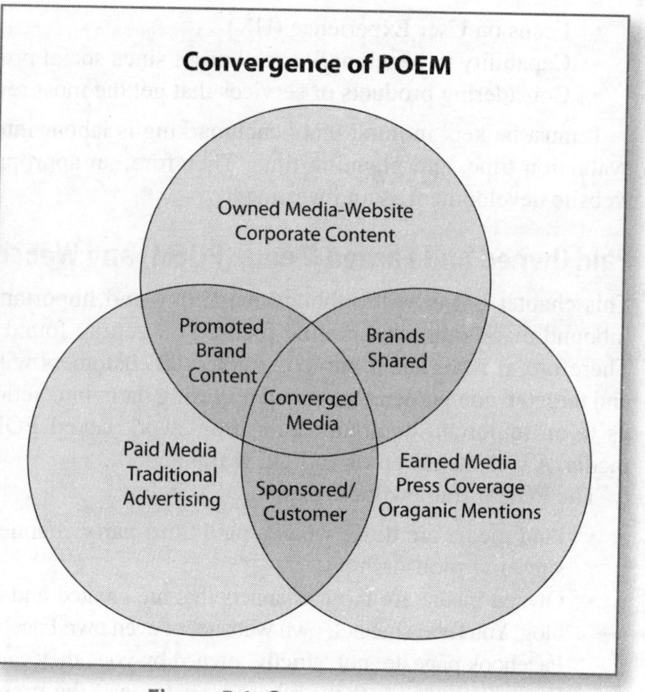

Figure 5.1 Convergence POEM

Website and Landing Page

The convergence of POEM framework underscores the importance of paid media since every part of the activity of lead-generation is important. This is where the role of landing page or L.P. comes in. While websites provide an overview of what you are (breadth), have tabs/pages that provide more information (length) and links (depth) to provide specific information. A landing page (LP) is a standalone web page, created specifically for the purposes of marketing or an advertising campaign. It is where a visitor *"lands"* when clicked on an ad or a similar communication. It is like the difference between multi-brand store and a single brand store. Multi-brand stores may encourage loss leaders and impulse purchase, whereas single brand stores are focused on and drive consumers to buy what they came for and not get distracted. For a marketer, conversion means convincing a visitor to do one specific act and one act only and not one of many things. It is about completing a single business-driven objective. Landing pages are designed with a single focused objective known as Call to Action (CTA). This simplicity makes landing pages the best option for increasing the conversion rates of campaigns. Usually a conversion centred design is adopted.

Conversion Centred Design – CCD[1]

> **Conversion Centered Design (CCD):** Conversion-centred design (CCD) is a discipline targeted specifically at designing experiences that achieve a single business goal.

Conversion Centred Design or CCD helps in designing experiences that guide the visitor towards completing that one specific action (CTA) , using persuasive design and psychological triggers to increase conversions. In other words, it's about persuasion. CCD needs a source and a destination. Source is any campaign in social media, Google Ad-words or mail, etc. The destination is landing page or LP. The reason for LP and not Home page is because the focus is on a single purpose with no distractions and making the navigation friction free and seamless. The end purpose is CTA or call to action that could be the likes of Register/Download/Call, etc.

Principles of Conversion Centred Design (CCD)

There are seven principles that govern CCD. A brief description of these seven principles is outlined below.

1. **Attention**: The headline should be powerful both textually and visually to hold attention. The design should focus on the action that is called for. In attention, an important element is attention ratio. It is

the ratio of the number of things you can do on a given page to the number of things you should do. When talking about marketing campaigns, you should only have a single goal (or CTA), and thus the Attention Ratio should be 1:1. Exhibit 5.3 shows on the left a cluttered WP and simple LP. It is advisable to minimize the number of links. It also recommended that an AB testing be done.

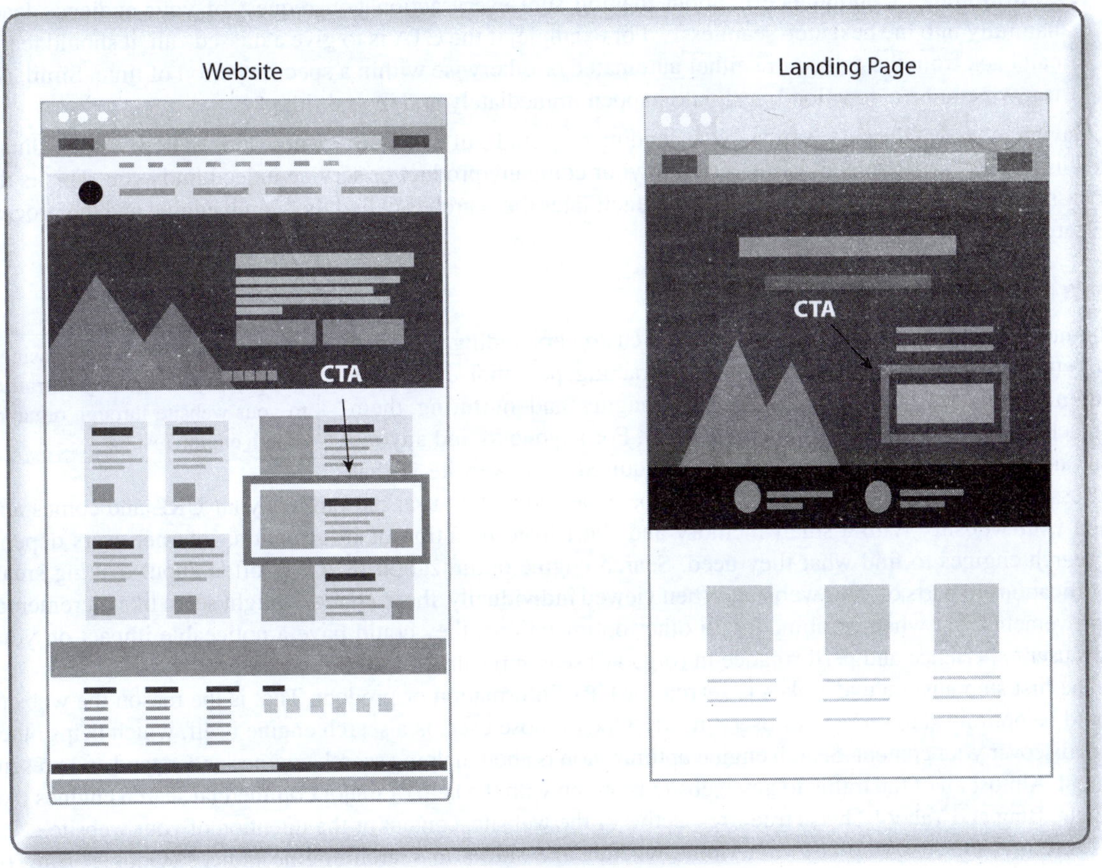

Exhibit 5.3 Cluttered WP and Simple LP

2. **Context**: Context is how well the initial above-the-fold (is the portion of a Web page that is visible in a browser window when the page first loads. The portion of the page that requires scrolling in order to see content is called below the fold.) Landing page experience delivers on the promise made. Context is the equivalent of designing an ad in traditional marketing giving prospects all the information they need in order to convert both pre-click and post-click. Content should follow the eye movement left to right and from top to bottom.
3. **Clarity:** Clarity implies that copy (text) should effectively communicate the value proposition.
4. **Congruence:** Congruence means alignment of context and clarity to remove all the distractions. It consists of a message match that is all about having a headline that closely matches the call to action of the upstream ad/email/any other communication. Design match is matching the visuals and colour palette of the visuals presented in the ad/email/any other communication. Continuity thread should be maintained with strong coupling (memory hook). It must be ensured that landing page headline maintains an attention long enough to deliver on the pre-click promise.

5. **Credibility:** Credibility leads to trust. Trust is an important factor and should be aligned with customer beliefs. For credibility, badges, testimonials and awards visuals/logos will help.
6. **Closing:** Closing refers to triggering an action or CTA. Area around CTA should be well designed. There should be no clutter or any confusing message around the CTA button. The copy should inspire a CTA in a bold way.
7. **Continuance:** Continuance is about making sure every action you request of your audience leads naturally into the next step seamlessly. For example, if the CTA is to give a missed call, it should lead a call back from the call centre either automated or otherwise within a specific period of time. Similarly, if it were to be a download, it should happen immediately and in real time.

Having looked at the details of website, landing page and call to action, we now look at how we coordinate and ensure that someone who is interested in your company/product or service indeed finds you. This is the process of searching and the primary tool that facilitates the search is called the search engine and the process as search engine optimization.

Search Engine Optimization (SEO)

> **SEO:** The practice of increasing the quantity and quality of traffic to your website through organic search engine results

Inbound marketing is marketing focussing on customers finding you (pull marketing) and therefore it is all about attracting potential customers with high-quality and targeted content, engaging and nurturing them into action which is that they are ready to buy. For anyone to find anyone else, an address or some co-ordinates are required. The website is that address or the coordinate. Besides, it cannot be expected that an user remembers your URL and comes and visits your website. With a small memory and short-lived retention of information, Internet users depend on search engines to find what they need. Search engine optimization (SEO) is often about making small modifications to parts of your website. When viewed individually, these changes might seem like incremental improvements, but when combined with other optimizations, they could have a noticeable impact on your site's user experience and performance in (organic) search results.

The first step anyone undertakes is search for URL/Information or product. That is the reason the website should be optimized to serve your users' needs. One of those users is a search engine itself, which helps other users discover your content. Search engine optimization is about helping search engines understand and present content. Almost all of the traffic to any website is driven with the help of major commercial search engines like Google, Bing and Yahoo! This is true irrespective of the website, content or the intention of your website.

Therefore, the first step is to determine whether the site is in search engine indices (Google, Bing or Yahoo). A site search for your site's home URL will show whether the site is in the index. If the site is not in the index, it could happen that some sites are missed. When crawlers miss a site, it is usually on account of one of the following reasons:

- The site is not well connected from other sites on the web.
- The site is newly launched and the SEs has not had time to crawl it yet.
- The design of the site makes it difficult for SEs to crawl its content effectively.
- SEs received an error when trying to crawl your site.
- A policy blocks SEs from crawling the site.

Since the search engines are the media/roadway to provide information about the website for people looking for what you have to offer, if search engines are not allowed or find it difficult to find the website for the content on offer, it means missing out on great opportunities.

SEO is the process of acquiring website traffic by organic and free search results on the search engines. Search engines do their bit to crawl every website on the Internet, however, they are not intelligent enough to understand every website. Search engines need some help from every website for a better assessment and relevant connection to the traffic intended. By applying proper SEO techniques by websites, search engines will complement their quest to acquire more traffic and thereby more business. Before getting into details, let us understand some of the key terms used by Google since Google is the most popular search engine.

Key Terms (Google)

- **Index** - Google stores all web pages that it knows about in its index. The index entry for each page describes the content and location (URL) of that page. To index is when Google fetches a page, reads it, and adds it to the index.
- **Crawl** - The process of looking for new or updated web pages. Google discovers URLs by following links, by reading sitemaps, and by many other means. Google crawls the web, looking for new pages, then indexes them (when appropriate).
- **Crawler** - Automated software that crawls (fetches) pages from the web and indexes them.
- **Googlebot** - The generic name of Google's crawler.

How do Search Engines Work?

Internet is a network of huge digital properties (web pages, images, videos or other files) with links between each other. Search engines send out "crawlers" or "spiders" to crawl the entire network and decipher the documents based on select criteria and stores it in its database to provide the search users with a list of relevant websites ranked on their relevance.

The crawlers or spiders referred above are not living entities or creatures but is a software that goes through and peruse the webpage content and hence are text driven. This software does multitasking of activities such as scanning, listing, filtering, relevance, storing (or indexing) and recovering when needed. This is what is seen when it is said that the search has "returned search results", basis scanning, listing, filtering, relevance, storing (or indexing) and recovering. In addition, they provide a quality score after assessing and computing scores for different components such as

- Website names and URL
- Page design
- Page content
- Meta tags
- Relevance of links
- Usability, etc.

As mentioned above, a search engine carries out a number of activities that can be described as—

- **Crawling** is derived from the dictionary meaning "to move forward on the hands and knees or by dragging the body close to the ground" and considered as the most important activity. This software crawls or examines closely the webpage content on a periodicity that is prewritten in its algorithm. Hence the crawler may not see or track updates of webpages as desired by us since it may not visit the website for a month or two. Besides, it cannot crawl Flash movies, certain types of images, Java Scripts, password protected pages and directories. Therefore, it is recommended that a keyword simulator test is run to determine recognizable content and non-recognizable content is done away. This will help better ranking index. Google has named its crawler as Googlebot.
- **Indexing** is a term in digital that refers to a giant database where relevant contents of the crawled pages are stored for a subsequent retrieval upon entering a related search string or keyword. Hence, this is where optimization plays a key role such that the content is recognized and indexed.

> **Googlebot:** The name for Google's Crawler.
> **Index:** An index is another name for the database used by a search engine. It contains information on all the websites the search engine was able to find. If a website is not in a search engine's index, users will not be able to find it using that search engine.
> **Meta tags:** Meta tags are snippets of text that describe a page's content; the meta tags do not appear on the page itself, but only in the page's code.

- **Search** is the process by the search engine of matching the keywords or key phrases searched with that of the pages indexed and stored in the database. A keyword or a phrase may be found in millions of pages/documents in the web. Therefore, there should be a relevance between the word searched and those in the page. The search engine algorithm measures and matches the relevancy with what it indexed and that inserted in the result page.
- **Search algorithm** is the step-by-step procedure used to locate specific data among a collection of data. Usually, search algorithms make use of a search and return a success or a failure status. The efficiency of a search algorithm is measured by the number of times a comparison of the search key is done in the worst case. In search engines, the algorithm measures and matches the relevancy with what is indexed, estimates probable answers and directs to an URL or a page with similar content by looking at Meta tags, Title tags, keyword density, links, etc. There are different types of search algorithms—on site and off site—that are a part of a much larger algorithm. As the name suggests, each algorithm searches different aspects of the own web page (on site) apart from actions taken outside of your own website that impact the search and ranking (off-site).
- **Retrieving** is the result that is visible and is shown as the output of the search algorithm described as above. Since different search engines have developed different set of algorithms, different results could be returned in different search engines.

Therefore, the two factors that influence the search engines and of SEO are—

- **Relevance—**Relevance is not mere matching the right word. As mentioned earlier, the algorithm estimates the probable contextual answers in terms of relevance to match the searcher's queries than a simple step of exact matching of the word alone.
- **Popularity—**Search engines take an algorithmic approach based upon a citation analysis to finding pages based on the assumption that if a query matches tens of thousands of documents, the searcher is likely to look at documents that are mentioned in other web pages, or those mentioned at least a few times. It also takes into account the number of times that a document has been read, or the number of times that it might have been linked to or mentioned or shared on a social network, or selected when shown in a set of search results.

As mentioned in the previous paragraphs, it must be reiterated that popularity and relevance are not measured manually and that search engines have created intelligent algorithms that mathematically predict these factors and provide numerical scores for the search engines.

Search Engine Success Factors

Every enterprise/product or service want their URL or product to be right on top when searched for. That is what had been defined as SEO earlier in this chapter, which is the process of making your site better for search engines. As the name suggests, there is a process of optimization which is how to get all the above parameters or influencers to perform at their best by using various techniques. We also need to understand that no single factor can directly contribute to search engine success. SEO success factors work in combination.

There are three major factors that will decide the success of your search engines optimization.

- On page optimization
- Off page optimization
- Violations

On Page Optimization

The factors that are basically under the control of website owner are on page optimization. Website content, website architecture and HTML are the broad areas of control that supports on page optimization.

> **On page optimization:** Measures that can be taken directly within the website in order to improve its position in the search rankings.

Website Content

Quality - The mantra for digital marketing as a whole is that "Quality content wins". When the content offered is of good quality, a solid foundation is laid that could be supplemented by other factors. Primarily, buying decisions are made basis the content more than anything else. A compelling reason needs to be offered to the user/consumer to consume your content and be satisfied with the value on offer. The question of "what is the value that is offered that other websites don't?" should be decided on the content of the website before it is offered. The uniqueness and value the content has will decide time spent and CTA.

Research - The basic step to write good content is to understand what the user wants to consume in your website. Keyword research is the way to understand what the user really wants to see on your website. There are multiple keywords research tool that will help you understand what exactly the customers are looking for. Google Keyword Planner is the best place to begin keyword research. Though it is designed for advertising, it can be used to research organic keywords by customizing results for one of the competitors. If a product or service, competitor's landing page and product category are entered, the search can be customized for a certain kind of keywords. While a bouquet of keywords for a particular offer will be returned, the enterprise needs to identify and segment appropriate keywords aligning with the content strategy. Exhibit 5.4 represents screenshots from Google Keyword Planner.

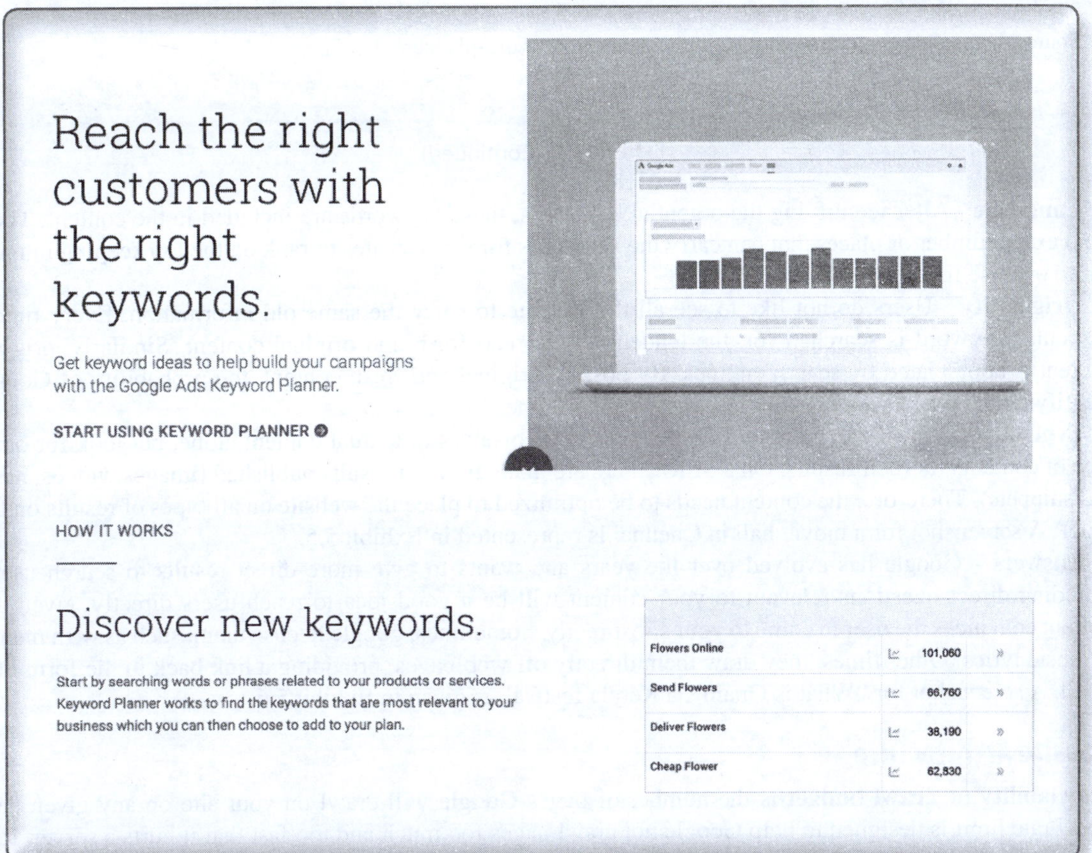

Exhibit 5.4 Google Keyword Planner

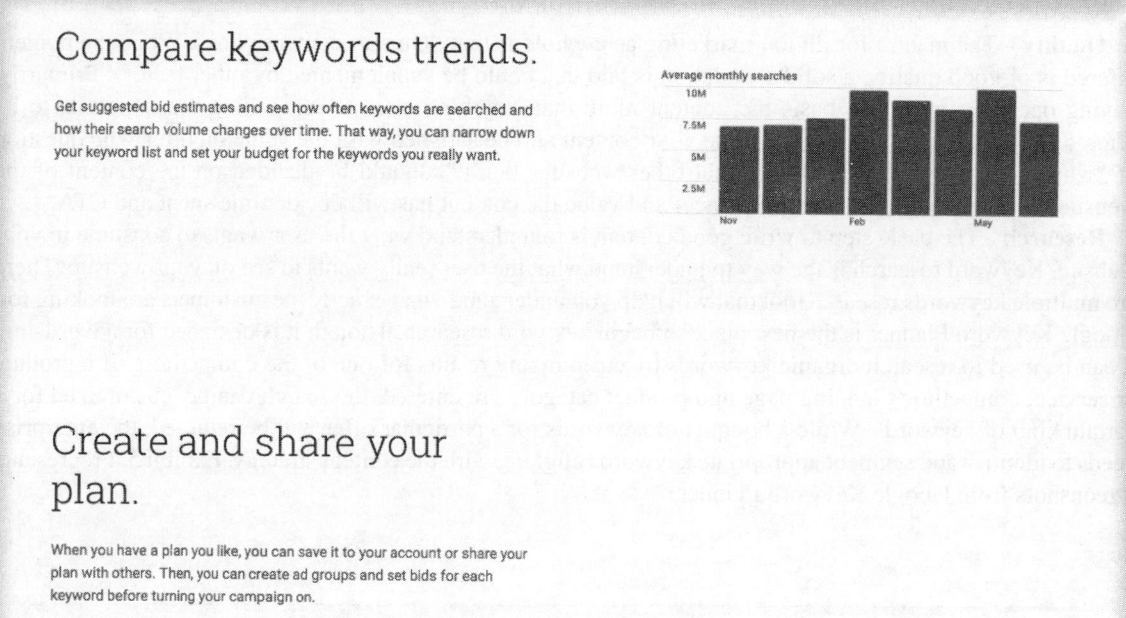

Source: https://ads.google.com/intl/en_in/home/tools/keyword-planner/

Exhibit 5.4 (Continued)

Language - After identifying the potential keywords, these keywords are included in the content. There is no exact number or places that can carry the keywords for the websites to rank on the top keeping in mind not to overuse the keywords directly.

Originality - Users do not like to see all the website to carry the same old information. Every time a particular keyword is searched for, the tendency is to read fresh and original content. Similarly, original content is appreciated by search engines. By posting original and fresh content, the probability of Google identifying the post as a top result gets significantly higher.

Type of content - Search engines do not restrict themselves to textual content alone, but look for other type of contents for their results. On a SERP, there are many types of results published (images, videos, news and snippets). Therefore, the content needs to be optimized to place the website on all types of results on the SERP. A screenshot for a movie hall in Chennai is represented in Exhibit 5.5.

Answers - Google has evolved over the years and wants to give more direct results to search users. Including direct questions relevant to your content will be a good idea to reach users directly, given the content convinces the user to come to your site directly. Sometimes, google license them, such as with menus or music lyrics. Other times, they draw them directly off web pages, providing a link back in the form of a credit. A screenshot for "What is Onam", a Kerala festival, is given in Exhibit 5.6.

Website Architecture

Crawlability or crawl budget is the number of pages Google will crawl on your site on any given day. Crawl rate limit is designed to help Google not crawl pages too much and too fast that it hurts a server. It is also based on trust and authority of a site information to search engines on not to crawl pages that contain URL parameters such as Flash movies, certain types of images, Java Scripts, password protected pages

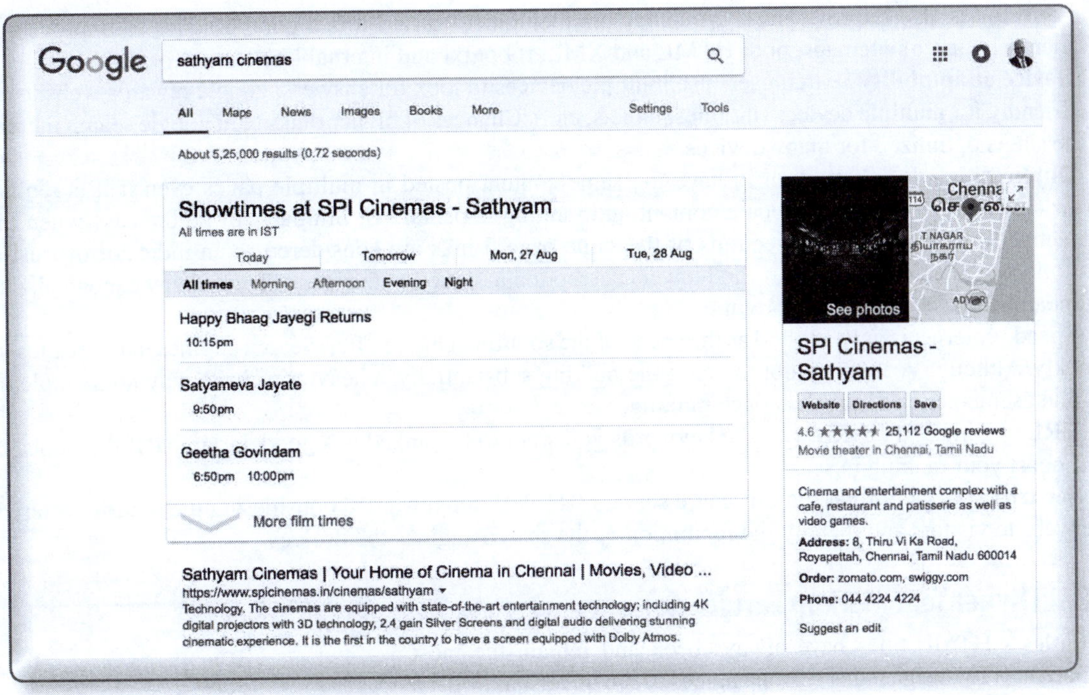

Exhibit 5.5 Screenshot for a Movie Hall

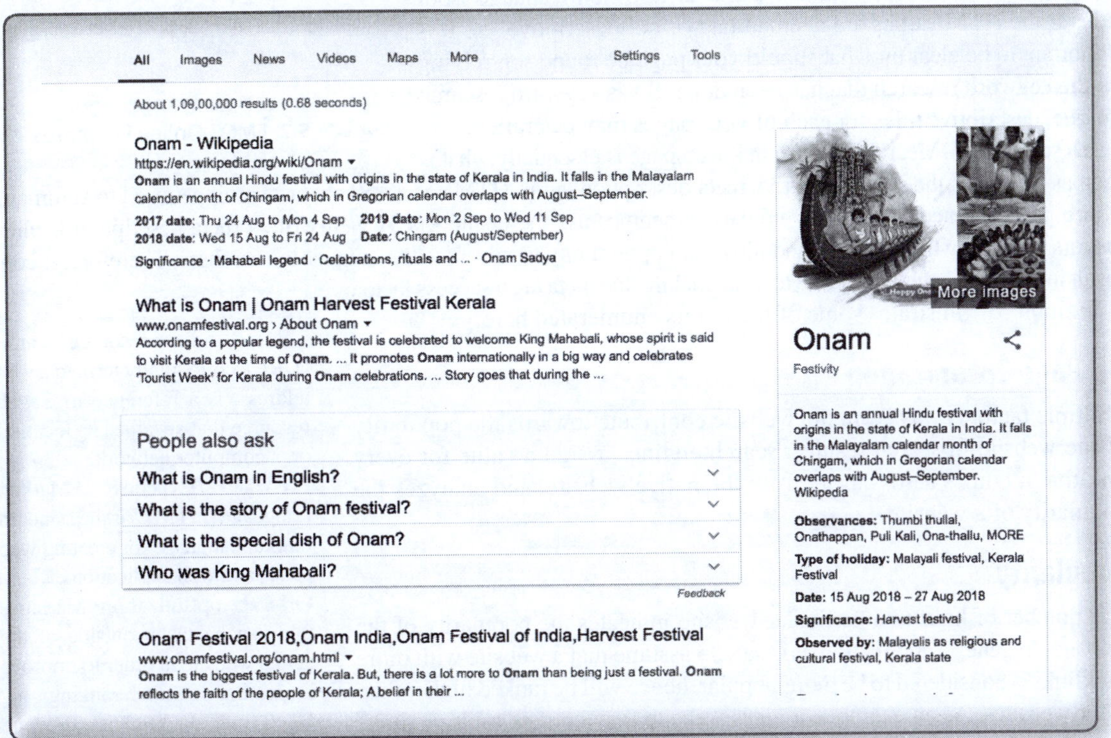

Exhibit 5.6 Screenshot of "What is Onam?

and directories also improve crawl efficiency. As mentioned earlier, it is a good practice to improve crawl efficiency by use of sitemaps, both HTML and XML, robot.txt and internal link structures.

Device adaptability Search users use multiple devices to look for answers, google rewards websites that are friendly for multiple devices (mobiles, tablets, etc.). Chances of higher ranking in google search increases if the site is optimized for many devices.

Duplication - It is better not to have the same content posted in multiple pages even if it is required. Crawlers identify them as duplicate content and ranking is penalized. Similar will be the case when there are active linking to different versions of the same page. Links are considered as an indicator of trust and authority and duplications distort (and lower) perception assigned to that page. That is why canonicalization (standardization) becomes important.

Speed - Internet is only as good as the speed of the solution it has to offer. Search engines like websites load quickly. Although speed may not increase the ranking substantially, a heavier website may not complement a good user experience and thus page ranking.

URLs - Having the URL with the keywords you want to be ranked is a good and impactful practice that will boost your ranking in search results.

Security - Websites that run on secure servers (HTTPS) are rewarded considering the security offered to the website visitors and thereby the reputation of the search engines themselves.

HTML (Hyper Text Markup Language)

Titles - HTML titles have always been and remain the most important HTML signal that search engines use to understand what a page is about. Bad titles on your pages are like having bad headlines for your communication (ad). Google is known to change your titles if the HTML titles are deemed bad or not descriptive! So it is important to be clear on what should your page be found for, relying on the keyword research that has been done. Basis keyword research unique, descriptive titles for each of your pages may be crafted.

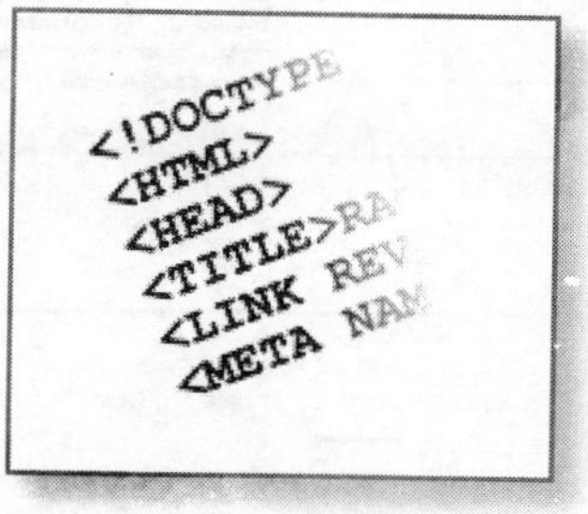

Figure 5.2 FMCG Online Purchases 2017

Descriptions - Meta description in a web page is essentially what is seen as a blurb in the search result. A meta description tag in HTML is a 160 character snippet used to summarize a web page's content and search engines sometimes use these snippets. A well-written meta description facilitate visitors to know what a page is and also is an opportunity to advertise the content to searchers. Therefore, it could result in additional clicks or traffic to a site making the meta tag a success factor.

Exhibit 5.7 illustrates some of the points enumerated here.

Off Page Optimization

Multiple factors away from the website contribute towards the popularity of the website in search results. Search engines assign a value for every link that it comes across away from the native website, and analyzes the popularity of a website.

Popularity

The number of links to a particular website indicates the popularity of the website. In generic application, it is safe to assume that a website with more backlinks is considered to be more popular, hence will be ranked higher than other websites. As an example, a news website may contain multiple links from different types of other website. The more popular and trustworthy the link offering website is, your website's chances of ranking higher goes up.

URL: A uniform resource locator (URL), colloquially termed a web address, is a reference to a web resource that specifies its location on a computer network.

HTML: Hypertext Markup Language (**HTML**) is the standard markup language for creating web pages and web applications.

Off Page optimization: Measures that can be taken outside of the actual website in order to improve its position in search rankings.

Back link: Backlink is a link one website gets from another website/source in Internet.

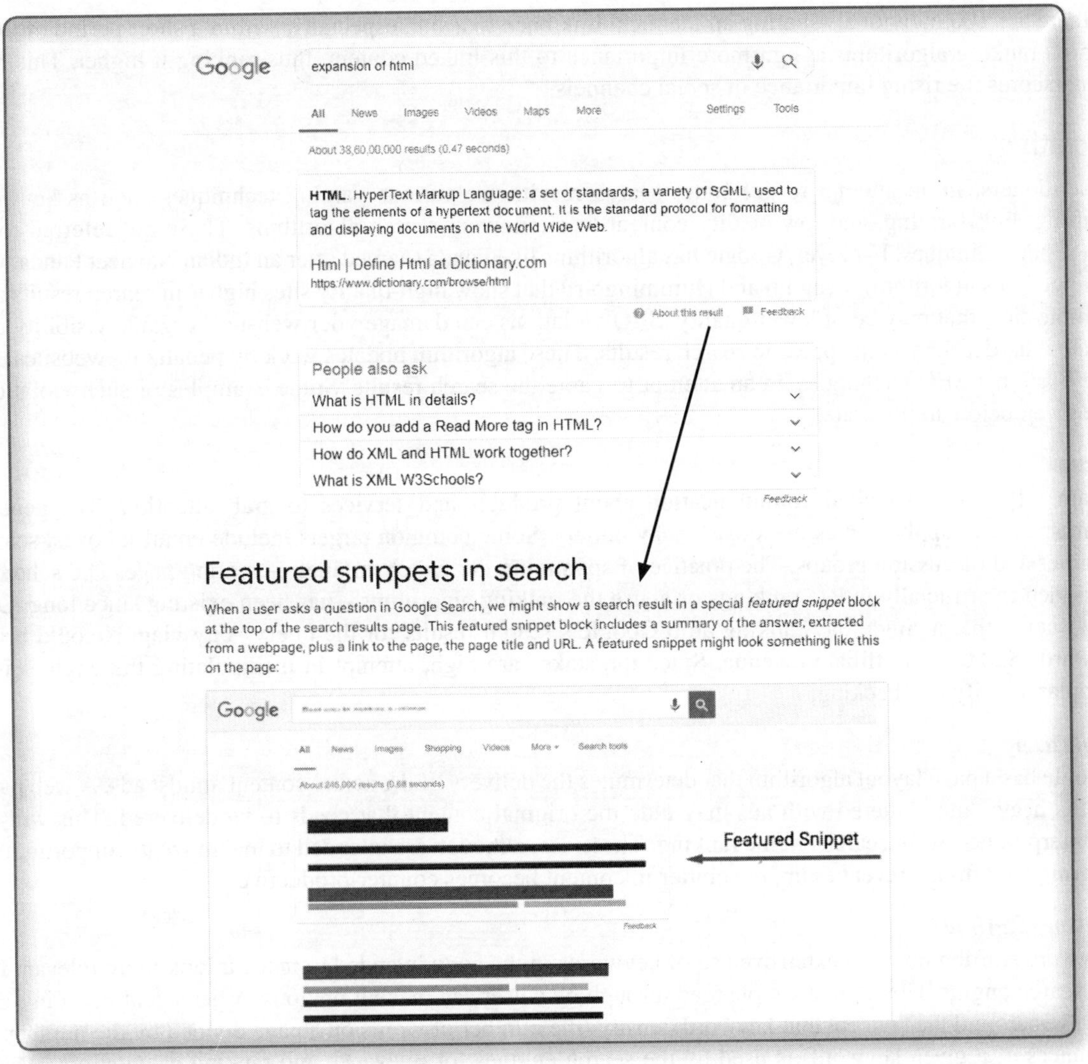

Exhibit 5.7 Screenshot of HTML

Trust Score

Internet contains a great deal of junk as much as it contains original content. As mentioned earlier, Google likes to reward original content and penalize others. Important parameter to measure the originality is the trust score of the website. Earning links from highly-trusted domains can result in a significant boost to this scoring metric. Universities, government websites and non-profit organizations represent examples of high-trust domains.

> **Trust Score:** TrustScore is an instant measure of your customer satisfaction based on service reviews you collect.

Sharing

Content sharing refers to distribution of webpage and blog content across relevant social media such as Facebook, Twitter, LinkedIN, and Google+ and implies an intent of building engagement and referral traffic. Shareability is the potential of a given piece of content to be transmitted, or shared, by a third party. Whenever a link to a website is shared on a public social media platform, it is taken note of by Google. For example, if there are 100 individuals sharing an identical link back to a site, especially, within a short period of time, search ranking algorithms assign more importance to this linked content, thus ranking it higher. This also underscores the rising importance of social channels.

Violations

Practitioners, in an attempt to get better search results use various gaming techniques such as keyword stuffing, link farming, and low-quality content to circumvent search algorithms. These are referred to as black hat techniques. However, Google has algorithms like Panda (named after an Indian Navneet Panda who patented this algorithm), Penguin and Hummingbird that show high-quality sites higher in search results and demote sites that may be of lower quality. SEO violations can damage your website's organic visibility and make it harder for you to appear in search results. These algorithm updates work by penalizing websites that use black hat SEO techniques, in an attempt to game the search results. Some examples of such violations are given below to illustrate.

Spam

Spam refers to unsolicited communication about products and services to grab attention. The general term spam can apply to messages over many outlets. Some common targets include email inboxes, search engines and discussion groups. The practice of spamming the search engines—creating pages and schemes designed to artificially inflate rankings or abuse the ranking algorithms—has been existing since long. One SEO noted that a single day ranking atop Google's search results for the query "buy viagra" could bring upwards $20,000 in affiliate revenue. Since the stakes are high, attempt in manipulating the engines is a popular activity like hacking.

Advertising

Google has a page layout algorithm that determines the delivery of the actual content amidst ads. A web page that is heavy and cluttered with ads may hide the original content that needs to be delivered. This will be counterproductive for search engine ranking. These ads, although are intended to maximize the opportunities to bring the affiliate revenues up, the clutter in content becomes counter-productive.

Keyword Stuffing

Keyword stuffing involves extensive use of keywords in the copy intended to make it look more relevant for the search engine. However, a simple read through by a user can make it obvious. A persistent myth in SEO revolves around the concept that keyword density (the number of words on a page divided by the number of instances of a given keyword) is used by the search engines for relevance and ranking calculations. Many SEO tools still feed on the concept that keyword density is an important metric. Despite being disproved, this myth continues. Google crawlers identify these stuffing patterns and penalize. It is recommended to ignore the keyword density and use keywords intelligently and with usability in mind. Earning one good editorial link from a source that does not think you're a search spammer is of better value than density.

Malpractice - Manipulative Linking

SEO practitioners, in order to increase their backlinks, create multiple websites and feed content and links back to the original website. Using of dummy websites as link sources attempts to exploit the search engines algorithms for link popularity and rank their respective website on the top of the search results.

However, as mentioned earlier, Google has algorithms like Panda, Penguin Hummingbird, etc. that show high-quality sites higher in search results and penalize by demoting sites that indulge in black hat practices.

SEO – Integrated Digital Marketing

Increasingly, the use of SEO is becoming important for the overall success of digital marketing and hence is referred to as Integrated Digital Marketing–IDM (somewhat like IMC). This can be seen by a changing paradigm of SEO over years. In mid-90s when very first SEO came into picture, manual submission, the Meta keywords tag, and keyword stuffing were all usual techniques necessary to rank well in the SERP. Then around 2004, for generating web traffic, some popular measures were anchor text associated link bombing, link buying from automated blog comment spam injectors, and creation of inter-linking websites. Post 2010, social media marketing (SMM) and vertical search inclusion have become methods of choice for SEO. The search engine algorithms are constantly updated and improved.

Social Media: As discussed in detail in the earlier chapter on Social Media Marketing, SMM is gaining importance because of the increased usage of viral marketing approach through Facebook, LinkedIn, Twitter, Yammer, and Google+. These social networking sites must be in line with the SEO best practices to entirely control SEO potential.

More the Links, Higher the Ranking Outdated: The more links with a view to ranking higher is not today's approach . We had discussed earlier in the chapter "Content Sharing" that referred to distribution of page and blog contents resulting in common belief of ranking high in the search results is changing. The concept of 'link' is changing in that respect. The intention and therefore the practice was to build as many links as possible. This resulted in what are called black hat practice some marketers relied on. Consequently, Google tweaked its algorithms, ending the practice of traditional link building practice. This came to be known as spamming. Even guest-blogging with a motive to generate links was counterproductive. Guest-blogging works well only if it is presented by an expert, and engaging with the targeted community. More than the content strategies generating the quality inbound links that stay as an important SEO element positively affect ranking.

The Implied Links

In Google terminology, regular backlinks are called "express links" (explicit) and brand mentions "implied links" (implicit). For example, if there is a brand called "BlueBook" and brand BlueBook is mentioned in other websites but there is no website for BlueBook, if in a query BlueBook is typed, Google notes this similarity and connection and provides an implicit link. To quote Search Engineland citing Gary Illyes, "......Thus, a resource in the group can be a target of an implied link without a user being able to navigate to the resource by following the implied link," as propounded by Navneet Panda and Vladimir Ofitserov (Patent granted March 25, 2014[2]). It is called implied linking because there is basically no link to go back to the source site.

> **Implied Link:** An implied link is a reference to a target resource, e.g., a citation to the target resource, which is included in a source resource but is not an express link to the target resource. http://sumo.ly/9COF via @monitorbacklink.

Brand Mentions and Online Citations

Brand mentions and online citation are important parts of content strategy and affect SEO and hence must be handled carefully and incorporated well into the site content. Brand mentions are generally connected to the products or services with an explanation of how those are connected to the content. So long as the brand or website name is used, a brand name or citation is created. Google Webmaster Trends Analyst Gary Illyes mentioned in his keynote at Brighton SEO in September 2017: "If you publish high-quality content that is highly cited on the internet — and I'm not talking about just links, but also mentions on social networks and people talking about your branding . ….. Then you are doing great."[3] Going forward, the following are expected to be the trend of the brand authority:

1. **Better judgement in brand authority:** Google does not give that much importance to the former practice of traditional link building. A new brand authority will rule in the form of brand mentions.
2. **No manipulation:** The anchor texts and links cannot be manipulated now. The black hat practice of linking to a site that is totally irrelevant to the source site is replaced by the brand mentions or online

citations. Once a brand is flawlessly woven in site content, the implied link should point to sites that must be relevant to the source site.

3. **Influencing the social signals through brand mentions:** Brand mentions or online citation are reckoned as important factors to leverage the social signals for SEO. The links that got generated through social media are no-follow links that do not affect the SERP rankings. But when any source content is shared, commented, tweeted, or cited socially with or even without these implied links, it must funnel to highest rankings. This entire process of back-linking through social media is called social media optimization.
4. **Online citation is an important factor for local SEO:** Local SEO targets potential customers of the small and medium sized enterprises. Citations are always good for local SEO. Here, the use of name, address, and contact number are taken into consideration by Google for a bigger picture.

However, the above does not mean that only brand mentions exist, and the traditional linking has become obsolete. There needs to be a balance between these two and an equal importance be given. Just avoid having a higher ratio in the express links to your brand mention to escape the possible danger of getting spammed that can affect your brand.

- Avoiding higher ratio of express links
- Use of visual content that go viral – balance of express links to brand mention
- Use of guest-blogging, social media, comments and RSS feeds that can go viral to promote the brand

Emerging Trends in SEO – Integrated Digital Marketing

- **Social media optimization has a new entrant, video optimization:** Although it had been mentioned earlier in the book under crawlability that crawlers sometimes are unable to recognize and hence rank some types of video content, certain types of images and related directories, technological advances today has made it possible to optimize video content, effectively distribute it, and rank them in meaningful ways.
- **Paid search redefined:** Paid searches usually appear on either side of the aisle vis-a-vis organic search. Again thanks to technological advances, co-optimization is now possible that follows the paid search initiatives for better outcomes on both sides of the aisle.
- **Use of data:** With emergence of specialized and advanced analytics programs, now there is new breed of qualified analytics professionals who have a capability to understand, mine, and use data efficiently. This provides the capability to share resources and steer a digital plan within restricted budgets for handsome RoI.
- **Other factors of modern SEO:** Behavioural targeting or retargeted marketing and contextual advertising using display advertising based on Artificial Intelligence that keeps track of search and page visit patterns of an individual using targeted keywords generated in organic search is also gaining ground. This can be seen in various e-commerce sites that provide not only a history of products searched but also suggestions for products.

Thus, a digital marketer would need to have a thorough understanding of not only the campaign but also the business models to be effective. Hence, SEO today is the face of integrated digital marketing.

> **Organic Search:** Method for entering one or several search terms as a single string of text into a search engine.
> **Paid Search:** Paid search marketing means you advertise within the sponsored listings of a search engine or a partner site.

SERP (Search Engine Results Page)

Inbound marketing is marketing focused on being found by customers, that is, it is all about attracting potential customers with high-quality and targeted content, engaging and nurturing them into action which is that they are ready to consume. As consumers, when we need something, whether it is a product, service, doubt or description/meaning, the first thing we do is to search on the Internet. Google is the most popular search engine today. Therefore, search becomes important in inbound marketing context. In the previous section, we looked at SEO that enables a high ranking of product, service, doubt or description/meaning searched for. When we search the place or the page where we find the result is called search engine results page (SERP).

Search engine results page (SERP) - When a searcher keys in a search query, the page that is displayed by a web search engine in response to that query is called SERP. The SERP lists in a certain order the responses to a keyword query, and the listing order is termed as search ranking. The results are normally ranked by relevance to the query. The page also exhibits other results that are advertisements.

The results exhibited are classified into two types, organic and paid search results and sponsored. Paid search results are those that are retrieved by the search algorithm. Sponsored results are advertisements. The results displayed on the SERP has a title (header), a link to the actual page on the Web besides a short description showing within the page the match of keywords with the content for organic results. The advertiser chooses what to display for sponsored results.

> **SERP:** Search engine ranking page/Search engine results pages (SERP) are the pages displayed by search engines in response to a query by a searcher

Exhibit 5.8 explains the above.

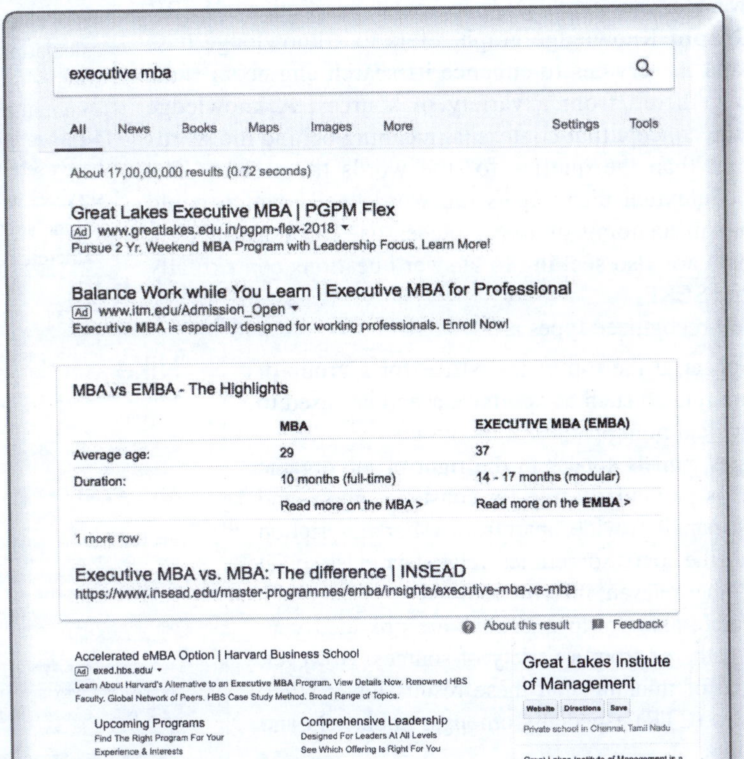

Exhibit 5.8 SERP Results Page

Since one search result can turn in a large number of responses, they run into multiple pages for a single query, for, in every hardware, there is a limitation on the number of results that can be viewed on a single page. Besides, an user can also restrict the number of results viewed per page. This implies lower ranking or relevance in each succeeding page.

Some of the key features of an SERP are:

Advertisements: Advertised search results related to your search query will show up on the top of the search results above or below the organic results. These will be arranged in the order of their ad rank which is a function of MaxCPC and quality score.

Featured Snippet: The principle of a snippet is to provide you a direct answer to a query that is not provided in the knowledge graph. The snippets can provide specific details that are located in the relevant web pages.

Images: This feature displays the images that are relevant to the query. The search engine picks up such images with the help of the Meta tags, ALT text and SEO.

Videos: Video results from websites such as YouTube, daily motion which carries videos relevant to your search query appears in this section of SERP.

Knowledge Graph: Knowledge graph refers to a knowledge base used by Google and its services to enhance its search engine's results with information gathered from a variety of sources. A knowledge graph is built on the concept that contextual meaning behind the words are more important than the queries for the words themselves. The example for the contextual meaning is the word "nail" which could mean parts of human anatomy or metal pieces used in construction. Thus the algorithms are also seeking to answer questions contextually for users within the SERP.

Algorithm: A process or set of rules to be followed in calculations or other problem-solving operations, especially by a computer

Knowledge graph: A knowledge base used by Google and its services to enhance its search engine's results with information gathered from a variety of sources

Some of the well-recognized types are:

- Carousels appear at the top of the SERP for a group of items that are related such as sportswear and are used to display individual mini profiles of the group.
- In many pages, panels appear to the right of the organic listings. This is particularly true for consumer goods and brands. These panels provide, apart from a short description of the brand, the logo, sometimes related brands, social profiles and other relevant information.
- Today in search, answers to questions are provided with information gathered from a variety of sources. However, there is a line of thinking that these results lower Click Through Rates (CTR) especially amongst publishers and content creators.

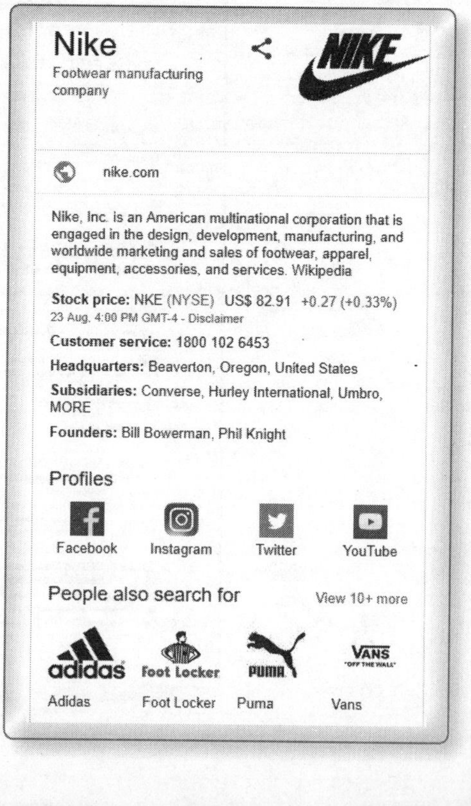

News: Search engine displays the news links relevant to your search query which are from Google news. Getting into such results is efforts on getting your branded message published by news partners and is different from SEO.

Product/Shopping Results

Search engine will display products, relevant pictures and direct link to buy in the SERP. These results are mostly sponsored.

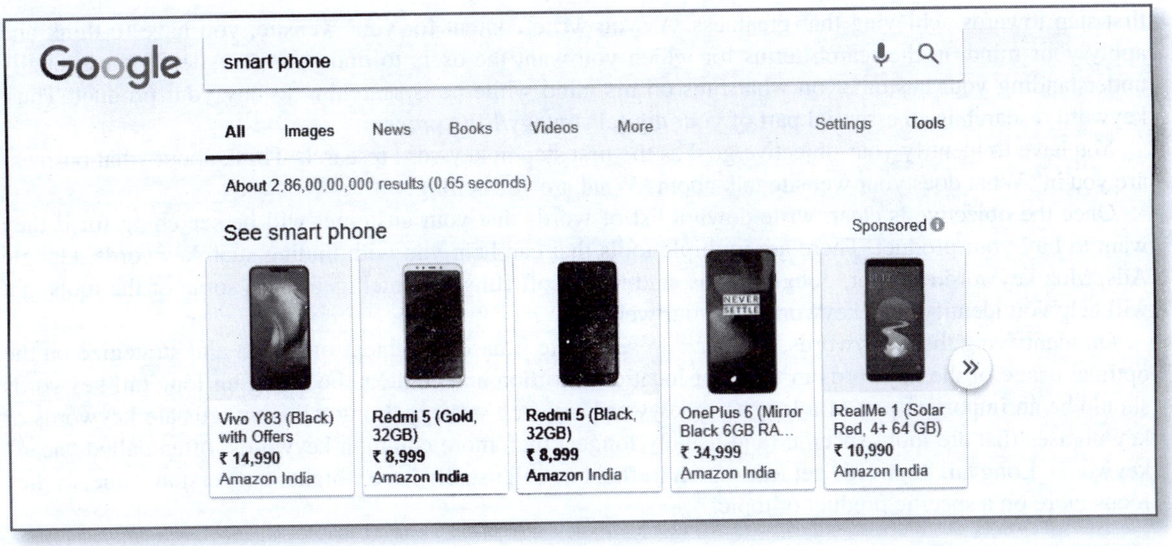

Site Links

Site links are links to different specific pages of the same website that are displayed along with the main link to the website relevant to your queries.

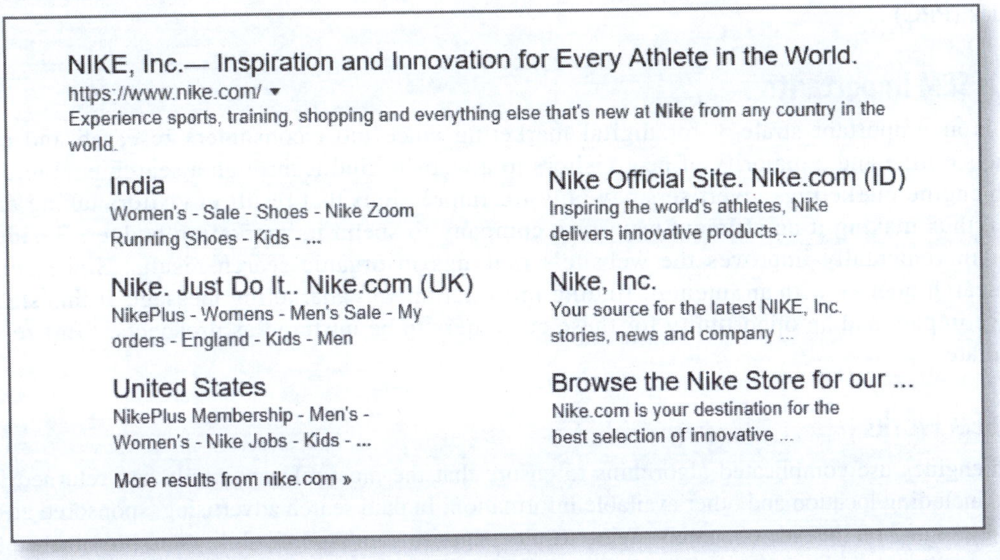

Thus, SERP tries to provide you with answers for your query in multiple ways and more direct ways. The understanding of search engines of your queries are developed and evolving into understanding the exact meaning of your query than the words. The SERP will provide you with choices of solutions in different formats in order to facilitate your problem solving.

Keyword Research

Although this has been covered earlier under Website, it is covered once again here from a SERP perspective. As you embark on SEO to make your website available on top of the SERP, keyword research forms the first step towards achieving that greatness. As you write content for your website, you have to think and apply your mind on the search terms for which you want the users to find your website. It is essentially understanding your customer on what runs on his mind while he is searching to buy your product. Thus, keyword research is an essential part of your digital strategy/SEO process.

You have to identify your objective/goal as the first step in keyword research. Think about what business are you in? What does your website talk about? What are you selling?

Once the objective is clear, write down a list of words that your customer will be searching for if they want to buy your product. There are multiple tools that can help you with finding such keywords. Google Ads, Moz keyword explorer, google trends, and Microsoft Bing ads intelligence are some of the tools that will help you identify such keywords for your website.

On identifying these keywords, you have to segregate it based on intent of search and strategize on the optimal usage of the keywords in terms of location, position and context. Focusing on long tail keywords should be an important part of a long-term keyword research strategy. Long tail keywords are keywords or key phrases that are more specific (and usually longer) than more common keywords, often called "head" keywords. Long tail keywords get less search traffic, but will usually have a higher conversion value, as they focus more on a specific product or topic.

Search Engine Marketing

Search engine marketing (SEM) is a digital marketing strategy used to increase the visibility of a website in search engine results pages (SERP). In the past, both organic search activities (such as SEO) and paid search were called SEM, now SEM refers almost exclusively to paid search that is also referred to as pay per click (PPC) .

Why Is SEM Important?

SEM is an important strategy for digital marketing since most consumers research and shop for products online and a majority of new visitors to a website find it through a search engine query. In search engine marketing, advertisers pay only for impressions that result in visitors taking an action (CTA), thus making it an efficient way for a company to spend its marketing budget. Besides, each visitor incrementally improves the website's rankings in organic search results. Since consumers enter search queries with an intent of finding information, any marketing message at this stage has a positive impact and an opportunity for these customers to be nurtured as prospects. SEM results are immediate.

How SEM Works

Search engines use complicated algorithms to ensure that the most relevant results are returned for each search, including location and other available information. In paid search advertising, sponsored ads appear at the top of and on the side of search engine results pages to gain more visibility and prominence than the organic results.

Let's say that you are a customer looking for a product or service online. You go to a search engine and type in your search terms (also known as keywords). In your search results page, you will come across various company ads whose keywords match the keywords in your search. These ads appear in prominent locations on the page – along with the other search listings that match your keywords. The paid listings are highly relevant to your specific search, making it likely that you will click on them. Two such examples are given in Exhibit 5.9.

> **SEM:** Search engine marketing (**SEM**) is a form of Internet marketing that involves the promotion of websites by increasing their visibility in search engine results pages (SERPs), primarily through paid advertising

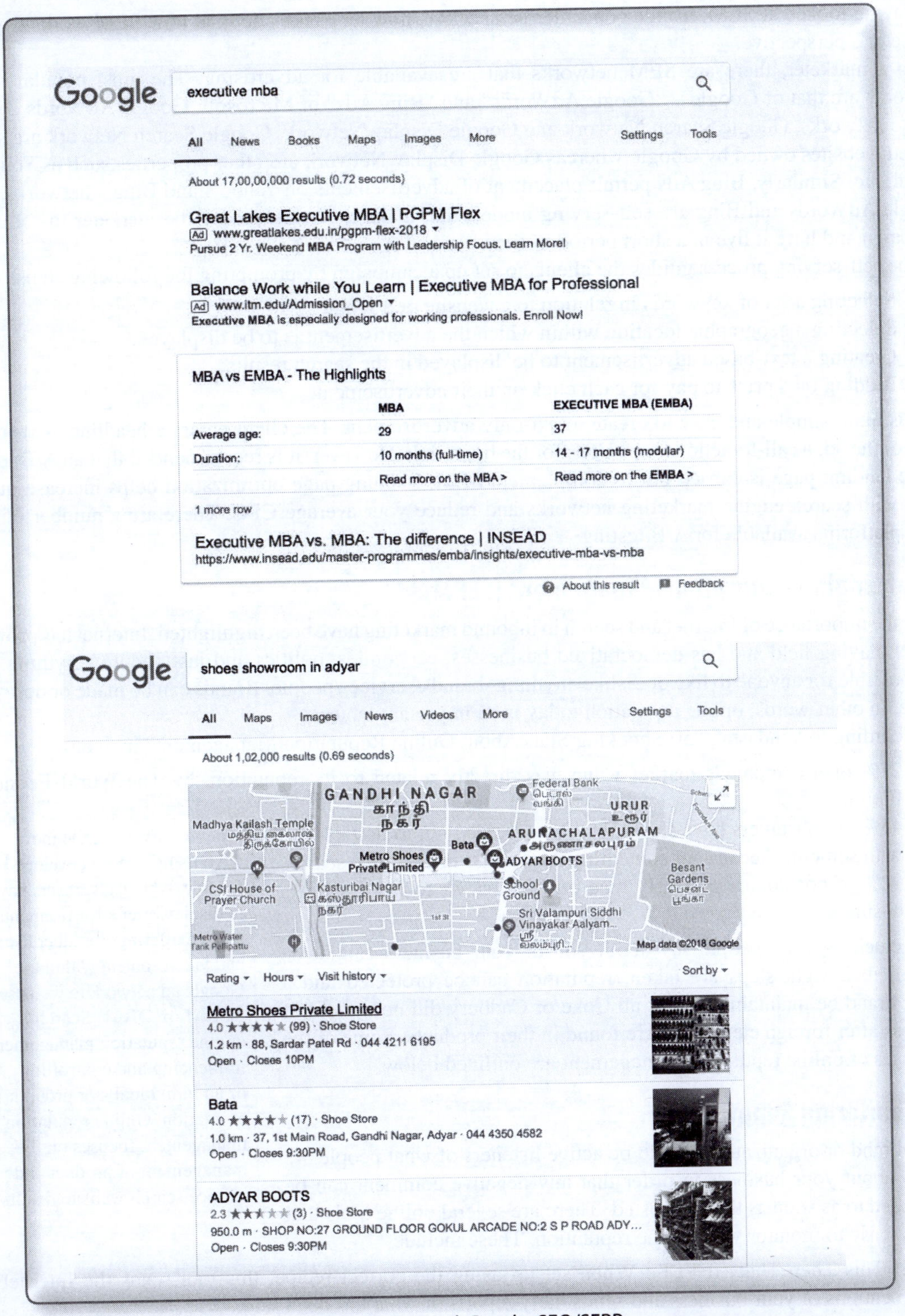

Exhibit 5.9 Search Results SEO/SERP

Having looked at SEM, from a consumer perspective, now let's take a look at how SEM works from the marketer's perspective.

To a marketer, there are SEM networks that are available for advertising. The most popular search networks are that of Google – "Google AdWords" and "Bing Ads" of Microsoft. Google AdWords consists of two networks, Google Search Network and Google Display Network. Google Search Network are search related websites owned by Google whereas Google Display Network are other properties such as YouTube, Gmail, etc. Similarly, Bing Ads permit placement of advertisements on Yahoo's and Bing's networks. Both Google AdWords and Bing are self-serving models that make it convenient for the marketer to set up the campaign and have it live in a short period of time.

The self-serving process guides the clients to set up a campaign by prompting the following steps:

1. Selecting a set of keywords in relation to a website or a product;
2. Selecting a geographic location within which the advertisement is to be displayed;
3. Creating a text-based advertisement to be displayed in the search results;
4. Bidding on a price to pay for each click on their advertisement.

It is quite simple and easy to create a text-only advertisement. The client enters a headline, text for the body of the ad, a call-to-action and a URL for the hyperlink. However, it is recommended that an A/B testing of the landing page is carried out to complement SEM. Landing page optimization helps increase quality score with search engine marketing networks and reduce your average CPC. There are a number of third party platforms available for A/B testing.

Search Engine Reputation Management (SERM)

So far the importance of Internet and search in inbound marketing have been highlighted. Internet has provided a level playing field and has democratized businesses, economies, politics and just about everything. It is now possible for anyone to like or dislike anything–brands/services/people. Brands can be made or destroyed online. In other words, online reputation today is an important factor.

According to Vendasta[4], "50 Shocking Stats About Online Reputation Management" includes:

- 25% of a company's market value was directly related to its reputation, by The World Economic Forum.
- 45% of consumers have stated that they decided not to do business with someone because of something they found in an online search.
- 92% of consumers regularly read online reviews to learn about a business.

In as much as what people say about you or your business cannot be controlled, if right steps are taken, reputation can be protected and a strong brand be maintained. After all Coke or Cadbury did not go out of business after foreign elements were found in their products. Some of the processes of online reputation management are outlined below.

> **Google Adwords:** Online advertising service developed by Google, where advertisers pay to display brief advertisements, service offerings, product listings, and video content within the Google ad network to web users.
> **SERM or ORM:** Search engine reputation management, influencing and controlling of an individual's or group's reputation. Online reputation management focuses on the management of product and service search website results.

1. Monitoring Reputation

Every brand or organization should be active listeners of what people are saying about your business in order that any negative comment can be responded to as soon as they're posted. There are several online tools that make it easy to monitor your online reputation. These include

- If This Then That (IFTTT): When set up using the correct recipe, this tool scans the Internet for mentions of your business and sends daily reports of what has been said.

- Me On The Web: Another tool that scans the Internet and a mail is received on mentions about the business.
- Ice Rocket: This tool lets you search the major social media platforms to see what people are posting about your business.

2. Optimizing Search Engine Results Pages (SERPs)

Another way to prevent negative comments from impacting the business is to make it harder for these negative comments to get attention by optimizing the top ten search results for the name of your business or creating implied links, brand mentions and citations. Once SERPs are locked, it will be harder for any other negative mentions to break in and search for your business online will be less likely to see a negative mention. The objective, therefore, should be to create several strong pages built around your brand name that all have the potential to rank.

> **Key Word:** Keywords are ideas and topics that define what your content is about. In terms of SEO, they're the words and phrases that searchers enter into search engines
> **SOP:** Standard operating procedure is a set of step-by-step instructions compiled by an organization to help carry out complex routine operations

These can be done by

- Creating social media profiles.
- Guest content and citations.
- Creating multiple websites of relevant key words.
- Contributing strong content on other reputed online publications.

3. Using Social Media and Listening to Customer

Social media is one of the most important facets of online reputation management. However, it is not enough to just have social media accounts but they must be actively used by building and maintaining an engagement. Social media allows building influences and trust with the customers thereby reducing the likelihood of negative comments. Still, if a complaint or a negative post is made, it must be discovered quickly and the complainant reached out to in double time and not blown off or swept under the carpet. This is the basic principle of a good service recovery.

Another benefit of using social media regularly is that it can make it easier to claim your SERPs positions. The more engagement there is on your social media accounts, the higher the likelihood your business is ranked higher.

4. Transparency and Taking Responsibility

One of the easiest and most powerful ways to build a positive reputation is to be willing to admit when wrong. Apologies can go a long way towards mending relationships with dissatisfied customers. It is not about the mistake made but is about handling the mistake correctly, being transparent, admitting it and taking a corrective action to reinforce trust.

Summarizing online reputation management, it is difficult and not easy. Better reputation equals better sales, better revenue and thus a healthy bottom line. It requires a constant vigilance and an awareness of what's being said about the enterprise. The organization (through competent and committed employees) should be committed to taking ownership of search engine results and the dissatisfied customers, as best as possible.

Chapter 2 of this book outlined web as an effective communicator and how the first web page built in 1989 by Tim Berners-Lee built contained information about world wide web (www) and web browser. This chapter covers the current technology and tools available that has taken the modest web page of Tim Berners-Lee to an important and integral part of digital or inbound marketing, beginning from planning and development of a website, optimizing it for search engine marketing to online reputation management. This chapter provides the platform for subsequent chapters on analytics, B2B, ecommerce, IoT, etc.

CHAPTER SUMMARY

- Inbound marketing is marketing focused on getting found by customers. That is, it is all about attracting potential customers with high-quality and targeted content, engaging and nurturing them into action which is that they are ready to buy.
- Anything that needs to be found needs an address and that address in inbound marketing is the website. Websites usually provide a map and directions to the premises of the enterprise so that visitors are less likely to have trouble finding your location.
- A website has a far wider reach than any other form of advertising. It is the face of an organization or a product and is almost the first contact point with your prospective customer/user. A good website helps establishing a credibility for the business and building a website is not expensive!
- A website is usually an amalgam of both source and destination of information and consists of—an overview of what you are—breadth, tabs/pages to provide more information–length, links–depth to provide specific information, facilitates visual content; Traffic is not restricted or limited (i.e. may not need log in credentials).
- Usually, a website is confused with a portal. Websites, are for driving traffic, whereas web portals are for limiting traffic to a specific group of users. Web portals generally require a user to log in, that facilitates the site to deliver a more specific content based on the user profile.
- While planning or designing a website, it is advisable to pay attention to details and it is imperative that detailed sitemap (visualization), primary navigation (functionality breakdown), ease of navigation—uncluttered, load time (GT Metrix), content management system, user interface (UI)/ user experience (UX) and interactivity are built in a website.
- Website benchmarking is essentially to gauge a website that gives a measure of where a website stands in relation to other websites, both direct competition, category or general.
- Some typical benchmarking parameters are site performance, marketing performance, financial performance, search performance and usability.
- POEM stands for paid, owned and earned media. A website is central to POEM framework. Paid media are those when a paid third-party channel is leveraged, such as advertising on third-party sites and sponsorships. Owned media are those channels that are created and controlled by you. Earned media are those wherein customers, the press and the public share your content, speak about your brand via word of mouth, and otherwise discuss your brand.
- It is a common misconception that we must maximize own and earned media than paid media. Every page, irrespective of paid, owned or earned should have a specific job to do along the prospect's journey to becoming a customer and justify RoI. Also, over years, the boundaries between paid-owned-earned media have blurred, resulting in convergence.
- While websites provide an overview of what you are (breadth), have tabs/pages that provide more information (length) and links (depth) to provide specific information, a landing page (LP) is a standalone web page, created specifically for the purposes of a marketing or an advertising campaign. It is where a visitor *"lands"* when they have clicked on an ad or a similar communication.
- Conversion Centered Design or CCD helps in design experiences that guide the visitor towards completing that one specific action (CTA), using persuasive design and psychological triggers to increase conversions.
- There are seven principles that govern CCD—Attention, Context, Clarity, Congruence, Credibility, Closing and Continuance.
- Search engine optimization (SEO) is about making small modifications to parts of your website. When viewed individually, these changes might seem like incremental improvements, but when combined with other optimizations, they could have a noticeable impact on your site's user experience and performance in (organic) search results.
- SEO is the process of acquiring website traffic by organic and free search results on the search engines.
- Search engines are not humans but software that crawl the web page content they are text-driven. They complete a number of activities that bring search results–crawling, scanning and storing (or indexing), measuring pertinence, and recovering.
- Basis the above parameters, they provide a quality score which is essentially calculating components of design. Higher the score, higher is the page ranking. The two factors that influence the search engines and of SEO are relevance and popularity.

- There are three major factors that will decide the success of your search engines optimization—on page optimization, off page optimization and violations.
- On page optimization - These are factors that are basically under the control of website owner. Website content, website architecture and HTML are the broad areas of control that supports on page optimization. In website content: quality, research language, originality type of content and problem solution are important. In website architecture: Crawlability, device adaptability non duplication, speed keyword URLs, security, HTML, and meta tags play an important role.
- In off page optimization - Popularity, trust score, sharing, violations, spam, advertising intrusions, keyword stuffing and malpractice (manipulative linking) play a role in page ranking scores.
- Increasingly, the use of SEO is becoming important for the overall success of digital marketing and hence is referred to as integrated digital marketing–IDM (somewhat like IMC (Integrated Marketing Communication).
- Emerging trends in SEO–IDM are video optimization: redefining of paid search, data analysis, bounce rate, site speed, content above the fold, display advertising, including behavioural targeting or retargeted marketing and contextual advertising.
- A search engine results page (SERP) is the page displayed by a web search engine in response to a query by a searcher. The main component of the SERP is the listing of results that are returned by the search engine in response to a keyword query, although the page may also contain other results such as advertisements.
- The results are of two general types, organic search and paid search (i.e., retrieved by the search engine's algorithm) and sponsored (i.e., advertisements). The results are normally ranked by relevance to the query. Each result displayed on the SERP normally includes a title, a link that points to the actual page on the Web and a short description showing where the keywords have matched content within the page for organic results. For sponsored results, the advertiser chooses what to display.
- The key features of an SERP are advertisements, featured snippet, images, videos, knowledge graph, news, product/shopping results and site links.
- SERP provides you with answers for your query in multiple ways and more direct ways. The SERP will provide you with choices of solutions in different formats in order to facilitate your problem solving.
- Search engine marketing (SEM) is a digital marketing strategy used to increase the visibility of a website in search engine results pages (SERP). In the past, both organic search activities (such as SEO) and paid search were called SEM, now SEM refers almost exclusively to paid search that is also referred to as pay per click (PPC).
- Search engine marketing is an important strategy for digital marketing since most consumers research and shop for products online and a majority of new visitors to a website find it through a search engine query. In search engine marketing, advertisers pay only for impressions that result in visitors taking an action (CTA), thus making it an efficient way for a company to spend its marketing budget.
- Search engines use complicated algorithms to ensure that the most relevant results are returned for each search, including location and other available information. In paid search advertising, sponsored ads appear at the top of and on the side of search engine results pages to gain more visibility and prominence than the organic results.
- There are what are called SEM networks that are self-serve operations. The two popular search networks that SEM professionals prefer are Google AdWords and Bing Ads. Google AdWords is actually two networks: Google Search Network and Google Display Network. The first network consists exclusively of search-related websites owned by Google, while the second include other properties such as YouTube and Gmail.
- Search engine reputation management (SERM) is about maintaining a good online reputation. If right steps are taken, reputation can be protected and a strong brand be maintained.
- Key factors in SERM are monitoring reputation, optimizing search engine results pages (SERPs), using social media, listening to customer, transparency and taking responsibility.
- Thus, online reputation management is difficult and not easy. Better reputation equals better sales, better revenue and thus a healthy bottom line. It requires a constant vigilance and an awareness of what is being said about the enterprise. The organization (through competent and committed employees) should be committed to taking ownership of search engine results and the dissatisfied customers, as best as possible.

CLOSING CASE

CASE LET

Mane Attraction

The special cosmetics and hair products categories were exciting for several reasons, the most significant of which was the high margins and high growth rate it promised. Consumers who believe they need special cosmetics or hair products do not mind spending that little bit extra for the emotional reassurance these products provided.

Mane Attraction was an online retailer of special cosmetics and hair products. It was one of the few companies that had understood this consumer and developed a retail environment especially for her. Recognizing that they had chosen a segment where the consumer is picky, the company had taken special care:

1. The range of products available on their site was vast, so consumers were assured of finding something.
2. Online retailing simplified the shopping experience, and the certainty of available stocks.
3. The consumer—already known to be picky and choosy—could shop at her convenience, adding to her retail experience.

Mane Attraction had everything planned out well and could only succeed. After two years in the business, this is how their numbers looked:

Parameter	Monthly Average
Visitors to site	8500+
Traffic from organic search	6000+ (70% of visitors to site)
Conversions	<2%
Revenue	Rs. 10 lakhs

While there was scope to increase visitor numbers and traffic from organic search, Mane attraction believed the low-hanging fruit was in increasing conversions. This could be done through discounts, promotions etc., since that is simplest way to convince a consumer hesitant to make a purchase. However, Mane Attraction wanted to ensure it hadn't missed a strategic opportunity by focusing on immediate sales. There was more to consider:

1. 93% of the traffic was new visitors. In a personal care category like this, consumers don't always make a purchase on their first visit. Even so, 7% of the traffic as returning visitors seemed low.
2. Most of these returning visitors came back to the site within two days of the first visit, not having made a purchase at that time.
3. Visitors returning after a longer gap were invariably repeat buyers. Encouraging, but insufficient in number.
4. 70% of visits to site from organic search indicated that new visitors were likely to be shopping around.
5. Different pages on the site had performed differently in terms of
   a. Share of visitors (new and returning)
   b. Bounce rates
   c. Conversion rates
6. Some pages drew high consumer interest in the product(s) featured. These were
   a. Pages with high share of new visitors.
   b. Pages with low bounce rates.
7. Recognizing that consumers would search for specific products at the first level and then specific brands, Mane Attraction had already developed display ads, focused on the main product groups. These covered:
   a. Hair colouring
   b. Hair Styling
   c. Hair maintenance
   d. Hair repair
   e. Cosmetics
   f. Accessories

With all this information, Mane Attraction sensed that returning visitors **might present** a **bigger** opportunity for conver**sion vs. increasing conversions** from all visitors. **Suddenly promotions and** dis**counts** were not the only **answers.**

Case Questions

1. If you were to advice Mane Attraction to double the number of returning visitors to 15% (from 7% now), what would you do?
2. What additional analysis would you carry out?

REVIEW QUESTIONS

1. What is inbound marketing and what is its relevance in website planning and development?
2. What is the difference between website and a landing page?
3. What are the parameters for website benchmarking?
4. What is a search engine and what parameters are important for a search engine?
5. What is SEO and what are the major factors that determine the success of SEO?
6. What are the emerging trends in SEO?
7. What is SERP? What are the key features of SERP?
8. What is SEM and how does it work?
9. What are SEM networks? Name one of them that you are familiar with.
10. What is SRM, what is its importance and which are key factors in SERM?

ACTIVITY QUESTIONS

1. Make the social group created in Chapter 4 assignment, a Product or Service with the same name and create a web page starting with a wire frame.
2. For the product or service thus created, design a landing page for the social media campaign.

KEY TERMS

AIMLA
Algorithm
Back link
Crawler
Conversion Centered Design (CCD):
Google Adwords
Googlebot
HTML
Implied Link
Index
Key Word
Knowledge graph
Load time
Meta tags
On page optimization
Off Page optimization
Organic search
Paid search
Page link
Platform
POEM
Portal
SEM
SEO
SERM or ORM
SERP
Site map
Snippets
SOP
Trust score
UI
URL
UX

REFERENCES

1. https://unbounce.com/conversion-centered-design/.
2. http://patft.uspto.gov/netacgi/nph-Parser?Sect1=PTO2&Sect2=HITOFF&p=1&u=%2Fnetahtml%2FPTO%2Fsearch-adv.htm&r=1&f=G&l=50&d=PALL&S1=08682892&OS=PN/08682892&RS=PN/08682892.
3. https://searchenginewatch.com/2017/09/27/the-last-word-on-fred-from-googles-gary-illyes/.
4. https://www.vendasta.com/blog/online-reputation-management-stats.

ADDITIONAL SUGGESTED READING

1. Carroll, D. (2012). *United breaks guitars*. Hay House, Inc.
2. Chaffey, D., & Ellis-Chadwick, F. (2012). *Digital marketing: strategy, implementation and practice* (Vol. 5). Harlow: Pearson.
3. Corcoran, S. (2009). Defining earned, owned and paid media. *Forrester Research, 16*.
4. Davis, H. (2006). *Search engine optimization*. "O'Reilly Media, Inc.".
5. Gupta Sunil and Davin Joseph (2015) Digital Marketing Harvard Business Publishing
6. Langville, A. N., & Meyer, C. D. (2011). *Google's PageRank and beyond: The science of search engine rankings*. Princeton University Press.
7. Marker, M. Online Reputation Management.
8. McCracken, D. D., & Wolfe, R. J. (2004). *User-centered website development: A human-computer interaction approach* (pp. 1-305). Upper Saddle River: Prentice Hall.
9. Teixeira, T., & Kornfeld, L. (2013). Managing Online Reviews on TripAdvisor - Harvard Business Review case.
10. Wilde, T., Morton, K. D., Lobacheva, Y., Zinovieva, N., & Meteer, M. (2012). *U.S. Patent No. 8,312,022*. Washington, DC: U.S. Patent and Trademark Office.

CHAPTER 6

WEB ANALYTICS

CHAPTER OBJECTIVES

After reading this chapter, you will be able to

- Assess web analytics as a technique and a tool
- Analyze the criticality of web analytics for businesses
- Understand the use of web analytics tools to study patterns of audience, acquisition, behaviour, and conversion
- Explain the use of data segmentation to analyze various layers of website traffic
- Define dashboard metrics and conversion tactics from goal setting to funnelling conversions and A/B testing methods
- Discuss social media analytics tools

OPENING CASE LET

CONVERSIONS VS. CLICKS

Advertisers who have discovered pay-per-click (PPC) advertising overnight become evangelists of 'digital advertising', virtuously declaring the control they have over their budgets and the ability to measure the 'return on investment' on their advertising spends. True, control and measurability, turbo-charge the realized value of advertising, but, as usual, the enthusiasm needs to be tempered with a dose of reality.

Typically, advertisers evaluate the RoI on the cost they incur per 'click'. PPC advertisers pay only for the click an online advertisement generates. Implicit in this are two assumptions–one, only those interested in the advertisement will click on the advertisement, and hence are likely to be warmer prospects than those who only 'see' the advertisement; two, all the clicks that are generated actually generate an evaluation of the offer conveyed in the advertisement, whether a transaction or a proposition. These two relate directly to the user action on the advertisement.

No such thing as an average CPC

Intuitively, it stands to reason that the propensity of an individual desiring to transact is greater among those clicking on a digital communication than those who do not. In a general sense, this is probably right too.

However, CPC, whether being bid or being bought, is typically computed on the average click-through-rate (CTR) of digital advertising. Thus, if CTR can be improved, CPC can be brought down.

In most buying situations though, the seller determines CPC based on their metric of average CTR. However, where the media selection is right, the CTR of the campaign may be higher than the metric the seller determines. In such an event, it might actually be more profitable for the advertiser to buy impressions rather than clicks, since, then the actual CPC is likely to be lower than what is being offered by the media seller.

All clicks are not made equal

In a campaign for a real estate company, automated bid tools showed the following three scenarios as promising opportunities for advertising:

Scenarios	Index of ...		
	CPC bid/ click	Clicks	Cost
1	100	100	100
2	100	95	95
3	97	73	71

On the face of it, all three scenarios are attractive since they had about the same CPC and the variability in the number of clicks between the scenarios is low. In fact, were the marketers to choose between the scenarios only on the basis of cost, chances are that Scenario 3 would be selected.

Scenario	Index of ...				
	CPC bid/click	Clicks	Cost	Conversions	Cost per conversion
1	100	100	100	100	100
2	100	95	95	500	19
3	97	73	71	100	71

However, the agency decided to do a test run across the three scenarios to assess how the impact would be on conversions for each of the plans. These results with business metrics added to them were as follows:

As is apparent from the above, conversions from the clicks generated in Scenario 2 are five times as many as from the other two scenarios. Consequently, the cost per conversion is a fraction of the cost incurred in the other two scenarios. Thus, from a business point-of-view, i.e. the actual addition to business value, the second scenario is far more attractive than the other two scenarios. Thus, a decision on a mere CPC basis may be good on the face of it , but is likely to have a negative impact on the bottom line.

Clearly, buying clicks merely on the cost-per-click metric without the attendant business value is a chimera that gives a false assurance that money is being well spent, when in actual fact, it is not.

Case Questions

1. Why do advertisers prefer PPC or pay per click?
2. What is the downside of PPC?

INTRODUCTION

Analytics is a noun and the dictionary meaning of analytics is "the systematic computational analysis of data or statistics". According to Wikipedia, "Analytics is the discovery, interpretation, and communication of meaningful patterns in data. Especially valuable in areas rich with recorded information, analytics relies on the simultaneous application" (https://en.wikipedia.org/wiki/Analytics).

WHAT WEB ANALYTICS IS

In the literature, we find several descriptions and explanations for web analytics and it will be difficult to find a single definition of web analytics. The easily understood and uncomplicated description would be—Web analytics is a detailed methodological study of online and offline patterns and trends. It is a technique that you can employ to collect, measure, report, and analyze your website data. It is normally carried out to analyze the performance of a website and optimize its web usage. Web analytics is used to track key metrics and analyze website visitors' activity and traffic flow. The data thus derived is used to generate reports and strategize campaigns.

The History of Web Analytics

Some of the important milestones in web analytics available from literature are

- **1990 – The Birth of The World Wide Web**
  Sir Tim Berners-Lee created the first dialogue of HTML code between the web user and the web server, i.e., the World Wide Web on the eve of Christmas in 1990. This invention led to the creation of Internet as we experience it today.
- **1993 – Log Files, Creation of Webtrends**
  At the early stages, the Internet was limited to mostly static pages with text and links. Therefore, when a page received a hit by a visitor, it was assumed that they were engaging with the entire contents of the page. With the advent of web technology, website owners became aware of this metric. Thus, log files were born. The invention of log file analysis paved a path that led to the beginning of web analytics for commercial purposes, and so WebTrends was introduced to the world in 1993.
- **1995 – Creation of Analog**
  Dr. Stephen Turner created Analog in 1995. It was the first log file analysis program to be completely free of charge. Analog made the reports generated through log files that were easily understandable by online business owners unlike the previous version of web analytics that could be decoded only by tech teams.
- **1996 – Birth of Hit Counters**
  In 1996, hit counter service came into the picture. Web-Counter was the first. This sparked the trend of odometer-style hit counters being displayed on website landing pages. Gradually, Accrue, Omniture, and WebSideStory were founded.
- **1997 – Javascript Tags**
  As websites started becoming a mixed combination of visuals and other such elements besides text and links, Javascript started

Log file: In computing, a log file is a file that records either events that occur in an operating system or other software runs, or messages between different users of a communication software.
Hit counter: A web counter or hit counter is a computer software program that indicates the number of visitors, or hits, a particular webpage has received. Once set up, these counters will be incremented by one every time the web page is accessed in a web browser.
Javascript Tags: The <script> tag is used to define a client-side script (JavaScript).
Web analytics: Web analytics is the process of analyzing the behaviour of visitors to a website. The use of web analytics is said to enable a business to attract more visitors, retain or attract new customers for goods or services, or to increase the dollar volume each customer spends.
Web server: A webserver is a program that uses HTTP (Hypertext Transfer Protocol) to serve the files that form web pages to users, in response to their requests, which are forwarded by their computers' HTTP clients. Dedicated computers and appliances may be referred to as webservers as well.

becoming a more popular and reliable method of data accumulation to generate reports on varied web traffics and trends. The monopoly still prevails in the web analytics market.

> **Web Analytics Association (WAA):** The Web Analytics Association (WAA) was founded to promote a global understanding of web analytics. The WAA strives to connect and empower an informed and involved web analytics community.

- **2004 – Creation of the Web Analytics Association (WAA)**
  By the beginning of the 21st century, web analytics was already established as the most important tool for web. The Web Analytics Association (WAA), now known as the Digital Analytics Association, was born.
- **2005 – Urchin Analytics Acquired by Google to Become Google Analytics**
  In March 2005, Google acquired Urchin and the world was introduced to Google Analytics only on November 14, 2005. When Google launched it, the service was free and eventually, it became the most widely used web analytics service in the market.
- **2012 – Universal Analytics**
  Seven years and millions of users later, Google launched Universal Analytics. This new version allowed tracking of users across multiple devices and platforms through user IDs. The feature also enabled monitoring of offline making customer data richer with the addition of demographic and other such useful information.
- **2016 – Machine Learning on Mobile**
  With the advent of analytics, mobile app analytics became the next logical progression. Machine learning into its app analytics gave marketers smarter insights about their customers showing more relevant metrics, with real-time monitoring. This eventually became a turning point in the analytics industry.

Importance of Web Analytics

Using web analytics, we can:

- Assess web content issues
- Derive an accurate perspective of website trends
- Monitor web traffic and user flow
- Demonstrate goals acquisition
- identify potential keywords
- Identify segments to be improved
- Identify sources of traffic

Web Analytics Purpose and Process

To quote W Edward Deming, the father of quality revolution, " In god we trust – All others bring Data". This is one of the major reasons for any business to adapt to web analytics. Analytics is used to optimize the website in order to provide better user experience resulting in better business. It gives the marketer an access to metric-driven report to measure visitors' activity on the website.

The process of web analytics follows and flows as shown below:

- Setting business goals
- Tracking the goal achievement
- Setting up the key performance indicators (KPI)
- Collection of relevant data
- Extracting insights and analyzing data
- Test alternatives
- Based on either data analysis or website testing, implement insights

ANALYTICS TOOLS

For an effective analytics process and flow, there are various tools that are available in the market that offer businesses the much needed insights. These tools are inexpensive and easy to use and have a plethora of useful insights.

Google Analytics

Google analytics was launched on November 14, 2005 after it acquired the company Urchin Software (https://www.sibiaanalytics.com/blog/google-analytics-11-years-later). In 13 years, it has become the most commonly used freemium tool by website owners. It provides a detailed statistics of the web traffic and enables you to track and measure visitors, traffic sources, goals, conversions and several other metrics. A brief history is given in Table 6.1.

Table 6.1

YEAR	MILESTONES
2005	Birth - Acquisiton of Urchin Analytics
2007	Synchronous Code for Google Analytics Released
2008	Advanced Segments and Custom Reporting
2009	Analytics API Released
2009	Intelligent Events Released
2009	Event Tracking Released
2009	Asynchronous Code for Google Analytics Released
2010	Google Analytics iOS SDK Released
2011	Real Time Reports Released
2011	Release of Google Analytics Premium
2011	Multi-Channel Funnel (MCF) Reports Released
2012	Content Experiment Released
2012	Data Import Released
2012	GA Android V2 SDK Released
2012	Urchin Discontinued
2012	Display Advertising support Extended
2013	Universal Analytics Launched
2013	Attribution Modelling Released
2014	Enhanced eCommerce Released
2016	New GA UI Launched
2016	Google Data Studio Launched
2016	GA Demo Account Introduced
2017	GA Intelligence Reports Released

(Source – Literature)

Why Google Analytics?

Google Analytics is one of the most popular tools used in digital marketing as this tool provides a complete insight about the visitors visiting and interacting with your site.

There are a plethora of reasons why Google Analytics is more preferable than any other analytics tool at the moment (https://www.logit.net/blog/). The top 10 being

1. Easy to use
2. Essential to understand where your customers are coming from
3. Customizable reports
4. Insights into visitors
5. Real-time visitor tracking
6. Automated data collection
7. Easy integration with third party tools
8. Extensive help documentation
9. Large Google community
10. (most importantly) It's Free!

The USP of Google Analytics

The customizable report feature is definitely a boon to any marketer and is one of the main USPs of Google Analytics. The software generates reports on the basis of a marketer's requirements mainly focusing on:

- Audience analysis
- Acquisition analysis
- Behaviour analysis
- Conversion analysis

Audience Analysis

Understanding the audience of your communication is important for any business irrespective of the industry they are in. Audience analysis on Google Analytics provides a thorough understanding of the audience, irrespective of the business. This enables the business to customize their business practices/offerings and increase customer retention. Google Analytics gives you an overview of the audience who visits your site along with their session history, page-views, bounce rate, etc. The audience can be tracked as shown in Exhibit 6.1, on various metrics, like:

- Age and gender
- Affinity reach
- Market segmentation
- Language and location
- New and returning visitors and their frequency
- Browsers and operating systems
- Mobile devices used
- Benchmarking channels, locations, and devices. Benchmarking allows you to compare your metrics with other related industries.
- Flow of user activity and engagement on the website

Acquisition Analysis

Acquisition analysis is another important analysis for a business that is advertising on several platforms at the same time. This analysis determines the various sources from where the web traffic originates. Acquisition analysis enables identifying the following:

- Insights on traffic from various channels, mediums or referrals
- Traffic from paid campaigns on Google and social media
- Traffic from search engines
- Information on triggered landing pages and geographical summary
- Social media traffic tracking
- Information and insights about plug-ins and their respective traffic

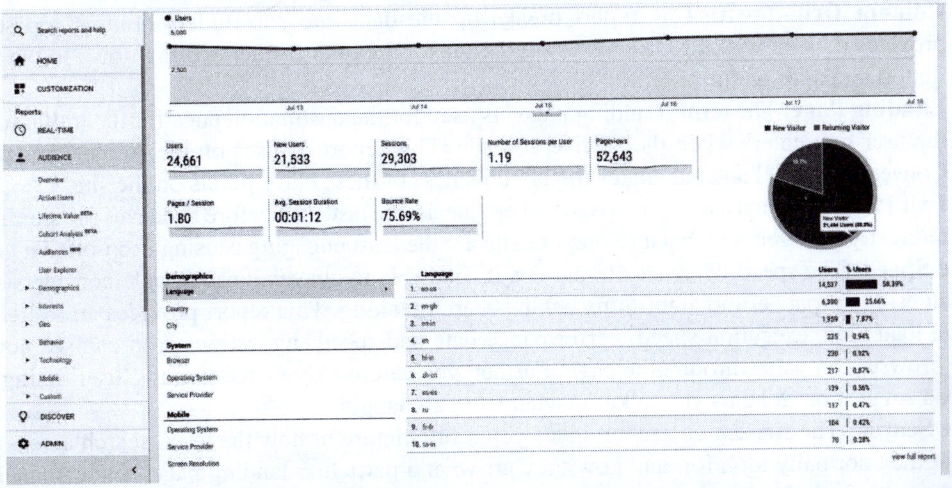

Source : Screen Shot Audience Analysis (GA)

Exhibit 6.1 Audience Analysis- Google Analytics

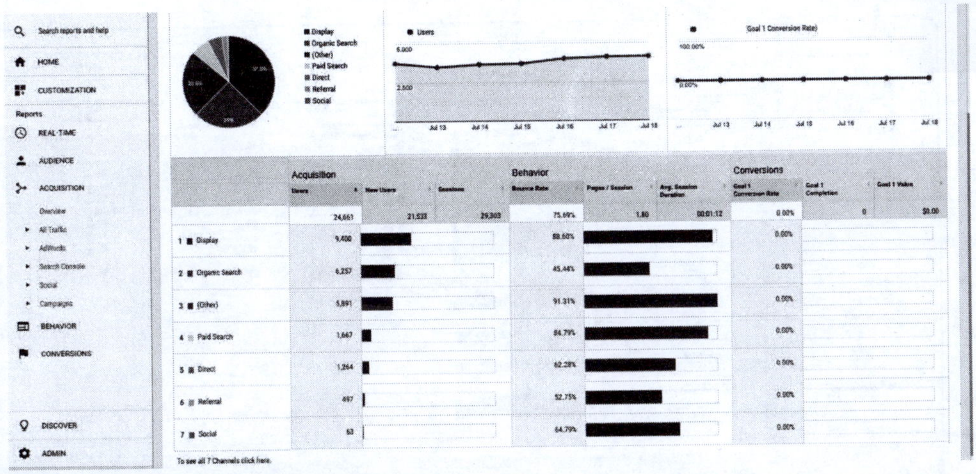

Source : Screen Shot Acquisition Analysis (GA)

Exhibit 6.2 Acquisition Analysis - Google Analytics

Behaviour Analysis

Behaviour analysis monitors users' activities on a website such as the most popular pages of a site or the bounce rate of each of these pages, the average time users spend on your site. The behavioural data may be broadly classified under the following four segments:

- **Site Content:** This report focuses on the site content and analyzes the same. It provides detailed interaction and insights on various important metrics like page views, unique page views, average time spent per page, number of entrances on a page, the page's bounce rate and exit percentage. It shows how many pages were viewed. Content drill-down is breaking up data into sub-folders.
  a. **Content Drill-down:** This report breaks up the data into sub-folders holding top sections. It provides data on which top sections are the most important further drilling down to the individual important pages on the site.
  b. **Landing Page:** The term 'Landing page" is used for the destination page for the traffic from where the user first enters when they arrive at a site. This report focuses on the Acquisition-Behaviour-Conversion model and calculates the effectiveness of these entry points on the site.
  c. **Exit Page:** Exit pages are those pages where the user is last seen before he leaves the site. This report indirectly tells you which pages on your site are the least engaging causing drop-offs on your site.
- **Site Speed:** The speed of a website plays a pivotal role in conversions. Google considers site-speed as an essential part of the algorithms behind search ranking. This report provides an overall view on page load time, execution speed, performance data and speed suggestions. You can see how quickly the browser can parse through the page. Further, you can measure page timings, user timings, and get speed suggestion. It helps you to know where you are lagging.
- **Site Search:** The site search section gives you a full picture of how the users search across your site, what they normally look for, and how they arrive at a particular landing page. You can analyze what they search for before landing on your website.
- **Events:** Events are visitors' actions within your site. These actions can be traced independently. The events report gives a complete analysis of the occurrences of such events like the most occurred event, number of occurrences, breakdown of pages where they occurred, the activities of an user before the event, i.e., the event flow. Examples of events are downloads, sign up, log-in, etc. Exhibit 6.3 provides a typical screenshot.

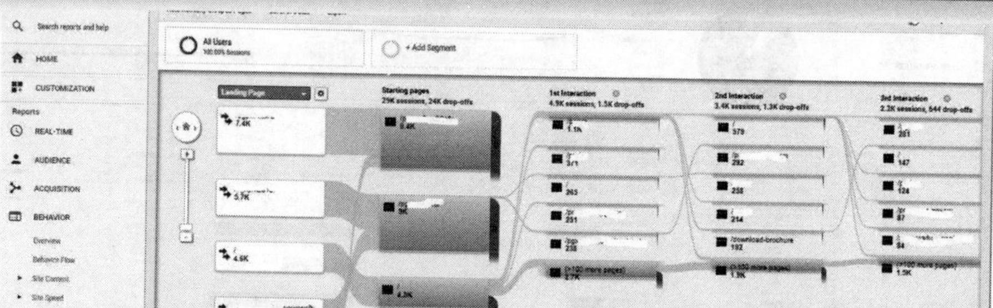

Source : Screen Shot Behavior Analysis (GA)

Exhibit 6.3 Behaviour Analysis - Google Analytics

Conversion Analysis

Conversion is a goal completion or a transaction by a user on your website that is important to a business' success. The conversion can be in the form of a download, sign-up, checkout, add-to-cart, etc. (event referred to earlier). The conversion analysis ultimately reports your website's overall business performance.

The conversion analysis provides a range of reports that helps in determining the various aspects of a business like:

- **Goals** – Goal can be defined as metrics that result in a profitable activity on the website. The goals need to be customized to track conversions. Each time a goal is achieved, a conversion is added. The goal analysis gives insight about various important metrics like:
  a. Goal URLs
  b. Reverse goal path
  c. Goal flow
- **eCommerce** – eCommerce analytics lets you derive at important data product performance, sale performance, transactions, billing amounts, purchase time and more. It gives a clear picture on the returns of your marketing dollars.
  eCommerce analytics brings into light various important aspects like:
  a. Product performance
  b. Sales performance
  c. Transactions
  d. Time taken to purchase
- **Multi-channel funnels (MCF)** – Funnels are the steps a user takes on a site to complete the goals. Usually, a conversion is credited to the last campaign or page or ad the user interacted with. But what were the webpages, searches or ads that the user indulged in prior to the conversion? MCF report provides details of webpages, searches or ads the user indulged in.
  For example, a user looked up a query on Google search page and landed on a particular website, but did not convert. Later on, he decided to buy the product and directly typed the website's name and made a purchase. All these steps can be traced on MCF.
  An MCF report gives insights on the following data:
  a. Assisted Conversion – In assisted conversion, one can find which channel has assisted the highest number of conversions.
  b. Top Conversion Path – Top conversion path report identifies which channel the user first interacted with prior to walking directly through the website and making a purchase.
  c. Time Lag Report – This report gives insights on how long did it take for a user/visitor to convert. It gives accurate information on the length of a business' online sales cycle.
  d. Path Length Report – This report shows the number of interactions an user/visitor indulged in prior to making a conversion.
- **Attribution** Different channels drive traffic to the site at different point of time during the conversion process. A few might drive traffic in the beginning while other in the middle and some towards the end. That does not mean only the channels that bring the last clicks should be considered as profitable channels. This is indicated by attribution modelling in Google Analytics.
  An attribution model is a set of rules that defines how credit for conversion goals gets attributed to each interaction during the conversion process.
  The various kinds of default attribution models are:
  a. Last interaction – This model gives 100% credit of the conversion to the last channel used by the user before converting.
  b. Last non-direct click – The credit for conversion is given to the last channel used by the visitor except when that channel is direct traffic.

c. Last AdWords click - The entire credit of the conversion is given to the most recent AdWord clicked upon by the user.
d. First interaction - 100% of the conversion credit is given to the first channel interacted by the user.
e. Linear – The conversion credit is divided equally amongst all the channels used by the user prior to the conversion.
f. Time decay – This attribution model provides a major chunk of the conversion credit to the channels that were most recently used by the visitor and the lesser portion goes to channels in the lookback window.
g. Position based – This attribution created a hybrid of the first and the last interaction models.

A screenshot of attribution model is shown in Exhibit 6.4:

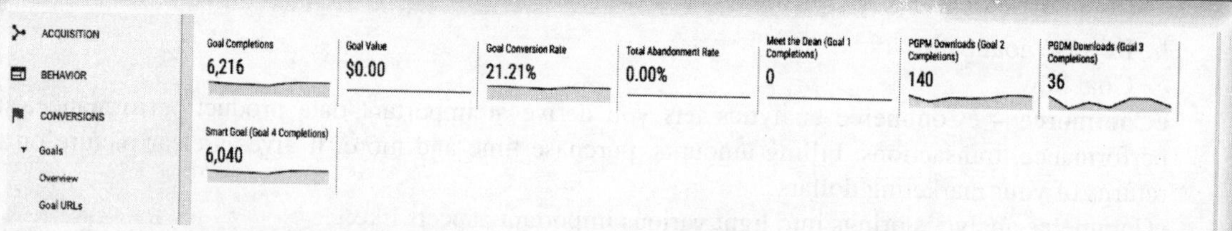

Source : Conversions Overview (GA)

Exhibit 6.4 Screenshot of Attribution Model

SEGMENTATION

A segment is the subset of your analytics data. Segmentation is the process that segregates the data to find the actionable items. For example, you can categorize your entire website traffic data as one segment for a "Country," or for a specific "City". Another segment can be those who visited particular web pages or interacted with specific parts of your site.

Segmenting helps you isolate and analyze subsets of data based upon a user's actions on your site. Segmentation can also be used to form audiences for your paid campaigns. For example, you can use segmentation isolate users who added a product to the cart but did not make a purchase. This audience can be used for the purpose of remarketing.

Data segmentation is very helpful in examining website traffic and respond to the component trends in the same. For a website, you can segment total traffic according to acquisition, goals, and channels. Following are the types of segmentation:

- **Organic Traffic** – It categorizes the organic traffic of the website. You can derive insights on which search engine works the best for your business and what the top keywords are.
- **Referrals Traffic** – This segment gives you the total traffic derived out of referrals on the website.
- **Direct Traffic** – This segment helps you identify the traffic that landed your website directly by typing the URL in Search.
- **Social Traffic** – With the social segment, you can analyze social traffic and get insights on which social media platform (Facebook, G+, Twitter, Pinterest, StumbleUpon, Reddit, etc.) is driving traffic to your website. Such data can be used to strategize social media campaigns.
- **Paid Traffic** – This segment captures traffic through paid channels.
- **Channels** - The channel source of those visits; including Direct, Referral, Social Media, Organic Search, etc.

DASHBOARDS

Dashboards are at-a-glance views of the trends of a business' key performance indicators. They provide a graphical representation of important data encapsulated in a single space.

Dashboard Implementation

Widget: An application, or a component of an interface, that enables a user to perform a function or access a service.

Google Analytics allows you to customize a dashboard as per your requirements. You can further customize these dashboards by creating widgets. Representative screenshots are shown in Exhibits 6.5 and 6.6.

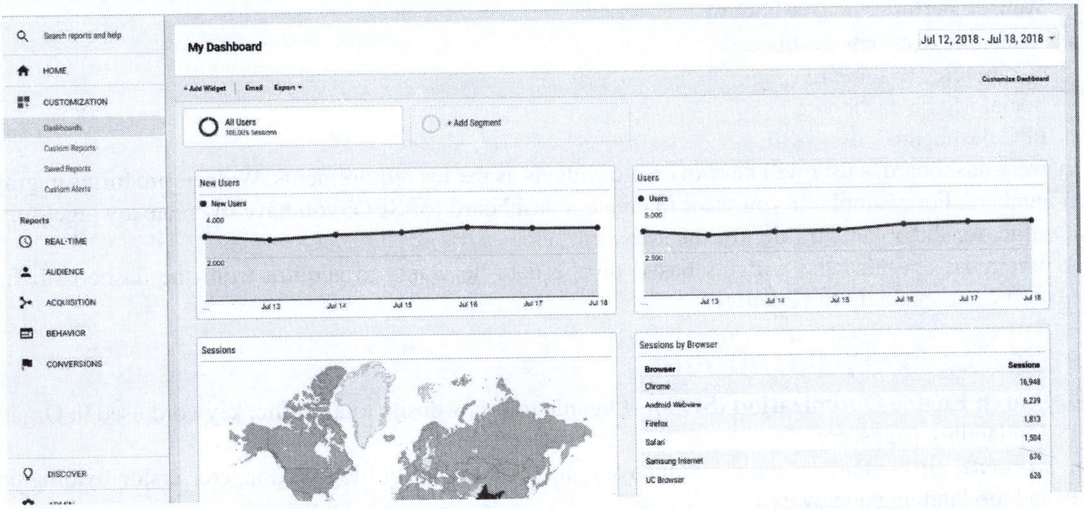

Source : Screenshot - Segmentation (GA)

Exhibit 6.5 Dashboard

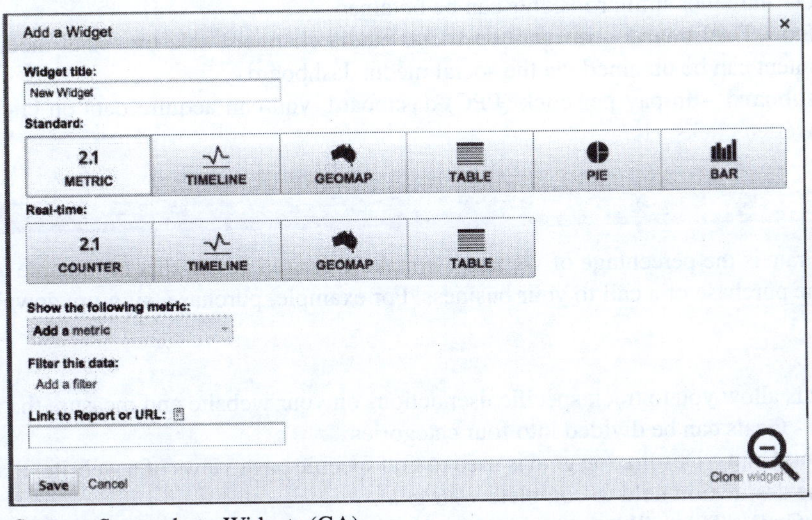

Source : Screenshot - Widgets (GA)

Exhibit 6.6 Widgets

Types of Dashboards

Each Analytics account can contain up to 50 shared dashboards per view. And each Analytics view can have a maximum of 20 private dashboards per user. Although Google Analytics allows a user to customize dashboards, there are a few dashboards that are most commonly used.

- SEO dashboard
- Content dashboard
- Website performance dashboard
- Real-time overview dashboard
- eCommerce dashboard
- Social Media dashboard
- PPC dashboard

In every dashboard, a user will have to create widgets as per his requirements. Widgets are forms in graphs or in numbers. For example, if you want to create a dashboard for SEO, you have to create a widget for the total traffic, for the organic traffic, for the keywords, etc.

A user must optimize the widgets based on the data he wants to acquire from the dashboard. Each dashboard can contain up to 12 widgets.

Metrics for Every Dashboard

- **Search Engine Optimization (SEO)** – Organic traffic, website total traffic, keyword used in Organic, Top landing pages, etc.
- **Content** – In content dashboard, you have to monitor traffic for blog section, conversion by blog post, and top landing page by exit.
- **Website Performance Dashboard** – Average page load time, mobile page load time, page load time by browser, and website server response time.
- **Real Time Overview Dashboard** – In real time overview, you can set a widget for real time traffic, real time traffic source, and real time traffic landing pages.
- **eCommerce Dashboard** – On an ecommerce dashboard, total traffic, landing by products, total sale by products and other similar insights can be obtained.
- **Social Media Dashboard** – Insights on social media channels, sale by social media, most socially shared content can be obtained via the social media dashboard.
- **PPC Dashboard** – In pay per click (PPC) dashboard, you can acquire data on clicks, impressions, CTR, converted clicks, etc.

CONVERSION

The conversion rate is the percentage of visitors who take a desired action that is valuable to your business, such as an online purchase or a call to your business. For example, purchase, sign-up, download, etc.

Goals

In analytics, goals allow you to track specific user actions on your website and measure the rate of success.

Goals Types - Goals can be divided into four categories:

- **Destination Goal** – Destination goal is used to find specific page views of a website. Place a destination URL in the destination field to complete your goal.
- **Duration Goal** – This will help to calculate the visitor engagement with the help of duration goal. If someone spends more than 10 minutes or longer on the webpage, then the goal is completed.

- **Event Goals** – Event goals are helpful for tracking visitor interaction with your event on the site. You should include at least one event to create this goal.
- **Pages/session Goal** – This will help to measure the visitor engagement with pages/session goal. Will load 5 page views/session counts as goal complete and can analyze how many goals are completed.

Exhibit 6.7 presents a screenshot of conversions against individual goals.

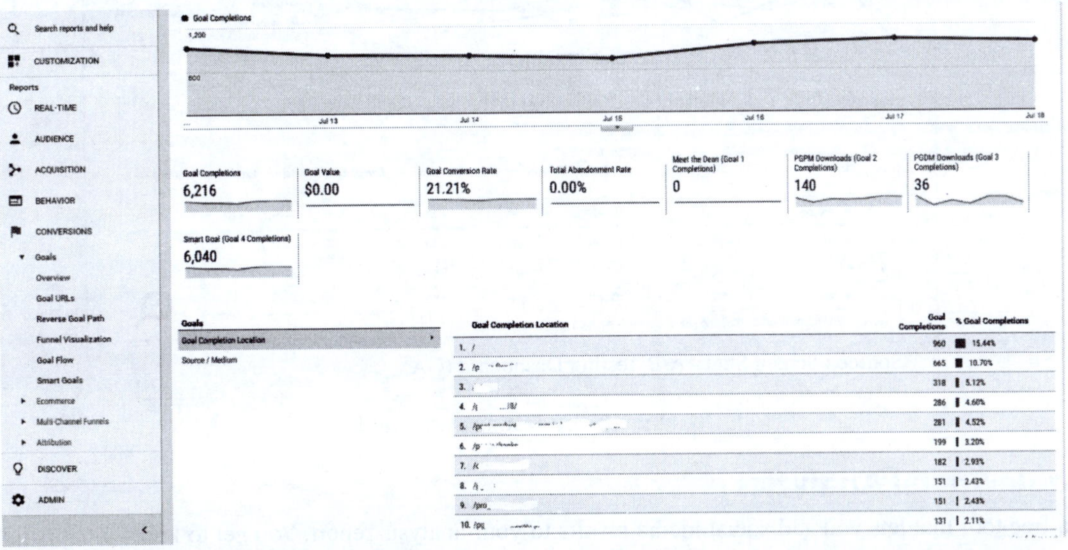

Source : Conversion Mapping Against Goals (GA)

Exhibit 6.7 Conversion Mapping

A/B TESTING

A/B testing is comparing between two versions of a web page to see which one gives better results. This A/B testing can build a huge difference in the marketing efforts especially ecommerce business.

> **Web page:** A hypertext document connected to the World Wide Web.

eCommerce sites apply A/B testing on products to find out which product has the potential to earn more revenue. And also this will be useful for AdWords campaign manager running two ads for the same campaign in order to know which of them works well.

A/B testing permits to extract additional data of your traffic. A/B testing will be run on headings, paragraphs, testimonials, call to action button, links, images, social icons, and awards and badges.

Exhibit 6.8 shows an A/B testing dashboard.

SOCIAL MEDIA ANALYTICS

Social media analytics involve gathering statistics from all the social media platforms to make decision about your business' ups and downs. Social analytics predicts customer's behaviour; find out business trends, and build plan to improve online reputation. Analytics metrics will help you identify the primary influencers within specific network channels. Let's find out the most popular social media analytics tools.

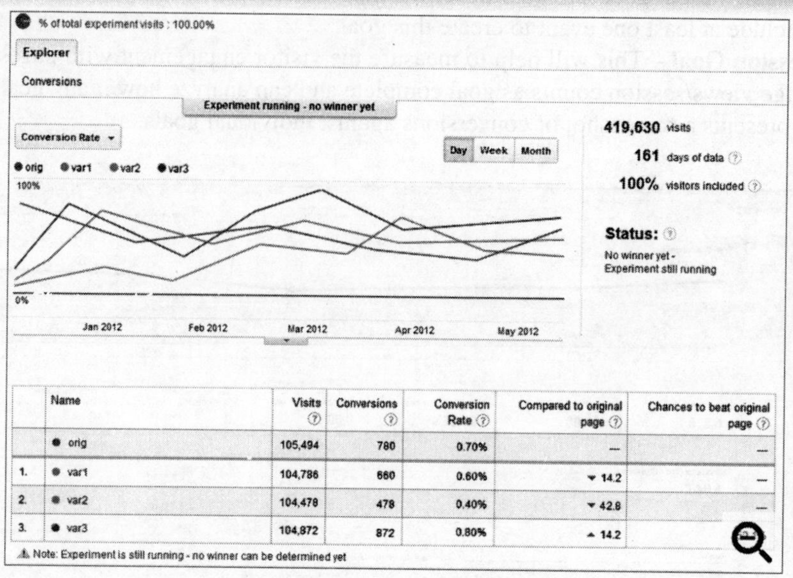

Source : Screen Shot - A/B Testing Dashboard (GA)

Exhibit 6.8 A/B Testing Dashboard

Google Social Analytics

It is a free tool that lets you add social media results to your analysis report. You get to know what is in air about your business, how many people interacted with your website through social media and how many liked and shared your content.

Sum All

It combines Twitter, Facebook, and Google Plus into one dashboard to give you an overall view of what people are talking about you on social media. Refer Exhibit 6.9 for visualization.

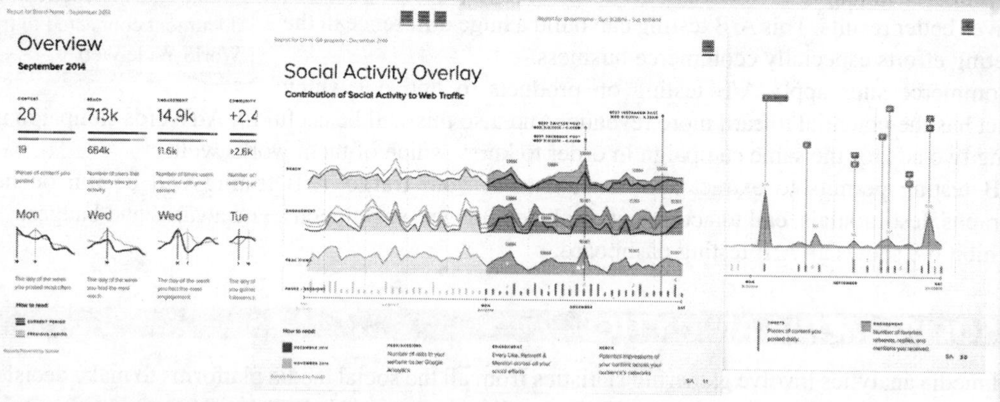

Source : Screenshot Social Media Analytics

Exhibit 6.9 Sum All

Google Plus

Google Plus creates an opportunity to connect with a community of customers and fans. It has a significant impact on SEO and search traffic volume. Google+ Pages created for various businesses through Google My Business make it easy for customers to find and connect with your business. Google My Business uses Search, Maps, and Google Plus to make your brand more visible in local search results.

Facebook Insights

Facebook Insights tool was designed to assist marketers know more about the target audiences, including aggregate information about geography, demographics, purchase behaviour and more. To get business information from Facebook Insights, page for your business is required to be set up. It provides you with the information about demographics, page likes, location and language, usage, purchases activity. And also you can see three different groups of people:

- People on Facebook
- People connected to your Page or event
- People in custom audiences you've already created

Exhibit 6.10 provides a screenshot for reference.

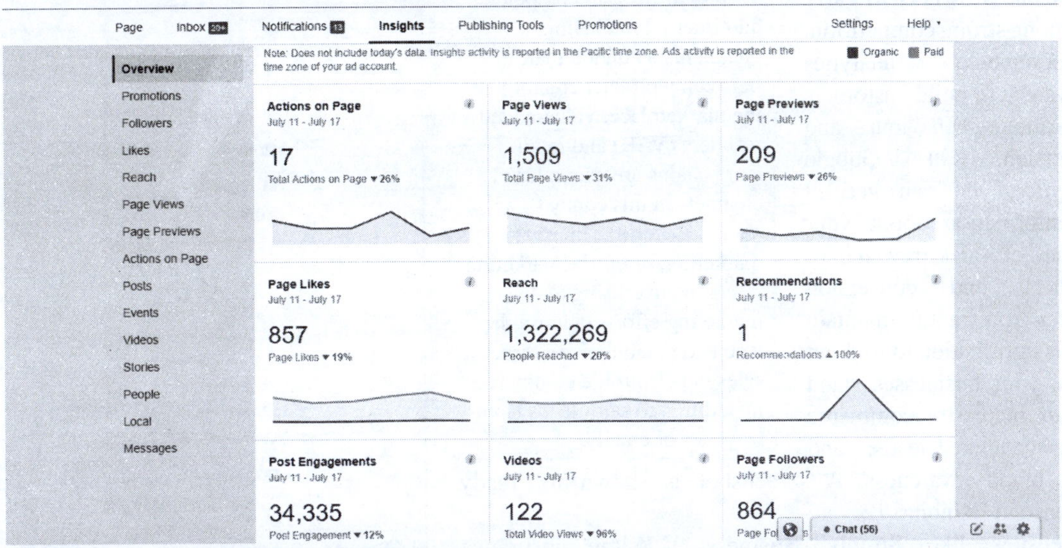

Source : Screen Shot FB Insights- FB Analytics

Exhibit 6.10 Facebook Insights Tool

Twitter Analytics

Twitter Analytics shows you total tweets of the month, followers, un-followers, top tweets, how many impressions of each tweets, engagement status. See Exhibit 6.11.

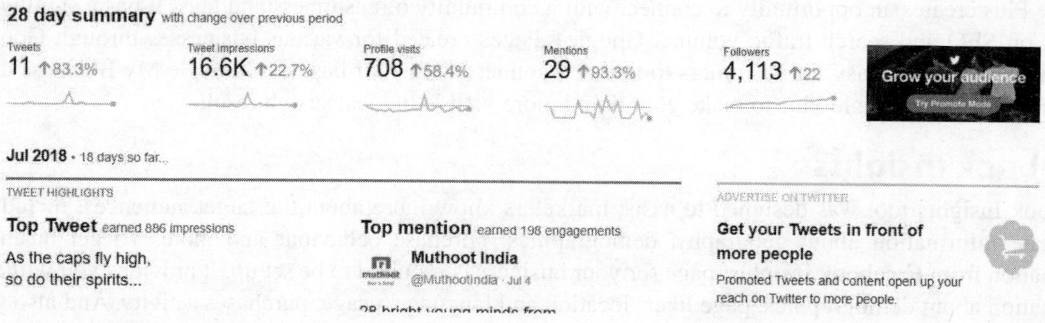

Source : Screenshot Twitter Analytics

Exhibit 6.11 Twitter Analytics

eCommerce Analytics

Web analytics play a key role for business owners to carry on among strong competition.

eCommerce analytics allows you to build customers acquisition, behaviour and conversion. In Google Analytics, you can get all the information about your amount of sales, revenue of products, and conversion sources. You want to maintain all this information to find out where your businesses stand and to increase ecommerce sales, generate leads, and boost brand awareness. A screenshot is shown for ready reference in Exhibit 6.12.

> **Web channels:** In computer and Internet marketing, a channel is a "middleman" between a product creator and the marketplace. Value-added resellers (VAR) and retail store chains are examples of channels in this context.
> **Web marketing:** Internet marketing, or online marketing, refers to advertising and marketing efforts that use the web and email to drive direct sales via electronic commerce, in addition to sales leads from websites or emails.

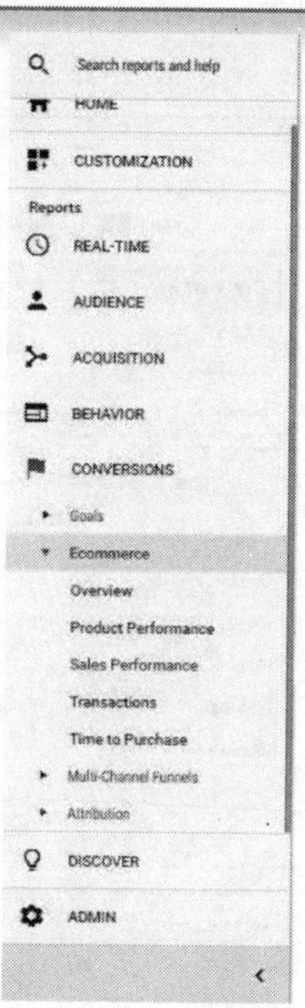

Source : Screen shot eCommerce (GA)

Exhibit 6.12 Google Analytics

Websites like Simply Business U.K.[1](an insurance service provider) and Entrepreneurs.com[2] offer beginners in ecommerce free infographics and tutorials on Google Analytics.

Mobile Analytics

Mobiles have emerged as one of the most significant tools in the past two decades. It changes the way people communicate and innovate. This has led to marketing driven by mobile apps.

> **Mobile Apps:** A mobile app is a computer program designed to run on a mobile device such as a phone/tablet or watch.

Mobile apps have proved easy to access and engaging. Webmasters and online business makers need to take support of mobile apps to make their way perfect. Once you are done with making a mobile app, you'll need to acquire new users, engage with them, and earn revenue. For this, you need mobile analytics. It helps marketers to measure their apps better. For example:

- How many people are using your app
- How to optimize user experience
- How to prioritize
- What operating system to focus on
- How to visualize navigation path, etc.

For reference a screenshot is given in Exhibit 6.13.

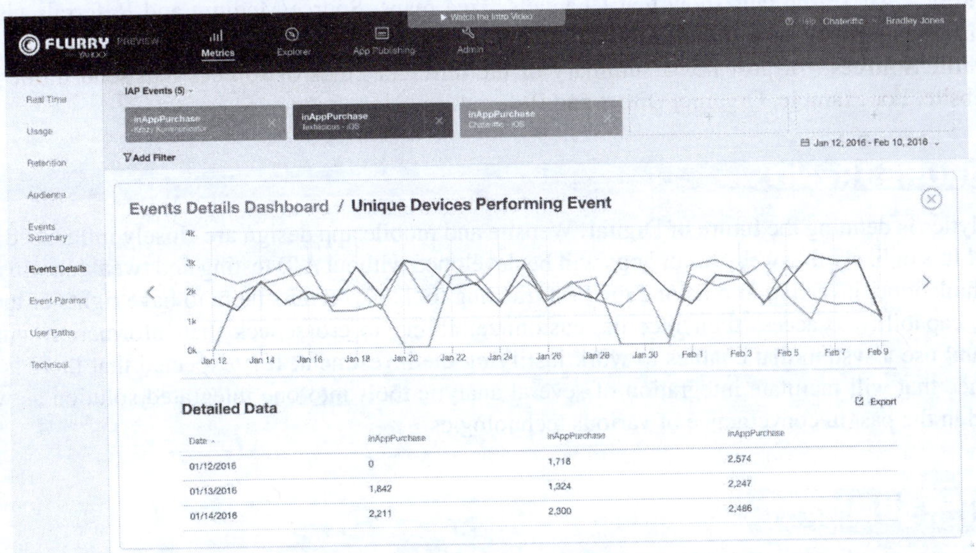

Source : Screenshot Mobile Analytics Platform

Exhibit 6.13 Mobile Analytics

After having understood the basics of web analytics and some of the important tools of web analytics, listed below are some of the important terminologies commonly in use or referred to.

Web Analytics Terminologies

- **Benchmarking** – This insightful tool helps to compare your website performance to previous results, industry trends.
- **Bounce Rate** – Visitors view only website home page and exit the site on that same page.
- **Click** – An amount of clicks on your website through search engines.
- **Conversion** – Conversion rate is the percentage of visitors who buy on the site. For example, purchase, registration, downloads, etc.
- **Direct Traffic** – Visitors who enter directly on your website in the address bar count as direct traffic.
- **Filter** – This will exclude/include particular IP or source from analytics reports.
- **Funnels** –This will help you to calculate conversion rates on specific user behaviours.

- **Goal** – A metric that track the success rate of sales.
- **Impression** – The display of the website results in search engine pages.
- **Keywords** – Keywords that users apply to find your website in search engines.
- **Landing Page** – The first page from where a visitor enters your website.
- **New Visitor** – The visitor who is visiting for the first time to the website.
- **Organic Traffic** – Traffic which comes from search engines like Google, Yahoo,etc.
- **Paid Traffic** – Traffic which comes from paid advertising like Google Ads, Bing Ads, etc.
- **Page View** – Number of times a visitor landed in page views.
- **Returning Visitor** –If session count is more than 1 time, the session will be defined as "Returning Visitor".
- **Time on Site** – It shows the amount of time that visitor spent on your website.
- **Tracking Code** – A small snippet of code paste into the top or bottom of HTML page.
- **Traffic** – All Traffic tabs show that Channels, Tree maps, Source/Medium and Referrals visitors to your website.
- **Traffic Sources** – It provides a summary of the different kinds of sources that send traffic to your website. For example, Organic, Direct and Referral.

FUTURE TRENDS

Web analytics is defining the future of Digital! Website and mobile app design are closely influenced by web analytics! It is unlikely that websites or apps will be developed without A/B testing and tweaking. Businesses have to think about investing into having the best tracking tool that permits them to have rights of their own statistics, capability to access their records, customize, ability to crosscheck that information with other sources and use a system that enables to work justifying the investment. It is expected that there is a huge white space that will facilitate integration of several analytic tools into one integrated solution as we have witnessed in the past in convergence of various technologies.

CHAPTER SUMMARY

- Web analytics helps provide insight into online/offline patterns and trends of visitors' activity in order to strategically optimize website performance and usage.
- The beginning of web analytics can be traced back to 1990, when Sir Tim Berners-Lee created HTML code for the beginning of Internet.
- The next notable advancement was in 1993, when log files came into existence and laid the corner stone for web analytics. This was enhanced through the creation of Analog in 1995 as that was the first log analysis file given free of cost.
- The innovations in 1996 and 1997 saw the birth of hit counters and JavaScript tags which aided significantly with data collection, and is relevant even today.
- In 2004, with the institution of the Web Analytics Association (now known as Digital Analytics Association), web analytics was established as an essential component for web optimization. Later in 2005, Google launched its very own analytics tool by buying out Urchin and establishing itself across all its products. In 2012, Google launched Universal Analytics to enable ease of collection and transmission of customer data.
- The integration of machine learning into Google Analytics in 2016 has steered the analytics industry on to a higher ground for breakthroughs.
- Web analytics is more than just analyzing customer data for web enhancement, it aids with content development, positioning, identify segments, etc.
- The web analytics process when integrated with a business process aids in a data-driven approach for establishing goals and furthering a business proposition.
- The use of each analytical tool is not only distinct in its function but also crucial to efficaciously monitor each platform that it was created for. The most

commonly used analytics tool by more than 60% of website owners is the Google Analytics tool.

- The four main key areas that Google Analytics enables a better understanding towards are audience analysis, acquisition analysis, behaviour analysis, and conversion analysis. Each component is useful in successful implementation of focussed marketing.
- Segmentation is the process that segregates the data to find the actionable items, and this provides an insight into web traffic based on the parameters of acquisition, goals, and channels.
- Dashboard is an interface showing graphical status of the trends of your business' key performance indicators. Dashboard implementation and appropriate customization through widgets will enable effective and easy interpretation of data. Every dashboard should be stacked with appropriate metric tools to ensure that the data gathered is accurately sorted.
- Tracking of conversions is possible through goal setting, and goals in analytics help measure the rate of success of your web pages. The four important goals that you have to build are destination goal, duration goal, event goal, and page/session goal.
- Funnels act as the passageway for goal completion. The multi-channel funnels report provides an insight into the joint working of marketing channels.
- A/B testing is like running an experiment between two or more pages simultaneously in order to discover which one has the potential to convert more.
- Social media analytics drives business decision making on the popular social media platforms, as this provides a definitive insight into specific network channels. Some popular choices are Google Social Analytics, Sum All, Facebook Insights, Twitter Analytics, etc.
- While ecommerce analytics let you figure out customers' acquisition, users' behaviour, and conversion, mobile analytics measures the traffic and interactions on a mobile app for building mobile-centric marketing strategies.

CLOSING CASE

CASE LET

Long Tail Does Not Mean Scatter Shooting

Digital search marketers often target long tail keywords (LTK) in the misguided belief that more-is-merrier. Nothing can be further from this, particularly, when mobile devices are the dominant content access mode.

The received wisdom is that LTK, because of their low search volume, attracts little competition. Ergo, it is believed that the search advertisement will not vie for positional prominence and hence have the entire audience for the LTK to itself, improving its click-ability. The logic, so far, is impeccable. However, the search for LTK is also likely a highly refined search, with the searcher addressing a specific need. In such an instance, even if the click through on the search listing occurs, the likelihood of the conversion is low, unless the listing addresses the specific query of the LTK searcher.

We observed this in a recent search campaign, where even though the click-through index dropped precipitously, by reducing the number of LTK, the actual conversions increased dramatically. The graph below shows this.

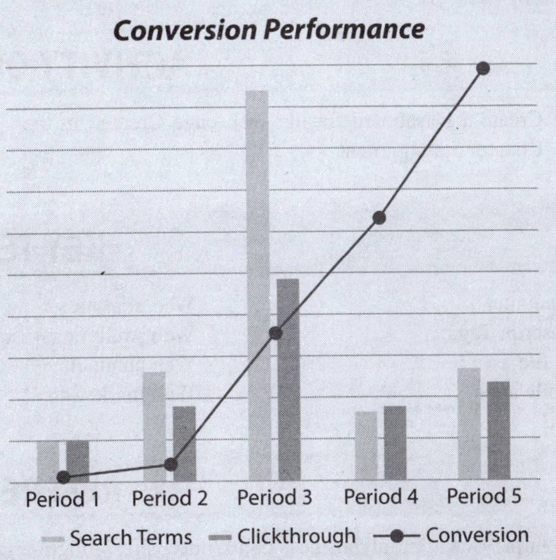

The number of search terms used (the ■ bars) were reduced as a part of a concerted optimization exercise. As expected, the click-throughs (the ■ bars) also declined.

However, notwithstanding the drop in the click-throughs, the number of conversions (the grey line) improved dramatically.

And what about search on mobile devices, particularly smartphones. Our experience shows that click-through rates for LTK is about 50% higher on mobile devices, while conversion is only around 40% of the conversion on desktops.

The net impact, despite the seemingly high click-through rates with LTK, the value realized by the advertiser is poor because of the low conversions with LTK. The net result is that, even on a pay-per-click model, the advertiser ends up with high wastage.

The way thus to optimize LTK is to examine the intent of each search term and use only those LTK search terms whose intent would be congruent to the advertising groups that are created for the campaign. Without such congruence, the probability of the search term converting would be low.

Case Questions

1. Why are long tail key words referred by digital marketers?
2. How do you optimize LTK?

REVIEW QUESTIONS

1. What is web analytics and how is it different from customer analysis?
2. What is the difference between analysis and analytics?
3. List different analytics tools that you have been exposed to.
4. What are the four main key areas of Google Analytics?
5. Why is offline data and patterns important in web analytics?
6. What is goal setting and what are the types of goal that should be set in web analytics?
7. What id MCF (Multi Channel Funnel) Report and what insights do they provide?
8. What is A/B testing and how does it aid in achieving your goal?
9. How is a dashboard created? List important parameters.
10. Why are mobile analytics important for ecommerce?

ACTIVITY QUESTIONS

1. Create a Dashboard for the Web page Created in the Chapter 5 assignment.
2. Do an A/B testing of the landing page designed in the Chapter 5 assignment.

KEY TERMS

Hit counter
Javascript Tags
Log file
Mobile apps
Web analytics
Web Analytics Association (WAA)
Web channels
Web marketing
Web page
Web server
Widget

REFERENCES

1. https://www.simplybusiness.co.uk/microsites/google-analytics-guide/.
2. https://www.entrepreneur.com/article/314343.

CHAPTER 7

DIGITAL ENGAGEMENT

CHAPTER OBJECTIVES

After going through this chapter, you will be able to

- Describe digital engagement, why engage and Net Promoter Score
- Explain effective digital engagement models
- Understand building capabilities for engagement marketing
- Discuss the 5-Step Process of email marketing
- Enumerate the role of POEM (Paid, Owned and Earned Media) in engagement marketing
- Analyze online reputation (ORM) – key to engagement

OPENING CASE LET

MONEYBAGS FINANCIALS

MoneyBags Financials is a Mumbai based advisory and publisher of several websites focused on investments. Their websites and other online advisory platforms provide free access to anyone interested in getting sound financial analysis and advice.

As this audience covers the small and easily identified community of investment advisors, MoneyBags' main marketing activity is email. This has been successful and MoneyBags enjoys a loyal following that regularly visits the site. The main challenge facing the company now is to increase traffic to its websites.

The most popular of MoneyBags' websites is www.smartscrooge.com. MoneyBags believes the site has enough analysis and other content to attract more traffic than it does now. However, since it uses email to drive traffic, the opportunity to increase traffic is limited by the size of this database. This is now about 10,000 distinct investment advisors.

Further, the audience for the site is now located in the top seven cities: New Delhi, Mumbai, Kolkata, Chennai, Bengaluru, Hyderabad and Ahmedabad. MoneyBags is unsure if expanding the geographic coverage of its email will drive traffic proportionately. Geographic expansion of database might also impact content communicated in the email as not all content might be relevant to everyone in the database.

The site has performed well, and seen about 4,000 sessions per week over a full year. There are some peaks—typically during Feb/Mar and during the festival seasons. MoneyBags usually increases its email frequency at this time, so it's not easy to determine how much of that increased traffic is due to email marketing and how much due to seasonal factors alone.

A closer look at traffic to the site:

Regional traffic

Region	Share
North	30%
West	40%
East	10%
South	20%

Traffic to site

Source	MoneyBags	Benchmark
Direct	20%	32%
Email	43%	12%
Organic Search	23%	28%
Referrals	12%	10%
Social	2%	3%
Other	-	15%

Benchmark covers sites comparable to smartscrooge.com

It is clear that email is the biggest traffic driver for MoneyBags, and is disproportionately high compared to the benchmark. Therefore, there is some doubt about expanding the email database and investing more into it, since the yield (ratio of emails sent to traffic) will soon plateau or drop.

In addition, there is a regional bias in email effectiveness, and it brought in more traffic in the West than in other regions. Therefore, email on its own cannot be expected to work equally well across the country.

The volume of direct traffic was more in the South than in other regions and more than email driven traffic. Clearly investment advisors responded differently to different marketing stimuli.

Organic search is the other significant driver of traffic. In an average month, the search volume for topics covered by www.smartscrooge.com is more than 2,10,000 across all the seven cities. The measured CTR to the site in these cities is about 1.4%. This translates into traffic of nearly 3,000 visitors.

The large volume of search and the current low CTR point to a potentially bigger opportunity in optimizing search than in expanding email activities—either database or mailing frequency. For all the knowledge and certainty MoneyBags seemed to have about finance, it seemed unsure about how to proceed.

Case Questions

1. Why would a financial services company want to have a web presence?
2. What additional data should be looked at before making a recommendation?
   a. Use Benchmarks from GT Metrix , monitor and then make the recommendation

INTRODUCTION

In Chapter 1, digital transformation has been discussed. It is all about data driven online marketing, collaborating and integrating across platforms for a seamless customer experience (CX) through their entire journey which is more important than satisfaction at individual touch points. Also Chapter 4 took us through engagement being a key measure in marketing. Simply stated, engagement is the interaction that consumers/customers have with products/services in various touch points, like share, comment, retweet, tag, mention, etc. leading finally to a seamless customer experience.

WHY ENGAGE

Customer engagement is important because (according to Convero Inc.), most products and services find it difficult to engage on account of not having a formal customer engagement program in place[1]. Gallup[2] reports that only 29% of B2B customers are fully engaged. Besides, there is a large gap in the engagement rate that is a function of industry, market and product (or service). A B2C product like a fashion accessory is likely to have a higher engagement than a B2B product or even another B2C product like real estate. Companies that excel at customer experience (thereby resulting in better engagement) grow revenues 4-8% above the market and also a customer life time value 6 to 14 times compared to that of detractors[3] (Bain & Co). A Salesforce.com report indicates that 75% consumers expect a consistent experience wherever they engage (e.g., website, social media, mobile, in person) and Accenture attributes Customer churn to the poor quality of customer service[4]. Besides all the above, Engagement also helps in—

- Communicating new features and updates
- Collecting feedback on existing product features
- Generating more revenue through upgrades or cross-sells
- Decreasing churn or increasing retention
- Improving Net Promoter Score

Engagement Rate and Net Promoter Score

One of the metrics of measuring the level of engagement is Net Promoter Score. According to Trackmaven, "… an engagement rate is a metric that measures the level of engagement that a piece of created content is receiving from an audience. It shows how much people interact with the content. Factors that influence engagement include users' comments, shares, likes, and more[5]. "The Net Promoter Score Scale"[6] is a process of asking the respondents (customers) to rate their likelihood of recommending a company/product to a friend or colleague by using a 0-10 point scale: The number on the scale that a customer chooses is then classified into one of the categories: "Detractors," "Passives," and "Promoters". The NPS system can be looked at as similar to a four-star online review, but the NPS scale gives a broader and a more accurate measure of customer's opinions.

> **NPS:** Net Promoter or Net Promoter Score is a management tool that is used to gauge the loyalty of a firm's customer relationships.

Score breakdowns

0 – 6: Detractors - Least satisfied customers. May not purchase again and could spread negative word of mouth if something is not done to improve their experience.

7 – 8: Passives - Are typically satisfied, but not to the extent that they become loyal. Susceptible to competitors' offers, but will spread neither negative nor positive word of mouth.

9-10: Promoters - Loyal and enthusiastic customers. They will spread good word of mouth about your company and can be brand advocates.

The Net Promoter Score is calculated by subtracting the percentage of detractors from the percentage of promoters, yielding a score between –100 to 100. A Net Promoter Score of –100 means every respondent is a detractor while a Net Promoter Score of 100 means everyone is a promoter. The Net Promoter Score is an indicator of a company's engagement and could be a first step in improving customer loyalty, which, as we saw in Chapter 1, is the cornerstone of Marketing 4.0 – *"from Awareness to Advocacy"*.

FOUR DIGITAL MARKETING MODELS

Given the importance of Engagement, Strategy& (subsidiary of PWC) has identified four digital marketing models[7]. They are Digital Branders, Customer Experience Designers, Demand Generators, and Product

Innovators. A company may focus on one or more of the above models and one of these models may represent the right marketing approach for that company.

- **Digital Branders** are marketers who focus on building brand equity and deep consumer engagement. These companies focus on digital multimedia experiences that connect consumers to the brand in new ways by realigning how they engage consumers, with a primary goal of attracting new consumers and deriving loyalty through multiple experiences.
- **Customer Experience Designers** use customer data and insights to create a superior end-to-end brand experience for their customers by building their business models around superior customer experience at multiple touch points.
- **Demand Generators** typically focus on driving online traffic and converting them into sales across channels efficiently to grow their share of wallet. All digital elements from website design, search engine optimization, mobile connected apps to engagement in social communities are tailored to increase sales and loyalty. They are focused on driving volume and efficiency.
- **Product Innovators** use digital tools to identify, develop, and roll out new digital products and services by employing digital interactions with consumers and gather insights that can shape the innovation pipeline.

Capabilities Spectrum

These digital marketing models are not industry-specific. In fact, companies in the same industry may choose different digital marketing strategies to go to market. For example, in the Indian telecommunications industry, Airtel aligns most closely with the Digital Brander model, Idea is Customer Experience Designer, Jio is a Demand Generator and a Product Innovator. Each of these companies has focused on a different set of capabilities to leverage their digital marketing strategies to building the right combination of processes, tools, knowledge, skills, and organization.

There are eight other marketing capabilities to support these models, which are relevant depending on which of the four digital marketing models a company applies. Of these, some focus on building insights and the others focus on execution based on those insights. They are—

> **PWC:** Pricewaterhouse Coopers

1. **Segmentation and needs assessment**, is the use of research tools to analyze transactions, identify customer pain points, and also interpret non-transaction data (from the social media). By understanding how customer subsets assess, purchase, and use products, the company can more directly target advertising, promotions, and content along the journey to purchase.
2. **Measurement (Journey Mapping)** is the development of consistent metrics across the consumer journey to purchase *viz.*, at home, on the go, and in stores. This capability also includes metrics for consumer engagement across paid media (e.g., advertising), owned media (such as the company website), earned media (coverage in other publications), or shared media (e.g., Facebook or YouTube). These metrics help quantify ROI across the digital marketing program.
3. **Real-time decision making** is the regular monitoring of social sentiment and brand health that enables adjustments during marketing campaigns—including branded media and in-store merchandising—to make them more effective.
4. **Personalization and targeting** is the creation of a unified view of the consumer across sales channels and digital touch points through integration of multiple data sources—including household data, shopping behaviour, mobile data, and web analytics. To improve target marketing, customer profiles can be augmented with social media data to improve specific promotions and offers.
5. **Optimized content** is the dissemination of branded content through multiple platforms of POEM to help easy search and navigation. Optimized content helps engagement with consumers to drive registration and sales across a variety of formats, for specific occasions or phases of life.

6. **Innovation** for richer consumer insights by leveraging social media help product development. Apart from product improvement, these insights enhance the customer's experience with the product.
7. **Social influence and advocacy** is to create, share content and mine social sentiment to further improve consumer engagement.
8. **Omnichannel experience** is implementation of marketing programs across channels by investing in technology, analytics, and human resource to support seamless mobile, social, and *e*-commerce experiences, that facilitates consumers to engage with the company wherever and whenever they want. Omnichannel experiences also include integrated marketing programs with third parties, along with broader media and trade-promotion strategies.

Since it may not be possible for every company to be good at all of the above digital marketing capabilities, focussing on the capabilities that align best with the firms' digital marketing model that works the best. For example, capabilities necessary to succeed as a Digital Brander will be different from those required by a Demand Generator. However, in general, these models require a set of supporting capabilities are developed as shown in Figure 7.1.

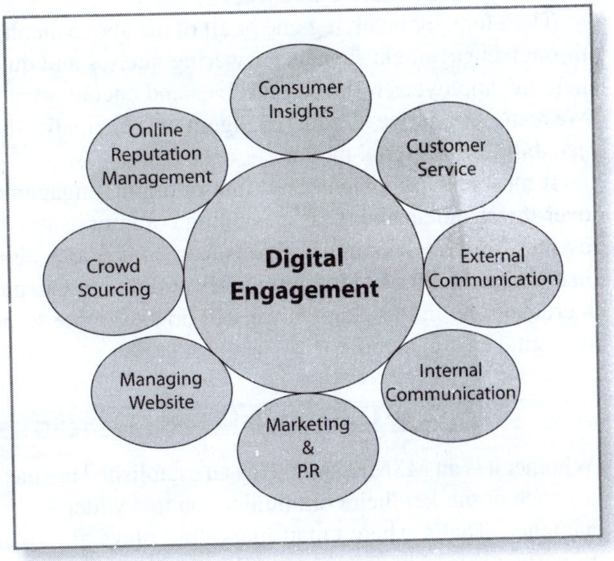

Figure 7.1 Digital Engagement

WHAT DIGITAL ENGAGEMENT IS

According to CIO White Paper review, " … digital engagement is often used as an umbrella term for all digital marketing done by corporate organizations. Digital engagement is the act of engaging people throughout their journey with a company or its offering. This often includes engaging with more customers that you win, serve and retain along the way. The customer is unlikely to see these business processes as separate entities even if the business is organized in that way"[8]. The key operating part of this definition is engagement throughout the customer journey with a company or organization that is the cornerstone of digital transformation.

ROI: Return of Investment

Is Engagement Marketing the Same as Social Media Marketing?

Social media can be a strong component of engagement marketing, since your audience is already engaged with social sites like Facebook, Pinterest, and LinkedIn., but not restricted to social media. As mentioned earlier, a robust marketing strategy will include a plan for the social media channels that best represent your brand's target personas and thus social media marketing is a subset of Digital Engagement and is a combination of many tools of the digital world such as:

- Email marketing
- POEM (Paid, Owned and Earned Media) including contact with third parties who run forums and sites, and establishing two-way partnership.
- ORM (online reputation management) i.e., getting people to give feedback, leave comments or vote/ rate things online using simple digital tools.
- Crowd Sourcing

- Blogs/Case studies/Whitepapers
- Press Release/Company News/Results/Industry Trends
- Illustrations and Infographics
- Vlogs/Podcasts
- Aggregators and Influencers

Therefore, by involving one or all of the above mentioned tools, it ensures not only customer management through engagement such as answering queries and questions but also about robust internal communication helping employees reskill themselves and encouraging knowledge sharing amongst peers and stakeholders. We can summarize digital engagement schematically as shown in Figure 7.1 that are the supporting capabilities for digital models.

It must also be remembered that in digital engagement, organizations often have relatively little control over the channels and messages being communicated, since digital engagement goes beyond programs run by the Corporate Communications team and is also about views, posts and ratings in POEM. That is where listening, adapting and learning tools outlined in Chapter 4 and online reputation management (ORM) play a crucial role. In this chapter, we will now examine some of the above mentioned digital platforms and tools of digital engagement.

EMAIL MARKETING

Whether it is an MSME, start up or an established business, it is always a challenge finding a cost efficient way to reach or market their communication to a wider audience. That's where email marketing plays an important role. An effective email marketing plan is key to promoting and growing a business and increasing revenue. Data of email users presented in Table 7.1 illustrates the potential of email.

Table 7.1 Email Data 2012-2016

In Billion	2012	2013	2014	2015	2016
Global e Mail Clients	4.37	4.66	4.96	5.27	5.59
Global e Mail Users	2.17	2.31	2.46	2.61	2.76
Avg User/ Client	2.01	2.01	2.02	2.02	2.03

Source : Statista

Against this, if active Facebook and Twitter users were to be compared, the following statistics emerge (Figure 7.2).

MSME: Micro, Small and Medium Enterprises

Comparing email users with users of FB and Twitter, it can be inferred that email users are higher than Facebook + Twitter combined. Highlights from 2017 data on email marketing indicate:

- 33% of email client market share is with Apple iPhone, followed by Gmail at 19% basis data for 1.44 billion opens. (Litmus 2016)
- 79% of US mail boxes are consumer email boxes. (Radicati, 2016)
- Constant contact survey in 2016 indicated that 49% of small business owners do not use email marketing data because they do not know where to begin. (Constant Contact, 2016)
- According to Barilliance data of August 2016, the best retargeting conversion rate happens when the first retargeting email is sent within an hour. (eMarketer, 2016)
- According to Acid.com survey, more than 86% of businesses surveyed indicate that they plan to increase their upcoming email marketing budgets. (Email on Acid, 2016)
- According to Litmus in 2016, mobile devices lead the pack at 54% of emails opened, webmail followed at 30% and desktop email opens were 16%. (Source: Litmus 2016)
- Brands that personalize promotional marketing emails experience 27% higher unique click rates and 11% higher open rates compared to those not personalized. (Experian, 2016)
- Survey respondents to Adobe's second annual email survey indicate that they check email while watching TV or while watching a movie (69%), in bed (57%), and on vacation (79%). Percentages are higher across the board for millennials (ages 18-34). (Adobe, 2016)

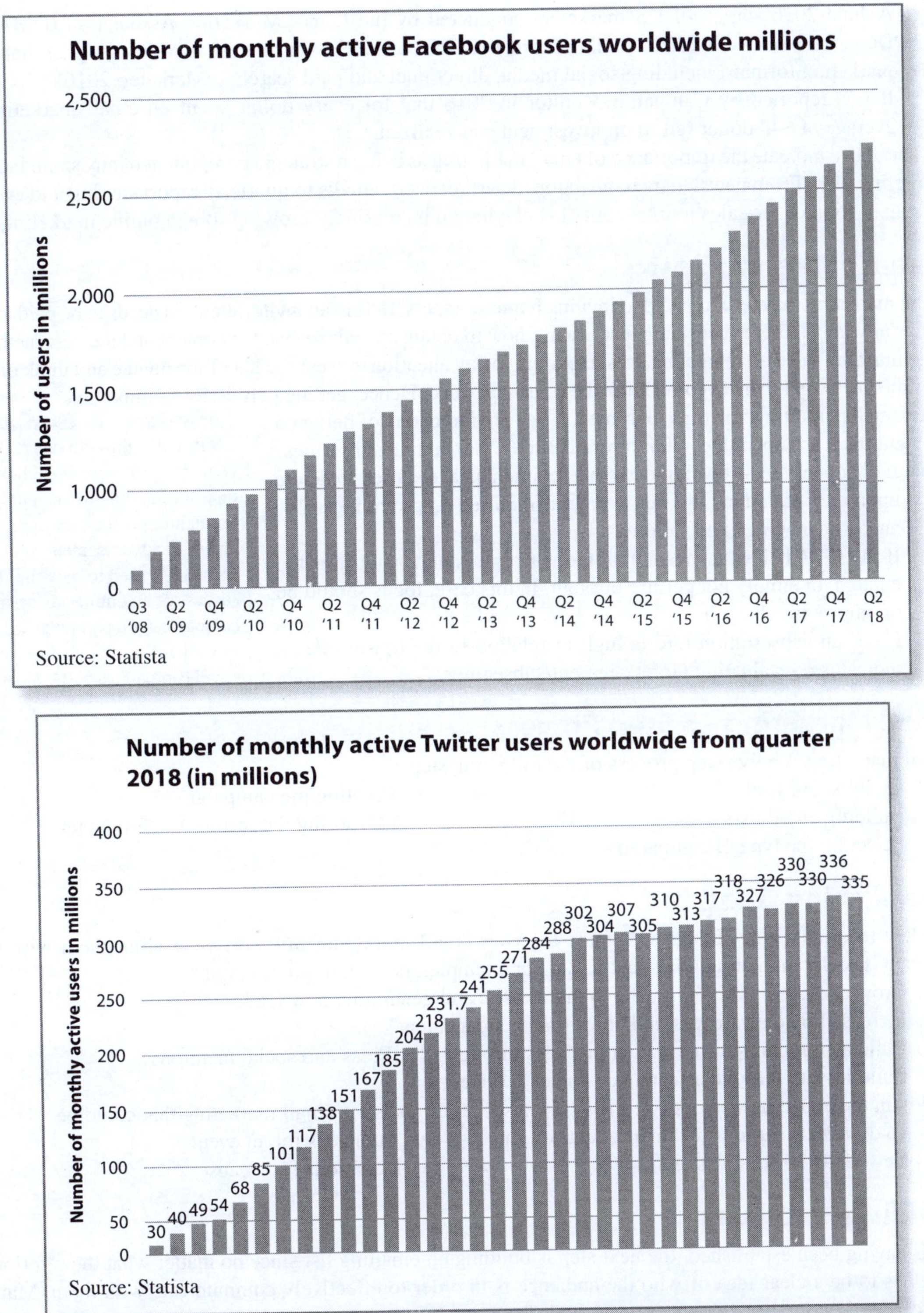

Figure 7.2 Number of Monthly Active Facebook and Twitter Users

- A June 2016 survey of US marketers conducted by the Direct Marketing Association (DMA) and Demand Metric found that email had a median ROI of 122% – more than four times higher than other marketing formats, including social media, direct mail and paid search. (eMarketer, 2016)
- It was reported by Campaign Monitor in 2016 that for every dollar spent on email marketing, an average of $44 dollar return on investment was realized.

The above indicate the importance of email marketing as being a strategic component of any small business marketing plan. From newsletters to abandoned cart recovery emails to quarterly report sharing and even the personalization of the sales journey, email is playing an increasingly growing role in online marketing.

Email Marketing Basics

Email marketing may be compared to inviting home strangers. Before an invite, attention needs to be paid to such details as who will be invitees (target segment), how to obtain an address list, the content and the best method of dissemination. In email marketing, it is important to pay attention to wear the hat of the invitee and think of what does the invitee get (benefit) or would it be a spam or junk? Hence, getting permission is important.

In email marketing, the three parameters that are indicators of being on the right track are open rate, click through rate (CTR), and unsubscribes.

- If the open rate is low, it means that recipients have started to delete upon receipt, indicating improvements required on providing value and/or managing expectations.
- If the CTR is low, it means that the message is either not targeted enough, or simply not getting through. In this case, focus should be on improving the copy.
- If the un-subscription rate is high in relation to the opt-in rate, it indicates re-evaluating target segment/subsegment.

> **CTR:** Click through rate (CTR) is the ratio of users who click on a specific link to the number of total users who view a page, email, or advertisement. It is commonly used to measure the success of an online advertising campaign for a particular website as well as the effectiveness of email campaigns.

Email Marketing - 5 Step Process

Email marketing is a five step process of the following steps:

- Establishing goals
- Building email lists
- Selecting the type of campaign
- Creating the campaign
- Measuring the results and follow up

Establishing Goals

The key to establishing the correct goals for your email marketing initiative is to align them with your company's wider marketing goals and KPIs. For example, the overall goals could be

1. Grow revenue by driving traffic to the website and generating new leads
2. Increase brand awareness and boost brand engagement
3. Build a community around your business through P.R., Press and social mentions
4. Build loyalty through effective customer service

Within the above framework, we may draw a subset of goals for email marketing that could be

- To drive new signups for the product/offering
- New leads for the sales team
- Attendees for an event
- Donations for a cause

Building Email List

Goals having been established, the next step is building an emailing list since no matter what the offering is, there has to be a clear idea of who the audience is in order to effectively communicate with them. Mailing lists can be imported or bought or even built from scratch. But, as mentioned earlier, in email marketing, the three parameters that are important indicators of effectivity are open rate, click through rate (CTR), and unsubscribes. Therefore, segmentation is important to split up the email list into more targeted groups by creating a more unified list by segmenting a larger leads list as

- Customer List (from leads basis specific parameters)
- Product Updates (from customer list)
- Newsletter
- Periodic Reminder List (weekly, bi-weekly, monthly, etc.)
- HTML (that may be preferred over text)

> **KPI:** Key Performance Indicator (KPI) is a measurable value that demonstrates how effectively a company is achieving key business objectives.

This division facilitates flexibility and ability to send more targeted communication, for, some customers may want both product and sales updates, while others might only want to hear about new versions. Thus, if the flexibility of choice is not given, there is this risk of losing them all-together. With a segmentation approach, a broadcast can be sent only to those who didn't open the last communication to find why, or to those showing interest a 2nd pitch. Test messaging can also be split amongst different groups in order to refine best practices. Beginners can take advantage of MailChimp's segmentation tools (https://mailchimp.com/resources/using-segmentation-to-improve-click-rate-and-increase-sales/) that can significantly increase the click-through rates. A 2-part formula for building an email list is offering a valuable incentive plus simple subscribe opportunities. Large email list may need to be supported with a compelling content such as first order discounts and upgrades like free or express shipping with prominent CTAs like header bars and sliders.

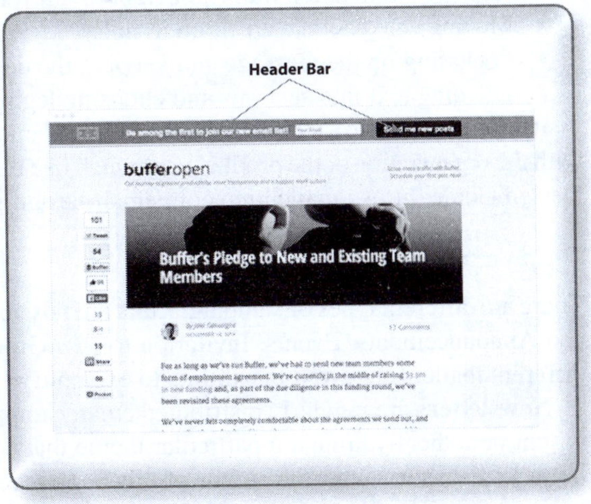

A slider is small box that 'slides in' to the bottom corner of your website and contains a call to action encouraging people to subscribe along with a field for visitors to enter their email address. An excellent tool for setting this up on owned websites is scroll box (https://sumo.com/app/scroll-box).

Having built a mailing list, the next step is the content and frequency of mailing that is in line with the KPIs and sub-goals as mentioned earlier in the chapter. These could be

- Upcoming events
- Recaps and photos from previous events
- Popular posts from social media, like Instagram or Facebook
- News coverage
- Details about featured or new products
- Holiday shopping guides

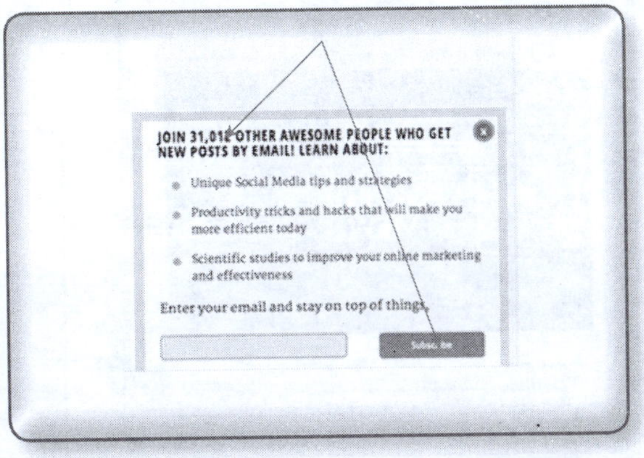

It will always be helpful to build some unique personality for emails, with branding elements, tone of voice, tongue-in-cheek humour, etc. while keeping it short and inspiring. The next step is to establish sending frequency and goals. The email marketing schedule will depend on the industry, the type of content, and the frequency for OTS (Opportunity to See). There are no hard and fast rules about how often the emails are sent, but if they are sent too often, as mentioned earlier in the chapter, there is a risk of low CTR or even un-subscription. Therefore, it is suggested to make a schedule. There are good scheduling tools available from Mailchimp, Salesforce and the like.

Designing Emails

Designing of emails will be a function of the campaign that is most appropriate. Some of the elements of a good campaign are

- Relevance of the campaign (Objective like lead generation, registration, subscription, etc.)
- Structuring for easy reading by laying out all elements in a hierarchy with the most important information or the main takeaway at the top like an inverted pyramid and following the eye movement (top to bottom and left to right/right to left for Arabic and Hebrew)
- Making conversion easy through links
- Focussing on the message and keeping the design simple
- Dividing text into sections and choosing legible fonts

It is better to create a template with branding elements incorporated such that the recipient relates the mailers with the organization or the product very much like the letter heads or business cards. For beginners, Mailchimp Design Guide (https://mailchimp.com/email-design-guide/) is recommended as a good reference point.

Types of Campaign

There are different types of campaigns that are possible and some examples are Newsletters, Marketing Offers and Announcements, Events, Invitation to join Groups, etc., basis the marketing objective. Screenshots of different mailers are given in exhibits to exemplify.

Newsletters are regularly distributed email campaigns that is usually about one main topic of interest and is sent periodically around a particular theme that could be reminders, products, travel, etc. As can be seen in the screenshot below, the author of this book received a campaign newsletter with the goal of keeping in touch with existing customers and a reminder to drive people back to your website. Arrows indicate some of the salient communication points.

Marketing Offers and Announcements are meant to trigger impulse purchase and actions in undecided universe.

Events' mailers are to communicate and trigger registrations.

Invitation to join Groups : In all these mailers, clear CTAs may be noted.

CTA: Call to action (CTA) is an instruction to the audience designed to provoke an immediate response

Testing the campaign is the next logical step after having created the campaigns and the mailers for the campaigns. It is recommended that the campaign be tested with different email clients (Google mail, Outlook, Apple mail, etc.) and also with different ISPs by sending test mails to friends and co-workers. From amongst the versions tested, the best version after A/B testing campaign may be chosen for the burst. It is also imperative that suitable actions be taken to ensure that mails are delivered avoiding spam filters. They are

- Paying attention to technicalities and using automated/triggered mails
- Using a recognizable sender name and avoiding *noreply@xyz.com*
- Using a good subject line/pretext
- Choosing a reliable ESP – Email Service Provider
- Getting a third party certification such as Return Path (https://returnpath.com/)
- Ensuring the sender is not a blacklisted sender
- Making sure the content is compliant with Terms of Use and consistent with the brand

The above is not an exhaustive list but is only indicative one to avoid spam filters.

Measuring Results

As they say, the test of the pudding is in its eating, having created, designed and executed an email campaign, the final act is to track and measure its effectivity. Generally, there are two ways/places to track the success of the email marketing campaigns:

1. An email marketing tool (such as Campaign Monitor)
2. Website analytics tool (such as Google Analytics)

In Campaign Monitor, there are a number of reports that can help track email campaigns but the most commonly used is the Snapshot report that reports on the following:

- Number of unique opens
- Number of bounces
- Number of emails not opened
- Open rate
- Click-through rate
- Unsubscribe rate

A typical screenshot is shown in Exhibit 7.1.

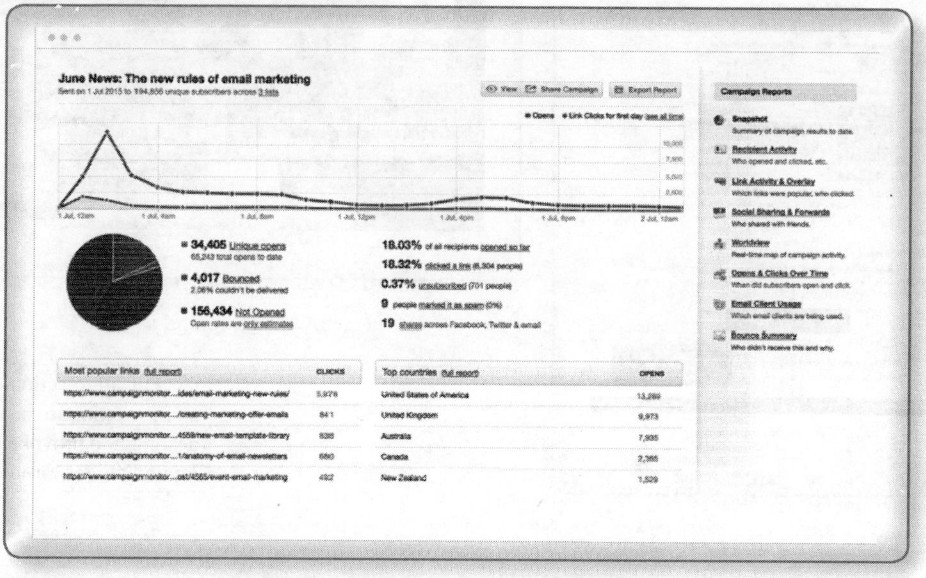

Exhibit 7.1 Campaign Monitor Screenshot

Having looked at email as an important tool of engagement marketing, we now move on to understand POEM as another tool of engagement.

POEM (PAID, OWNED AND EARNED MEDIA)

Media play an important role in Engagement Marketing Digital or otherwise. Media is an essential part of IMC (Integrated Marketing Communication) or IDC (Integrated Digital Communication) as they are the vehicles or channels of communication. In the digital engagement and marketing context, media are categorized in three buckets that are popularly referred to as POEM.

POEM is an acronym for Paid, Owned and Earned Media. POEM is emerging as an important channel of digital marketing particularly in B2B, high end products and services where content plays a crucial part in end of the funnel activities leading to purchase that include blogs, white papers, webinars, demo videos, etc. None of these buckets of media types are new, but what is new is the increasing prominence given to owned and earned media while paid media has always dominated in the past. The strength of content lies in its relevance and a possibility to be non-intrusive (like zoo-zoos). It creates traffic through a desire to consume quality content. These can be as follows:

Paid Media (Native content) is simple placement in a format native to the online channel or publisher. Paid or bought media are media where there is a payment for visitors, reach or conversions through search, display ad networks or affiliate marketing. In the offline format, traditional media like print and TV advertising and direct mail remain important paid media. Pay per Click (PPC), search engine advertising and banners are some of the popular forms of paid advertising.

Paid media are measured depending on the platform used for advertising. For promoted social media posts, internal analytics software is offered by many social networks. Facebook, LinkedIn, Twitter and Pinterest all have built-in analytics. For Instagram, besides its own analytics tool, there are third-party Instagram analytics tools such as Social Bakers (https://www.socialbakers.com), Quintly (https://www.quintly.com) are available. For PPC, Google AdWords offers analytics of paid campaigns and Bing Ads covers Yahoo! and Bing. There are also a number of tools such as SEMRush or SpyFu that track paid search performance in addition to organic search and SEO efforts.

Owned Media (content) - This is media owned by the brand or the organization. In digital, this includes a company's own websites, blogs, white papers, webinars, mobile apps or their social presence on Facebook, Linked In or Twitter. Offline owned media may include brochures or retail stores.

Although Chapter 6 covers various tools available for analytics, a quick summary of measuring owned media is that most of the time, it can be done in the analytics platform of the social network that is being used. Owned media analysis can also be done with analytic tools such as Brandwatch (https://www.brandwatch.com/brandwatch-analytics/) that covers Facebook, Twitter, and Instagram. This allows in-depth analysis of owned media channels, as well as those of the competitors since the ultimate goal behind content and social marketing strategies is not restricted to likes and retweets but to move consumers along their journey. While the traffic that comes from social media can be tracked, it is important to separate traffic from owned and earned media that can be tricky. Nonetheless, by analyzing the owned vs earned mix, the effectiveness of the content and marketing can be improved significantly. However, as outlined in Chapter 6, dedicated social analytics tools developed in-house can provide detailed analysis that helps measure the efforts in greater detail.

> **IMC:** Integrated Marketing Communication is simple concept that ensures that all forms of communications and messages are carefully linked together.
> **PPC:** Pay per click is a model of Internet marketing in which advertisers pay a fee each time one of their ads is clicked.
> **SEM Rush:** SEMrush is a powerful and versatile competitive intelligence suite for online marketing, from SEO and PPC to social media and video advertising research.

Earned Media (Viral content) is essentially viral marketing with rich media content – videos, cartoons, caricatures, graphics, etc. Any mention of the brand that are outside owned channels falls into earned media. This will include a variety of sources, including news sites, forums, blogs, and social media. In traditional marketing, earned media has been the name given to publicity generated through PR invested in targeting influencers to increase awareness about a brand. Earned media also includes word-of-mouth that can be stimulated through viral and social media marketing. This includes conversations in social networks, blogs and other communities. Earned media may have or include different types of partners such as publishers, bloggers and other influencers including customer advocates. However, earned media are different from other forms of conversations both online and offline.

Any social analytics tool, like Brandwatch Analytics (https://www.brandwatch.com/brandwatch-analytics/), is an easy way to monitor the mentions across the web excluding own channels. In measuring earned media, one of the primary sources of the information is the voice of the customer, that facilitates further insights from the captured data. An overview can be obtained by measuring share of voice that gives an understanding of earned mentions, vis-à-vis industry and the competition. Another important aspect of earned media is PR and reputation management. This is usually measured by assigning an advertising value equivalency (AVE) to web mentions. AVE is a measure commonly used in the public relations industry to 'measure' the benefit to an advertiser from media coverage of a PR campaign by measuring the size of the coverage gained, its placement and calculate what the equivalent amount of space, if paid for as advertising, would cost. Often a multiplier is also used factoring the medium, credibility factor, timing of the coverage, etc. We must also understand that not all mentions will be positive and should be monitored for any negative mentions to monitor reputation and proactively take actions. This is covered separately in the next section, i.e., online reputation management or ORM. Keeping track of the most shared content such as top stories, tip hashtags help to understand the audience preferences and the content that have engaged them enabling reaching out to these influencers as advocates. By comparing owned versus earned hashtags, a hashtag/key phrase strategy can be formulated.

For better efficacy paid, owned and earned media can be integrated, for example, through crowd sourcing of idea and content or incentivizing influencers. Thus, monitoring paid, owned and earned media leads to an understanding of the buzz around the brand and how it can be influenced. Table 7.2 and Figure 7.3 capture the summary of POEM.

Table 7.2 POEM Comparison

POEM				
Media Tpe	**Description**	**Examples**	**Role**	**Benefits**
Owned Media	The Channel Company or Brand Controls	Websites Mobile Sites. Blogs, Twitter, etc.	Building Long Term Relations	Control Cost Niche Long Term Versatility
Paid Media	The Channel Company or Brand pays to leverage	Display Ads. Paid Search. Sponsorships, etc.	Catalyst that feeds owend media and creates earned media	On demand. Can scale qickly. Control
Earned Media	Customers Become Channel	WOM. Buzz. Viral. Social	Listen & respond Result of coordinated owend and paid media	Credible & transparent. Reputation Management is important

Online reputation management (ORM) is about comments, vote, rate, like and the feedback received and left online using simple digital tools. Wikipedia defines ORM as "online reputation management (or monitoring) is the practice of monitoring the Internet reputation of a person, brand or business, with the goal of suppressing negative mentions entirely, or pushing them lower on search engine results pages to decrease their visibility". In a nutshell, it is about what is being talked about individuals, brands or organizations, online!

ORM is important as

1. It plays a major role in protecting the brand equity, since brand equity is all about a set of stored values that consumers associated with a product/ service and these associations add value beyond the basic product functions due to investments in marketing the brand that create some strong, favourable, and unique brand associations in memory.

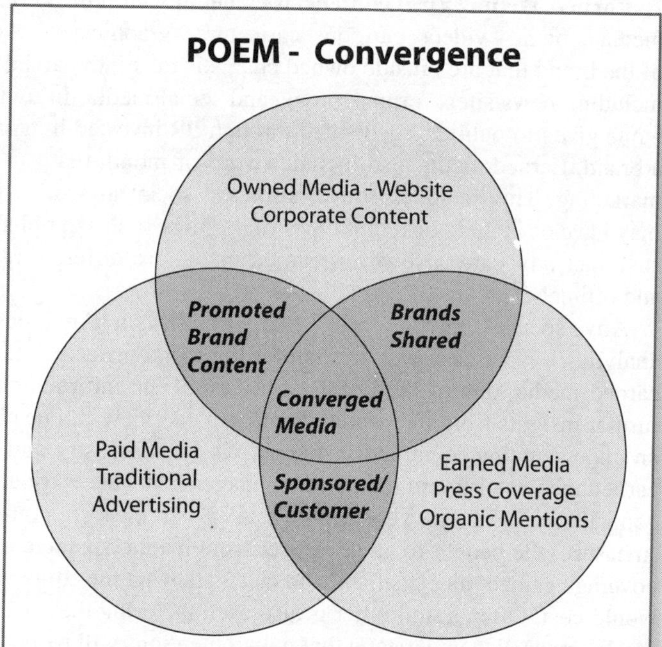

Figure 7.3 POEM Conversion

2. 70% of consumers trust other consumer opinions that are posted online.
3. According to literature, over 1 billion people search Google every day and 45% of them find something that prevent them from doing business with someone.
4. 50% of consumers spend 75% or more of their total shopping time conducting online product research.
5. At any given time, prospects, customers and competitors are online including unhappy/dissatisfied customers.

The effect of bad customer experience or reviews would not only result in losing customers but also result in loss of revenue as illustrated in Figure 7.4.

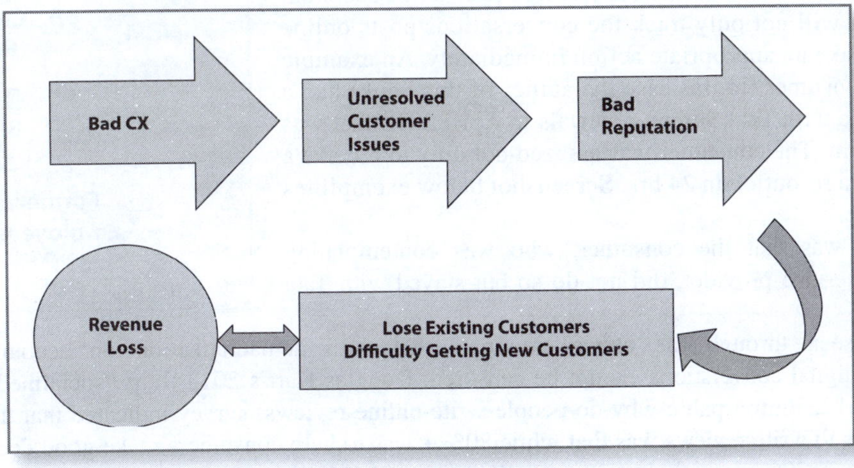

Figure 7.4 Effect of Bad CX

ORM uses the principle of Listen, Adapt and Learn (Chapter 4) for reputation monitoring, damage control, branding, review management, search protection, etc., through keyword based monitoring in social media, news, blogs and forums.

What is ORM?

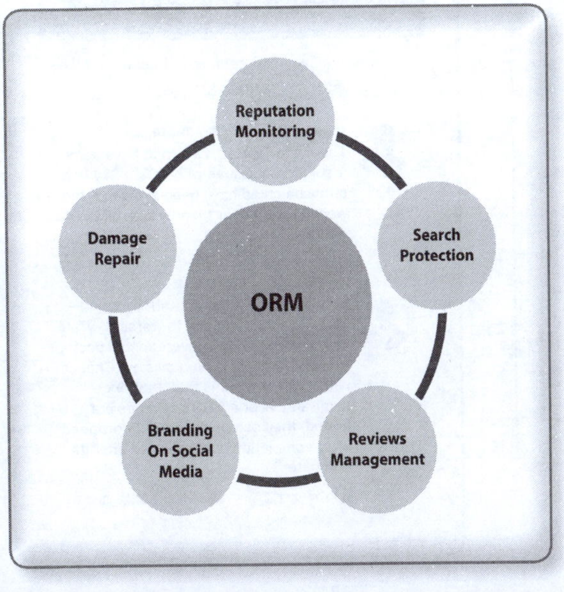

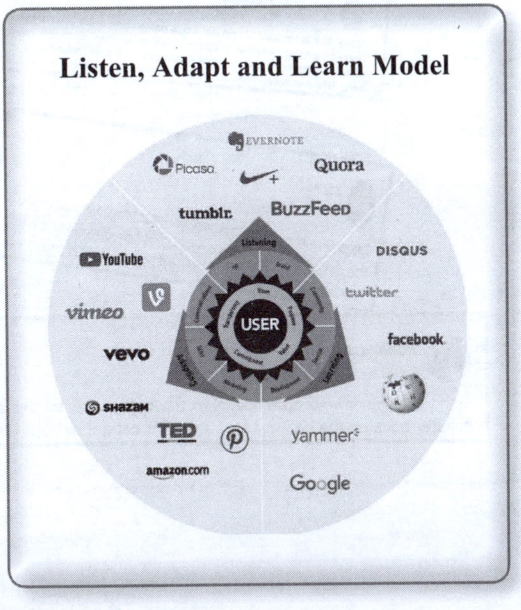

Digital conversations originate from multiple forums like social media, customer reviews, blogs, former employees, dissatisfied customers and a host of other sources. Using Listen, Adapt and Learn model, it is possible to track these conversations. But more important than tracking is listening to them and taking appropriate action. For example, a random visit to Facebook or following Twitter would show posts from individuals and communities that may not be complimentary to organizations. Given below are some screenshots from Twitter and Facebook. A good ORM will not only track the conversations/posts online but also will take an appropriate action immediately. An example of this is, a consumer (in this case the author of this book) had a bad experience with Tata Sky on renewals in April 2018 that was Tweeted by him. The consumer was amazed not only to receive a reply but also a resoution in 24 hrs. Screenshot below exemplifies the experience.

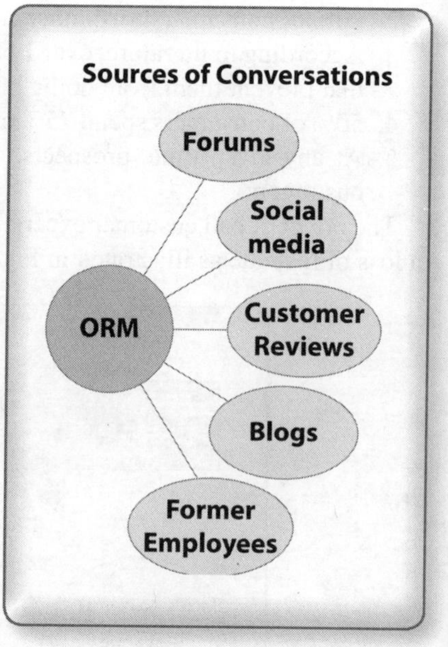

The result was that the consumer, who was contemplating changing the service provider, did not do so but stayed with Tata Sky.

We have seen through the above examples that with demacratization on account of digital technologies, digital converstions cannot be censored. Douglas Karr's 2013 (http://socialmediatoday.com/douglaskarr/561225/infogrpahic-why-do-people-write-online-reviews) survey indicated that the motivation for respondents to write reviews was that while 80% + was to help consumers make good decisions and to share experiences, 70% was to help companies improve and 62% was to get a company to listen. In as much

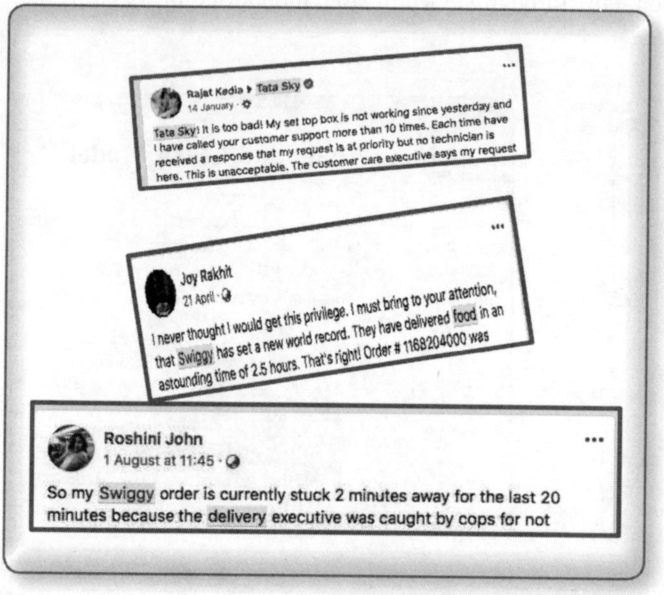

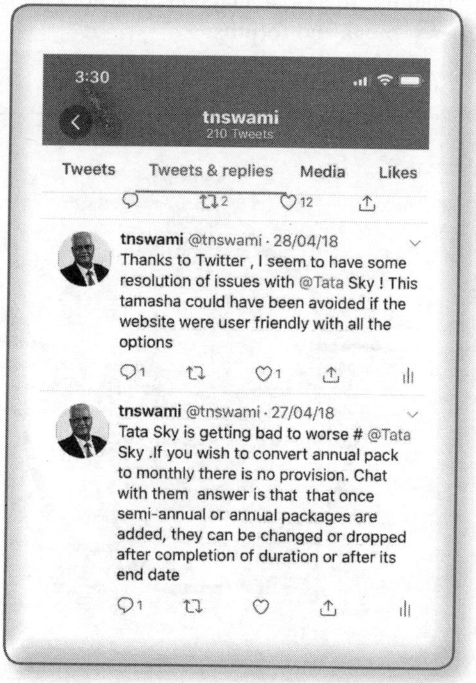

as the social conversations cannot be stopped or censored, proactive measures can be taken to manage online reputation. Two of important proactive measures of managing ORM are

- Search Protection
- Review Management

In search protection, through available online tools such as "Spy Bot", it is possible to do Brand Keyword Protection that ensures positive results on search engines when brand name and related phrases are searched. Brand Yourself (www.brandyourself.com) offers software that facilitates Removal/Replacement/Burial of search results showing negative reviews or opinions or bad PR. However, these tools are not recommended, for, they are perceived as contrary to best practices under self-regulation. But on a positive note, Rich Snippets can be generated that show authorship and Microformats compliance to show Google validated data about your brand when searched, thus pushing up your SE ranking.

Review management is an important part of the Listen, Adapt, and Learn model. As a part of the standard operating procedure, it will be a good practice to put in place automated processes that collect and consolidate onsite/online feedback, customer reviews from the website and social media. This Integrated Review Solution enables highlight/improve visibility and discoverability of positive customer feedback on line/site, initiate search protection and removal of bad reviews. Besides, there are on-site tools available to have integrated reviews publishing across all managed social media . This is part of the POEM management and include offsite reviews besides managing rebuttals and positive review publishing across third-party sites. Review management, if not possible in-house, digital PR agencies that specialize in all of the above can be outsourced. These agencies also facilitate and actively trigger reviews from satisfied customers, boost conversions and provide valuable feedback. Since consumers trust online reviews more than paid content, these agencies also facilitate incentive in exchange for reviews. Another way to trigger customers to review is by placing CTAs on relevant pages as well as redirect customers to business listings on Google Places, Yelp, CitySearch, and other listings.

Apart from social media marketing being an important and integral part of digital marketing, social media are important listening posts since most conversations and reviews happen in social media and POEM including own website. The following are important for ORM in social media:

- Social media channels be well managed; If in-house expertise is lacking to explore ghost-run by experts and agencies.
- Initiate community development activities that are relevant to the business and sometimes for a social cause and awareness programs.
- Building fans, fan clubs, followers and likes.
- Initiate customer engagement through
  - Social posts
  - Getting the buzzword out
  - Campaign specific postings across socio-sphere

The closing case ".sucks" illustrates different dimensions of online reputation management and exemplifies the "*decoy*" phenomenon.

Damage Control

Notwithstanding all the actions taken, the moment of truth is that negative mentions can happen at any touch point during the customer journey, the cardinal principle in Services Marketing namely "Service Recovery" needs to be put in place. This in digital context is "Damage Control" which is nothing but, damage having happened how best it may be controlled. While there are no standard templates available, the following will be helpful:

- Addressing bad PR and negative comments through dialogue control. That is about having designated spokesperson to whom all the conversations forwarded and *suo moto* actions or replies avoided.

- Connect with disgruntled customers to exhibit transparency, empathy and warmth and explore to get the reviews off. This may also be done through an appropriate external agency if in-house resources are a constraint.
- Negative Review Burial/Replacement
- Ensuring that negative reviews are taken down or replaced by positive ones on third-party sites
- Developing microsites to diverting traffic
- Development of campaign and purpose specific websites/microsites
- Flooding the first page of the search engines with positive, branded content
- Content management in POEM through articles, videos, press releases, photos, etc.
- Tips, tools, helpful tutorials, and other useful content

Integral part of damage control is to respond and interact by
- Listening to what is being said
- Responding to both positive and negative comments
- Accepting mistakes and errors
- Being respectful and displaying a helpful, friendly demeanor
- Quickly offering a solution to any problems

Quick and timely response allows proactively manage the brand, organization and control negative effects besides building relationships and demonstrating a caring attitude. It also provides an opportunity for others to appreciate the firms'/brands' point of view.

This chapter is focussed on three important activities of digital engagement through email marketing, POEM and online reputation management (ORM) with examples to give an idea of what it takes to meaningfully engage with the target consumer/market. Besides those covered in this chapter, there are other digital activities such as blogs, case studies/Whitepapers, press release/company news/results/industry trends, illustrations and infographics, vlogs/podcasts and social media channels, that are covered in other chapters (content marketing, social media marketing, etc.).

CHAPTER SUMMARY

- Customer engagement is important since most products and services find it very difficult to engage on account of not having a formal customer engagement program in place.
- Engagement also helps in communicating new features and updates, collecting feedback on existing product features, generating more revenue through upgrades or crosssells, decreasing churn or increasing retention, improves Net Promoter Score.
- Engagement rate and Net Promoter Score are the process of asking the respondents (customers) to rate their likelihood of recommending a company/product to a friend or colleague by using a 0-10 point scale.
- The number on the scale that a customer chooses is then classified into one of the categories: "Detractors," "Passives," and "Promoters". The Net Promoter Score is an indicator of your company's health and could be the first step in improving customer loyalty.
- Given the importance of engagement, Strategy& (a subsidiary of PWC) has identified four digital marketing models. They are Digital Branders, Customer Experience Designers, Demand Generators, and Product Innovators.
- Digital Branders are marketers who focus on building brand equity and deep consumer engagement.
- Customer Experience Designers use customer data and insights to create a superior end-to-end brand experience by building their business models around superior CX at multiple touch points.
- Demand Generators typically focus on driving online traffic and converting them into sales across channels efficiently to grow their share of wallet.
- Product Innovators use digital tools to identify, develop, and roll out new digital products that can shape the innovation pipeline.
- There are eight other marketing capabilities, which are relevant. They are 1. Segmentation and

needs assessment, 2. Measurement, 3. Real-time decision making, 4.Personalization and targeting, 5. Optimized content, 6. Innovation, 7. Social influence and 8. Advocacy and omnichannel experience.

- Digital engagement is the act of engaging people throughout their journey with a company or its offering.
- Digital engagement is done through a host of activities like email marketing, POEM (Paid, Owned and Earned Media), ORM (online reputation management), crowd sourcing, blogs/case studies/whitepapers, press release/company news/results/industry trends, illustrations and infographics, vlogs/podcasts Twitter.
- Email users are greater than Facebook plus Twitter combined. Highlights from 2017 data on email marketing indicate the criticality of email marketing as being a strategic component of any small business marketing plan.
- Email marketing may be compared to inviting home strangers. Thus, before an invite attention needs to be paid to such details as who will be invitees (target segment), how to obtain an address list, the content and the best method of dissemination.
- In email marketing, it is important to pay attention to wear the hat of the invitee and think of what does the invitee get (benefit). Would it be a spam or junk? etc.
- If the open rate is low, it means that recipients have started to delete upon receipt, indicating improvements required on providing value and/or managing expectations.
- If the CTR is low, it means that the message is either not targeted enough, or simply not getting through. In this case, focus should be on improving the copy.
- If the un-subscription rate is high in relation to the opt-in rate, it indicates re-evaluating target segment/sub-segment.
- Email marketing is a five step process of establishing goals, building email lists, selecting the type of campaign, creating the campaign and measuring the results.
- Establishing goals is the key for email marketing initiative to align them with the company's wider marketing goals and KPIs.
- Goals having been established, the next step is building an emailing list. Mailing lists can be imported or bought or even built from scratch.
- Beginners can take advantage of MailChimp's resources.
- A 2-part formula for building an email list is a valuable incentive plus simple subscribe opportunities.
- A slider is a small box that 'slides in' to the bottom corner of the website and contains a call to action encouraging people to subscribe along with a field for visitors to enter their email address.
- A content list is then prepared in line with the KPIs and sub goals. It will always be helpful to build some unique personality for emails, like the branding elements, tone of voice, tongue-in-cheek humour, etc. while keeping it short and inspiring.
- The next step is to establish sending frequency and goals. The email marketing schedule will depend on the industry, the type of content, and the frequency for OTS (opportunity to see). There are good scheduling tools available from Mailchimp, Salesforce and the like.
- Designing of emails will be a function of the campaign that is most appropriate like the relevance of the campaign (objective like lead generation, registration, subscription, etc.).
- It is better to create a template with branding elements incorporated such that the recipient relates the mailers with the organization or the product very much like the letter heads or business cards. For beginners, Mailchimp Design Guide (https://mailchimp.com/email-design-guide/) is recommended for reference.
- Different types of campaigns are newsletters, marketing offers and announcements, events and calendars invitation to join groups and the like and actions taken to ensure that mails are delivered avoiding spam filters.
- Success of the email marketing campaigns are measured through email marketing tool such as Campaign Monitor and website analytics tool such as Google Analytics.
- POEM (paid, owned and earned media) plays an important role in engagement marketing digital or otherwise.
- Paid media (native content) is simple placement in a format native to the online channel or publisher. Paid or bought media are media where there is investment to pay for visitors, reach or conversions through search, display ad networks or affiliate marketing.
- Owned media (content) are media owned by the brand or the organization. In digital, this includes

a company's own websites, blogs, white papers, webinars, mobile apps or their social presence on Facebook, LinkedIn or Twitter.

- Earned media (viral content) is essentially viral marketing with rich media content: videos, cartoons, caricatures, graphics, etc. Any mention of the brand that are outside owned channels falls into earned media. This will include a variety of sources, including news sites, forums, blogs, and social media.
- For better efficacy, paid, owned and earned media can be integrated through crowd sourcing of idea and content or incentivising influencers. Monitoring paid, owned and earned media leads to an understanding of the buzz around the brand and how it can be influenced.
- Online reputation management (ORM) is about comments, vote, rate, like and the feedback received and left online using simple digital tools.
- Wikipedia defines ORM as "Online reputation management (or monitoring) is the practice of monitoring the Internet reputation of a person, brand or business, with the goal of suppressing negative mentions entirely, or pushing them lower on search engine results pages to decrease their visibility". In a nutshell, it is about what is being talked about individuals, brands or organizations, online!
- ORM uses the principle of Listen, Adapt and Learn for reputation monitoring, damage control, branding, review management, search protection, etc., through keyword based monitoring in social media, news, blogs and forums.
- Digital conversations originate from multiple sources like forums, social media, customer reviews, blogs, former employees, dissatisfied customers and a host of other sources. Using Listen, Adapt and Learn model, it is possible to track these conversations. But more important than tracking is listening to them and taking appropriate action.
- Digital converstions cannot be stopped. However, proactive measures can be taken to manage online reputation. Two of important proactive measures are search protection and review management.
- Review management is an important part of the Listen, Adapt, and Learn model. As a part of the standard operating procedure, it will be a good practice to put in place automated processes that collect and consolidate onsite feedback, customer reviews from the website and social media.
- In ORM, it is important that social media channels be well managed; If in-house expertise is lacking, it is suggested to explore ghost-run by experts and agencies; Initiate community development activities that are relevant to the business and run social cause and awareness programs; build fans, fan clubs, followers and likes; Initiate customer engagement through social posts, getting the buzzword out and campaign specific postings across socio-sphere.
- Damage Control – Not withstanding all the actions taken, the moment of truth is that negative mention can happen at any touch point during the customer journey. Thus, damage having happened how best it may be controlled by addressing bad PR and negative comments through dialogue control; connecting with disgruntled customers to exhibit transparency, empathy and warmth and explore to get the reviews off; Burial/Replacement of Negative Review; Development of campaign and purpose specific websites/microsites; Flooding the first page of the search engines with positive, branded content.
- Integral part of damage control is quick and timely response that allows proactively manage the brand, organization and control negative effects. It builds relationships and demonstrates a caring attitude. It also provides an opportunity for others to appreciate the firms'/brands' point of view.

CLOSING CASE

CASE LET

Sucks Domain

First reaction of most to the domain name ".sucks" is that this is the most controversial domain name on the Internet. The question whether the domain 'dot sucks' belong on the Internet that members of Congress, the Federal Trade Commission, and even of the organization that approved it in February—the Internet Corporation for Assigned Names and Numbers (Icann)—are now asking (http://fortune.com/2015/05/20/dot-sucks-web-address/)."Icann says it approved the .sucks domain because no one objected," the *Wall Street Journal* reports. "Now, it says doesn't have authority to block the domains or control the pricing." Meantime, in 2010 Junior Hawkins created a facebook page with a mission of showing the world Apple sucks! https://www.facebook.com/AppleComputersSuck.

Industry experts call the domain extortionary as it's forcing businesses and others to pay a premium for "[name].sucks" website addresses since they fear that malcontent and critics are likely to pick up the domain name, and employ the site for bringing disrepute for a brand, person, or firm. According to Wall Street Journal (https://blogs.wsj.com/digits/2015/05/19/new-domain-sparks-icann-debate/), while typically domain names cost less than $100, Vox Populi, the company that owns the rights to sell "dot sucks" domains, suggests $2,499. These led Icann in 2015 to ask governmental authorities such as the Federal Trade Commission and the Office of Consumer Affairs in Canada to investigate Vox Populi's practices.

Thus as the future of "dot sucks", and the power of the non-profit partnership that has managed web domains for nearly two decades hangs in the balance. Already, buyers have been reported to have claimed such websites as "starbucks.sucks," "jpm.sucks," and "reeses.sucks,". According to Vox Populi, some of the companies most sought after for a "dot sucks" address, are:

1. Apple
2. Google
3. Microsoft
4. Facebook
5. Comcast
6. Walmast
7. CocaCola
8. McDonald's
9. Sony
10. Amazon

A full list of available web domains approved by Icann can be found at (http://data.iana.org/TLD/tlds-alpha-by-domain.txt).

The Vox Populi website https://get.sucks also advertises its intention is to "foster debate and share opinions."

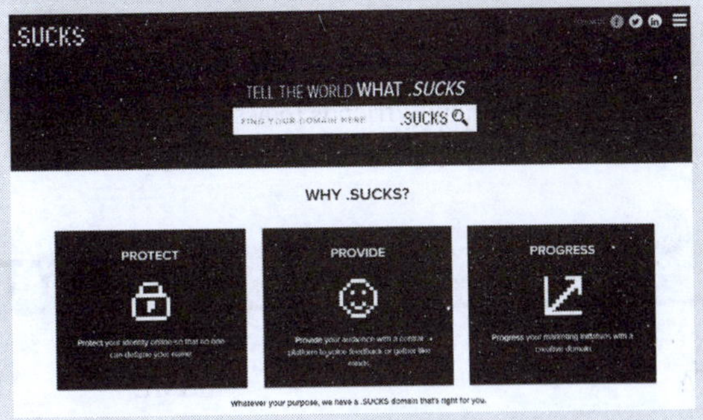

Case Questions

1. What is the advantage in creating/buying controversial/disruptive domain names?
2. Is it prudent to create/buy controversial and disruptive domain names?

REVIEW QUESTIONS

1. What is digital engagement and why is digital engagement important?
2. What are engagement rate and Net Promoter Scores? How is Net Promoter Score measured or expressed?
3. Explain each of the four digital marketing models of engagement by Strategy&.
4. What are the 8 capabilities that an organization need to build and explain each one of them?
5. Which are the different digital tools in the digital world that are used in digital engagement?
6. On the basis, some of the 2017 data, explain the relevance and importance of email marketing.
7. What are the 3 basic parameters that indicate email marketing is not working?
8. Explain each of the 5 steps of email marketing process.
9. What are the criteria for designing good emails?
10. Explain various types of email campaigns.
11. What is POEM and explain each one of them?
12. What is ORM and why is it important?
13. Which are the various sources of conversation in ORM?
14. What is importance of search protection and review management?
15. Why are social media important in ORM and how do you manage them well?

ACTIVITY QUESTIONS

1. Design an e-mailer for the product/service created in Chapter 4 assignment and do a campaign by mailing 25 - 50 of your family/friends to assess the response to your product/ service.
2. Using Campaign Monitor or Google Analytics measure the results/efficacy of the mailer campaign done as above.

KEY TERMS

CX
CTA
CTR
IMC
KPI
MSME
NPS
PPC
PWC
ROI
SEM Rush

REFERENCES

1. http://www.converoinc.com/#fancyboxID-2.
2. https://news.gallup.com/businessjournal/225068/why-b2b-customers-important-part.aspx?g_source=link_NEWSV9&g_medium=TOPIC&g_campaign=item_&g_content=Why%2520B2B%2520Customers%2520Are%2520the%2520Most%2520Important%2520Part%2520of%2520M%26A.
3. http://www2.bain.com/infographics/five-disciplines/.
4. https://www.accenture.com/us-en/strategy-index.
5. https://trackmaven.com/marketing-dictionary/engagement-rate/.
6. https://customergauge.com/net-promoter-score nps/?__hstc=166525089.039551fac660bb5ffd7d2f9e47c2903a. 1544524135411.1544524135411.1544524135411.1&__hssc=166525089.1.1544524135411&__hsfp=2825255773.
7. https://www.strategy-business.com/article/00241?gko=20aae.
8. https://whatis.ciowhitepapersreview.com/definition/digital-engagement/.

CHAPTER 8

DIGITAL CONTENT MARKETING

CHAPTER OBJECTIVES

After going through this chapter, you will be able to

- Define what content marketing and storytelling are and why content marketing in digital
- Analyze top priorities and challenges for content creators
- Discuss content marketing strategy and content strategy
- Explain content mapping based on the customer journey
- Describe the stages of content creation and the metrics for each stage

OPENING CASE

CASE LET

NIKE – BREAKING 2

Nike's campaign "Breaking 2" from 2017 is a great example of how the combination of influencer and content marketing works. As a part of launching their new shoe, the Zoom Vaporfly Elite, Nike live streamed an attempt to complete a marathon in less than two hours. It was live streamed on Facebook and Twitter, while the behind-the-scenes photos were shared on Instagram throughout.

They signed up three runners - Eliud Kipchoge, Zersenay Tadese, and Lelisa Desisa – for this campaign. They were made a part of this marathon race. Nike made it easy for viewers to follow the race with the hashtag #Breaking2. Nike even created a custom Nike Vaporfly Elite shoe emoji.

While Nike's core audience or the customer base could be athletes or sports enthusiasts, the campaign's message was so powerful that it reached millions around the world, and not just runners or athletes. The campaign was about unlocking human potential, to push oneself beyond and Nike struck the right cord. Anyone with an Internet access could join the race which inspired a much broader audience.

The result: One week after the campaign, here is what happened:

- Nike garnered 584,000 mentions on social media
- The hashtag was used over 400,000 times with 87% of the comments positive and a remarkable 2 trillion impressions.
- The shoe did well achieving 5.2 times more digital content engagement in the days following the attempt.
- Nike's core audience or the customer base could be athletes or sports enthusiasts, but the campaign's message was so powerful that it reached millions around the world, and not just runners or athletes. The campaign was about unlocking human potential, to push oneself beyond and Nike struck the right cord. Anyone with an Internet access could join the race which inspired a much broader audience.

Case Questions

1. What made Nike's campaign successful?
2. What is the role of niche influencers in such content marketing campaigns?

INTRODUCTION

Earlier in Chapter 2, we learnt that communication has been an essential component in marketing, and Kotler crafted the mantra of marketing as "CCDVTP" or "Create, Communicate and Deliver Value to a Target market at a Profit". Products create value, value is communicated through integrated marketing communication or IMC. Chapter 2 also outlined the evolution of IDC from IMC in the digital age.

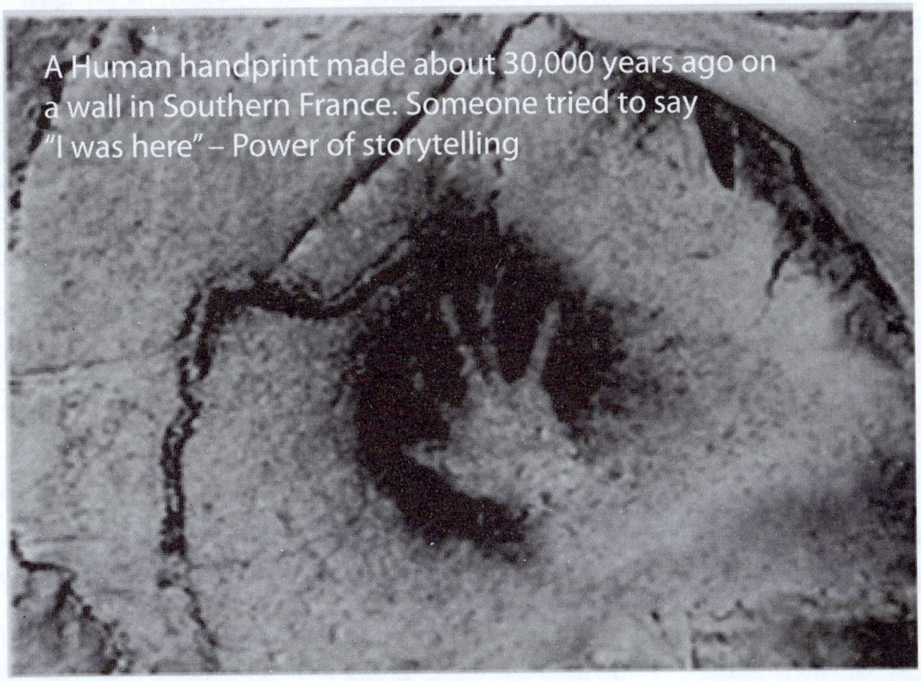

Figure 8.1 Power of Storytelling

EVOLUTION OF CONTENT THROUGH THE AGES

Since the time of Adam and Eve, people have been trying to influence others, utilizing whatever means available to them at that point in time. Human voice was the first, which is now known as word of mouth. In the stone age, pieces of sharp stones were used by natives, for etching images and markings on trees, on stones and in caves that may have appeared as random. However, these primitive images had stories to tell, communicated ideas and insights on life in that period. These have endured several ages and civilizations. These also demonstrated the power of images and messages in storytelling and propagation of ideas! These seem to be the first evidence of marketing and advertising, for, they influenced the perception and behaviour! Through millennia, advances in technology contributed to the evolution of communication, each altering the way business was carried out and the way businesses communicated with their customers.

Great persuaders have existed throughout history and they have created or destroyed nations – Lincoln or Hitler, for example. History stands testimony to anyone, anywhere in the world who was better at expressing their ideas could muster and accumulate wealth that was unprecedented in history. However, a farmer who ploughed better than his neighbour or a factory worker who assembled widgets faster than the person next to them could not create more wealth in comparison. Thus, the one skill that can separate an individual from the knowledge or technology that he creates/uses or from his peers is the art of persuasion—combining words and ideas to ignite people's imagination. This also includes the digital presentation tools like PowerPoint, unlike drawing pictures on cave walls as was done thousands of years ago and illustrated above. Thus, storytelling is not new but goes back 2,000 years ago to Aristotle (Carmine Gallo, 2018).

When we were children, we enjoyed listening to audio tapes of nursery rhymes by Preeti Sagar, watched Jungle Book/Mowgli cartoons in movie halls or television, read Chandamama Comics, etc. These were essentially aids for storytelling and this storytelling happens in the industry today, for example, SAP, a giant business software company that's global, recently created a position titled Chief Storyteller. Today no tech company can compete by communicating with an average customer using engineering terms and talking to them about business software that is complex and hard to understand. The vehicle of story is used, that of a narrative to better sell those products. According to Gallo, this was also found at Google while interviewing Avinash Kaushik, one of the top executives at Google who was also the leading web analytics expert in the world. According to Kaushik, "…, we can have all the data in the world. We can have better data than anyone else. But if we cannot communicate that data to a customer and show them how it applies to their world and make their business better, then we have failed. Then all that data doesn't matter to our company" (Gallo, 2018).

Central to storytelling or any piece of communication is ***CONTENT*** – voice, text, image or a combination thereof. In India, Chandamama comics in various Indian languages stands testimony to the power of content marketing and the fact that content marketing has been around for a long time, much before the Internet. Content is all about longevity, relation building and consistency.

WHAT CONTENT MARKETING IS

The Content Marketing Institute defines content marketing as "… *a strategic marketing approach focused on creating and distributing valuable, relevant and consistent content to attract and retain a clearly-defined audience — and, ultimately, to drive profitable customer action"*.

A closer look at the definition conveys that content marketing is a long-term strategy that focuses on building a strong relationship with the target audience by giving them high-quality content that is relevant to the target audience on a consistent basis. That is, when a purchase decision is made by the consumer, purchase of your offering should be preferred over that of the competitors.

In other words, content marketing is an excellent tool for customer care and engagement. The foundation of content marketing is based on a tenet of quality content and storytelling and this activity has been around longer than the term itself using tools that were the best at that time whether it was a stone, indigo, paper or computer (now). Benjamin Franklin's publishing the yearly Poor Richard's Almanack in 1732 to promote his printing business is chronicled as the oldest and first known advertising (Content Marketing Institute).

Content Marketing: A strategic marketing approach focused on creating and distributing valuable, relevant and consistent content to attract and retain a clearly-defined audience and, ultimately, to drive profitable customer action.

Source : Content Marketing Institute

Figure 8.2 First Known Print Ad

In India, B Dattaram and Co. started in Mumbai in 1902 is claimed to be the oldest existing Indian agency, and its release of Jabakusum Hair Oil print advertisement as one of the oldest advertisements.

The importance of content in storytelling and advertising is reflected in the following advertisement of J. Walter Thomson Ad in 1903. Wikipedia page on History of Advertising captures the journey through the early years of evolution of advertising.

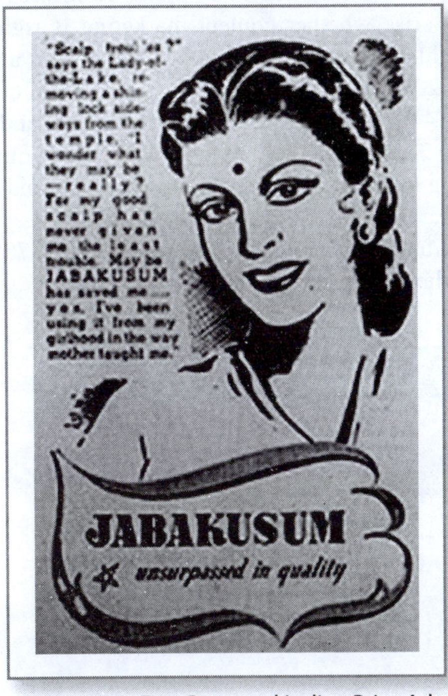

Figure 8.3 First Reported Indian Print Ad

Figure 8.4 JWT Ad 1903

While the above exemplify traditional communication, digital content has also made a significant progress ever since Video Cassette Recorders (VCRs) became popular in delivering video content in 70s as shown in the KPCB infographic below.

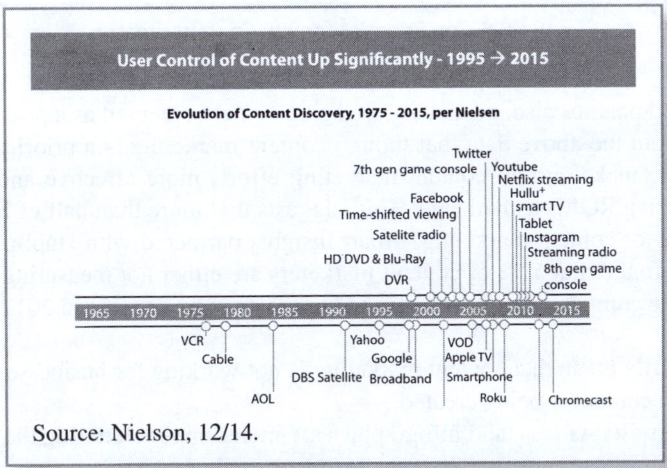

Figure 8.5 Evolution of Content

WHY CONTENT MARKETING

"Irrespective of B2B or B2C , 73 % Top Priority for B2C & 60 % for B2B" (Content Marketing trends 2016 – Content Marketing Institute)

Every time someone Googles something, millions and millions of results present themselves. And yet, only the top ten are seen. Thus, though content marketing has been important and many businesses have been using it for a number of years, the question still may arise whether content marketing is right for all businesses, both B2C and B2B. According to Smart Insights, content marketing has become an almost universal tactic, with almost 90% of companies using it in 2016, and reporting even more likelihood of utilizing in 2017. According to their study, "Every minute, 1440 WordPress blogs are published, and 500 hours of content are uploaded to YouTube. Although there are 38 million searches on Google every minute, the vast majority of these go to major established sites, leaving many brands competing with thousands and thousands of other content providers to come top of the pack".

A 2016 content marketing data by Content Marketing Institute indicated that in North America, 73% of B2C companies indicates creating more engaging content as their top priority.

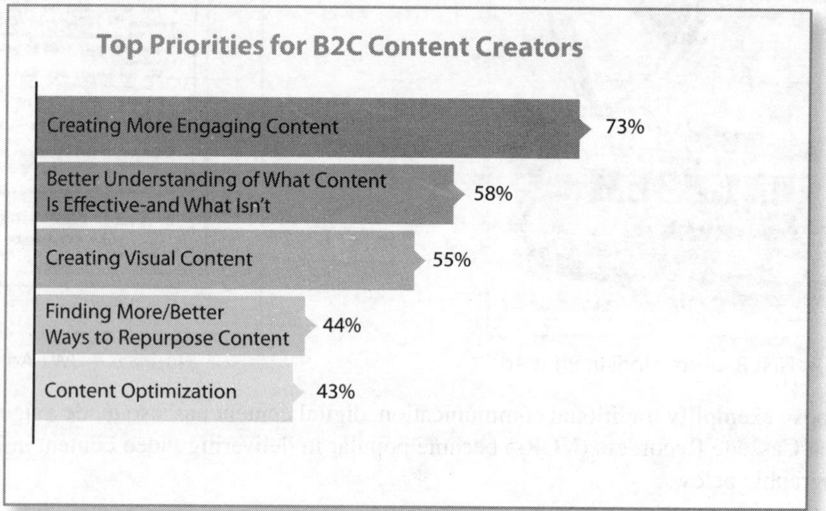

Figure 8.6 Top Priorities for B2B Content Creators

Similarly, for B2B companies also, producing engaging content emerged as a priority in 2017.

It can be inferred from the above data that though content marketing is a priority for these companies, 52% companies wish to make current content marketing efforts more effective and compelling. Another inference is that measuring ROI is a challenge! This suggests that more than half of B2B content marketers are unsure of effectivity of content marketing. Smart Insights partnered with HubSpot to survey European content marketers, and found that 51% of content marketers are either not measuring ROI or are struggling to do so. Yet, 70% of the companies surveyed planned to create more content in 2017 than they did in 2016 suggesting that

- It doesn't necessarily mean that content marketing is not working for businesses.
- Perhaps too much content is being created.
- Substandard blog posts, videos, and infographics are increasingly cluttering the online environment.

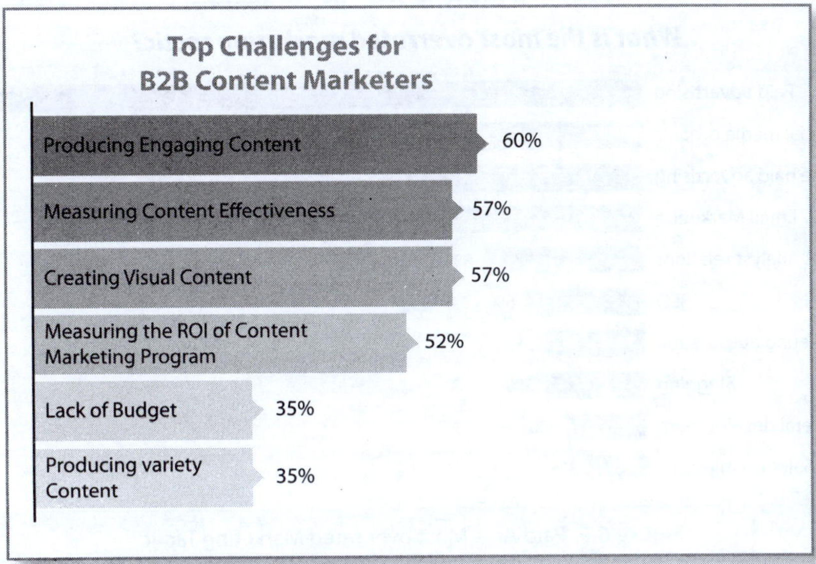

Figure 8.7 Top Challenges for B2B Content Marketers

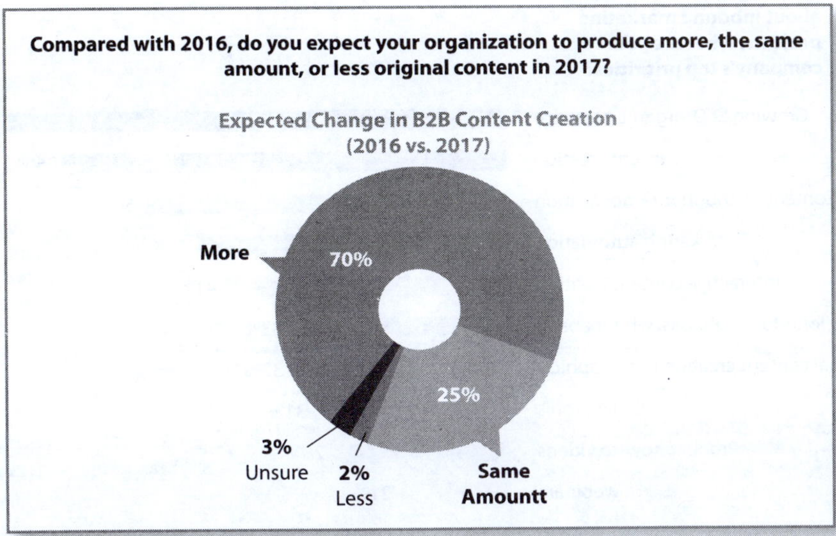

Figure 8.8 Expected Change in B2B Content Creation

The need of the hour, therefore, is that a lot of time and energy needs to be devoted to create effective content and to stand apart from the crowd. Another factor to be considered for clutter and pedestrian content seems to be paid advertising—sort of the antithesis of content marketing.

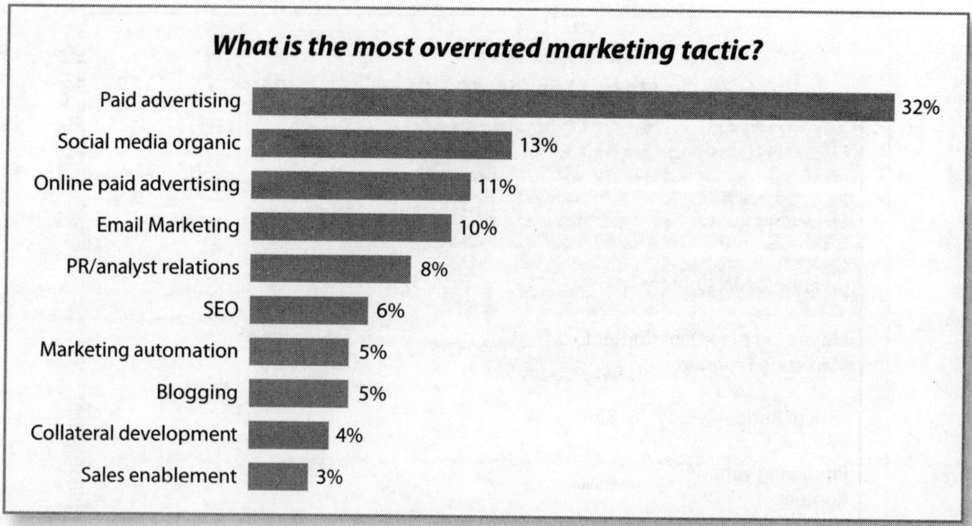

Figure 8.9 Paid Ad – Most over rated Marketing Tactic

To further indicate that content marketing is working for many businesses, SEO and blog creation emerged as the top two inbound marketing priorities for marketers.

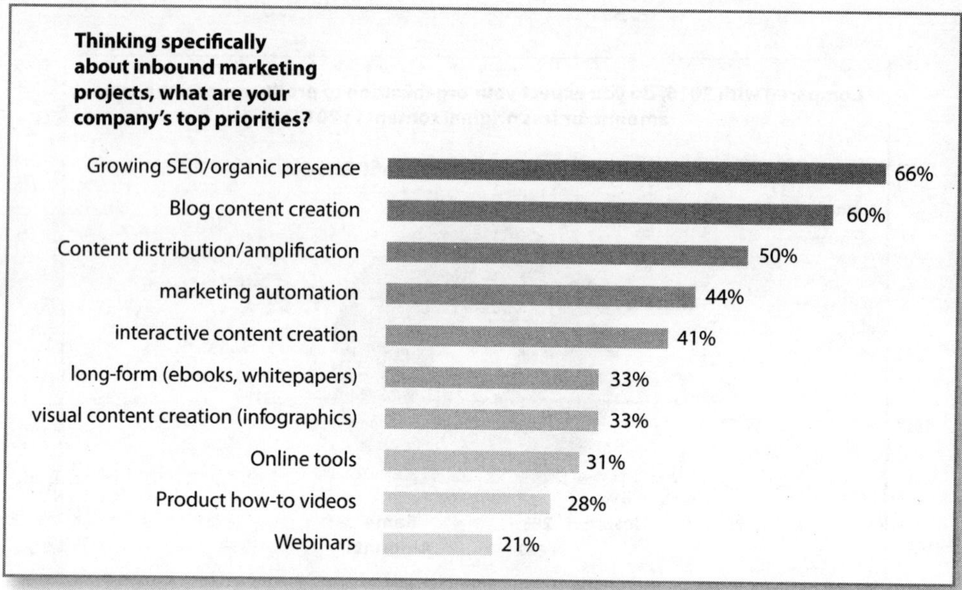

Figure 8.10 Company's Digital Priorities

Thus, irrespective of whether B2B or a B2C company, a content marketing strategy that can benefit the ROI is needed.

Content Marketing Strategy

Content marketing is a component of the overall integrated digital communications and it requires a strategy of its own. Content marketing strategy is different from content strategy in that content marketing strategy goes beyond:

- creating, distributing and sharing content in order to engage audiences, generate leads, improve branding, and other marketing goals you can serve with content marketing.
- the normal analyses across customer journey, customer life cycle and/or the different customer experience touchpoints.

Essentially, a content marketing strategy looks how content marketing (not content) can be used in a strategic way and integrate with other marketing, customer and sales strategies. Content Marketing Institute (CMI) provides some key points on CMS tips and a noteworthy one amongst these tips is: "Your strategy should outline your key business and customer needs, and how your content efforts will address them." Infographic below captures their key takeaways.

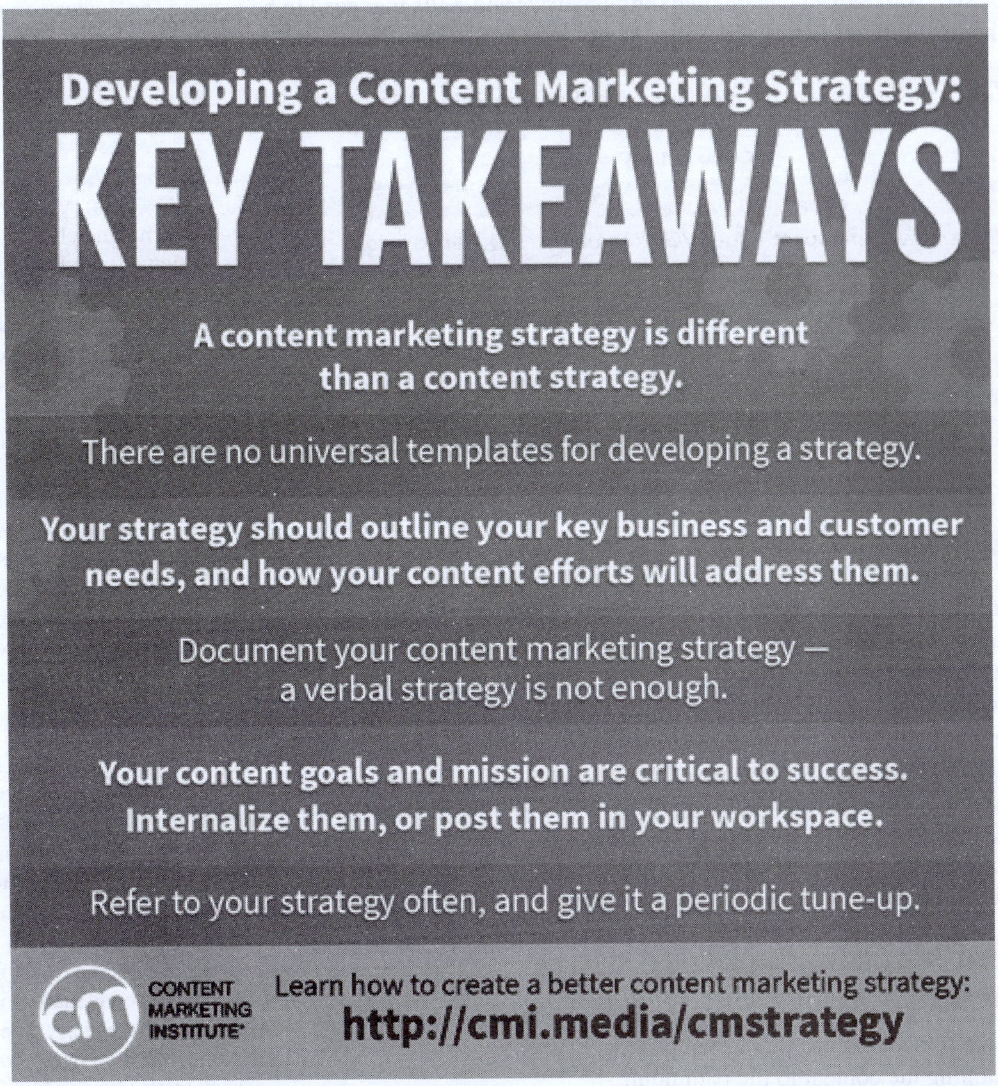

Source: CMI – Free

Figure 8.11 Key Takeaway– Content Strategy

Buying Persona and Preferences

Literature indicates that there are no universal templates for creating CMS; Nevertheless a good starting point is to define "Who the buyer personas are and what their content needs and preferences are?". This helps identify the type of information different types of buyers seek during their buying journey. For example, which of the following of traffic building, conversion optimization, event marketing, lead generation and management, email marketing, social media marketing, marketing automation, customer service, etc. can be improved by a better usage of content and content marketing. This also helps map the customer touchpoints, preferred communication channels, and to some extent, the content formats.

Key Performance Indicators

The next step is to look at content marketing metrics and KPIs that need to be gauged for success, in relation with other marketing metrics and KPIs. As per Oracle Eloqua's (https://www.i-scoop.eu/content-marketing/measuring-return-roi-content-marketing/content) content grid, different content marketing metrics differ according to the stages and business goals as shown in Table 8.1:

Table 8.1 KPIs

Awareness	Consideration	Closure
Traffic/Page views/Time spent	Opens/Click throughs	Qualified leads
Content downloads	Enquiries	Sales calls/Meetings
Inbound links/Page rank	Form submission rate	Active pipeline
Fans/Followers	Funnel conversion	Closed deals
Mentions/Comments /Shares		Size, value and frequency of the deal

Buying Persona: A buyer persona is not merely a description of your buyer. Built from the real words of real buyers, a buyer persona tells you what prospective customers are thinking and doing as they weigh their options to address a problem that a selling company resolves.
Click Through: The action or facility of following a hypertext link to a particular website, especially a commercial one.
Content Mapping: The process of delivering the right **content**, to the right people, at the right time.
Customer Journey: The customer journey is the complete sum of experiences that customers go through when interacting with your company and brand. Instead of looking at just a part of a transaction or experience, the customer journey documents the full experience of being a customer.
Inbound: Inbound marketing is a technique for drawing customers to products and services via content marketing, social media marketing, search engine optimization and branding.

Organizational and Industry Landscape

Although Table 8.1 is indicative of some typical metrics used in content marketing, it is important to speak a common language across all marketing and even business efforts. It is important to know organizational processes, stumbling blocks, competitor data, management goals, customer insights, business stakeholders, teams, external partners, overall marketing priorities, etc. in order to succeed. Besides, knowing the changing industry landscape is critical. That is, how buyer's persona is impacting and evolving the buyer's journey in the industries the customers are active in. For example, looking at the evolutions in the B2B services industry, while content plays a clear role, Key Account Management is being considered as a priority in B2B services industry. Such questions and insights need to be covered in crafting content marketing strategy.

Content Mapping based on the Customer Journey

Thus, content mapping is a three–step process of

1. Mapping the content to the pain point.
2. Mapping (the right type of) content for that problem.
3. Mapping the content to the buying cycle.

The above mapping moves the focus away from the marketer and to the customer journey that the marketer is trying to reach. Hubspot (https://blog.hubspot.com/marketing/content-marketing-plan) provides a list of 50 odd tools of content marketing some of which are mailers, blogs, whitepapers, infographics, reviews, quotes, quizzes, polls, podcasts, photo collages, etc. It is important to analyze what content is needed to address the pain point across the customer journey and the buying cycle and integrate the content with branding purposes (often overlap since each touchpoint has a branding dimension as well). A suggested framework will be

- Making an inventory of existing content and other resources or pieces of information that can be turned into content.
- Setting up the proper content planning, collaboration and scheduling processes.
- Developing a narrative that takes into account the brand's promise and unique value proposition.
- Linking the brand with the business goal and customer intent through content. Establish the tone of voice, style (guide), etc.
- Automating specific marketing processes, often triggered, using the right content at the right time on the right place.
- Planning a content strategy for different channels since each channel has specific characteristic, technical aspects, usage patterns, etc.
- Making sure the content gets found by and shared with the different buyer personas and target audiences.

Content mapping is the process of understanding the target audience so that content can then be created for each stage of their journey culminating in buying of the product. It is an established marketing dictum that seldom do consumers graduate straight from discovery to buying. Instead, the consumer usually passes through stages in their decision journey, discovers the website, considers and evaluates products and competition, influenced by a retargeting ad, and then decides to buy.

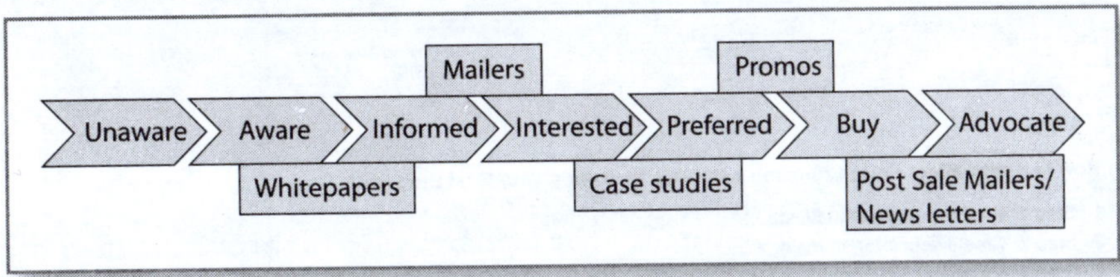

Figure 8.12 Content Mapping

As mentioned earlier, content marketing, if done well, can also be effectively utilized to build brand awareness, engagement, and evangelism since the duration of the customer journey can range from a few weeks to sometimes even months. Under the circumstances, traditionally, content marketing is a top-of-funnel strategy as illustrated in Figure 8.13.

Sales funnel has three stages and the type of content at every stage will need to be crafted accordingly:

1. Awareness
2. Consideration
3. Decision

Awareness Stage Content

The first stage in the consumer buying journey cycle is awareness. In this stage, 75% of the customers are looking for information to know about the offering and are not necessarily ready to buy yet or even ready to opt-in to the mailer list or newsletter. Here a powerful content is needed in creating an awareness for the offering or the organization. Typically, for creating awareness, long phrases/full sentences are used rather

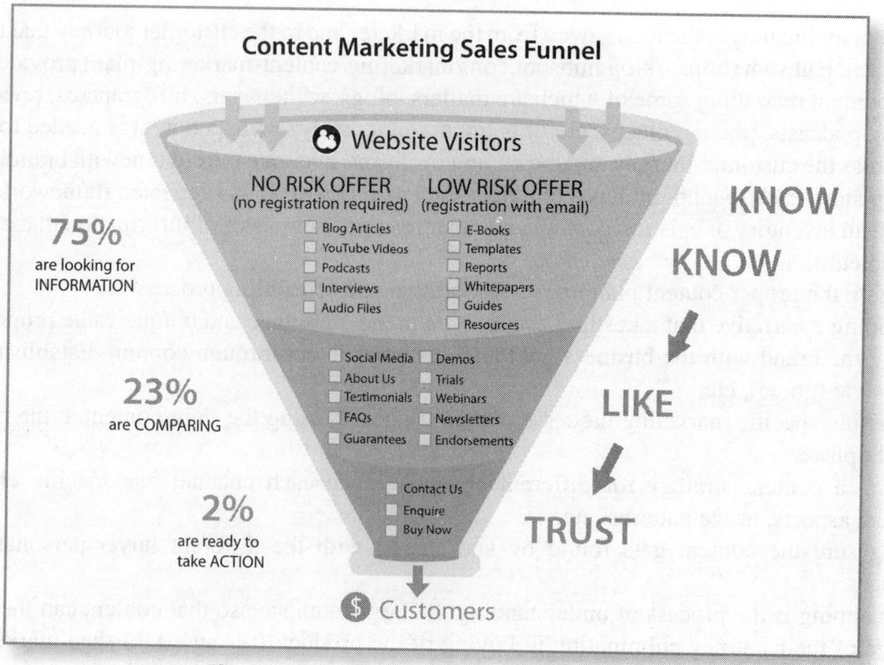

Figure 8.13 Content Marketing Sales Funnel

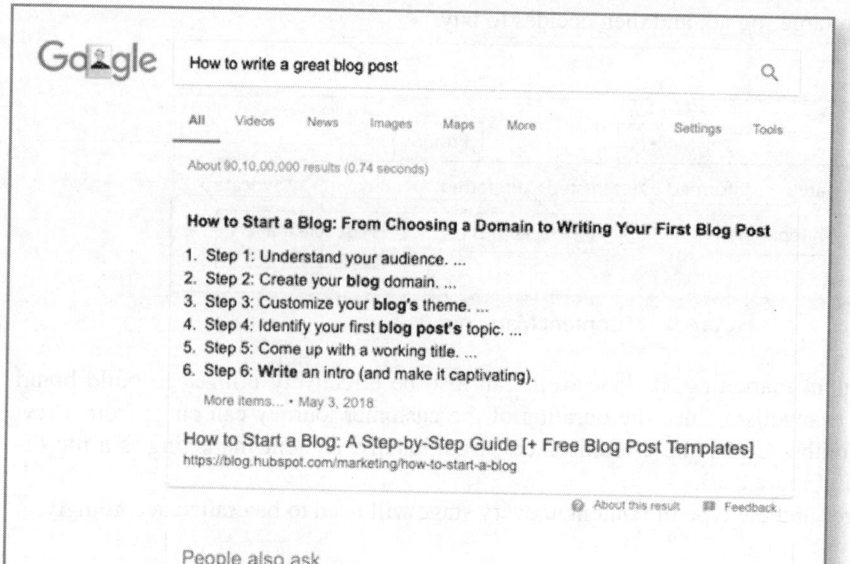

Figure 8.14 How to Write a Good Blogpost

Sales Funnel: It refers to the buying process that companies lead customers through when purchasing products. A **sales funnel** is divided into several steps, which differ depending on the particular **sales** model.

than single words or phrases. For example, a search for "How to write a great blog post" on Google by the author of this book showed:

The HubSpot Google snippet being right on top will be clicked by most searchers underpinning as an example of how a full sentence search with a powerful SEO together works for building brand awareness. A click on the HubSpot, showed the following screenshot!

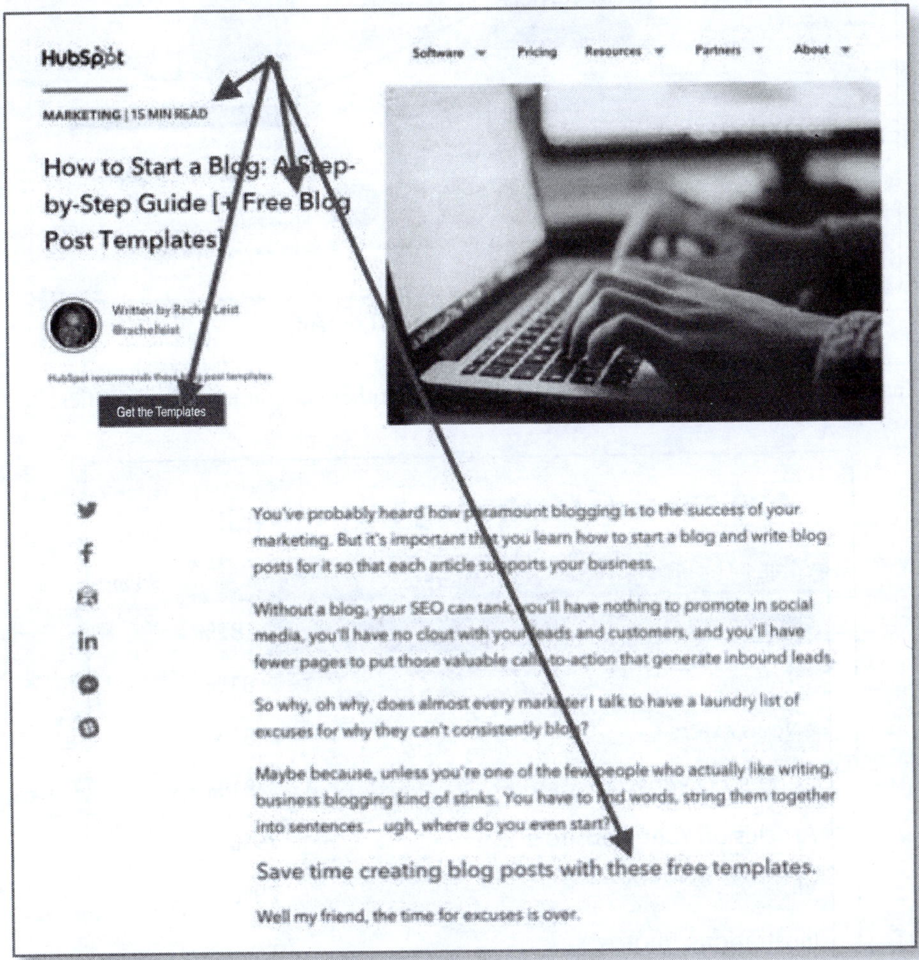

Figure 8.15 Hubspot Google Snippet

The screenshot above is an excellent example of how HubSpot, in their content, thought of everything including the offer of a free blog post templates and a reading time estimate. All those details help to motivate and instil a level of interest in the person who arrives on the page for HubSpot. Awareness stage metrics to look for will be traffic/page views/time spent, content downloads, inbound links/page rank, fans/followers, mentions/comments/shares.

Awareness Stage Metrics
Traffic/Page views/Time spent
Content downloads
Inbound links/Page rank
Fans/Followers
Mentions/Comments/Shares

Social media content is another good way to build brand awareness since 76% and 42% of people use Facebook and Twitter, respectively, daily and people do not necessarily go onto social media platforms to see product posts or buy products; but well-crafted content helps in creating awareness and leveraging the community.

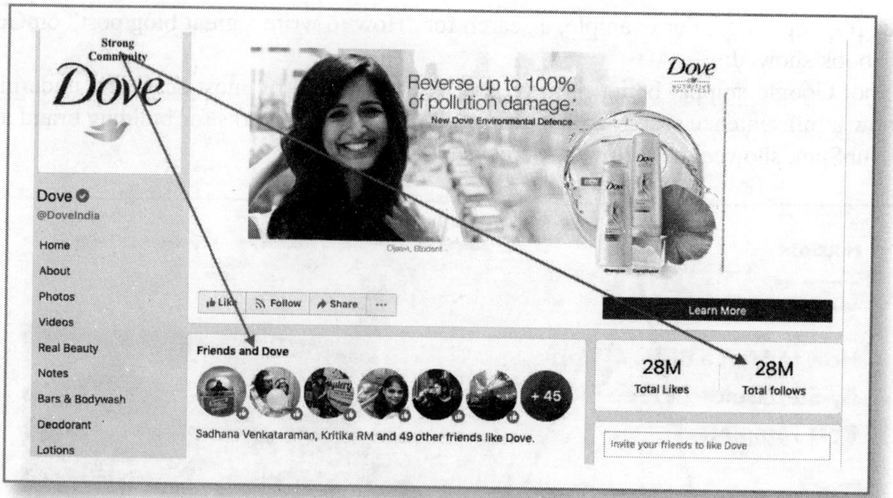

Figure 8.16 Social Media Content

A Smart Insight study shows the following data for use of other content marketing tactics.

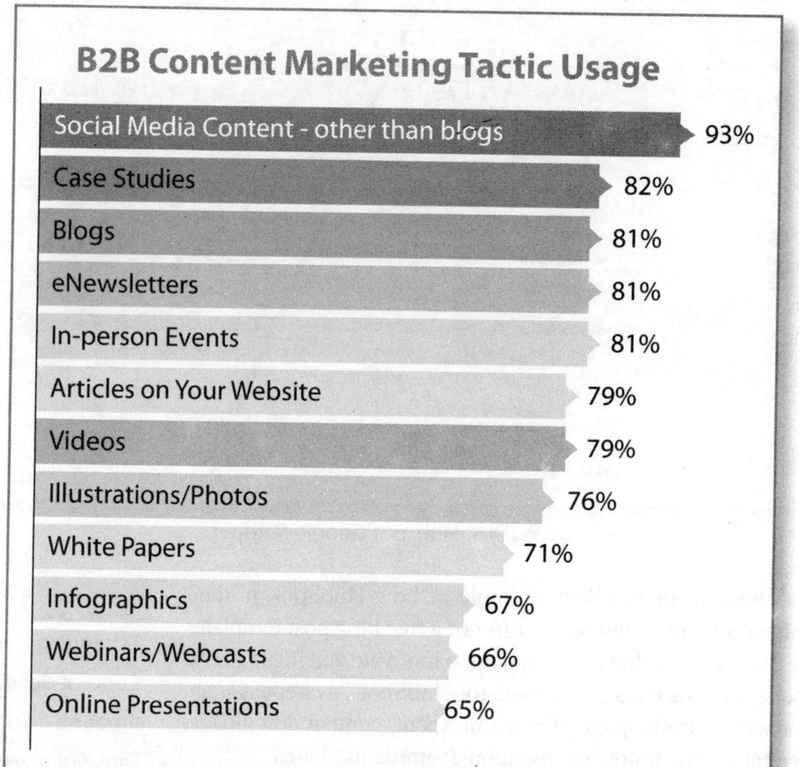

Figure 8.17 B2B Content Tactics

Consideration Stage Content

Consideration Stage Metrics
Opens/Click throughs
Enquiries
Form submission rate
Funnel conversion

After awareness, the next stage in consumer journey is consideration, for, once the consumer becomes aware of the offering or the organization, the chances of purchase improves significantly. However, being in consideration set alone does not guarantee final purchase or acquisition. The consumer still needs to be guided through the sales/purchase funnel. Thus, the role of content marketing at this stage and the focus should be on newsletter sign-ups, number of returning visitors, form submissions, and resource downloads.

Click throughs, enquiries, downloads, etc. are indicative of the interest of your current prospects. To sustain this interest, it is necessary to create content to continue attracting people who are interested in the offerings. Content like e-books and newsletters, for instance, do a remarkable job of building trust during the consideration phase because of the way information is presented, they convey views, they are brand communications and indeed the tone of voice. A consistent newsletter also creates an ongoing conversation with your prospects. While the prospect may not be ready to buy yet, signing up for your mailers, e-books and similar content indicate that the prospects are likely considering the offering. The data base generated in this process of signing up allows to stay in contact with prospects during the consideration phase, improving the probability converting the prospects.

E book: An electronic book is a book publication made available in digital form, consisting of text, images, or both, readable on the flat-panel display of computers or other electronic devices. Although sometimes defined as "an electronic version of a printed book", some e-books exist without a printed equivalent.

Long-tail keywords are recommended in SEO during the consideration phase since

- Long-tail keywords focus on audience who are in the consideration phase more than their counterparts.
- Long-tail keywords are less competitive, which means you have a higher chance of ranking for them in addition to being cost effective.

Decision Stage Content

Closure Stage Metrics
Qualified leads
Sales calls/Meetings
Active pipeline
Closed deals
Size, value and frequency of the deal

All the above activities should culminate and fructify to physical purchase and payment and is the final stage of the buying cycle or it is conversion optimization of your content marketing efforts. The metrics to be considered at this stage will be qualified leads, sales calls/meetings, active pipeline, closed deals, size value and frequency of the deal.

In this stage, longer keywords or even sentences rather than words or phrases help since generally speaking, the longer the keyword, the more interested someone is in buying from you. For example, a search for "how to start an e-commerce store." – the first result will be from Shopify that it is an ecommerce platform where beginners and experts alike build their online stores.

A click on the result takes the prospect to their blog post with CTAs right through the top-fold.

One of the CTAs in the middle of the content is for a webinar!

This is followed up with another CTA in the middle of the content that encourages visitors to start their 14-day trial right away.

This example of Shopify is to illustrate the process and the effectivity of Content and Content strategy at the decision or closure stage of the customer journey funnel, when there are undecided customers in the universe who need to be provided with a trigger for action beginning with long-tail, high-commitment keywords and including compelling CTAs within that content.

Webinar: A seminar conducted over the Internet

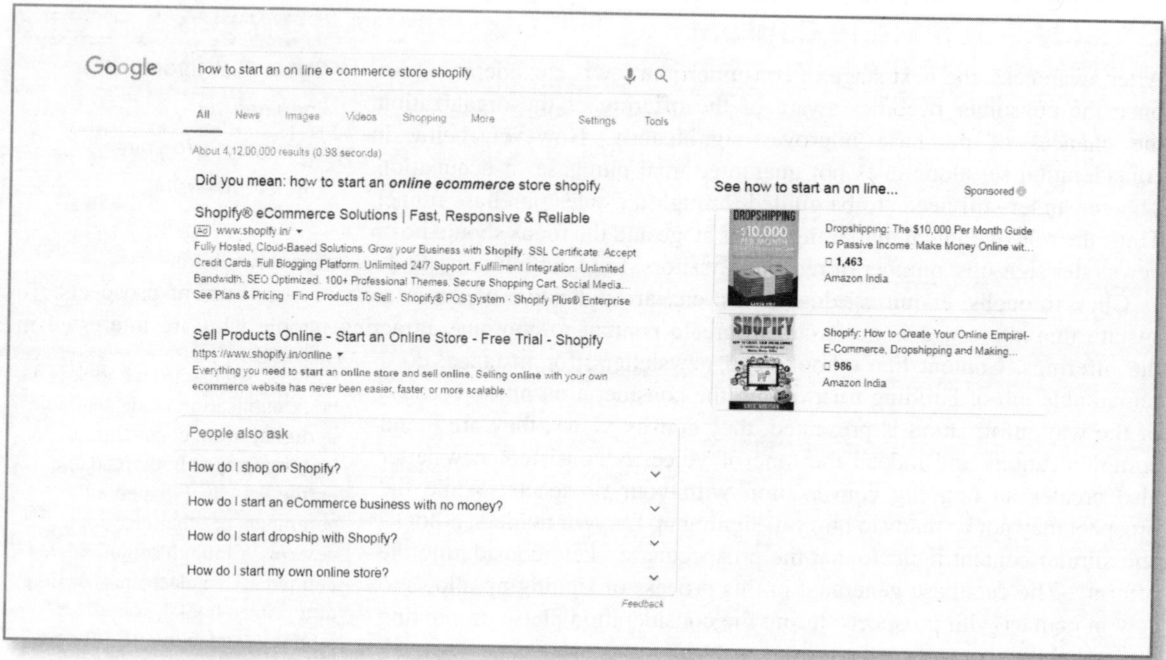

Figure 8.18 Setting up e-Commerce Store

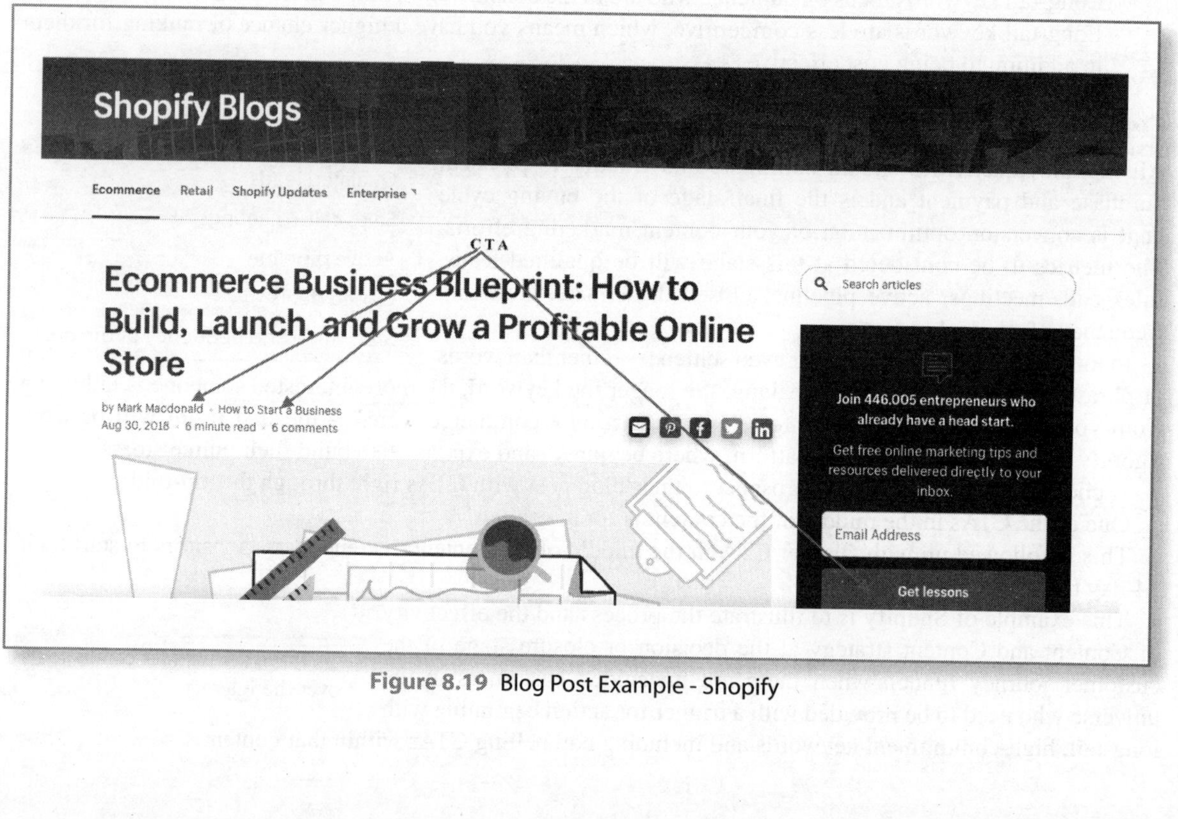

Figure 8.19 Blog Post Example - Shopify

Figure 8.20 Importance of CTA

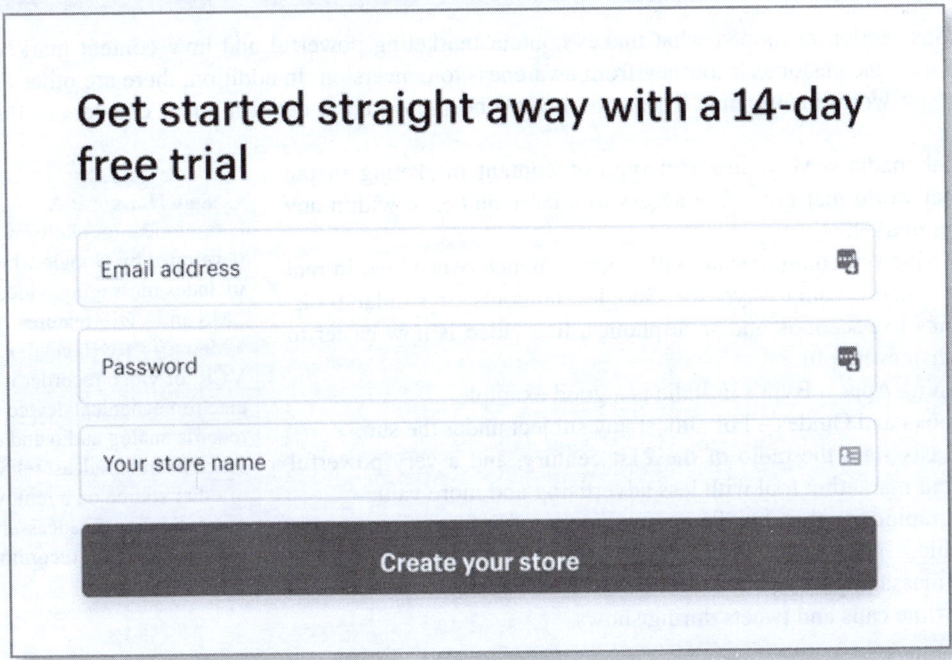

Figure 8.21 Create Your Store

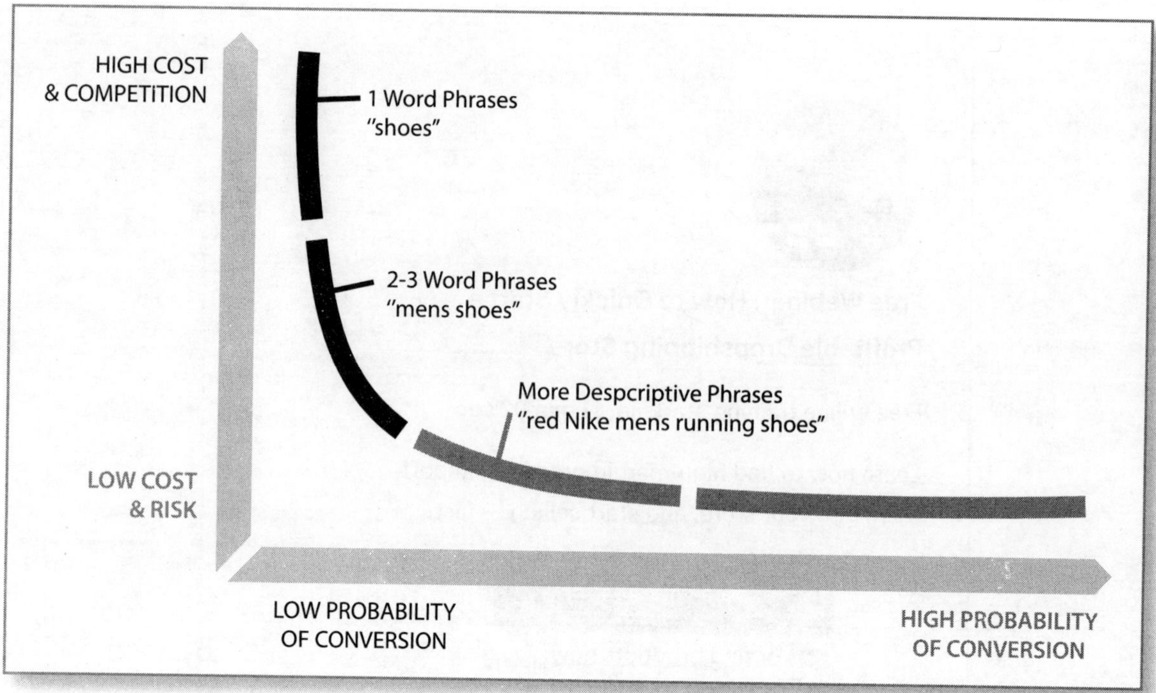

Figure 8.22 Long Tail Words Impact

OTHER PLATFORMS

The previous section examined what makes content marketing powerful and how content marketing can be used to map the customer's journey from awareness to conversion. In addition, there are other tools and media that are worth mentioning. These are or have been covered in detail in other chapters of this book. They are

- Social media – very powerful type of content marketing in the digital world that gives free access to a large audience within any target market.
- Live video to communicate with your audience over video in real time without using Skype or Google Hangouts or similar tools. Thanks to Facebook and smartphones, live video is now easier to use than ever before.
- Learning Apps – Byju's in India is a good example.
- E-Books and Guides – For almost any subject under the sun.
- Podcasts - are the radio of the 21st century, and a very powerful content marketing tool with less advertising and more value.
- Infographics – that bundle many pieces of information in one graphic.
- Text messaging.
- Real time calls and tweets during shows.

Google Hangout: A communication platform developed by Google which includes messaging, video chat, SMS and VOIP features
Video Casette Recorder: A VCR, or video recorder is an electromechanical device that records analog audio and analog video from broadcast television or other source on a removable, magnetic tape videocassette, and can play back the recording.

ADDITIONAL CONTENT MARKETING UTILITIES

Google Analytics

It is important to pay attention to analytics to know the performance of the current so as to fine tune and iterate what is working well. Google Analytics is usually a one stop shop that will provide all of the necessary information such as page views, unique page views, average time spent, entrance, bounce rate, exit percentage, etc.

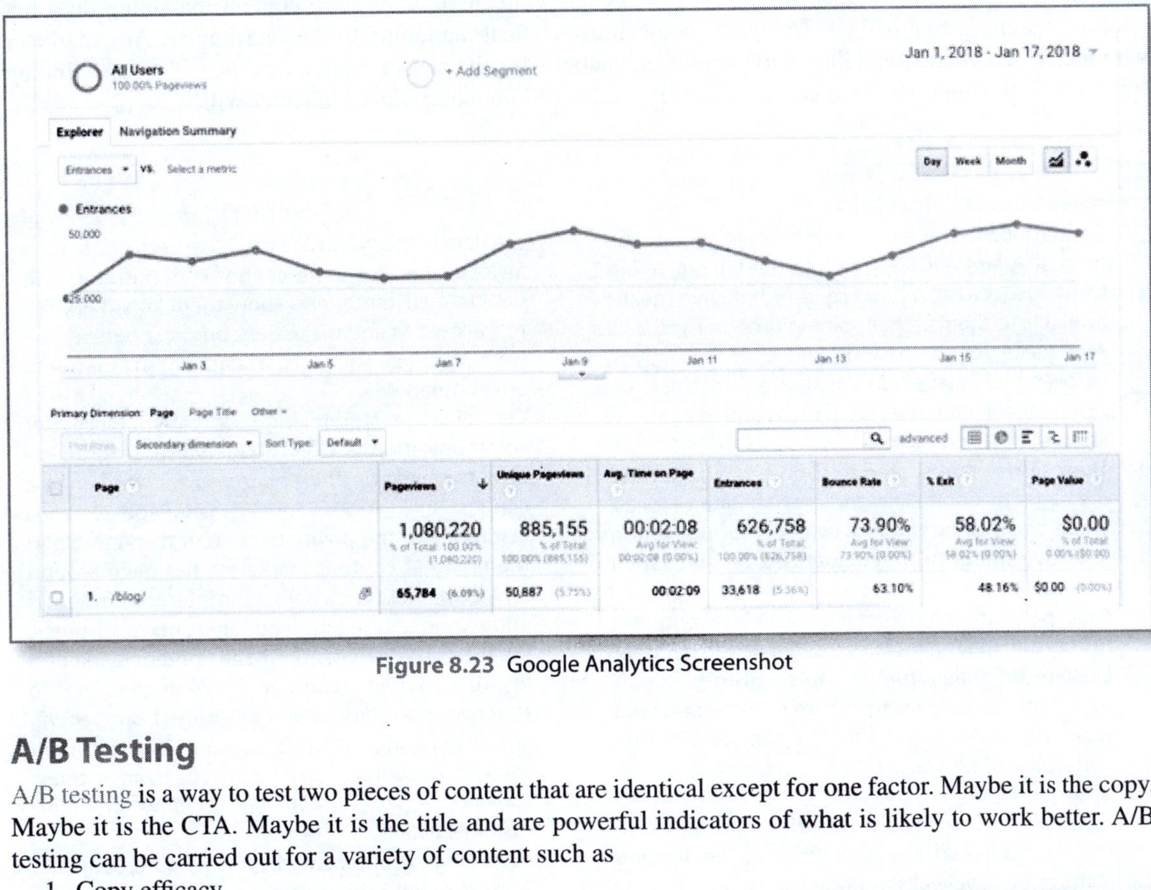

Figure 8.23 Google Analytics Screenshot

A/B Testing

A/B testing is a way to test two pieces of content that are identical except for one factor. Maybe it is the copy. Maybe it is the CTA. Maybe it is the title and are powerful indicators of what is likely to work better. A/B testing can be carried out for a variety of content such as

1. Copy efficacy
2. Landing pages
3. Form design
4. Headline and body copy
5. Impact of testimonial
6. Impact of social proof
7. Impact of email security seal
8. Final page design
9. Free sign up design
10. Button colour design

The above is an indicative list and not an exhaustive one. Suffice to say that A/B testing can be performed on any creative.

> **A/B Testing:** Sometimes called split testing Compares two versions of a web page to see which one performs better. You compare two web pages by showing the two variants (let's call them A and B) to similar visitors at the same time. The one that gives a better conversion rate wins!

Content Schedule and Scheduling

With a plethora of activities in a campaign, it is easy to lose track of various activities since a lot of time and money is spent on content marketing. With an organized content schedule, helpful analytics, and regular A/B testing, the content marketing efforts will have a better chance of success. There are several online tools such as CoSchedule that are available.

This chapter covered through examples, gives an idea of what it takes to be a good content marketer by differentiating between content marketing strategy and content strategy. Also content marketing does not burn a huge marketing budget. Today, anyone can use content marketing to their advantage. Any marketer who focus their energy on telling good stories, no matter what the platform or context is, will create winning strategies in the long run. As it is said, shouting louder will not help! Shouting better will!

CHAPTER SUMMARY

- Content has evolved through ages. Since the time of Adam and Eve, people have been trying to influence others, utilizing whatever means available to them at that point in time. In the Stone Age, pieces of sharp stone was used by natives, who etched images and markings on trees, on stones and in communicated ideas and insights on life in that period.
- These also demonstrated the power of images and messages in storytelling and propagation of ideas! These seem to be the first evidence of marketing and advertising, for, they influenced the perception and behaviour!
- Great persuaders have been irresistible throughout history and they have created or destroyed nations– Lincoln or Hitler, for example. History stands testimony to, anyone, anywhere in the world who was better at expressing their ideas could muster and accumulate wealth that is unprecedented in history.
- Today, storytelling includes the digital presentation tools that are used, like PowerPoint unlike drawing pictures on cave walls as done thousands of years ago. Storytelling is not new but goes back 2,000 years ago to Aristotle.
- When we were children we enjoyed listening to audio tapes of nursery rhymes by Preeti Sagar, watched Jungle Book/Mogli cartoons in movie halls or television, read Chandamama Comics, etc. This happens there in the industry today, for example, SAP, a giant business software company that is global, hired in 2018 for a position titled Chief Storyteller.
- According to Avinash Kaushik, one of the top executives at Google who was also the leading web analytics expert in the world "..., we can have all the data in the world. We can have better data than anyone else. But if we cannot communicate that data to a customer and show them how it applies to their world and make their business better, then we have failed. Then all that data doesn't matter to our company"
- Central to storytelling or any piece of communication is ***CONTENT*** – voice, text, image or a combination thereof. In India, Chandamama comics in various Indian languages stands testimony to the power of content marketing and the fact that content marketing has been around for a long time, much before the Internet. Content is about longevity, relation building and consistency.
- What is content marketing? The Content Marketing Institute defines content marketing as "*... a strategic marketing approach focused on creating and distributing valuable, relevant and consistent content to attract and retain a clearly-defined audience — and, ultimately, to drive profitable customer action*".
- According to Content Marketing Institute, Benjamin Franklin's publishing the yearly Poor Richard's Almanack in 1732 to promote his printing business was the oldest and first known advertising.
- In India, B Dattaram and Co. is claimed to be the oldest existing Indian agency, started in Mumbai in 1902 and its release of Jabakusum Hair Oil print advertisement as one of the oldest advertisements.
- Why content marketing in digital? According to Content Marketing Institute, "Irrespective of B2B or B2C, 73% Top Priority for B2C and 60% for B2B.
- According to Smart Insights, content marketing has become an almost universal tactic, with almost 90% of companies using it in 2016, and even more likelihood of utilizing in 2017.

- According to Smart Insights study, "Every minute, 1440 WordPress blogs are published, and 500 hours of content are uploaded to YouTube. Although there are 38 million searches on Google every minute, the vast majority of these go to major established sites, leaving many brands competing with thousands and thousands of other content providers to come top of the pack".
- A 2016 content marketing data by Content Marketing Institute indicated that in North America, 73% of B2C companies indicates creating more engaging content as their top priority.
- Companies wish to make current content marketing efforts more effective and compelling because 52% of B2B content marketers report measuring ROI as among their top challenges and more than half of B2B content marketers are unsure of effectivity.
- Smart Insights partnered with HubSpot to survey European content marketers, and found that 51% of content marketers are either not measuring ROI or are struggling to do so. Yet, 70% of the companies surveyed planned to create more content in 2017 than they did in 2016.
- In short, it does not necessarily mean that content marketing is not working for businesses, perhaps too much content is being created, substandard blog posts, videos, and infographics are increasingly cluttering the online environment.
- Content marketing is a component of the overall integrated digital communications and it requires a strategy of its own. It is also different from content strategy in that content marketing goes beyond creating, distributing and sharing content in order to engage audiences, generate leads, improve branding, and other marketing goals you can serve with content marketing.
- A content marketing strategy goes beyond the analyses across customer journey, customer life cycle and/or the different customer experience touchpoints. Essentially, a content marketing strategy looks how content marketing (not content) can be used in a strategic way and integrate with other marketing, customer and sales strategies.
- Considering there are no universal templates for creating CMS, a good starting point is to define "Who the buyer personas are and what their content needs and preferences are." This helps identify the type of information different types of buyers seek during their buying journey.
- The next step is to look at content marketing metrics and KPIs that need to be gauged for success, in relation with other marketing metrics and KPIs.
- It is important to know organizational processes, stumbling blocks, competitor data, management goals, customer insights, business stakeholders, teams, external partners, overall marketing priorities, etc. in order to succeed.
- Besides, knowing the changing industry landscape is critical. That is, how the buyer's journey of your buyer persona is evolving in the industries your customers are active in and your business is active in.
- Content mapping based on the customer journey is a three-step process of mapping the content to the pain point, mapping (the right type of) content for that problem, mapping the content to the buying cycle. This moves the focus away from the marketer and to the customer journey that the marketer is trying to reach.
- HubSpot provides a list of 50 odd possible ways of content marketing some of which are mailers, blogs, whitepapers, infographics, reviews, quotes, quizzes, polls, podcasts, photo collages, etc.
- It is important to analyze what content is needed to fulfil different business goals across the customer journey or for branding purposes often overlap since each touchpoint has a branding dimension as well.
- Content mapping is the process of understanding the target audience so that content can then be created for each stage of their journey culminating in buying of the product. It is an established marketing dictum that seldom do consumers graduate straight from discovery to buying. Instead, the consumer usually passes through stages in their decision journey, discovers the website, considers and evaluates products and competition, see a retargeting ad, and then the decision to buy happens.
- Content marketing, if done well, can be effectively utilized to build brand awareness, engagement, and evangelism considering the customer journey can take a few weeks or sometimes even months. Under the circumstance, traditionally, content marketing is a top-of-funnel strategy.
- There are three basic stages of content creation: awareness content, consideration content and decision content.
- In awareness content stage, 75% of the customers are looking for information to know about the

offering and are not necessarily ready to buy yet or even ready to opt into the mailer list or newsletter.

- Awareness stage metrics are traffic/page views/ time spent, content downloads, inbound links/ page rank, fans/followers, mentions/comments/ shares.
- In consideration content stage, the consumer needs to be guided through the sales/purchase funnel. This is the role of content marketing at this stage and the focus should be on newsletter sign-ups, number of returning visitors, form submissions, and resource downloads.
- Consideration stage metrics are Opens/Click Throughs, Enquiries, Form Submission rate, Funnel Conversion. Long-tail keywords in SEO also work during the consideration phase.
- In decision content stage, it is conversion optimization of your content marketing efforts.
- Closure stage metrics are qualified leads, sales calls/meetings, active pipeline, closed deals - size, value and frequency.
- In this stage, longer keywords or even sentences rather than words or phrases help since generally speaking, the longer the keyword, the more interested someone is in buying from you.
- Other platforms commonly used are
  - Social media – Very powerful type of content marketing in the digital world that gives free access to a large audience within any target market.
  - Live video to communicate with your audience over video in real time without using Skype or Google Hangouts or similar tools. Thanks to Facebook and smartphones, live video is now easier to use than ever before.
  - Learning Apps – Byju's in India is a good example.
  - E-Books and Guides – For almost any subject under the sun.
  - Podcasts are the radio of the 21st century, and a very powerful content marketing tool with less advertising and more value.
  - Infographics – that bundle many pieces of information in one graphic.
  - Text messaging.
  - Real time calls and tweets during shows.
- Additional utilities are Google Analytics, A/B testing and scheduling.

CLOSING CASE

CASE LET

Lead Pages

Lead Pages is a technology company that designs mobile friendly landing-page templates and offers testing services in digital marketing domain. It lets you build high-converting landing pages, sign-up forms, and other conversion assets that send new leads directly to tons of your web services simultaneously. The platform helps businesses to significantly enhance their reach.

With heavy competitions from major players like HubSpot and InfusionSoft, Lead Pages had to do something out of the box to be profitable and successful. But in its initial years, Lead Pages did not have the kind of money or resources that its competitions were spending in order to acquire clients. This is when the CEO of Lead Pages, Clay came up with an idea – "a content team of 4 people who can outperform a sales team of 80 people at conventional companies".

The basic objective of the campaign was to leverage on inbound marketing as against the traditional outbound marketing which was being used by Lead Pages' competitors. So, Lead Pages created a set of content marketing assets for this campaign. It included:

- Seven marketing courses, 2 ebooks, 10 case studies, and 8 info-graphics, all offered free-of-cost.
- Weekly webinars covering plethora of topics on digital marketing.
- Popular marketing blog which mainly covered lead generation, A/B testing, and a wide range of similar topics.
- Conversion Cast: A marketing podcast run by the world-famous podcaster Tim Paige.

Lead Pages' Content Marketing Resources

So, what was the end result? This strategy of Lead Pages proved to be highly successful. Their marketing assets were a huge hit among their target audience. It was a small team of content marketing professionals with focussed and a result-oriented approach. Hence, their acquisition cost was extremely low, as compared to their competitors who were spending a lot on outbound marketing.

In just under 3 years, Lead Pages acquired 35,000 customers. The company's business growth was remarkable and as a bootstrap start-up, Lead Pages generated revenue in excess of $16 million in 2015. In the year 2016, Lead Pages was declared as the #148 fastest growing company in the US. Till date, Lead Pages continues to be one of the top technology companies that offers landing pages and testing services.

Case Questions

1. Why was Lead Pages content marketing strategy a huge hit?
2. What are some of the high value content marketing assets for a technology company such as Lead Pages?

REVIEW QUESTIONS

1. What is content marketing?
2. Why is storytelling important in content marketing?
3. Why is content marketing important?
4. What have been the top priorities and challenges for Content Creators in 2017?
5. What is content marketing strategy? What is content strategy and what is the difference between the two?
6. What are content mapping and customer journey?
7. What are the stages of content creation in customer journey and what are the metrics for each stage?
8. What are the various platforms used in content marketing strategy?
9. Discuss some of the content marketing utilities that will be useful.
10. What is A/B testing and how is it important in content marketing strategy?

ACTIVITY QUESTIONS

1. Write a blog of approximately 300 words on benefits of the product/service created in Chapter 5 assignment and create your own account in Wordpress.com to post it.
2. Basis Dashboard created in the Chapter 6 Assignment, create an Infographic.

KEY TERMS

A/B Testing
Buying Persona
Click Through
Content Marketing
Content Mapping
Customer Journey
E book
Google Hangout
Inbound
Sales Funnel
Video Casette Recorder
Webinar

REFERENCES

1. Gallo, C. (2018) The Secret to Great Communication: Be Like Aristotle http://knowledge.wharton.upenn.edu/article/the-secret-to-great-communication-skills/.
2. Gardner James https://unbounce.com/a-b-testing/shocking-results/.
3. Google Analytics.
4. i – Scoop https://www.i-scoop.eu/content-marketing/measuring-return-roi-content-marketing/content.
5. Keiner Perkins Internet Trends, 2017 https://www.kleinerperkins.com/perspectives/internet-trends-report-2017.
6. Latka, Nathan - The 40 Best Free Online Scheduling Tools" (http://nathanlatka.com/best-50-free-online-scheduling-tools/).
7. McGill , J How to Develop a Content Strategy: A Start-to-Finish Guide https://blog.hubspot.com/marketing/content-marketing-plan.
8. Pulizzi, J (2016) The History of Content Marketing https://contentmarketinginstitute.com/2016/07/history-content-marketing/.
9. SmartInsights Essential 2017 Content Marketing Statistics, https://www.smartinsights.com/content-management/content-marketing-strategy/essential-2017-content-marketing-statistics/.
10. What is Content Marketing https://contentmarketinginstitute.com/what-is-content-marketing/.
11. Wikipedia History of Advertising https://en.wikipedia.org/wiki/History_of_advertising.

CHAPTER 9

DIGITAL AND BUSINESS MARKETING (B2B)

CHAPTER OBJECTIVES

After going through this chapter, you will be able to

- Understand B2B marketing and how it is different from B2C
- Define ecommerce and discuss its evolution
- Assess digital marketing strategies relevant to B2B/ecommerce/edistribution
- Describe content management—tools and strategy
- Analyze digital marketing for the millennial decision makers
- Discuss the role of artificial intelligence, analytics and algorithmic marketing

OPENING CASE LET

APPLE'S USE OF CONNECTORS

Nearly all electronic devices use Universal Service Bus (USB) connectors for enabling connectivity between devices and power sources. Apple Computers, on the other hand, for the most part eschews USB connectors and favours connectors that it designs for itself, even though it provides USB ports for connecting non-Apple products. The rationale for this approach range from the infirmities associated with USB ports to consumer experience to proprietary spare parts.

Of importance, though, in the context of B2B marketing is how suppliers of connectors would want to engage with Apple. A general manufacturer of commodity connectors is unlikely to curry any favour with Apple, even if they are offered free, simply because these connectors do not fit Apple's vision of the role of connectors in its products.

On the other hand, a connector supplier willing to adapt to the needs of Apple would likely find a ready audience with Apple. Even though, Apple will drive a hard bargain in the pricing, such a supplier would be at an advantage since it will be one among very few suppliers willing to adapt to Apple, and therefore, Apple needs the supplier as much as the supplier needs Apple. Thus, the supplier would be able to realize a reasonable price for his product and, on an average, be more profitable than other connector manufacturers.

Case Questions

1. Why does Apple eschew USB Connectors?
2. Given the above, why would a supplier of connector engage with Apple?

INTRODUCTION

Each of the elements in this chapter is independent. B2B marketing is a specific topic, the other topics nevertheless have a bearing on B2B marketing as well as B2C marketing, and almost any aspect of digital marketing, either as a component or as a facilitator. Thus, an attempt has been made looking at each of these topics independently and drawing analogies appropriate and connecting them.

Digital marketing is most of the time associated with consumer products (B2C). It is seldom considered to be B2B. However, in the global and Indian context, B2B contributes to well over 60% of the GDP. In the Indian context, for instance, business marketers serve the largest markets of all and also provide a large chunk of employment[1],[2].

- Products - $ 570 billion (INR 36.83 trillion or 3.68 lac crores)
- Employment :11.7 million (2013 Economic Survey)
- Services – US$ 1.02 trillion Ca 66 lac crores (2013 Eco Survey)
- IT /ITES - $ 231 billion(14.9 lac crores)
- IT /ITES employment – 13.7 million jobs

In this context, marketing statistics and trends show the industry's shift towards a more digital strategy. Let us look at some of the statistics.

- Mobile commerce makes up 30% of all U.S. ecommerce. (Internet Retailer, 2015) (Source: https://www.hubspot.com/marketing-statistics)
- 67% of B2B marketers say they see at least a 10% increase in sales opportunities through lead nurturing, with 15% seeing opportunities increase by 30% or more. (Demand Gen Report, 2014) (Source: https://www.hubspot.com/marketing-statistics)
- B2B marketers now heavily rely on content market tactics to bring in leads and grow the lead pool. 70 % of B2B marketers say that their priority in the next 12 months is converting leads to customers.
- Email remains a top tactic used by B2B marketers who want to reach potential clients and remain top-of-mind as that prospect moves along the sales funnel.
- B2B companies that blogged 11+ times per month had almost 3X more traffic than those blogging 0-1 times per month (HubSpot).
- 31% of B2B marketers use marketing automation to increase revenue (Statistica - https://www.statista.com/study/26613/b2b-marketing-in-the-us-statista-dossier/).

Given the sheer size and volume of the market and transactions, it is not a wonder that Marty Holmes, former CMO of HP, said, "B-to-B Marketers Must Think Like Consumer Companies"[3]. He added--

> **Digital Marketing:** Refers to advertising delivered through digital channels such as search engines, websites, social media, email, and mobile apps

- "Behind every business ("B") is a consumer ("C") who expects to receive a total customer experience. ….
- The Internet has been a great equalizer. This power shift means that we can no longer talk at our customers; we must talk with them.
- As technology and social media have advanced and consumers have risen to the top of the marketing pyramid, the distinction between B-to-B and B-to-C brands is no longer relevant.
- Companies that deal indirectly with consumers must now evolve their mindsets from B-to-B to B-to-P--Business-to-People…

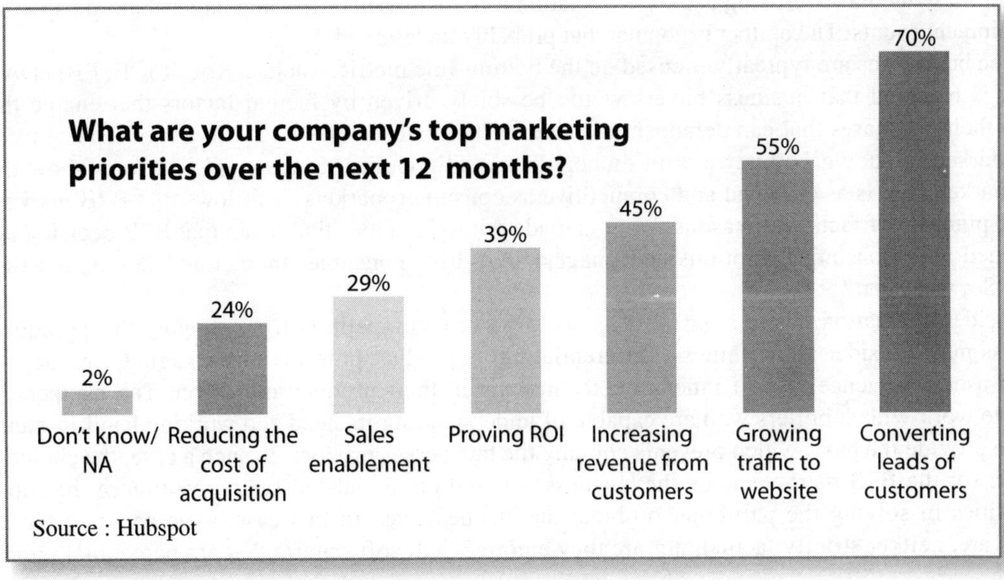

Figure 9.1 State of Inbound 2017

- While this change in approach must begin within marketing departments, it should also be ingrained into the larger company culture to create a brand experience that encompasses products, services and employees".

While we can keep looking at all the statistics and the quotes, let us now look at B2B and digital.

WHAT B2B MARKETING IS

B2B (business-to-business) marketing is marketing of products to businesses or other organizations for use in production of goods, for use in general business operations (such as office supplies), or for resale to other consumers, such as a wholesaler selling to a retailer. In simple terms, B2B marketing is the sale of one company's product or service to another company.

B2B marketing is different from B2C on several levels. For example, in case of B2B:

- The target segment is well known, and is fewer compared to B2C
- Involves complex decision making process
- Purchase decision is mostly made by a small group of individuals or perhaps one
- More reliance on the sales staff
- Much longer sales cycle
- Is largely driven by demand
- Purchase decisions are rational and may or may not be factual
- Has fewer need based segments

Traditionally, B2B had been more of a relationship based marketing and in fact the epithet "Boring to Boring" marketing is not unheard of. The reason being, B2B does not have the glitzy cachet that consumer marketing or Business-to-Consumer (B2C) marketing derives from its

B2B (business-to-business) marketing: B2B (business-to-business) marketing is the marketing of products to businesses or other organizations.

need for mass-media advertising and the association it has with celebrities and larger-than-life sporting and entertainment events. The epithet is popular, but probably undeserved.

Since businesses are typically focused on the bottom-line metrics such as RoI, RoCE, EBITDA, PBT, etc., it is believed that business buyers would be solely driven by factual factors that enable them to justify their purchases that can demonstrate value on their chosen metric. If this hypothesis be true, then B2B marketing should be strewn with monopolies or oligopolies. Since empirical facts show that the B2B marketplace is as crowded and competitive as consumer markets, it follows that B2B marketing is not the pinnacle of facts and reasons that it is made out to be. Does that mean that B2B decision making is imbued with consumer emotions and imagery that drive consumer marketing? This is not the case either. So, what is it?

Consider a situation where a business wants to prevent competitors from copying their product. The business may consider many things—differentiating its product in terms of packaging, product design, unique user experience, use of innovative technology in their product and so on. The business would prefer to work with suppliers who are capable of understanding its need and working hand-in-hand with them to provide the basis which prevents copying the businesses product. In such a case, the choice of the supplier (or the B2B marketeer) by the business is based on the businesses perception of the supplier's capabilities in solving the particular problem the business has. In this case, as is apparent the choice criteria are, neither strictly factual, nor are they emotive, but, soft criteria that are perceptual rather than factual.

B2B marketing abounds with these types of perceptual decision frameworks. It is in identifying and successfully implementing marketing programs around these decision frameworks that the B2B marketeer derives joy from.

PERCEPTUAL DECISION FRAMEWORKS IN B2B MARKETING

The world of B2B marketing comprises commodities, intermediate products, finished goods and services. Similarly, the consumers of these products have diverse needs. Opportunities for marketeers, thus, exist in product design as well as segmenting their markets.

Product design can be viewed along two axes.

1. The level of differentiation of the product
2. The criticality of the product to the buyer

Factual and perceptual factors will vary where the product is on these two axes. Consider, for example, iron. A steel mill making basic steel for use in low-technology application is likely to have some basic specifications. Such steel mill will only be concerned with whether the specifications are met and will base its purchasing decisions mainly along factual parameters and would possibly sacrifice higher specifications to lower its price. On the other hand, consider a steel mill focused on making high precision steel used in high-technology application. Such steel mill will demand high adherence to specifications and would pay a premium for partners who it believes will be consistent in delivering to the specifications.

The difference in the two cases is that in the case of the low-grade steel producer, the consequence of not achieving high quality is not high. Therefore, this producer maximizes on the factual factors. The high-technology steel producer, not only requires input materials that meet high specifications, but also needs a dependable source of supply. Dependability is not merely physical, but also a belief that a vendor will deliver products of the same quality, on time every time.

Exhibit 9.1 shows the relationship between factual and perceptual in B2B marketing.

Low Value added + High criticality = Moderately higher price on criticality	High Value added + High criticality = High Value realization
Low Value added + Low criticality = Low price realization	High Value added + Low criticality = Price realization supplier industry led

Exhibit 9.1 Value Addition Versus Price Matrix

B2B is not one-to-one Marketing

Figure 9.1[4] shows the full chain of B2B marketing and the multiplicity of providers. The significance of this figure is that, unlike in the case of a consumer, a B2B marketeer is both a consumer and a marketeer.

Since B2B consumers are institutions, the decision makers span several functions with sometimes competing objectives. Typically, the environment for a B2B buying decision will involve the users, the buyers and the financiers. Each of these functions could have competing objectives. Simplistically, for example, the users would comprise the individuals who have to use the material purchased by the company and convert it to another product that is used by the businesses' customers. In their decision making, such users receive inputs from various sources within the business in taking a decision—the marketing function, customer support and service functions. Procurement function is usually focused on reducing the cost to the company, while maintaining other parameters and the finance function is focused on rationalizing cash flows and reconciling payments. The successful B2B marketeer has to address all these functions in marketing his products. Thus, marketing functions in the B2B environment are also structured differently from those in consumer marketing businesses.

INTERNET AND B2B MARKETING

Technology has always been a part of B2B marketing. Even before the existence of Internet, B2B purchases of primary commodities happened through exchanges that were automated to a significant extent. Some services, notably financial services, used automation extensively in creating differentiation and providing services to their customers.

The rise of Internet has not only hastened these processes, but also, taken automation to areas such as search for vendors, assessing supplier viability, etc., which used to be more of a manual task earlier. Such automation is not only on the demand side, but also on the supply side, where marketeers have access to many tools to identify prospects and pitch their services to them online.

A survey[5] done by the Business Development Bank of Canada neatly summarizes the diversity of uses the Internet has on B2B marketing.

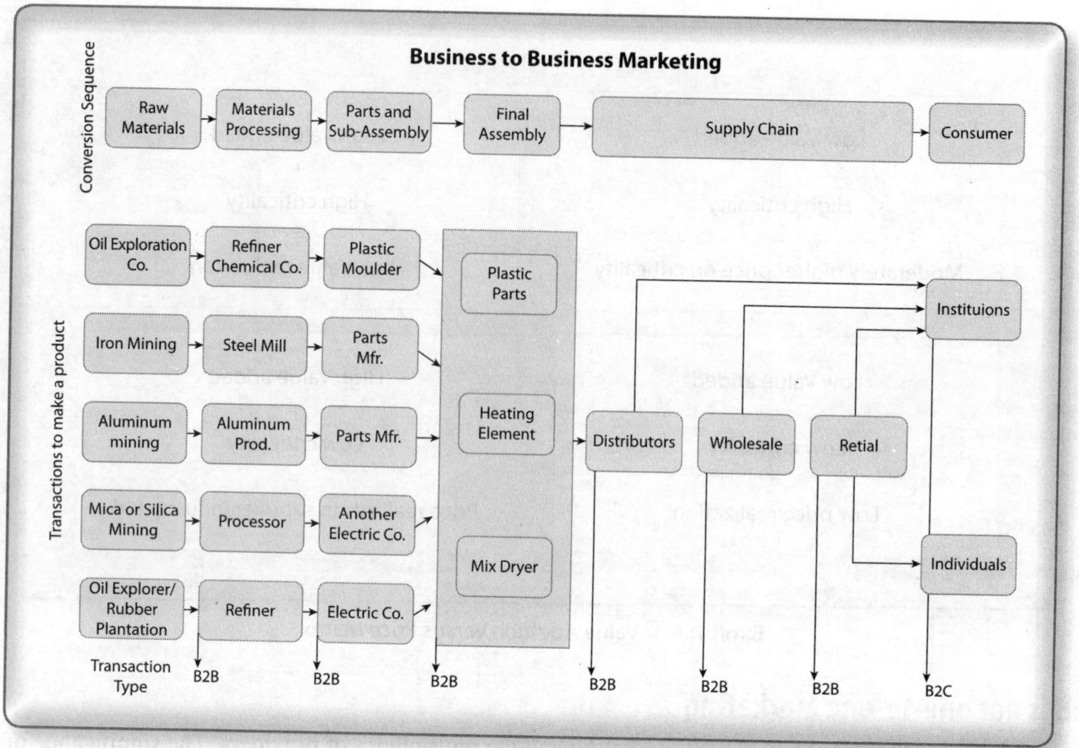

Exhibit 9.2 Business to Business Marketing

ECOMMERCE

Electronic commerce or ecommerce is the marketing, buying and selling of merchandise or services or the transmitting of funds or data over the Internet. eCommerce is truly the child of the Internet. Simply put, the Internet is to ecommerce, what the steam engine was to locomotion and the internal combustion engine was to personal transport.

A Brief History of eCommerce

The seeds of ecommerce were sown in 1995 with the launch of eBay and Amazon, with two diametrically opposing views of online commerce. eBay sought to make entrepreneurs of everybody, while Amazon sought to make consumers of everybody. The people, of course, embraced both visions and the two pioneers enjoy a near hegemony of the ecommerce space.

While the two biggies of ecommerce rule media headlines, they also showed the way to other entrepreneurs on the potential from Internet. So much so today, the ecommerce space ranges from mom-and-pop players to the large multi-nationals. It is the democratizing power of the Internet that allows all to co-exist, without allowing any one dominant force to subsume the less endowed players.

Along the way ecommerce has spawned other ecommerce enterprises such as payment gateways, mobile wallets, logistics, data analytics among others, as well as new and innovative services and products like ride sharing, food delivery, homestays, fitness monitors, etc.

E-commerce: The marketing, buying and selling of merchandise or services or the transmitting of funds or data over the Internet

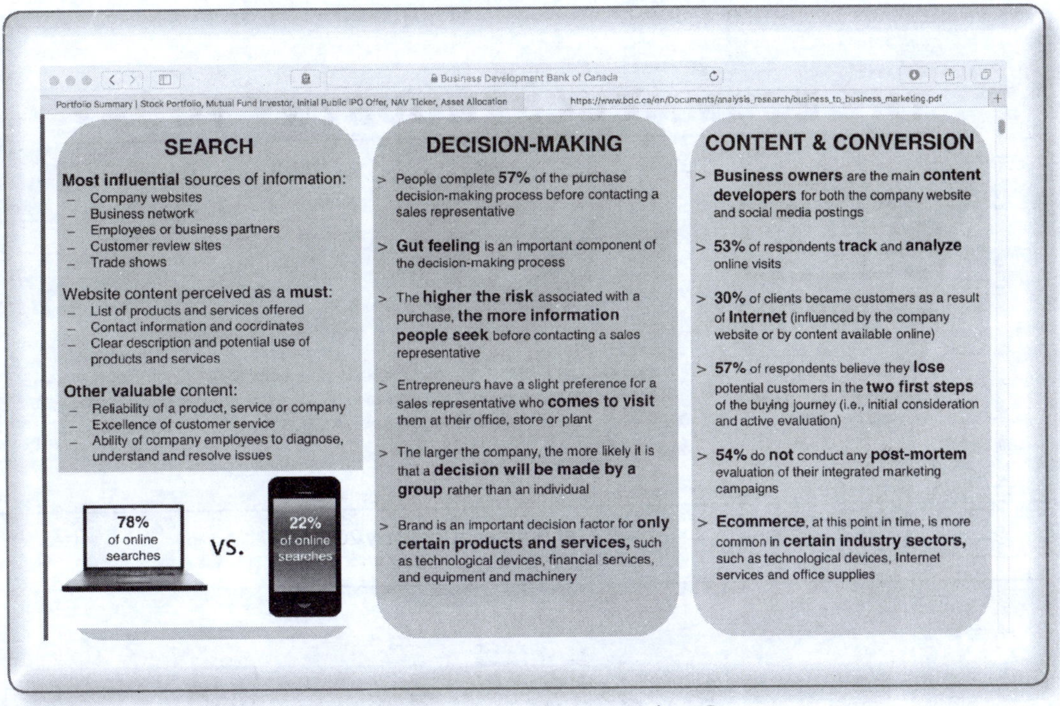

Exhibit 9.3 eCommerce Decision Making Process

Even though ecommerce is mainstream today, it still is quite small in the overall scheme of retailing globally. eMarketeer estimates[6] that 2017 eretail sales of US $ 2.35 trillion was only 10% of the total retail sales of USD 23.40 trillion. It further estimates, that while eretail sales will grow faster than conventional retail, eretail will still be less than 15% of total retail sales by 2020.

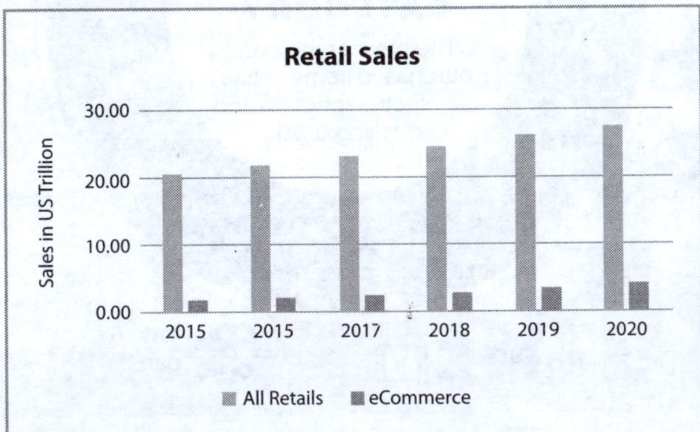

Source : EMarketer

Figure 9.2 Growth eCommerce Retail 2015- 2020

Notwithstanding the relatively small size of ecommerce in overall retail sales, today, ecommerce sales spans the entire spectrum of consumer goods[7].

HubSpot[8] has put together some interesting data on ecommerce and B2B on the Internet. These are summarized in Exhibit 9.5 (to include infographic of HubSpot data – Exhibit 9.5).

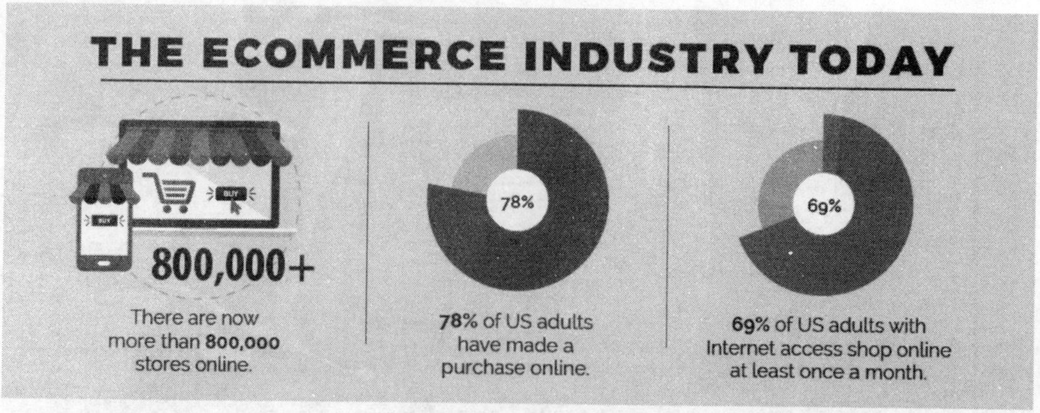

Exhibit 9.4 eCommerce Industry 2018

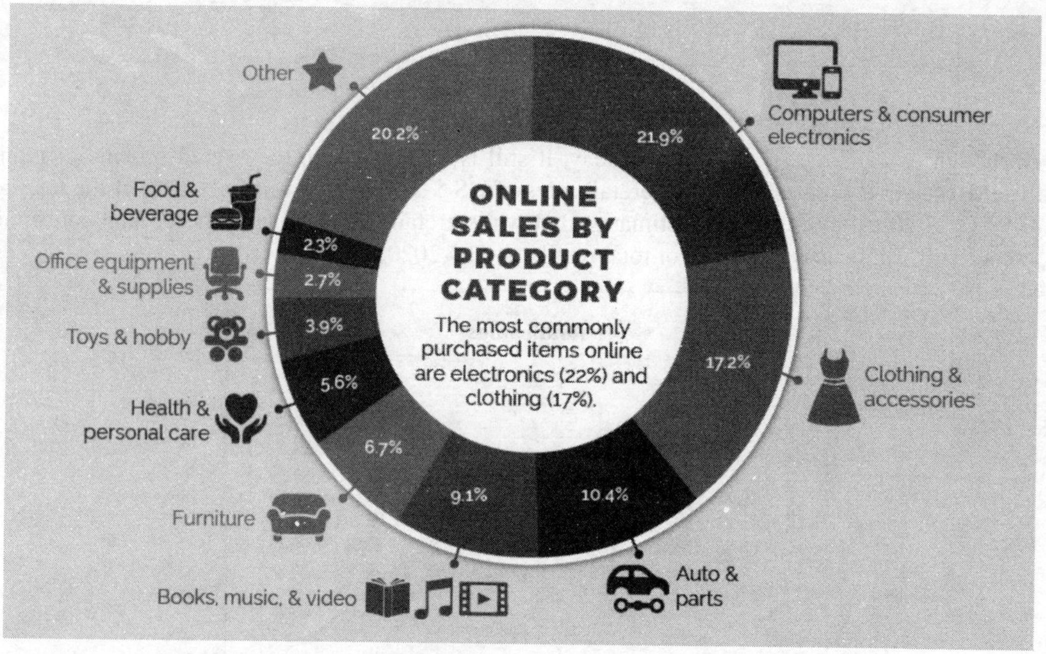

Exhibit 9.5 Online Sales by Product Category - 2018

What Makes eCommerce Tick

Popular perception is that ecommerce works because purchasing online is cheaper than buying on the street.

The reality is somewhat more complex. Yes, many online merchants, particularly the aggregators like Amazon, Ali Baba, Flipkart, etc., make low price a key selling point. In most cases, though, these low prices are an attempt to aggregate consumers and, in fact, impacts the organization negatively, since the low costs are subsidized by the aggregator offering discounts. This gravy train stops sooner or later and with it the low prices too. In fact, the perception that online prices are lower than retail prices, may not always be true too as a survey in the US discovered[9].

If it is not low prices, then what drives ecommerce. Very simple convenience, any time shopping and ubiquity drives ecommerce.

Consumer life-styles today are vastly different from even 25 years ago. These life-styles place enormous demands on one's energy and mobility, so the convenience of shopping from one's desk or one's home is always greater than having to go to a shop. Coupled with better customer service, greater reliability of products and the preponderance of consumer reviews, the need to have tactile or sensory reassurance of the product one is buying has also reduced and hence the need to visit a shop. Together, with the ability to buy online at any-time of the day, ecommerce is an attractive option for many consumers.

Another unique feature that is feasible with ecommerce is the availability of difficult to find products and brands. Most retailers tend to stock the faster moving and more popular products and brands. Niche brands or specialty products are stocked by few and far between. Thus, consumers looking for uncommon products would need to visit many retail outlets before they find what they are looking for. The Internet enables to find such retailers easily making even rare to find products ubiquitous.

Success in eCommerce

Contrary to the instant Internet millionaires' stories portrayed in popular media, success in ecommerce requires hard and systematic work. While no realistic data seems to exist on the failure rate in ecommerce, some believe it is as high as 75%. That itself might seem an underestimate since in 1983 a study by a leading consulting company estimated that it took 68 ideas to get one commercially successful product.

These rules are common for any product, online or offline. Having gotten the product right how should one approach ecommerce.

eCommerce Building Blocks

The building blocks of ecommerce can be conceived as shown in Figure 9.3:

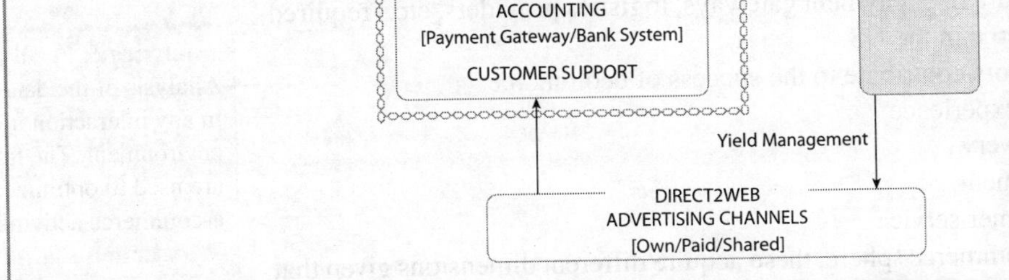

Figure 9.3 Building Blocks of eCommerce

The core of an ecommerce system is the Transaction Platform, which is also sometimes referred to as an ecommerce website or a store front. The other key components of making ecommerce work are a 'Drive-to-Web' (DtW) strategy, a well-developed analytics and feedback loop and integration with third-party eretailers such as aggregators like Amazon, Flipkart, etc.

We will first describe the system and then address what the key factors are that contribute to the success of the system.

Transaction Platform: The Transaction Platform is the virtual store where customers would interact with marketeer. Like a store in real life, the virtual store too contains displays of products for sale and pay for the merchandise. However, since, unlike in real-life stores, a consumer cannot get the goods from the virtual store, the Transaction Platform will have facilities for consumers to know if the goods have been sent and when they would receive it. Additionally, it will also have redressal systems to resolve consumer queries.

The transaction platform is created through appropriate databases and systems, owned by the marketeer as well as third parties such as warehouses, shippers, banks, etc., that are critical to successful functioning of any commercial activity.

Drive-to-Web: Building a transaction platform is a necessary, but, not a sufficient condition for successful ecommerce. To achieve success, the ecommerce venture needs revenues and consumers who provide the revenues. The DtW component performs this essential function using appropriate digital strategies that have been discussed in Chapter 3 of this book.

Analytics and Feedback Loop: This is the critical difference between 'brick-and-mortar' commerce and ecommerce. Since any interaction can be captured in a digital environment, successful emarketeers analyze the data that comes out to continually optimize their ecommerce activities. Two key areas of optimization are 'Funnel Management' or improving the conversion of visitors to paying customers on the transaction platform and 'Yield Management' on the DtW activities. Yield Management refers to incrementally improving the performance of the DtW activities so that these efforts continually increase the flow of visitors to the transaction platform.

While these are the critical revenue functions of the analytics of an ecommerce, other areas of application of analytics are in managing the functioning of the ecommerce site itself. For example, download speeds are very critical to whether users will buy from the site or not. Analytics is used to monitor these and fix any technical issues that could be impacting the performance of the site. With the emergence of cloud computing and multiple access devices, this aspect of analytics is as important as the revenue functions of analytics.

eDistribution: In the early days of ecommerce, the marketeers site was the only presence on the Internet from where the marketeer could sell his products. More recently, 'marketspaces' have emerged. Such marketspaces are large ecommerce players aggregating smaller emarketeers and providing access to the consumers of the marketplace. This enables small ecommerce players take advantage of the scale provided by these marketplaces without significant incremental investments by them. Thus, for example, a small operator in India could sell his wares to consumers in the US without making investments in the eInfrastructure (e.g. payment gateways, logistics providers, etc.) required for ecommerce in the US.

Four factors contribute to the success of ecommerce:

- User experience
- Discovery
- Fulfilment
- Customer service

In the ecommerce sphere, these acquire different dimensions given that there is no 'friendly' sales assistant to answer questions that prospective consumers may have.

Analytics & Feedback Loop: Analysis of the data captured in any interaction in a digital environment. The findings are used to optimize the e-commerce activities.
Transaction Platform: The virtual store where customers interact with the marketer

User Experience (UX) is a phrase that describes the end result of the consumer experience and it includes the entire consumer behaviour that is associated with choice processes of consumers. In an ecommerce context, this means providing consumers with the necessary information, tools and facilities in an easy to understand and use manner.

The first phase of the UX exercise is to map the consumer journey and how consumers would interact with the transaction platform during their journey. This map is then translated into templates that define the elements or artefacts that consumers will require to be able to interact with the site. As shown in Exhibit 9.3 the template, should have two components, a schema that shows how the consumers will interact with the site, also called a User Interface (UI), and process that define what functionalities are expected from the back-end systems, databases and processes will be architected and designed. These in turn help in determining the technology stack to be used and the kind of infrastructure (e.g. servers, connectivity, etc.) to be deployed for the project.

The next step in the UX design stage is to render the UI into a graphic design consistent with the brand style and to enhance the engagement of consumers with the site. Good graphic design not only brings the product alive to consumers, but also, enhances desirability. Both lead to higher conversions.

After poor business decision, most surveys show that UX is the second biggest reason why ecommerce initiatives fail.

The next component of ecommerce is discovery. The range of tools available for this has been dealt with extensively in Chapter 3. Key for ecommerce in this activity is the ability of the marketeer to use these tools to build a robust database for continuous marketing and enhance the reputation and imagery of the brand using social media tools. The latter becomes important since most digital marketing is one-to-one and is need based. Therefore, opportunities to create a brand aura are difficult. In this absence, the voice of satisfied consumers becomes a strong element in promoting conversions.

eDistribution, in addition to its obvious advantage of extending the reach of the marketeer, is also an important tool in enabling discovery. Most marketplaces use sophisticated algorithms to promote their marketplace participants like search engines do. Exhibit 9.6 shows one such example of a marketplace promoting brands.

As Exhibit 9.6 shows brands that are unknown, Saucony and Fluke, are juxtaposed along with their better-known rivals like Nike and Puma, which they could not have otherwise afforded given the large marketing budgets of the latter brands.

> **User Experience (UX):** Describes the end result of the consumer experience and includes the entire consumer behaviour that is associated with choice processes of consumers

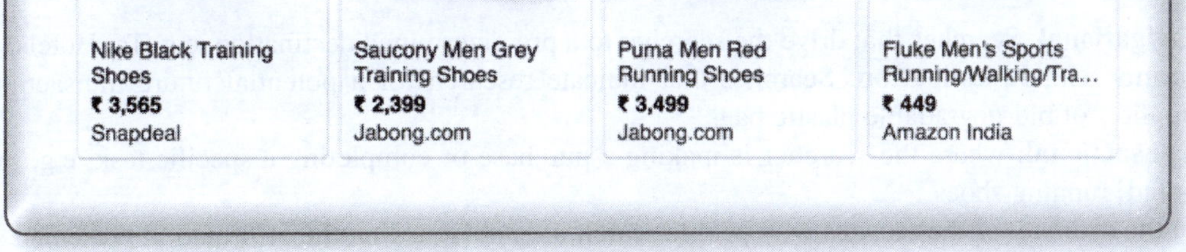

Exhibit 9.6 Search Results - Training Shoes

A great fulfilment experience not only makes for a loyal customer, but also enhances the reputation of the eMarketeer, particularly since at the end of a sale consumers only walk away with the expectation of the product and not the product itself. Thus, it behooves upon the eMarketeer to keep consumers informed of when they will receive the product through all possible channels throughout the logistic process.

It is the goal of all marketeers to have satisfied customers. Sometimes, however, even the best marketeers slip up. When that happens, the difference between happy customers and dissatisfied customers is great customer support and resolution of issues, whether it is product returns, exchanges, wrong accounting, etc. An excellent policy for ecommerce is, 'the consumer is always right'. This is simply because the power of the Internet to amplify good and bad experiences is enormous. Given that, the potential losses from consumer fraud will be insignificant compared to the losses that result from negative consumer feedback, blasted across the Internet.

Is eCommerce only for Those with Deep Pockets

This exposition of ecommerce could seem foreboding in view of the detail and painstaking activities to be undertaken, all of which involve significant costs, raising the question of how small entrepreneurs can afford this.

Obviously, doing everything ground up would involve significant costs. However, in the world of automation engineered by the Internet, many of the common tasks are provided by off-the-shelf platforms. These off-the-shelf platforms perform the entire gamut of tasks an ecommerce entrepreneur would require and are available in different sizes and different price-points, ranging from free to very large numbers with trailing zeroes limited only by the appetite of those who would pay.

Thus, ecommerce can be bootstrapped even on a shoe-string budget if the principles of what makes ecommerce tick are fully understood and applied with diligence.

CONTENT MANAGEMENT

The Internet is principally a means of information exchange. This exchange of information is the bedrock of any transaction, whether it is knowledge seeking or performing transactions. Content management refers to the principles and processes by which this information is created, deployed, stored and refreshed on the Internet.

The Creation of Content

The consumer of the content should be the core for creating any content. Content should be designed on the basis of why the consumer wants the information, where the consumer wants the information and what the consumer is going to do with the information.

Why Consumers Want Information?

Research shows that web searches can be classified in four categories:

1. **Informational**: Searches that answers question or clarifies an uncertainty, e.g. why does the earth rotate.
2. **Navigational**: Searches that drive the searcher to a pre-determined destination, e.g. Taj Hotels.
3. **Commercial Investigation**: Searches that indicate research for a potential future transaction, e.g. suppliers of bid-degradable plastic bags.
4. **Transactional**: where the searcher is making a purchase or completing a specific task, e.g. price of [brand] running shoes.

Given the diversity of the reasons why people search, it is obvious that the information presented should be tailored to the search.

While this much is obvious, how the information should be presented is not so clear, and is often mired in myths of human attention spans.

Most scientific research shows that theories of short human attention spans are not backed by empirical data. In fact, the researches show that how humans apply attention to different tasks depends very much on what the individual brings to that situation. Given this it follows that if a searcher is searching for something particular, the searcher's attention span will be relative to the importance he places on getting the information.

Having said that, attention span is not a given merely because of interest. Research published[10] by ASCD (formerly, Association for Supervision and Curriculum Development) shows that the human attention has evolved to quickly recognize and respond to sudden, dramatic changes that signal physical predatory danger, and to ignore or merely monitor the steady states, subtle differences, and gradual changes that don't carry a sense of immediate alarm.

This research goes on to summarize what an attentional system must do, viz:

- quickly identify and focus on the most important item in a complex environment
- sustain attention on its focus while monitoring related information and ignoring other stimuli
- access memories that aren't currently active, but that could be relevant to the current focus
- shift attention quickly when important new information arrives

Therefore, it is important to present content aligned to how consumers process and engage with it and not to be distracted by the myths of short attention span.

Where do They Want the Information?

In today's hyper-connected world, content is consumed

- On a wide range of devices – desktops, laptops, TVs, mobile phones, smart phones, tablets, etc.,
- Different locations – offices, homes, on commutes, in restaurants, etc.
- Different technologies – wired or wireless broadband, mobile data, browser versions, operating systems, etc.
- via a browser or an app

The content that is created requires customizing and adapting for these combinations for maximizing consumer interaction. This does not mean that for each combination content needs to be created anew; today's content creation technologies allow for the content to be modified according to the consumption environment on-the-fly and is usually referred to as 'responsive design'.

What are They Going to Do with the Content?

Apart from creating content in line with consumer needs for the information, it is also important to focus on the format in which the content is created, particularly on the Internet, where content can be presented in multiple formats—words, graphics, video or a combination of these. This is best determined by how complex the content to be presented is. For example, pricing information can be shown in words; video would be more appropriate for instructions on how to use a product; an infographic may be apposite for showing the myriad benefits of a product, etc.

Content is not just restricted to information, but elements of interaction that one may want from searchers. For instance, in an ecommerce site, one would expect consumers to buy. The design and presentation of the artefact that enables this is also content and should be integrated to the entire experience of consuming content. Similarly, content should include widgets and other devices that facilitate sharing of content, saving of content, etc. so that the experience the searcher has is complete and in consonance with their intention for using the content.

THE TECHNOLOGY OF CONTENT MANAGEMENT

The phrase that "Content is the king" has almost become redundant now. Still, not many B2B companies have embraced or leveraged on a powerful content marketing strategy. In a 2017 survey, only 37% of companies have a documented content marketing strategy (Content Marketing Institute). Now content strategy is not all about posting few blogs or writing something on social media. A good content management strategy begins with documenting an editorial calendar for at least the next three to six months. This helps in bringing the various stakeholders on to the same page and thereby to work on a content strategy that aligns with the overall marketing plans of the organization.

Most B2B companies are still miles beyond their B2C counterparts when it comes to engaging or reaching out to their clients through social media. While B2C attract the customers through colourful campaigns, powerful social media messages and advertisements, some B2B companies have not even explored having their presence in various social media platforms. In particular, the power of LinkedIN is huge when it comes to B2B marketing. LinkedIN not only helps in posting information or sharing, it helps hugely in finding quality B2B leads through its LinkedIn Sale Navigator. It is one of the most trusted social media platforms for finding B2B quality leads.

Similarly, platforms such as Twitter, Facebook, Slideshare, YouTube, Blogs, etc. can be effectively used to engage or even reach out to potential customers. It is also to be noted that leveraging the power of social media does not mean being present on every platform that is out there and spamming the channels with content; it is the responsibility of the content marketing team to come up with a clear content marketing strategy that would help their business or product. Content is truly about quality rather than quantity.

One example of how social media can help B2B business is General Electric's Facebook campaign, which proves the power of social media marketing. GE's tagline on Facebook read "We love science, technology innovation and hearing from you! So, say hello." This simple social media campaign resulted in nearly 1.5 million likes for the page. Such campaigns reach your potential customers and creates a strong brand identity for the company.

Below are list of trends that suggest the importance of content marketing in today's time:

Content Marketing Trends[11]

- 91% of B2B marketers used content marketing in 2017 (Statistica).
- B2B companies that blogged 11+ times per month had almost 3X more traffic than those blogging 0-1 times per month (HubSpot).
- 49% of B2B marketers say articles are the most effective type of content for moving prospects through the sales funnel (Statistica).
- 53% of B2B marketers say their content marketing strategy is successful (Content Marketing Institute).
- 76% of B2B marketers prioritize content quality over quantity (Content Marketing Institute).
- 90% of B2B marketers say the leading attribute of content marketing effectiveness is "audience relevance" (Statistica).
- 55% of B2B marketers say they are unclear on what content marketing success or effectiveness looks like (Content Marketing Institute).

> **Content Marketing:** Marketing focused on creating, publishing, and distributing content for a targeted audience online.
> **Facebook:** A popular free social networking website that allows registered users to create profiles, upload photos and video, send messages and keep in touch with friends, family and colleagues.
> **LinkedIn:** A social networking site designed specifically for the business community. The goal of the site is to allow registered members to establish and document networks of people they know and trust professionally.
> **Social Media:** Computer-mediated technologies that facilitate the creation and sharing of information, ideas, career interests and other forms of expression via virtual communities and networks.
> **Twitter:** A free micro blogging service that allows registered members to broadcast short posts called tweets. Twitter members can broadcast tweets and follow other users' tweets by using multiple platforms and devices.

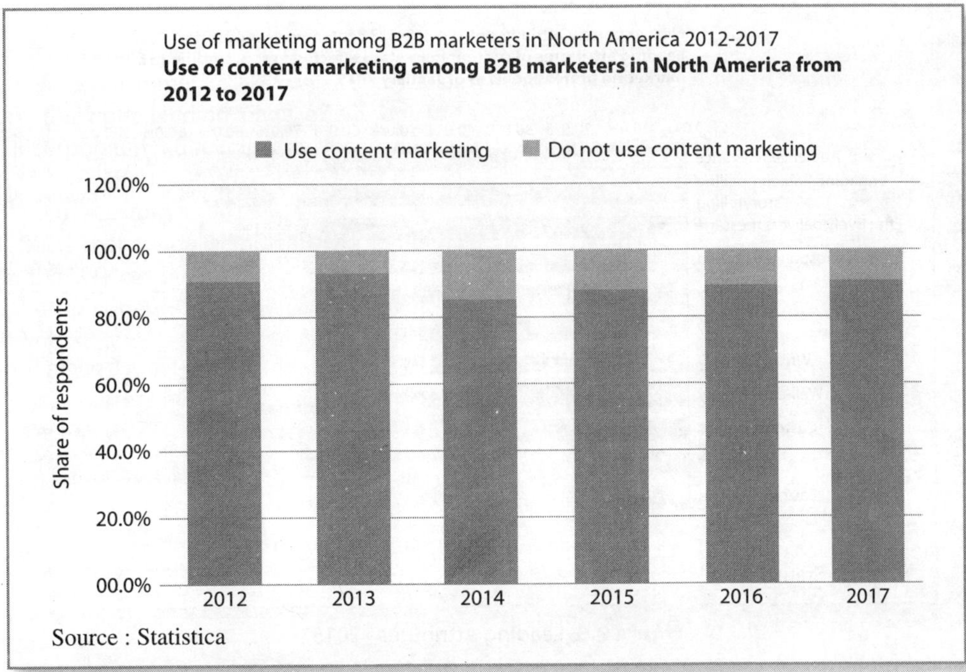

Figure 9.4 Percent Use of Content Marketing - B2B

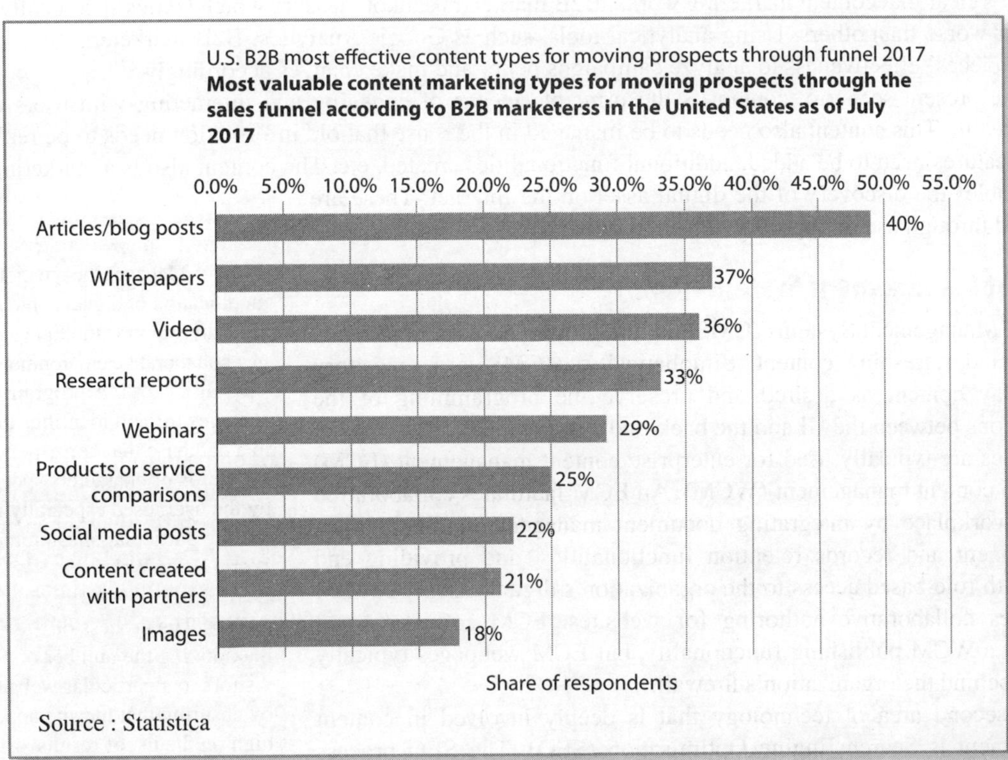

Figure 9.5 Effective Content B2B

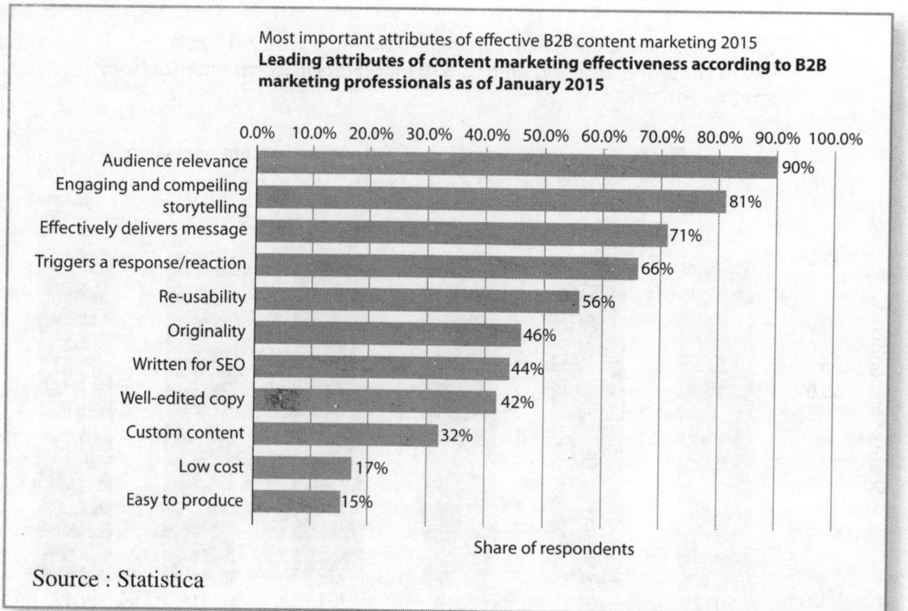

Figure 9.6 Leading Attributes - 2015

One challenge B2B marketers face is analyzing and measuring the effectiveness of the content strategy. While it's clear that content marketing works, B2B marketers cannot measure which tactics specifically work better or worse than others. Using analytical tools, such as Google Analytics, B2B marketers can measure content pieces' effectiveness to analyze campaigns better and make changes accordingly.

In the present scenario, content is the principle means of engaging and interacting with users in the digital realm. This content also needs to be managed in the sense that old information needs to be replaced, newer features need to be added, additional functionalities created, etc. The content also is a marketing tool as it enables the discovery of the digital asset on the Internet. These are achieved through use of appropriate technology.

Content Management Systems (CMS)

Content Management Systems (CMS) are the primary tool for deploying, storing and refreshing content. Simplistically, a CMS is a repository to display content as desired and preserve the programming of the interactions between the UI and the back-end systems.

CMSes are typically used for enterprise content management (ECM) and web content management (WCM). An ECM facilitates collaboration in the workplace by integrating document management, digital asset management and records retention functionalities, and providing end users with role-based access to the organization's digital assets. A WCM facilitates collaborative authoring for websites. ECM software often includes a WCM publishing functionality, but ECM webpages typically remain behind the organization's firewall.

The second area of technology that is deeply involved in content management is Search Engine Optimisation (SEO). The SEO process primarily allows search engines to 'crawl' digital assets using software

Content Management System (CMS): Manages the creation and modification of digital content. It typically supports multiple users in a collaborative environment.

Search Engine: A program that searches for and identifies items in a database that corresponds to keywords or characters specified by the user, used especially for finding particular sites on the World Wide Web.

Search Engine Optimzation (SEO): The process of maximizing the number of visitors to a particular website by ensuring that the site appears high on the list of results returned by a search engine.

known as 'bots'. This crawling allows the search engines to index the pages and display theme appropriately when users search for information using the search engines. The technology also allows the pages in the website to be refreshed, depending on competitive situations, so that the website is dynamic to changing consumer tastes and interests.

Content and Digital Marketing Strategy for the Millennial decision makers:

Most organizations have decision makers that are less than 30-35 years old. Some of the start-up CEOs in the Technology space is perhaps even younger. Do you think cold calling followed by emails are going to work in such scenarios? Certainly not! It is mandatory to have a strong content and digital marketing strategy if you want to cut through all the noise.

Here are some of the basics.

Having a rich and engaging content is a must across:

- Website – Should also be fast, secure and designed for mobiles, not just mobile friendly and must be optimized for SEO.
- Social Media Platforms
- Blogs, Case Studies and White Papers
- Info Graphics
- Podcasts, Live streams and Videos
- Mobile Apps

Table 9.1 Revolving your Digital Marketing Strategy

	Changing Drivers B2B	
Head	**Traditional Marketing**	**Digital Marketing**
Strategy	Sales Led, Outbound	Inbound & Informed Buyer
Marketing	Push, Disjointed	Pull, Customized
Channel	Offline, Brick & Motar	Digital & Offline integration
Operation	Manual, Siloed data	Automated, tech enabled, Realtime
Metrics	Activity Based, periodic	Result based, continuous
Organisation	Siloed	Integrate
Skills	Street Smart	Tech & Analytical
Culture	Rigid, Top Down	Flexible & Agile

Artificial Intelligence (AI), Analytics and Algorithmic Marketing

Of these three, AI and Algorithmic Marketing are at their nascent stages and there is a wide ranging debate on whether these disciplines will work for marketing as very little is known about consumer choice processes for them to be codified with any degree of predictability.

In its October 2017 insights on Digital Marketing and advertising, in the Gartner Hype Cycle[12] (GHC) it places AI for Marketing in the 'Innovation Trigger' region and does not even recognize the existence of Algorithmic Marketing. GHC places the closest discipline to Algorithmic Marketing, Programatic Direct Advertising, in the 'Trough of Disillusionment'.

Algorithmic Marketing: An approach for scientifically managing a full range of marketing issues
Analytics: The discovery, interpretation, and communication of meaningful patterns in data
Artificial intelligence (AI): Intelligence demonstrated by machines, in contrast to the natural intelligence displayed by humans and other animals
Case study: A process or record of research into the development of a particular person, group, or situation over a period of time
Info graphics: Graphic visual representations of information, data or knowledge intended to present information quickly and clearly
Mobile App: A computer program designed to run on a mobile device such as a phone/tablet or watch.
Podcasts: Also called netcast, is an episodic series of digital audio or video files which a user can download and listen to

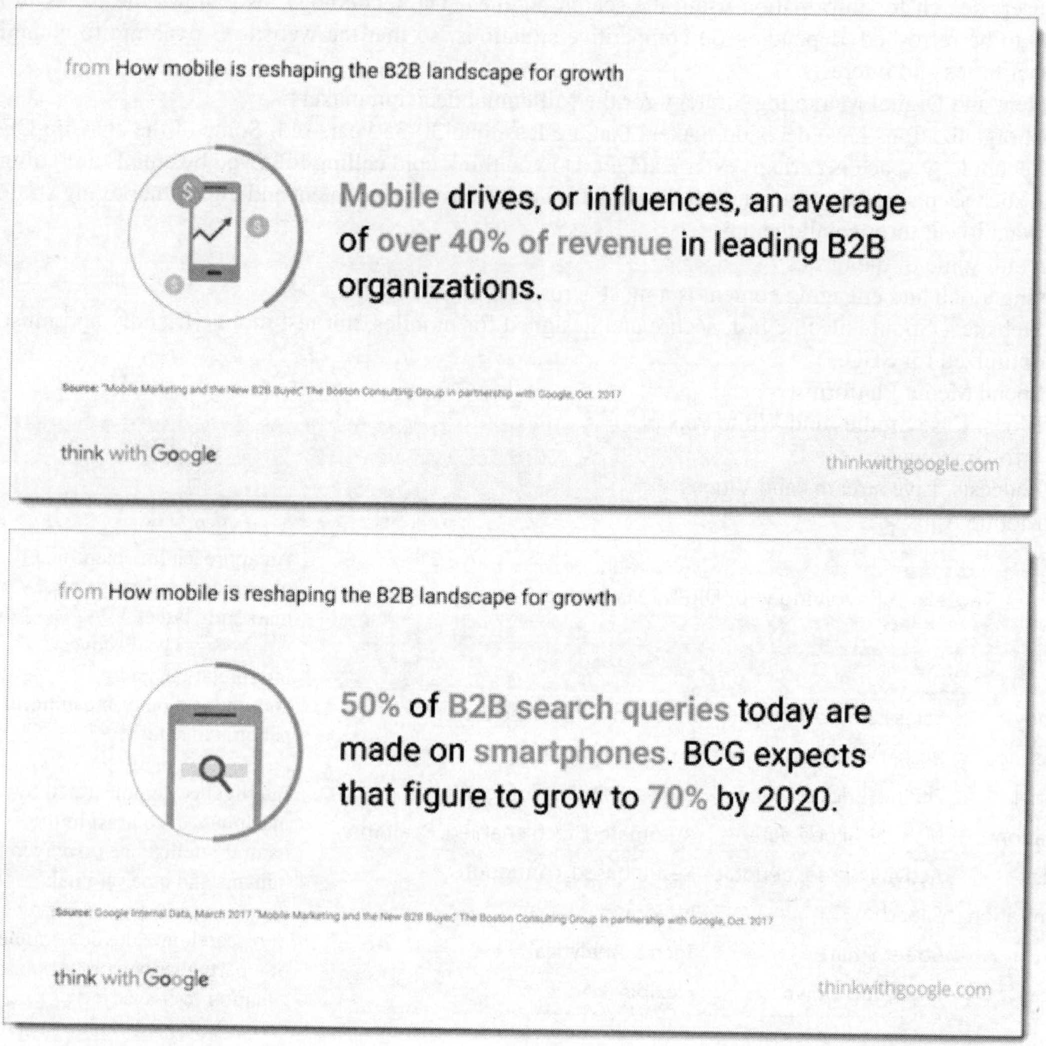

Source : Google

Exhibit 9.7 Mobile Critical Driver - B2B

Analytics, however, has a deep tradition in marketing from its very early days in its efforts to understand consumer behaviour and measure the potential impact of marketing stimuli such as advertising, product changes, etc. In view of its importance, a separate chapter has been included on Analytics in this book which is the next chapter.

AI is a nascent development in the marketing landscape. Currently, there appears to be no use cases of AI in marketing. However, it does not mean that such use cases cannot be developed. To understand where AI may find application in marketing, one needs to understand AI itself. Simply put, AI is a system by which

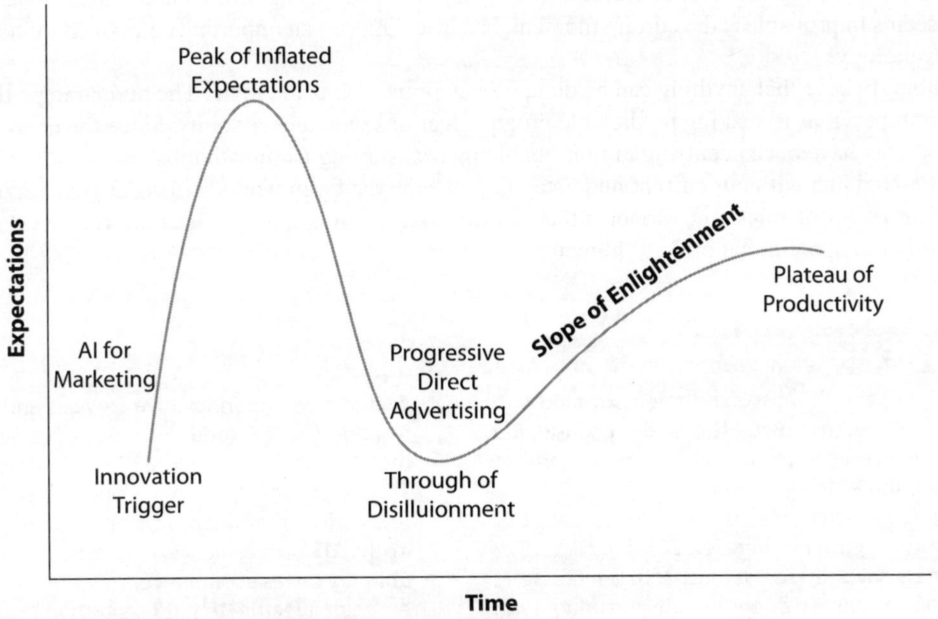

Source : 5 Insights from Gartner Hype Cycle for Digital Marketing and Advertising, 2017

Figure 9.7 Insights from Gartner Hype Cycle

an action is triggered without the need for collecting data, processing it and programming decision outcomes based on the processing. Thus, on the face of it, much of consumer behaviour can be covered by AI. For example, on any given day, many people walk into shops, but walk out without buying anything. A potential application of AI, in such a scenario, may be the assessment of the probability of a walk-in actually buying a product or not and triggering actions based on that assessment.

It is Gartner's assessment that, while AI-enabled technologies and techniques have the potential to transform the practice of marketing as we know it, AI for marketing is in the Innovation Trigger phase. Players in this area liberally promote "intelligent" capabilities within their offerings with varying degrees of precision and truth.

Similar is the case with algorithmic marketing.

By definition, an **algorithm** is a set of instructions for carrying out a particular task. It is, for the most part, deterministic, predictable, and not subject to chance. It works for all cases and is presumed to give a correct answer. It works well in certain situations such as stock trading, where a common application of algorithms is in trading. Algorithmic trading happens when large transactions are placed, and a trader initiates a trade just before the transaction hits the exchange, to take advantage of the transaction that has been placed. Therefore, it fulfils all criteria for an algorithm to perform.

Algorithm: A process or set of rules to be followed in calculations or other problem-solving operations, especially by a computer

Internet Marketing: A form of marketing and advertising which uses the Internet to deliver promotional marketing messages to consumers

Social Media Marketing (SMM): A form of Internet marketing that utilizes social networking websites as a marketing tool

White papers: An authoritative report or guide that informs readers concisely about a complex issue and presents the issuing body's philosophy on the matter. It is meant to help readers understand an issue, solve a problem, or make a decision.

However, developing set of predictable instructions to construct algorithms and hence scale marketing activities seems improbable at the current moment, because it misses an important component of marketing—human psychology!

Innovators' believe that anything can be done if one applies mind and logic. The human logic though, has so far been impervious to making predictable prognostications with any certainty. Since the dawn of history, eureka moments have been occurring in improbable places, starting from bath tubs.

It is estimated that with our current understanding of how the brain works, efforts at generalizing human behaviour into a set of rules and variables that you can play with is likely to account for less than 10% of what is *really* going on in that brain of humans!

CHAPTER SUMMARY

- Digital marketing is most of the time associated with consumer products (B2C). It is seldom considered as B2B. However, in the global and Indian context, B2B contributes to well over 60% of the GDP.
- Mobile commerce makes up 30% of all U.S. ecommerce. (Internet Retailer, 2015), 67% of B2B marketers say they see at least a 10% increase in sales opportunities through lead nurturing, with 15% seeing opportunities increase by 30% or more.
- B2B marketers now heavily rely on content marketing to bring in leads and grow the lead pool. 70% of B2B marketers say that their priority in the next 12 months is converting leads to customers.
- Given the sheer size and volume of the market and transactions, according to Marty Holmes former CMO of HP "B-to-B Marketers Must Think Like Consumer Companies".
- Technology has always been a part of B2B marketing. Even before the existence of Internet, B2B purchases of primary commodities happened through exchanges that were automated to a significant extent. Some services, notably financial services, used automation extensively in creating differentiation and providing services to their customers. The rise of Internet has only hastened these processes.
- Electronic commerce or the e-commerce is the marketing, buying and selling of merchandise or services or the transmitting of funds or data over the Internet.
- Democratizing power of the Internet allows all players, large or small to co-exist, without allowing any one dominant force to subsume the less endowed players.
- eCommerce now has spawned other ecommerce enterprises such as payment gateways, mobile wallets, logistics, data analytics among others, as well as new and innovative services and products like ride sharing, food delivery, homestays, fitness monitors, etc.
- The perception that online prices are lower than retail prices, may not always be true as per a survey in the US. Convenience, any time shopping and ubiquity drives ecommerce.
- An unique feature that is feasible with ecommerce is the availability of difficult to find products and brands that retailers tend not to stock. The Internet enables to find such retailers/products easily.
- While no realistic data seems to exist on the failure rate in ecommerce, some believe it is as high as 75%.
- The core of an ecommerce system is the Transaction Platform, which is also sometimes referred to as an ecommerce website or a store front. The other key components of making ecommerce work are a 'Drive-to-Web' (DtW) strategy, a well-developed Analytics and feedback loop and integration with third-party eretailers such as aggregators like Amazon, Flipkart, etc.
- The Transaction Platform is the virtual store where customers would interact with marketeer. Drive-to-Web: Building a transaction platform is a necessary, but, not a sufficient condition for successful ecommerce. To achieve success the ecommerce venture needs revenues and consumers who provide the revenues. Analytics and Feedback Loop: This is the critical difference between 'brick-and-mortar' commerce and ecommerce.
- In the early days of ecommerce, the marketeers site was the only presence on the Internet from where the marketeer could sell his products. More recently, 'marketspaces' have emerged. Such marketspaces are large ecommerce players aggregating smaller emarketeers and providing access to the consumers of the marketplace.

- Four factors contributing to the success of ecommerce are user experience, discovery, fulfilment and customer service.
- User experience (UX) is a phrase that describes the end result of the consumer experience and it includes the entire consumer behaviour that is associated with the choice processes of consumers—that in ecommerce context is providing the necessary information, tools and facilities in an easy to understand and use manner.
- The first phase of the UX exercise is to map the consumer journeys and how consumers would interact with the transaction platform during their journey. The next step in the UX design stage is to render the UI into a graphic design consistent with the brand style and to enhance the engagement of consumers with the site. The next component of ecommerce is discovery.
- The Internet is principally a means of information exchange. This exchange of information is the bedrock of any transaction, whether it is knowledge seeking or performing transactions. Content management refers to the principles and processes by which this information is created, deployed, stored and refreshed on the Internet.
- Web searches can be classified in four categories: Informational, Navigational, Commercial Investigation, and Transactional. Because of the diversity of the reasons why people search, it is obvious that the information presented should be tailored to the search.
- Given theories of short human attention span, it is important to present content aligned to how consumers process and engage with it and not to be distracted by the myths of short attention span.
- It is also important to focus on the format in which the content is created, particularly, on the Internet, where content can be presented in multiple formats—words, graphics, video or a combination of these.
- Ninety one percent of B2B marketers used content marketing in 2017. Forty nine percent of B2B marketers say articles are the most effective type of content for moving prospects through the sales funnel, 53% of B2B marketers say their content marketing strategy is successful and 76% of B2B marketers prioritize content quality over quantity.
- Content Management Systems (CMS) are the primary tool for deploying, storing and refreshing content.
- Given most organizations have decision makers that are less than 30-35 years old. Some of the start-up CEOs in the technology space is perhaps even younger, it is important to have a strong content and digital marketing strategy for millennial decision makers.
- AI and Algorithmic Marketing are at their nascent stages and there is a wide ranging debate on whether these disciplines will work for marketing.
- An algorithm is a set of instructions for carrying out a particular task. It's, for the most part, deterministic, predictable, and not subject to chance. However, developing set of predictable instructions to construct algorithms and hence scale marketing activities seems improbable at the current moment, because it misses an important component of marketing—human psychology!
- However, they are useful as a pricing tool by Airline's Apex fares and Uber Surge pricing.

CLOSING CASE

CASE LET

Bugaboo: An International Hit Without Deep Pockets

Bugaboo was founded in 1997 in the Netherlands by Max Barenbrug, a man who was dissatisfied with the baby strollers he saw around him. His basic insight was that most strollers were being pushed by men and the strollers he saw were too short for men to be pushing. Moreover, the strollers themselves were uncomfortable and flimsy.

Starting with these insights he designed a stroller that could be pushed by anybody (either tall or short), be comfortable for the passenger (i.e. the baby) and be durable. His design was such a hit that very soon it was being used widely in Denmark, where one of Bugaboo's customers was Kari Boiler, an American working in an advertising agency in Amsterdam.

This American, took her Bugaboo to the United States on a vacation in 2001. While she was using her stroller, the story goes, a man driving a Porsche stopped his car and asked her where he could buy one. That is when this American woman looked around and had the same epiphany as the original designer of Bugaboo. On her return to Denmark, Kari Boiler met Max Barenburg and offered to represent them in the US.

Thus, in 2002, Bugaboo was launched in the US by Kari Boiler. Her first act in marketing Bugaboo was putting it in the hands of people who the media followed. Her real coup, though, was getting the Bugaboo into the iconic TV programme, Sex and the City. She got the opportunity when one of the characters got pregnant in the programme and, would therefore need a stroller. She promptly got in touch with the props department of the programme and got the stroller placed in the programme.

Kari Boiler did not stop with just putting the stroller in the programme. She also knew that there would be widespread interest and people would be searching for the stroller on Google. Sure enough there were enough searchers for, "that cute stroller in Sex and the City", and sales started taking off, even though the Bugaboo, at US $ 700 is thrice or more expensive than other strollers.

Since its early days, Bugaboo has added luggage to its product line, using the same design philosophies as in designing the stroller. The brand enjoys the same reverence among its users as iPhone has among its users.

Case Questions

1. How was Bugaboo marketed in USA?
2. What is the learning from the case?

REVIEW QUESTIONS

1. What is the importance of B2B in the global and Indian context?
2. How is digital marketing important in B2B context?
3. Why should B-to-B marketers must think like consumer companies?
4. How has technology fueled B2B?
5. What is ecommerce? Is it B2B or B2C?
6. What is a transaction platform?
7. What factors contribute to the success of ecommerce?
8. What is UX or user experience?
9. What is content marketing and what is its importance in B2B context?
10. What is Content Marketing System – CMS?
11. What is Algorithmic Marketing and where does it find its use currently?

ACTIVITY QUESTIONS

1. Build your own ecommerce website using free Wordpress or Shopify templates.

KEY TERMS

Algorithm
Algorithmic Marketing
Analytics
Analytics & Feedback Loop
Artificial intelligence (AI)
B2B (business-to-business) marketing
Case study
Content Marketing
Content Management System (CMS)
Digital Marketing
eCommerce
Facebook
Info graphics
Internet Marketing
LinkedIn
Mobile App
Podcasts
Search Engine
Search Engine Optimzation (SEO)
Social Media Marketing (SMM)
Social Media
Transaction Platform
Twitter
User Experience (UX)
White papers

REFERENCES

1. http://www.tradingeconomics.com/india/indicators; http://data.gov.in/.
2. http://mospi.nic.in/Mospi_New/site/home.aspx.
3. https://www.forbes.com/2010/09/22/social-media-zappos-sap-branding-advertising-marketing-employees-marty-homlish-cmo-network.html#53fa3dbe7975.
4. Adapted from Business to Business Marketing Management; Second Edition; Alan Zimmerman and Jim Blythe.
5. https://www.bdc.ca/en/Documents/analysis_research/business_to_business_marketing.pdf.
6. https://www.emarketer.com/Article/Worldwide-Retail-Ecommerce-Sales-Will-Reach-1915-Trillion-This-Year/1014369.
7. https://www.webpagefx.com/blog/general/the-evolution-of-ecommerce/.
8. https://www.hubspot.com/marketing-statistics.
9. https://lifehacker.com/is-it-actually-cheaper-to-order-everything-from-amazon-1451086140.
10. "What Brain Research Says About Paying Attention" by *Robert Sylwester and Joo-Yun Cho*; Education Leadership December 1992/January 1993 | Volume **50** | *Number* **4 Students at Risk,** *Pages 71-75.*
11. https://www.ironpaper.com/webintel/articles/15-b2b-marketing-statistics-relevant-2018/.
12. https://www.gartner.com/smarterwithgartner/5-insights-from-the-2017-gartner-hype-cycle-for-digital-marketing-and-advertising/.

CHAPTER 10

THE DIGITAL BUSINESS

CHAPTER OBJECTIVES

After going through this chapter, you will be able to

- Describe Marketing 4.0—from traditional to digital
- Understand the principle of cohorts
- Define millennials and how they will likely impact the future of business
- Give an overview of Industry 4.0 and IoT & Analytics—Key trends that are shaping the future of business
- Discuss the adoption of these influences and what opportunities and challenges they present

OPENING CASE

CASE LET

5G IS GOING TO DAZZLE THE WORLD—ARE YOU READY?

Here's how immersive smartphones, autonomous cars and billions of intelligent sensors could transform your life[1].

The fifth generation of cellular technology, 5G, will offer much more than faster phones. Its first phase, scheduled to begin in 2019, will improve smartphone responsiveness. Soon after, 5G may also start to enhance many other aspects of your daily life, from automotive safety to your entertainment and your view of reality.

For instance, your 5G smartphone will be able to stream ultra high-definition video at gigabit speeds, with enough consistency to enable immersive virtual reality experiences. In a subsequent phase, 5G could also provide a dependable link between autonomous vehicles, allowing cars to share their "intentions" and communicate directly with one another—and even with pedestrians—for safer, more efficient commutes.

How did we get here? Qualcomm has helped introduce new generations of cellular technology nearly every decade since we began using cell phones in the 1980s, each generation more advanced than the last. In 4G LTE, the current iteration of mobile Internet, Qualcomm's technologies helped bring gigabit speeds, streaming video and live TV to your phone.

5G, however, won't just be another "G" delivering faster speeds. Qualcomm has been building technologies and facilitating industry standards that will allow 5G to unite billions of devices, with the potential to transform not only your smartphone but also your home, vehicle, job, industry and community.

A NEW REALITY

Do you need 5G to access virtual and augmented reality? Not technically, but our current generation of wireless Internet does not have the power to fully bring them to life. That is because extended reality—an umbrella term encompassing virtual reality, augmented reality and everything in between—pushes connectivity to its limits. It requires a uniform high-speed connection, increased network capacity and minimal delays.

"With immersive VR and AR, you need high speeds and for something to happen right away when you push a button or move your head," says Durga Malladi, a senior vice president of engineering at Qualcomm Technologies, Inc.

5G will be able to support virtual teleconferencing: Imagine virtually entering the same room as friends and family.

Say you're streaming a basketball game to your headset and receiving a 360-degree view of the court. But you don't want to just watch the game; you also want to pause the action and brush shoulders with players. 5G will have the potential to provide enough capacity and low latency for you to immerse yourself in the game without delays or data congestion. Who wants to enter a virtual world, after all, only to be dragged out by slowed movements or scenery glitches?

Extended reality enabled by 5G will also be able to support virtual teleconferencing. Imagine virtually entering the same room as friends and family, with few delays or dropped connections. With the addition of haptic gloves — accessories that allow people to touch and feel in virtual reality — you might even be able to hold your child's hand while you're in another country.

"The high speeds and low latency enabled by 5G are necessary to have photorealistic extended reality experiences on sleek mobile headsets," Malladi says.

Smart Cities Will Talk To Us

FURTHER ALONG IN OUR 5G FUTURE, wearable technologies will join forces with the massive Internet of things, IoT, allowing billions of intelligent, connected sensors to do more than tell you how many steps you've walked or how fast your heart is beating. "Wearables today provide limited information," Malladi says. "But with 5G massive IoT, they'll be able to connect to what's going on around us all of the time."

This is the 5G future: Sensors could constantly interact with your wearable devices and with one another, creating the ability to monitor everything from your morning commutes to your factory goods to your children. A simple vibration from a wearable on your wrist, for instance, could tell you that only one bike remains at your usual bike-share location. As you rush over, the same device might caution you to be aware of cars speeding through the nearest intersection.

"With 4G LTE you can already connect sensor data," Malladi says, "What's transformational about 5G massive IoT is its ability to scale to billions of connected sensors."

"One sensor becomes infinitely more impactful if we're able to connect its data to sensors throughout the world, and use A.I. to detect trends and build scenarios," Malladi adds.

5G massive IoT will have the ability to scale to billions of connected sensors

How would this play out? A chain of sensors could track and optimize goods as they move from their sources to your home. Take your clothes, for instance. At the beginning of the supply chain, sensors in the ground and in machinery could connect over the 5G network to farm cotton more efficiently. Self-driving trucks with sensors could then transport the raw cotton to a factory, where a wireless automated robot could transform the raw material into samples, based on size and pattern. Designers fitted with AR glasses

> **Augmented reality:** A technology that superimposes a computer-generated image on a user's view of the real world, thus providing a composite view

could collaboratively turn the rough samples into templates for an entire production run. Finally, the shirts could be uploaded to an online shelf, where you could try them on using a VR device. This entire process, from farm to closet, would be brought to you by the 5G network.

A Dream Commute

5G WILL ALSO ENABLE ultrareliable and low-latency communication. Autonomous vehicles and high-precision manufacturing, among other use cases, will need these qualities to thrive.

5G, at a later stage, could allow autonomous vehicles to establish a direct link between each other that bypasses network towers and diminishes urgent communications delays. This means a vehicle could instantly receive alerts to stop or change course if a collision seems imminent, even if the danger is beyond the range of its cameras and radar. In addition, 5G-enabled vehicles could connect with smart city infrastructure like traffic lights and street signs, improving traffic management.

With 5G communications between autonomous vehicles, cars could share their intentions and know intended paths, allowing them to plan more safely and efficiently. "A vehicle could make decisions based on not just where other cars are," Malladi says, "but also where they are planning to go."

How would this affect your daily routine? Steering wheels could disappear, with cars redesigned as living spaces: basically couches or offices on wheels. With 5G-enhanced mobile Internet, your car will be able to stream ultra high-definition video, and even VR, while you travel. Passengers could easily work as they ride, perhaps changing the entire nature of their commutes.

As the first 5G-enabled devices are released, 5G will be on the cusp of changing the world in countless ways. And fully immersive virtual worlds, massive networks of connected sensors and safer roadways are just the beginning. Qualcomm is designing technologies and developing standards that will make 5G a wireless network that supports bold innovations for decades to come.

"Qualcomm is building underlying 5G technology that will enable new use cases beyond what we can imagine today," Malladi says.

(Source for the caselet – NY Times[10])

Case Questions

1. What are the advantages of 5G technology?
2. Why is 5G called technology of future?

INTRODUCTION

Digital technologies have revolutionized the way we have lived and worked and impacted every individual and business. Today, for individuals, marketing professionals and organizations to be distinctive and to stand apart, they must adopt and adapt to the convergence of technologies and leverage them effectively. This book is therefore intended to trace back and connect to the traditional marketing concepts that are fundamental and relevant to the digital world of today. This chapter discusses the integration of Marketing 4.0 that is from 'Traditional to Digital' with Industry 4.0 that is primarily being smart and connected.

MARKETING 4.0 – FROM TRADITIONAL TO DIGITAL

Professor Philip Kotler, who is the acknowledged Guru of Marketing, codified the academic principles of marketing. Kotler, in his book, describes how marketing has evolved from product-driven marketing (1.0) to customer-centric marketing (2.0) to human-centric marketing (3.0). Marketing 3.0 was essentially driven by the Internet that enabled the age of participation and collaboration (Chapter 1).

- Social media provided people at large to create new ideas and talk to each other
- People trusted each other more than marketers
- Economic recession (sub-prime) had shaken some of the core values

Marketing 3.0 inspired marketers to embrace and explore human centric marketing with digital and social media as enablers in this transformation.

Simultaneously, Industry 4.0 was gaining ground. Industry 4.0 is best described as convergence of two worlds that had been disconnected: Information Technology *(IT)* and Operational Technology *(OT)*. With hyper-connected digital industry, the bridging of digital and physical, cyber-physical production systems and the Industrial Internet of Things as parts (and names) described this fourth industrial revolution as the convergence of IT and OT = IoT. Once again the enabler being the Internet. These advanced applied technologies have opened the gates through big data and analytics to new and fresh insights into who our customers are and how they make decisions. The big data and analytics provided an opportunity to create more personalized and customized products and services. Kotler and his coauthors propound that *"Marketing 4.0 is a marketing approach that combines online and offline interaction between companies and customers. In the digital economy, Marketing 4.0 blends style with substance. While it is imperative for brands to be more flexible and adaptive due to rapid technological trends, their authentic characters are more important than ever[2]."* They provide new approach as discovering the new rules of marketing that is

- Stepping out and creating Wow moments - by being connected
- Building a loyal customer base by – From 4 Ps & AIDA to 4 As
- Shaping the future of customer choice - through user experience anthropology and multichannel marketing

Thus ***Marketing 4.0*** maps out an approach that is leading customers from ***Awareness to Advocacy***. Industry 4.0 was about from ***Exclusive to Inclusive*** and ***Marketing 4.0*** is about ***Awareness to Advocacy.***

Table 10.1 captures the journey of Marketing 1.0 to Marketing 4.0.

Table 10. 1 Marketing 4.0

	Marketing 1.0 Product Centric	Marketing 2.0 Customer Centric	Marketing 3.0 Value Centric	Marketing 4.0 Traditional to Digital
Objective	Sell products to the masses	Satisfy customers & brand loyalty	Meet emotional and rational needs of consumers	From awareness to advocacy
Enabling Forces	Industrial Revolution	Information technology	Connectedness of consumers	Digital technologies & social networking
How marketers see the market	Mass market	Smarter consumers & mass market	People instead of segments	Multi-tasking, connected & informed consumers
Key Marketing Concept	Product driven market	Differentiation	Value of product to consumer emotions	Touch points & hybrid channels
Value Proposition	Functional	Functional & emotional	Functional, emotional & rational	Customer journey - CX & UX
Consumer Interaction	Mass Communication	Micro segmentation	Consumers collaborate with each other	Collaboration & Co creation
Power of Branding	Marketers/ Companies	Marketers/ Consumers	Consumers	Consumers/Users

TARGET AUDIENCE AND SEGMENTS

According to Kotler (2014), the shortest definition of marketing is CCDVTP, i.e., "Create, Communicate, Deliver Value to a Target Market at a Profit." Target market/audience is important to any marketing activity and target audience is a broad group of consumers classified along easily determinable criteria such as demographics or geography that indicates the potential of the group to consume a particular brand or category. Segments are sub-groups, within these audiences that share a common characteristic—attitudinal, lifestyle orientation, usage habits, etc.—which influence the propensity of the consumer to use a particular brand, in preference to others. Such an analysis enables the positioning of brands to stand out in a cluttered marketplace.

If an example of toilet soap is taken, the target audience for a brand may be defined by criteria such as sex, age, socio-economic status, ethnicity, etc. In the Indian context, Lifebuoy, Dettol and Rexona, three different brands, may have the same demographic definition of the target audience. This information to consumers is only about the names of these products, without providing the consumer a reason to prefer one over the other. Further research and analysis could show that some consumers in their target audience are more concerned about thorough cleaning after excessive exposure to the elements; some on removal of germs; and others wanting to feel fresh, etc.

As is apparent, these cleaning needs are not demographic specific, but more to do with the consumer's attitudes or mindset. Thus, for a brand to engage with consumers, it needs to go beyond demographics and offer a solution that they are looking for, based on their attitudes. Since such attitudes are not discernible at a superficial level, brands look for markers that define attitudes. For example, an active outdoor life could be the marker for exposure to the elements; motherhood could be the marker for germs/care, etc. These markers not only help define the brand's promise, but also help communicate the promise to the consumers.

COHORTS—A MACRO TYPOLOGY

Cohort is an ancient Roman military unit, comprising six centuries, equal to one tenth of a legion. Marketing has borrowed this word from this ancient origin, to mean, a group of people who share a common characteristic or experience within a defined period (e.g., are currently living, are exposed to a phenomenon irrespective of their socio-economic condition, etc).

On the face of it, it would seem that this is no different from 'target audience' or 'segment'. This would be a wrong reading of the definition, since target-audience and segment is typically contextual, i.e., consumers of a product; beneficiaries of a government programme; patients for a drug, etc.

A cohort, on the other hand, is defined by the commonality of a world view that is common across members of the group and is often generational. Thus, when we talk of our generations we refer to them as the 'freedom-fighter' generation; post-independence generation; yuppies; etc. Each of these cohorts immediately brings to mind a stereotype that is likely to be common across all members of the cohort who share common values for significant life events such as religion, consumption, marriage, politics, education, etc. Typically, these common characteristics are not affected by the size of the group or the rate of change in the size of the group. Thus, the world views of the cohort change enmasse rather than individually and are shaped by the external events they encounter, rather than their personal experiences.

Millennials are a generational cohort defined by their age, a common predictor of differences in attitudes and behaviour. Age describes the individual in two different ways, their life stage—a young single adult, married with children, retiree, etc., and their belonging to a group who were born around the same period.

Age cohorts enables researchers analyze changes in views over time; how different experiences during their growing-up affect and shape their view of the world. For example, if one takes the freedom-fighter generation in India, the views of pretty much everyone born between, say, 1910 and 1945, would have been influenced by the events around them and would be significantly different from the views of say those born between 1945 and 1970, i.e. the period after independence.

Cohorts provide an ability to understand attitudinal changes across generations and their impact on behaviour. Younger and older adults differ in their views at a given point-in-time. Age cohorts allow investigators to examine how today's older adults felt about a given issue when they themselves were young, thus allowing to contrast how the views might differ from the young people of today from those of several generations ago. As an example, consider how the freedom fighter generation may have viewed patriotism in their youth compared with how today's youth views patriotism. Thus, millennials in the context of this book need to be understood as cohorts.

MARKETING FOR MILLENNIALS—THE GENERATION OF THE 21ST CENTURY

Like in all other spheres where updated editions are given progressive numerical numbers, current consumers can be called Consumer 2.0[3] (Chapter 1). A 2017 Nielsen Study in US indicates that though online for FMCG shopping is pervasive and all generations and income levels are shopping online, 61 % are millennials.

The term 'millennials' was most likely coined in the US and it specifically refers to those born after 1980. Figure 10.1 shows different age cohorts classified by their years of birth in the US.

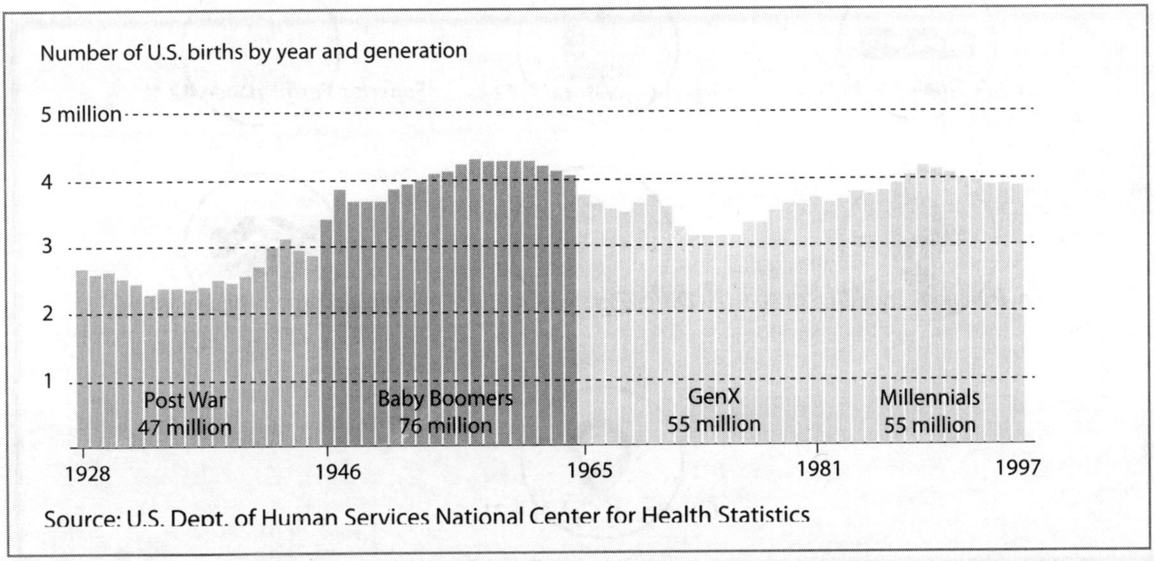

Figure 10.1 Number of US Births by Year and Generation

While a US centric definition of generational cohorts may not apply to all countries equally, the time periods can be more or less applied across countries, since they coincide with globally epochal events. Thus, in India, for instance, the period 1928 – 1946 could correspond to the freedom movement; 1946 – 1965 – the Post-Independence generation; 1965 – 1981 – the License-Raj generation; 1980 – 1995 – the Liberalization generation and post 1995 – the Millennials.

The Millennial Drivers

A global survey by Nielsen[4] in 2016 shows Indian millennials to be among the most optimistic about their future compared to their peers. The survey showed that:

- 78% of Indian millennials perceived their financial situation to be better than 'five years ago' compared to the global average of 55%.
- 36% of the Indian millennials felt they had the ability to spend freely compared to 14% of their global peers who felt so. Correspondingly, only 14% of Indian millennials felt that they had just enough to cover their basic expenses compared to 35% global average.

Other survey findings showed that millennials as a cohort were willing to pay premium prices for premium products, both as a means of self-esteem and as projecting their status.

Figure 10.2 shows what connotes premium to the millennials around the world. While this may not be India specific, anecdotal evidence suggests that the same trends may apply to India too with an Indian flavour, that ensures they get value!

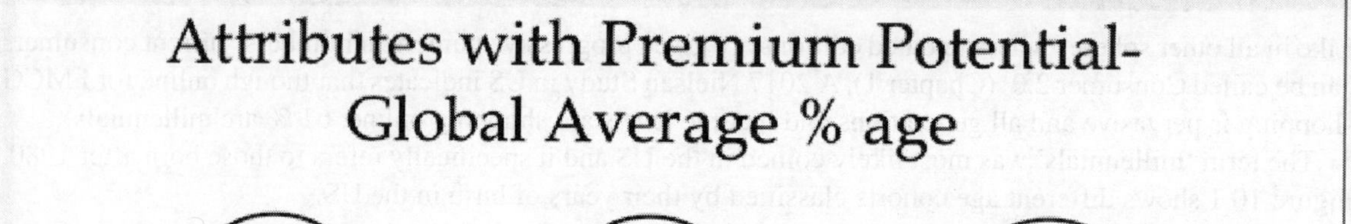

Data Source: http://www.nielsen.com/content/dam/nielsenglobal/eu/docs/pdf/Nielsen%20Global%20Premiumization%20Report%20December%202016.pdf- Graphic - authors

Figure 10.2 Premium Potential – Global Average

Not surprisingly, millennials having been born in the Internet era, are highly sophisticated users of technology. Not only does this lead to rapid adoption and absorption of technology, but also extends their horizons.

In a not-for-publication survey conducted by a leading technology company in 2010, one of the millennial survey respondents told the researcher that, "… unlike your generation, my generation lives in many windows", implying their ability to absorb widely disparate information simultaneously. Very often, older people dismiss this as a lack of attention. In reality, though, it explains the multiplicity of influences in their lives.

One of these, at seeming odds with their high self-esteem needs, is their tendency to shared services such as rides and accommodations as opposed to owning them out-right. Closer examination shows that this is not a contradiction, but in reality the millennials' way of projecting their social concern by sharing available resources, rather than locking up such resources for individual use.

In Chapter 1, we discussed about Consumer 2.0 who are encountered online are the same people who walk into a store, call on the telephone, or order from mail order catalogue. They are doing exactly the same what people have been doing for many years—communicating with each other. The shift is that technology has enabled them to communicate faster, over distances, over mobile phones, and in non-grammatical texts and emojis. The millennials best describe Consumer 2.0 as discussed in Chapter 1.

Consumer 2.0 expects companies to have an online presence, they prefer to shop online (for majority of purchases), and they expect the ecommerce sites to be quick or they do not hesitate to migrate. Consumer 2.0 seeks user-reviews to inform brand choices, and is likely to spend time into researching potential products and purchases. Consumer 2.0 is starting to expect a social media presence, they love innovation and reward innovative brands. Consumer 2.0 is moving from horizontal screen to vertical screen (monitor to phone). Consumer 2.0 expects these technological advances to become a part of their consumer experience (CX). Technology is not treated as novel or new, they are just expected to be there. These consumers are called ***Digital Natives***, a word coined by Marc Prensky[5] in 2001. They have spent their entire lives surrounded by and using computers, videogames, digital music players, video cams, cell phones, and all the other toys and tools of the digital age.

They are

- Wired and born with a keyboard
- Tech savvy, discerning and comfortable with different media and platforms
- Multi-tasking; Want it all and want it now and in control
- Flexible
- Of short attention span and fickle
- Vocal
- Dual personality and anonymity when they choose to be

Therefore, they expect

- Simplicity
- Convenience
- Interactivity
- Consistency
- Value

THE MILLENNIAL GENERATION—OPPORTUNITIES AND CHALLENGES

Every generation presents opportunities and challenges. The Millennial Generation is at a similar cusp.

The Emerging Landscape of E-Retailing and the Millennials

India is at the top of A.T. Kearney Global Retail Development Index 2017[6], replacing China which occupied that slot there for a long time. This has been possible due to a favourable foreign investment environment, a strong economic growth and a boom in consumption mainly on account millennials. This appropriately sums up the Indian retailing landscape described by A.T. Kearney Global Retail Development Index 2017!

AT Kearney Global Retail Development Index is reinforced by IBEF (India Brand Equity Foundation) September 2017[7], updates that the Indian retail industry has emerged as one of the most dynamic and fast-paced industries with the entry of several new players and India's retail market is expected to grow at a Compound Annual Growth Rate (CAGR) of 10 percent to $1.6 trillion by 2026 from $641 billion in 2016.

An Indiaretailing.com[8] 2016 estimate of revenues from eretailing currently pegged at $15 billion is expected to grow up to $60 billion by 2020. A report by Forrester also expects the eretailing market to reach $64 Billion by 2021. The inflection points for the above phenomena of markets to deepen, according to Matrix Partners was, reaching a critical mass of at least 20 million daily active users on the Internet in 2011. This coupled with mobile Internet users exceeding desktop Internet users by mid-2012 to early 2013 made a number of business models attractive. Matrix Partners further forecast that by 2021, at least another 30 billion dollar ecommerce companies are expected to be created in India.

This growth is being driven by Indian millennials leading India's smartphone revolution. An astounding 84 percent of them are already reliant on mobile broadband. A Morgan Stanley Research shows millennials spend an average of 17 hours a week online. They may be young, but many of them are already the chief wage earners in their households and contribute approximately 70 percent of respective household income.

This tidal wave of youth is driving an economic transformation. Since they have disposable income and access to broadband and data services, they sit in cafés, browsing social media accounts on their smartphones while shopping for new shoes, gadgets, apparel or even new homes online. Another Morgan Stanley report, based on its AlphaWise survey and analysis of the habits of India's millennials and the potential implications of their preferences concludes that "Indian Millennials could become the largest disruptive force in India for years to come, and this trend is still in its nascent stages,". As the largest millennial population in the world, the sheer number of India's 18- to 35-year-olds doubtlessly will hold significant sway over the country's immediate economic future.

Millennials are in a place where the existential concerns that defined previous generations—security and belongingness—can be put behind and they can go forth towards the self-actualization needs posited by Maslow. Thus, they are better educated and are economically more self-sufficient than previous generations.

This underlying drive to self-actualization, coupled with the economic wherewithal, can be seen in their perceptions of what signifies value. While the generations of their parents and grandparents sought value in asset creation and standing apart, the millennials generation attaches value to social good and sustainability.

Equally, technology has enabled cutting the wire that tethers people. Millennials have embraced this and entire industries are being disrupted as a consequence. While ride share and apartment share have captured popular imagination, the disruption has been secular across industries—food delivery, music, entertainment, computing, fashion, personal grooming, et al.

Marketers need to recognize these generational influences on millennials and develop their brand stories and product offerings along these axes. At the same time, they should be aware that change is the constant mantra and that today's success is not guaranteed for tomorrow given the pace of disruption being brought about technology. This is the essence of ***Marketing 4.0*** mapping out an approach that is leading customers from ***Awareness to Advocacy***.

Various data presented in the book highlights digital marketing challenges and opportunities with millennials.

THE INTERNET-OF-THINGS (IOT)

IoT has been in the news for the last several years. Like many hoary phenomena, the origin of IoT is lost in time. Kevin Ashton, Director of Auto-ID Centre, a think-tank promoting the use of RFID technology believes that he was the first to use the term in 1999. At that time his use of the term was linking RFID technology to supply chains using the Internet to improve efficiency of the supply chain. He has subsequently expanded the insight to a more nuanced view of collecting data without human interference through sensors and processing them for decision making. This he believes would greatly reduce waste, loss and cost. Quite obviously, the Internet has to be at the centre of this because, while sensors can compile data, the data needs to be processed and exchanged between devices to enable the vision of automated decision making in the use of devices.

What is IoT?

Wikipedia defines the Internet of Things as the network of physical devices, vehicles, buildings and other items, embedded with electronics, software sensors and network connectivity that enable these objects to collect and exchange data.

In 2013, Global Standards Initiative on Internet of Things[9] (IoT-GSI) defined IoT as "the infrastructure of the information society", creating opportunities for more direct integration of the physical world into computer-based systems, and resulting in improved efficiency, accuracy and economic benefit.

Legal scholars suggest looking at 'Things' in IoT as an "inextricable mixture of hardware, software, data and service". These devices collect useful data with the help of various existing technologies and then autonomously flow it between other devices. Current market examples include smart thermostat systems and washer/dryers that use Wi-Fi for remote monitoring.

> **Internet of Things:** It is defined as the network of physical devices, vehicles, buildings and other items, embedded with electronics, software sensors and network connectivity that enable these objects to collect and exchange data.
>
> **RFID:** RFID (radio frequency identification) is a form of wireless communication that incorporates the use of electromagnetic or electrostatic coupling in the radio frequency portion of the electromagnetic spectrum to uniquely identify an object, animal or person.

So, what is IoT really? Consider the simple task of switching on lights in one's home. This activity has a switch and a lamp. Grid power is connected to the switch and when it is switched on, electricity is consumed by the lamp and it lights up. By and large, in today's world, this activity is manual, or at best, one uses a remote control.

An IoT-enabled system would function differently. For instance, the switch can be programmed to go on and off in many different scenarios – at specified times or when the ambient luminosity is at specified thresholds or when human presence is detected or in a combination of these. The information of whether the lights are on or off can be transmitted to an app that can be accessed by a smart phone and the app can be used to re-program the system or take other decisions by the user.

Despite its early start, the adoption of IoT is still nascent. It is estimated that globally 23.14 billion devices are IoT enabled. That impressive number, though, represents only 0.06% of all the potential devices that can be IoT enabled. This is the cause for rosy prediction that the market for IoT enabled devices will be as big as US $ 6 trillion by 2025. The predicted value though is over three times as much, just in cost savings.

Adoption of IoT

IoT has been adopted largely by businesses. However, consumer applications are emerging with the launch of devices like Alexa, Apple TV, Google – Echo, among others.

Key business adoption of IoT has been in workplace sensors to enable and manage utilities and improved office productivity and efficiency. These applications are also used extensively in retail environments.

Industrial organizations, particularly in chemical and food processing industries, usage of IoT is in minimizing operational risk and plant downtime.

IoT is used in the healthcare industry to monitor patients by connecting critical care equipment and imaging systems. Such systems, not only monitor the patients, but also alert practitioners of potential malfunction in the equipment. Remote medical monitoring is an area where investments are accelerating.

Business users expect adoption of IoT would help them improve business efficiency, innovation and access to newer markets. However, a study shows that just about 1% of all the data that is being generated by the sensors is being analyzed and very large untapped potential exists to use the data for prediction and finding new applications. Figure 10.3[10] shows projections of IoT expenditure by different industries.

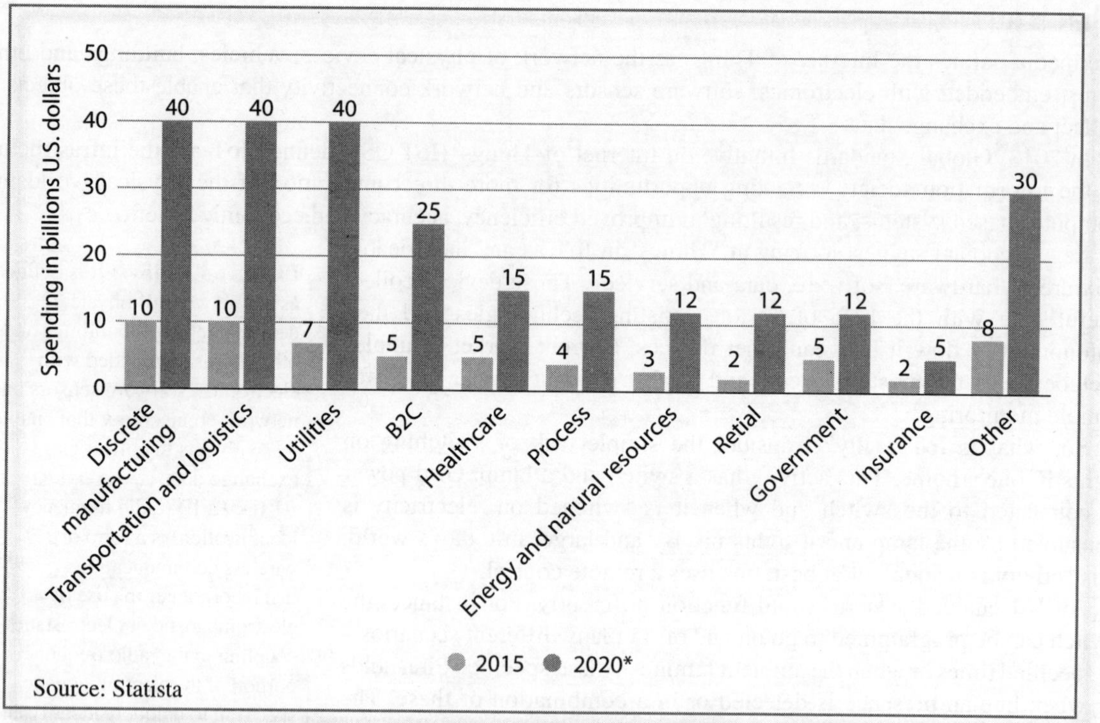

Figure 10.3 Projections of IoT Expenditure by Different Industries

IoT and Consumer

Consumer applications of IoT have been somewhat slow but are beginning to pick up pace. "Uses of the IoT that were previously impractical will increasingly become practical," said Roy Schulte, vice president and distinguished analyst at Gartner. According to him, the IoT is relevant in virtually every industry, although not in every application. While there will be no purely 'IoT applications', there will be many applications that leverage the IoT in some small or large aspect of their work.

Imagine your washing machine sending you options of detergents to buy based on the clothes you wash, a TV suggesting the right cable package suitable for you, your microwave oven sending you information on recipes and diet recommendations. All these are possibilities in a not so far future. There will be unlimited data that brands can acquire when the capacity of IoT is fully and completely exploited.

Internet of Things will educate the brands on what the customers exactly wants by analyzing their patterns and choices at microscopic levels and what really drives them to their choices. This way the brands will be able to customize and personalize their strategy and communications down to every individual consumer. The flexibility that IoT offers in terms of its own adaptability to change in the customer behaviour is in itself a huge advantage for brands to measure and analyze what the customer will need even before he actually realizes that he needs it. Please refer to Steve Jobs' quote in Chapter 3.

What if your refrigerator says you need to restock even before you realize you have exhausted everything? And even better when it says what you need to buy and gives you recommendations. Well the opportunities are endless. The relevancy and real time responses will produce the most personalized and effective brand-consumer interaction like never before.

Apart from the much hyped driverless cars, some major areas of consumer applications of IoT are:

Health Care: An extension of patient care systems in hospitals, in-home elder care is being IoT enabled by combining inputs from a microphone, motion sensor, paging service and real-time streaming data to monitor elders. The system can send alerts to adults or caretakers as and when required. An example is i-Doctor, a device that can be attached to a smart phone with an app and could substitute a BP monitor, ECG and sonography. It will transmit the results real time to your doctor besides storing the data on your phone. According to John Bates, CMO, Software AG, in 10 years' time we could be living in a world of sensors and connected human beings.

Home Security Systems: Nearly 25% of U.S. broadband households have an active security system. Sixty-five percent of the remaining plan to buy a smart home device within the year. Such systems, in addition to the traditional alarm systems have cameras connected to apps that can view activity remotely.

Smart Homes: The applications here range from the earlier example of lighting and utility management to voice activated cooking appliances, pet care, etc.

Wearable Tech: Wearable tech like smart watches are picking up quite smoothly. Augmented reality and virtual reality have introduced new perks in the smart glasses. At the same time, healthcare monitoring is the added selling point of smartwatches.

Smart home device: A residence that uses Internet-connected devices to enable the remote monitoring and management of appliances and systems, such as lighting and heating.

Wearable tech: Wearable technology (also called wearable gadgets) is a category of technology devices that can be worn by a consumer and often include tracking information related to health and fitness. Other wearable tech gadgets include devices that have small motion sensors to take photos and sync with your mobile devices.

Virtual reality: The computer-generated simulation of a three-dimensional image or environment that can be interacted within a seemingly real or physical way by a person using special electronic equipment, such as a helmet with a screen inside or gloves fitted with sensors.

TECHNOLOGY IN SPORTS

Cricket Twenty20 Cricket World Cup 2014, that was held in Bangladesh brought us a new technological innovation—of the stumps lighting up each time the bails were knocked off, either by the wicket-keeper or otherwise. With conventional bails, it was difficult for the umpire to decide when the bail is 'completely dislodged' from the wicket. But now, with the help of sensors combined with LED technology, the umpire can take a decision without a shadow of doubt. Another example of such a technology is Babolat's Play Pure Drive Racquet System in Tennis, a smart product that looks like a regular racquet on the outside; however, sensors integrated into the handle allow players access to a lot of information and analysis through a smartphone application, such as power, impact locator, type and number of strokes.

Personal Assistants and Cobots

Personal assistants have been in the market for quite a while. Siri, Alexa, and Google Assistant are making rapid progress in development. With IoT, the functionalities of these can increase manifold for many routine habits like finding misplaced objects, reminders of chores, preparation of lists, etc.

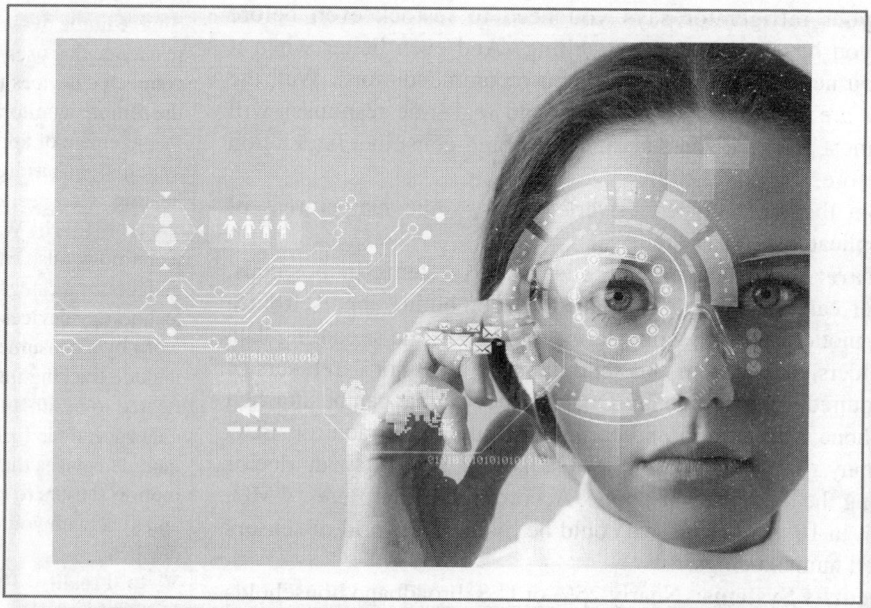

The concept of IoT is going to shake up the way businesses and consumers interact, and blur the boundaries between the physical and digital realms. But there is little understanding yet of how this much-hyped technology will play out for companies and their customers.

The race in developing machine learning artificial technology capabilities such as those being built by Apple and Google points to a far closer interaction between IoT and human beings. Apple CEO Tim Cook has said very clearly that they will not use data in certain ways. However, they would have no option if others are not going to play by the rule. So, soon our glasses are going to have the most intimate information about us and everything around us, and this data will definitely be used.

Cobots: A cobot or co-robot (from collaborative robot) is a robot intended to physically interact with humans in a shared workspace. This is in contrast with other robots, designed to operate autonomously or with limited guidance, which is what most industrial robots were up until the decade of the 2010s.

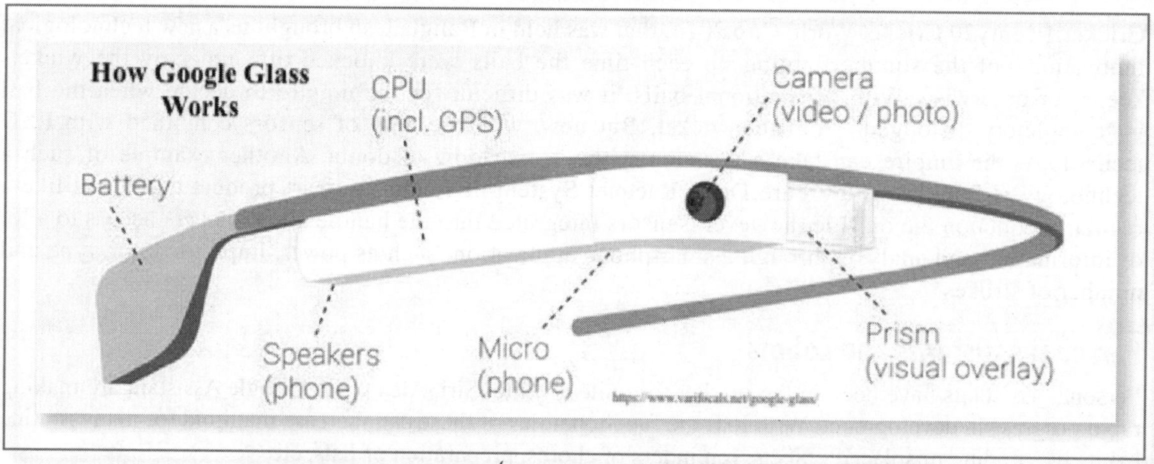

There is going to be a world where sensors will eventually be able to record biological data directly from human beings, such as glucose levels and blood pressure, potentially flagging health issues before the person knows about them. This could have wide-ranging implications for healthcare, insurance, and even mental health.

The Scale of Industries of Future

- Rise of the Cobots - digital assistants everywhere
- From Diagnosis to Wellness methods
- Biotechnology - BT will become larger than IT by 2025
- Growth of Virtual & Augmented Reality - will overtake TV & Media by 2025
- Rise of Smart Infrastructure - 152 K devices connect to the Internet every minute. IoT will rule.
- Global Economic shift From G7 (Group of 7) to D7 (Digital 7 that will include India)
- Shift to the "experience" economy - all about Usage Intelligence (UI) and usage ease (UE or CX)

PLC: An industrial computer control system that continuously monitors the state of input devices and makes decisions based upon a custom program to control the state of output devices

Usage Intelligence (UI): A user interface (UI) that involves some aspect of artificial intelligence (AI or computational intelligence). There are many modern examples of IUIs, the most famous (or infamous) being the Microsoft Office Assistant, whose most recognizable agentive representation was called "Clippy".

Challenges in IoT Adoption

Hardware Compatibility Issues: Data capturing majorly occurs through various sensors, PLCs, etc., which are connected to IoT gateways to collect and transmit data to the cloud. Enterprises need to meticulously identify the equipment, hardware, and existing legacy machines based on their goals and business outcomes. When there are legacy machines that do not have the said PLCs and sensors involved, the IoT implementation challenge becomes more critical. Adding external sensors to the legacy machines is one quick work around, but it will not be full proof, making it a very challenging task. Therefore, identifying the physical devices and understanding the associated compatibility issues before IoT implementation is highly recommended.

RTU: A multipurpose device used for remote monitoring and control of various devices and systems for automation. It is typically deployed in an industrial environment and serves a similar purpose to programmable logic circuits (PLCs) but to a higher degree.

Data Connectivity Issues: Data connectivity is a critical IoT implementation challenge. It involves how IoT devices talk to the gateway and the Cloud and what data format do they generate. Most IoT gateways available are compatible with GPRS and Wi-Fi/LAN, but legacy devices depend on PLCs, telemetry systems and RTUs to generate data. So, the need is for a suitable edge layer that translates transport and data format protocols to send data to the IoT platform. Defining the right combination of these protocols before proceeding with an IoT implementation will help in going a long way.

Apart from the issues of data transfer between systems, the speed at which the data is transmitted is also a critical factor. Delays in data transfer can slow down processing for real time actions that could lead to losses far greater than equipment damage alone.

Incorrect Data Capture Difficulties: Let's consider that the entire setup did not face any challenges and the system is up and running, but there can still be the issue of incorrect data capture creeping up. Because of some untoward incident or the inability of the software to handle certain anomalies in run time, incorrect data gets recorded. This results in inaccurate analytics that may not help in taking better decisions. This IoT implementation challenge can be a major decision influencer for the enterprises as well as the customers.

Analytics Challenges: The real value of an IoT solution is realized through actionable insights derived from the collected IoT data. This demands a high-performance analytics platform that is capable of handling the ginormous amount of data to be added in the solution at a later point. Data analytics partners need to keep this in mind while devising the IoT implementation architecture to involve data processing, cleansing and representation. Thus, leaving enough space for extensibility to add real-time or predictive analytics to an IoT solution can help solve this critical IoT implementation challenge.

Data Security Issues: This is not the least of the issues. In a connected world, the risk of the data being stolen is the least of the problems. Ill-intentioned thieves of data can use the data to cause enormous damage by using the stolen data to make people or machines do things they are not supposed to do. Hence, IoT service providers need to ensure that data is not only going to be safe, but also ensure that it cannot be processed or manipulated un rogue actors.

CHALLENGES FOR MARKETERS

With endless data and greater insights from multiple channels and sources, marketers will face a great challenge in strategizing and using the right tools. With the scope undefined, the tools to acquire and analyze data from different channels need to be built, which once again opens up greater opportunities.

Big data will be a challenge to analyze and the level of personalization will result in a huge number of communications and strategies in place. To manage the number of variables in a market and to personalize it to an individual's level is a humongous task and will be a great challenge for marketers around the globe. Therefore, one may even say that we are moving from *Customization to Customerization*.

We need to understand that it is not just the number of devices that are going up but also the types of devices. To harness all this information from so many sources is a challenge that the industry will look forward to as the insights they are going to get will be worthwhile.

Notwithstanding all the above, overall technology is transforming every conceivable space or activity.

INDUSTRY 4.0

Thus so far the focus has been on consumers and B2C. In Chapter 1, we said "Digital transformation means business transformation" and "Digital transformation is a fundamental shift in how a firm delivers value and drives revenue." Examples of Starbucks redesigning the layout of their stores to accommodate the logistics of "order ahead" customers, and Hilton wanting to allow customers to unlock doors through their app have been cited. Digital transformation has not only touched the lives of consumers as we have seen in the last few chapters, but has also impacted various industries in more than one way. Marketing 4.0. has been discussed, the buzzword in the industry is Industry. 4.0.

Let us consider the example of an automobile. The first automobiles came into use in the early 1900s, nearly 300 years after the beginning of the industrial age. While the industrial age dawned with mechanization, automobile manufacturing heralded the mass production era in manufacturing. Henry Ford, the putative father of mass production proclaimed, "Any customer can have a car painted any colour that he wants so long as it is black." As we saw in Table 10.1 earlier in this chapter, this situation gave way to the era of Marketing 2.0 (circa 1960) that was the era of STP (Segmentation, Positioning, Targeting) and 4Ps of marketing. This was to cater to an increasingly diverse consuming class with different tastes and wants. And now, as the millennials take root as the drivers of consumption, mass customization (as against standardization) is upon us.

The transition from mechanization to mass-production to mass-segmentation to mass-customization is referred to as the different eras of manufacturing. Thus, if mechanization was Industry 1.0, the era of mass-customization is Industry 4.0.

Exhibit 10.1 captures the key characteristics of this evolution.

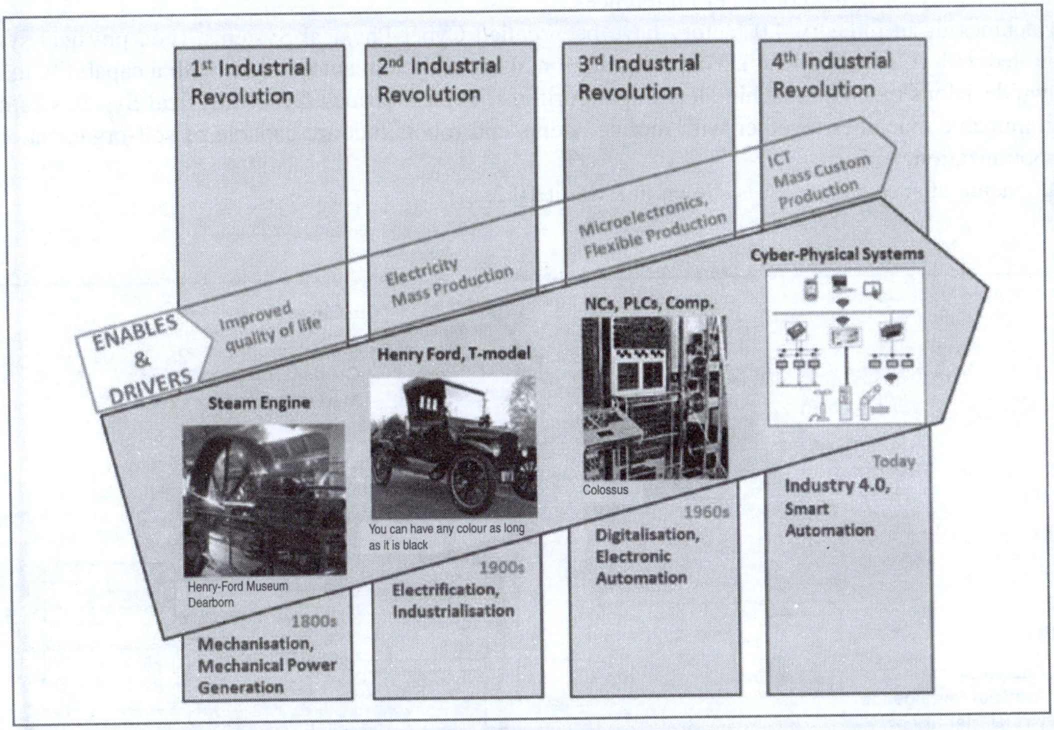

Exhibit 10.1 Evolution Industry 1.0 - 4.0

According to McKinsey[11], "Industry 4.0 is the next phase in the digitization of the manufacturing sector, driven by four disruptions: the astonishing rise in data volumes, computational power, and connectivity, especially new low-power wide-area networks; the emergence of analytics and business-intelligence capabilities; new forms of human-machine interaction such as touch interfaces and augmented-reality systems; and improvements in transferring digital instructions to the physical world, such as advanced robotics and 3-D printing" .

In layman's terms, Industry 4.0 is where everything is "Smart" and "Connected" – home, workplace and cities. In fact, IBM (mainly a B2B company) has been leveraging the SMART concept in their B2C communications in the last few years. According to Andrew Ng[12], Co-founder of Coursera, "AI is the new electricity".

The Building Blocks of Industry 4.0

Imagine an assembly line in a factory, where each product being assembled on the line is different. This is so antithetical to even the concept of the assembly line that it is mind-blogging. Yet that is the ultimate dream of Industry 4.0.

To achieve this the concept of the assembly line is being replaced by the concept of a re-configurable manufacturing system. The onset of Industry 2.0 saw production lines with machines performing specific tasks to produce only one product. In its avatar as Industry 3.0, flexible production systems with programmable machines (e.g., CNC machines, machines with Logic Controllers, etc.) were added to the assembly line. This development allowed production of a variety of different products but offered no flexibility in how much of each product could be manufactured in a single run. Reconfigurable manufacturing systems replace these approaches to manufacturing to adapt their hardware and software components so that output can be matched to the constantly changing consumer preferences.

Machines in an Industry 4.0 factory have been called Cyber-Physical Systems, (i.e., physical systems integrated with ICT components). This integration makes the system autonomous with a capability to make its own decisions based on machine learning algorithms. Typically, such Cyber-Physical Systems comprise programmable machines together with mobile agents and robots that are capable of self-organization and self-optimization.

A schema of such a system[13] is shown in Exhibit 10.2.

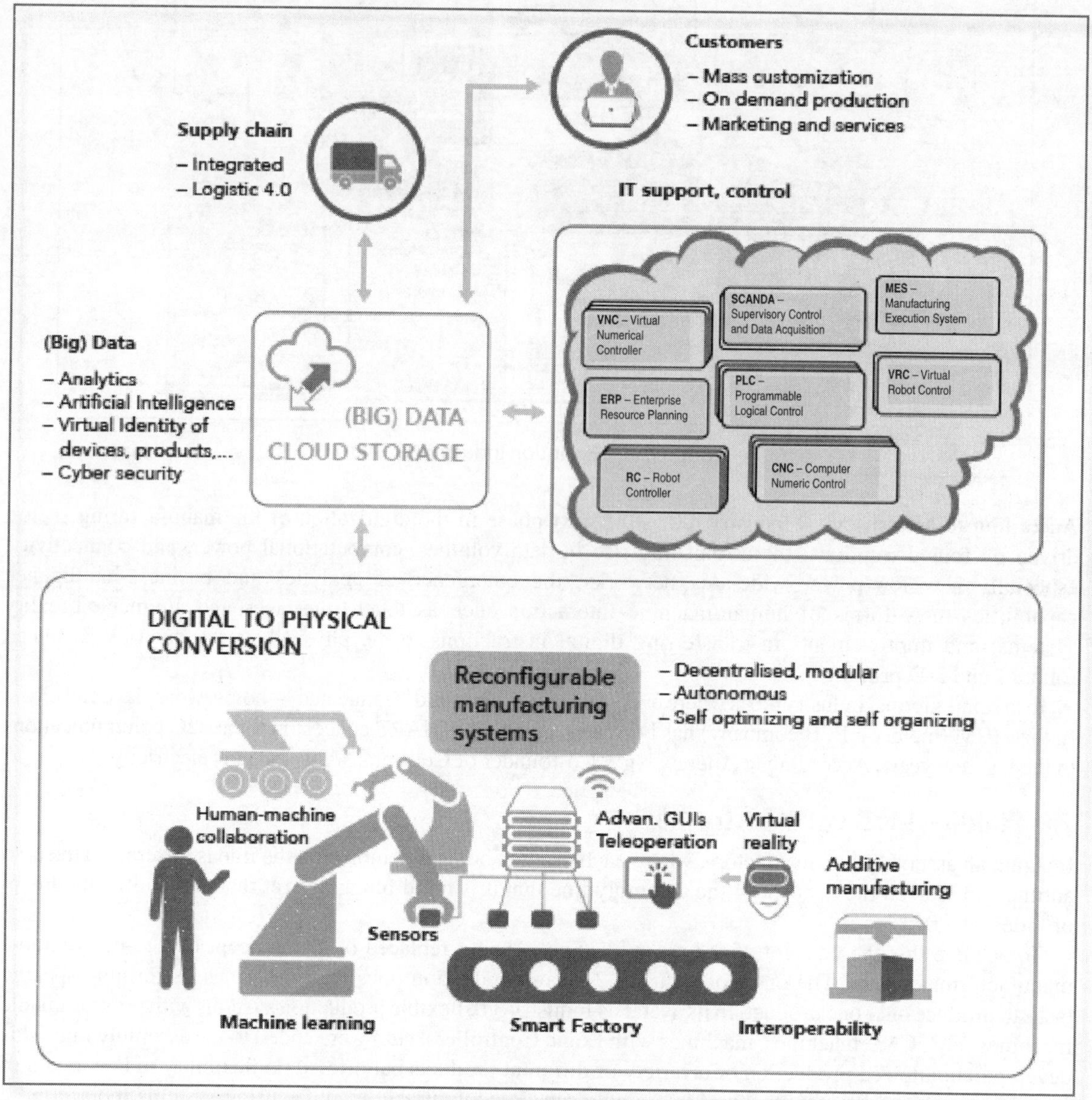

Exhibit 10.2 Cyber Physical System - Industry 4.0

Cyber-Physical Systems: A mechanism that is controlled or monitored by computer-based algorithms, tightly integrated with the Internet and its users

Internet of People (IoP): Refers to the digitalization of relationships between people and the collection, processing and application of personal data. It forms a network of collective intelligence and stimulates interactive communication among our digital selves through digital devices, the Internet and sharing of data.

The key characteristics of Industry 4.0[14] are:

- Interoperability: The ability of machines, devices, sensors, and people to connect and communicate with each other via the Internet of Things (IoT) or the Internet of People (IoP).
- Information transparency: The ability of information systems to create a virtual copy of the physical world by enriching digital plant models with sensor data. This requires the aggregation of raw sensor data to higher-value context information.
- Technical assistance: First, the ability of assistance systems to support humans by aggregating and visualizing information comprehensively for making informed decisions and solving urgent problems on short notice. Second, the ability of cyber physical systems to physically support humans by conducting a range of tasks that are unpleasant, too exhausting, or unsafe for their human co-workers.
- Decentralized decisions: The ability of cyber physical systems to make decisions on their own and to perform their tasks as autonomously as possible. Only in the case of exceptions, interferences, or conflicting goals, are tasks delegated to a higher level.

The evolution of Industry 4.0 is expected to bring about the following benefits to the manufacturing sector:

1. Cost reduction
   a. production costs by 10-30%
   b. logistic costs by 10-30%,
   c. quality management costs by 10-20%.

2. Shorter time-to-market for the new products
3. Improved customer responsiveness
4. Enabling a custom production at mass volumes without significantly increasing overall production costs
5. More flexible and friendlier working environment
6. More efficient use of natural resources and energy

All the above, therefore is expected to impact Digital B2B Marketing in a significant way, some of which are outlined below:

Smart Cities - Connected devices, services, and solutions

- **Energy**
  - Virtual power plants
  - Energy storage solutions
  - Energy-efficient heating, cooling, and hot water systems
- **Buildings**
  - Connected home appliances
  - Connected building solutions
  - Smart homes
- **Mobility**
  - Connected parking

- Intermodal transportation
  E-mobility
- Environmental monitoring
- Fleet management
- **E-governance**
  - City data platform
  - Community app
- **Safety and security**
  - Safety and security solutions
  - Disaster management

Industry 4.0 and Forecast for Businesses

- **Automobiles**
  - Electric cars, with around 20 moving parts compared with 2000 + for the traditional fossil fuel variety, would impact the automobile components industry.
  - The impact on the auto component industry will affect the global alloys steel sector (including ore and ferro alloys).
  - Most cars will be made from recycled steel, as a result of which, ore and ferro alloy companies will face viability issues.
  - Oil behemoths are likely to default on their loans if oil consumption declined (elimination unlikely).
  - Renewable energy will kick-start a long-term coal decline and large coal corporates employing thousands will face financial crisis.
  - Electric vehicles will come with an unlimited warranty implying once you buy a vehicle, you would not need to buy another for quite some years.
  - Uber and OLA have already established an asset sharing model and the cost to commute will become the 'next telecom' (virtually free).
- **Financial Services**
  - Banks will become a concept rather than a place, banks will become more about systems than people.
  - Oil-based economies (Saudi Arabia, Iran, Iraq, Russia, Nigeria, etc.) will go into a crisis impacting terror funding and the world may become a more peaceful place.
  - The large steel, oil and coal sector debt will become NPAs.
  - People will increase renting of assets (over buying these) and prefer pay as you use model.
  - 3D printing will even out the wage arbitrage between developed and developing nations.
  - The world likely move towards deflation arising out of an abundance of money and relatively limited spending.

A McKinsey Survey in 2015 of 300 Global Business Leaders indicate the following readiness levels of readiness with respect to Industry 4.0.

- 48 % of manufacturers consider ready
- 78 % of suppliers are prepared

Compare the above with a Participant Survey (September 6, 2017) one of the authors during a priming session for Industry 4.0 for a reputed Indian Giant in EPC sector.

Exhibit 10.3 What emerges is that India is not yet Industry 4.0 ready.

ANSWER CHOICES	RESPONSES	
I am aware and somewhat exposed	18.75%	3
I am aware but not exposed	12.50%	2
I am not aware	62.50%	10
My company has some Industry 4.0 initiatives	6.25%	1
Total Respondents: 16		

Exhibit 10.3 India Industry 4.0 Readiness

In summary, there is only one conclusion viz. digital transformation is business transformation and the earlier a country adapts digitization, the better it will be for its economic transformation.

CHAPTER SUMMARY

- Marketing 4.0 is a marketing approach that combines online and offline interaction between companies and customers. In the digital economy, Marketing 4.0 blends style with substance. While it is imperative for brands to be more flexible and adaptive due to rapid technological trends, their authentic characters are more important than ever.
- Industry 4.0 is best described as convergence of two worlds that had been disconnected, Information Technology *(IT)* and Operational Technology *(OT)*.
- According to Kotler (2014), the shortest definition of marketing is CCDVTP, i.e., "Create, Communicate, Deliver Value to a Target Market at a Profit."
- Target audience is a broad group of consumers classified along easily determinable criteria such as demographics or geography that indicates the potential of the group to consume a particular brand or category. Segments are sub-groups, within these audiences that share a common characteristic, attitudinal, lifestyle orientation, usage habits, etc., which influence the propensity of the consumer to use a particular brand, in preference to others.
- Millennials are a generational cohort defined by their age a common predictor of differences in attitudes and behaviour. Age describes the individual in two different ways, their life stage, a young single adult, married with children, retiree, etc., and their belonging to a group that were born around the same period.
- Like in all other spheres where updated editions are given progressive numerical numbers, current consumers can be called Consumer 2.0. The term Customer 2.0 came into being sometime in 2009.
- A global survey by Nielsenin 2016 shows Indian millennials to be among the most optimistic about their future compared to their peers. The survey showed that 78% of Indian millennials perceived their financial situation to be better than 'five years ago' compared to the global average of 55%.
- 36% of the Indian millennials felt they had the ability to spend freely compared to 14% of their global peers who felt so. Correspondingly, only 14% of Indian millennials felt that they had just enough to cover their basic expenses compared to 35% global average.
- Not surprisingly, millennials having been born in the Internet era, are highly sophisticated users

of technology. Not only does this lead to rapid adoption and absorption of technology, but also extends their horizons.

- Consumer 2.0 are called Digital Natives, a word coined by Marc Prensky in 2001. They have spent their entire lives surrounded by and using computers, videogames, digital music players, video cams, cell phones, and all the other toys and tools of the digital age.
- India is at the top of A.T. Kearney Global Retail Development Index 2017, replacing China which occupied that slot for a long time.
- This growth is being driven by Indian millennials leading India's smartphone revolution. An astounding 84% of them are already reliant on mobile broadband. A Morgan Stanley Research shows millennials spend an average of 17 hours a week online. They may be young, but many of them are already the chief wage earners in their households and contribute approximately 70% of respective household income.
- The essence of Marketing 4.0 is mapping out an approach that is leading customers from Awareness to Advocacy.
- Wikipedia defines the Internet of Things as the network of physical devices, vehicles, buildings and other items, embedded with electronics, software sensors and network connectivity that enable these objects to collect and exchange data.
- A prediction is that the market for IoT enabled devices will be as big as US $ 6 trillion by 2025. The predicted value though is over three times as much, just in cost savings.
- Key business adoption of IoT has been in workplace sensors to enable and manage utilities and improved office productivity and efficiency. These applications are also used extensively in retail environments.
- Consumer applications of IoT have been in Healthcare, Home security, Smart Homes, Virtual Reality, Sports and many other fields.
- The scale of industries of future are expected to be
  - Rise of the Cobots - digital assistants everywhere
  - From Diagnosis to Wellness methods
  - Biotechnology - BT will become larger than IT by 2025
  - Growth of Virtual & Augmented Reality - will overtake TV & Media by 2025
  - Rise of Smart Infrastructure - 152 K devices connect to the Internet every minute. IoT will rule.
  - Global Economic Shift From G7 (Group of 7) to D7 (Digital 7 that will include India)
  - Shift to the "experience" economy, all about usage intelligence (UI) and usage ease (UE or CX)
- "Digital transformation means business transformation" and "Digital transformation is a fundamental shift in how a firm delivers value and drives revenue."
- The transition from mechanization to mass-production to mass-segmentation to mass-customization is referred to as the different eras of manufacturing. Thus, if mechanization was Industry 1.0, the era of mass-customization is Industry 4.0.
- In layman's terms, Industry 4.0 is where everything is "Smart" and "Connected" – homes, workplace and cities.
- Industry 4.0 is expected to impact Digital B2B Marketing in a significant way, smart cities—connected devices, services, and solutions.
- Industry 4.0 will impact with electric cars, the automobile components industry. The impact on the auto component industry will affect the global alloys steel sector. Renewable energy will kick-start a long-term coal decline and large coal corporates employing thousands will face financial crisis. Electric vehicles will come with an unlimited warranty implying once you buy a vehicle, you would not need to buy another for quite some years. Uber and OLA have already established an asset sharing model and the cost to commute will become the 'next telecom' (virtually free).
- To sum up, there is only one conclusion, i.e. digital transformation is business transformation.

CLOSING CASE CASELET

CASELET - IOT & INDUSTRY 4.0

Looking to Industry for the Next Digital Disruption[15]

SAN RAMON, Calif. — When Sharoda Paul finished a postdoctoral fellowship last year at the Palo Alto Research Center, she did what most of her peers do — considered a job at a big Silicon Valley company, in her case, Google. But instead, Ms. Paul, a 31-year-old expert in social computing, went to work for General Electric.

Ms. Paul is one of more than 250 engineers recruited in the last year and a half to GE's new software center here, in the East Bay of San Francisco. The company plans to increase that workforce of computer scientists and software developers to 400, and to invest $1 billion in the center by 2015. The buildup is part of GE's big bet on what it calls the "industrial Internet," bringing digital intelligence to the physical world of industry as never before.

The concept of Internet-connected machines that collect data and communicate, often called the "Internet of Things," has been around for years. Information technology companies, too, are pursuing this emerging field. I.B.M. has its "Smarter Planet" projects, while Cisco champions the "Internet of Everything."

But GE's effort, analysts say, shows that Internet-era technology is ready to sweep through the industrial economy much as the consumer Internet has transformed media, communications and advertising over the last decade.

In recent months, Ms. Paul has donned a hard hat and safety boots to study power plants. She has ridden on a rail locomotive and toured hospital wards. "Here, you get to work with things that touch people in so many ways," she said. "That was a big draw."

GE is the nation's largest industrial company, a producer of aircraft engines, power plant turbines, rail locomotives and medical imaging equipment. It makes the heavy-duty machinery that transports people, heats homes and powers factories, and lets doctors diagnose life-threatening diseases.

GE resides in a different world from the consumer Internet. But the major technologies that animate Google and Facebook are also vital ingredients in the industrial Internet—tools from artificial intelligence, like machine-learning software, and vast streams of new data. In industry, the data flood comes mainly from smaller, more powerful and cheaper sensors on the equipment.

Smarter machines, for example, can alert their human handlers when they will need maintenance, before a breakdown. It is the equivalent of preventive and personalized care for equipment, with less downtime and more output.

"These technologies are really there now, in a way that is practical and economic," said Mark M. Little, GE's senior vice president for global research.

GE's embrace of the industrial Internet is a long-term strategy. But if its optimism proves justified, the impact could be felt across the economy.

The outlook for technology-led economic growth is a subject of considerable debate. In a recent research paper, Robert J. Gordon, a prominent economist at Northwestern University, argues that the gains from computing and the Internet have petered out in the last eight years.

Since 2000, Mr. Gordon asserts, invention has focused mainly on consumer and communications technologies, including smartphones and tablet computers. Such devices, he writes, are "smaller, smarter and more capable, but do not fundamentally change labour productivity or the standard of living" in the way that electric lighting or the automobile did.

But others say such pessimism misses the next wave of technology. "The reason I think Bob Gordon is wrong is precisely because of the kind of thing G.E. is doing," said Andrew McAfee, principal research scientist at M.I.T.'s Center for Digital Business.

Today, GE is putting sensors on everything, be it a gas turbine or a hospital bed. The mission of the engineers in San Ramon is to design the software for gathering data, and the clever algorithms for sifting through it for cost savings and productivity gains. Across the industries it covers, GE estimates such efficiency opportunities at as much as $150 billion.

Some industrial Internet projects are already under way. First Wind, an owner and operator of 16 wind farms in America, is a GE customer for wind turbines. It has been experimenting with upgrades that add more sensors, controls and optimization software.

The new sensors measure temperature, wind speeds, location and pitch of the blades. They collect three to five times as much data as the sensors on turbines of a few years ago, said Paul Gaynor, chief executive of First Wind. The data is collected and analyzed by GE software, and the operation of each turbine can be tweaked for efficiency. For example, in very high winds, turbines across an entire farm are routinely shut down to prevent damage from rotating too fast. But more refined measurement of wind speeds might mean only a portion of the turbines need to be shut down. In wintry conditions, turbines can detect when they are icing up, and speed up or change pitch to knock off the ice.

Upgrades on 123 turbines on two wind farms have so far delivered a 3 percent increase in energy output, about 120 megawatt hours per turbine a year. That translates to $1.2 million in additional revenue a year from those two farms, Mr. Gaynor said.

"It's not earthshaking, but it is meaningful," he said. "These are real commercial investments for us that make economic sense now."

For the last few years, GE and Mount Sinai Medical Center have been working on a project to optimize the operations of the 1,100-bed hospital in New York. Hospitals, in a sense, are factories of health care. The challenge for hospitals, especially as cost pressures tighten, is to treat more patients more efficiently, while improving the quality of care. Technology, said Wayne Keathley, president of Mount Sinai, can play a vital role.

At Mount Sinai, patients get a black plastic wristband with a location sensor and other information. Similar sensors are on beds and medical equipment. An important advantage, Mr. Keathley said, is to be able to see the daily flow of patients, physical assets and treatment as it unfolds.

But he said the real benefit was how the data could be used to automate and streamline operations and then make better decisions. For example, in a typical hospital, getting a patient who shows up in an emergency room into an assigned bed in a hospital ward can take several hours and phone calls.

At Mount Sinai, GE has worked on optimization and modeling software that enables admitting officers to see beds and patient movements throughout the hospital, to help them more efficiently match patients and beds. Beyond that, modeling software is beginning to make predictions about likely patient admission and discharge numbers over the next several hours, based on historical patterns at the hospital and other circumstances—say, in flu season.

The software, which Mount Sinai has been trying out in recent months, acts as an intelligent assistant to admitting officers. "It essentially says, 'Hold off, your instinct is to give this bed to that guy, but there might be a better choice,'" Mr. Keathley explained.

At a hospital like Mount Sinai, GE estimates that the optimization and modeling technologies can translate into roughly 10,000 more patients treated a year, and $120 million in savings and additional revenue over several years.

The origins of GE's industrial Internet strategy date back to meetings at the company's headquarters in Fairfield, Conn., in May 2009. In the depths of the financial crisis, Jeffrey R. Immelt, GE's chief executive, met with his senior staff to discuss long-term growth opportunities. The industrial Internet, they decided, built on GE's strength in research and could be leveraged across its varied industrial businesses, adding to the company's revenue in services, which reached $42 billion last year.

Now GE is trying to rally support for its vision from industry partners, academics, venture capitalists and start-ups. About 250 of them have been invited to a conference in San Francisco, sponsored by the company, on Thursday.

Mr. Immelt himself becomes involved in recruiting. His message, he says, is that if you want to have an effect on major societal challenges like improving health care, energy and transportation, consider GE.

An early convert was William Ruh, who joined GE from Cisco, to become vice president in charge of the software center in San Ramon. And Mr. Ruh is taking the same message to high-tech recruits like Ms. Paul. "Here, they are working on things they can explain to their parents and grandparents," he said. "It's not a social network," even if the GE projects share some of the same technology.

Source for the Caselet – NY Times on line

Case Questions

1. How did GE exploit IoT differently?
2. What were the challenges in Mt. Sinai Hospital and how did IoT help?

REVIEW QUESTIONS

1. What is your understanding of Marketing 4.0, what is its essence and how is it different from earlier versions of Marketing viz. 1.0, 2.0 and 3.0.?
2. What is the shortest definition of marketing and how do you relate it to the 4Ps of marketing?
3. Describe a millennial and why do we call them Consumer 2.0?
4. What is the difference between cohorts and segments?
5. What is the impact of millennials' behaviour on shopping and retail development index?
6. What is IoT and what is its impact in the consumer and business economy of India?
7. What is your understanding of Industry 4.0?
8. What is the impact of Industry 4.0 in the consumer and business economy of India?
9. How is Industry 4.0 expected to impact automobile and financial services sectors?
10. Explain "Digital transformation means business transformation".

ACTIVITY QUESTIONS

1. Compare a fit bit, smart watch and a smartphone using sensors to track health and exercise parameters by going through their respective details on their websites on how they work.
2. Visit http://smartcities.gov.in/ to understand GOI Smart City initiative and the road map for cities in your state.

KEY TERMS

Augmented reality
Cobots
Cyber-Physical Systems
Internet of People (IoP)
Internet of Things
PLC
RFID
RTU
smart home device
Usage Intelligence (UI)
Virtual reality
Wearable tech

REFERENCES

1. https://paidpost.nytimes.com/qualcomm/5g-is-coming.html.
2. https://medium.com/@diana.salacka_95611/what-is-marketing-4-0-e7007b32f79d.
3. Ryan,Damien and Jones Calvin (2009), *Understanding Digital Marketing –Kogan Page*, New Delhi.
4. http://www.nielsen.com/content/dam/nielsenglobal/eu/docs/pdf/Nielsen%20Global%20Premiumization%20Report%20December%202016.pdf
5. Marc Prensky, (2001) "Digital Natives, Digital Immigrants Part 1", On the Horizon, Vol. 9 Issue: 5, pp.1-6, https://doi.org/10.1108/10748120110424816.
6. https://www.atkearney.com/global-retail-development-index.
7. https://www.ibef.org/industry/ecommerce.aspx.
8. https://www.indiaretailing.com/2018/02/19/retail/e-retailing-market-likely-surge-two-fold-three-years/.
9. https://www.itu.int/en/ITU-T/gsi/iot/Pages/default.aspx.
10. Source: https://www.statista.com/statistics/666864/iot-spending-by-vertical-worldwide/.
11. http://www.mckinsey.com/business-functions/operations/our-insights/manufacturings-next-act.
12. http://www.mckinsey.com/global-themes/future-of-organizations-and-work/the-evolution-of-employment-and-skills-in-the-age-of-ai.
13. Source: http://online-journals.org/index.php/i-jim/article/viewFile/7072/4532.
14. https://en.wikipedia.org/wiki/Industry_4.0.
15. https://www.nytimes.com/2012/11/24/technology/internet/ge-looks-to-industry-for-the-next-digital-disruption.html?pagewanted=all&_r=1&.

CHAPTER 11

DISRUPTIVE DIGITAL TECHNOLOGIES AND IMPACT

CHAPTER OBJECTIVES

After going through this chapter, you will be able to

- Demystify MarTech a.k.a Marketing Technology
- Discuss AIMLA (Artificial Intelligence, Machine Learning and Analytics)—The new mantra for technology
- Learn artificial intelligence using machine and deep learning—supervised and unsupervised learning
- Illustrate technology in sports, supply chain, blockchain and bitcoins
- Explain the impact of technology in marketing on jobs and traditional marketing
- Analyze career in marketing: going digital traditionally and career choices

OPENING CASE LET

ARTIFICIAL INTELLIGENCE CAN PRODUCE AMAZING CONTENT - FROM WEATHER AND LOCAL NEWS TO RECIPES

Ask Alexa or Siri

A 2 ½ year old kid who has just learnt to speak, takes mom's smartphone and asks Siri to play a song. The child has learnt this from "Ask Alexa or ask Siri" through TV commercials. In industry AI is used in the financial world for uses ranging from fraud detection to improving customer service by predicting what services customers will need. Today all of us are getting used to technology that is being adopted in our everyday life being powered by AI – may it be Alexa of Google or Siri of Apple. Whether it is the weather forecast from Alexa or directions from Siri, the technology that enables this is natural language generation (NLG). NLG is a software that automatically creates a written narrative from data.

NLG is a subset of artificial intelligence that transforms input data into language/languages that sound as natural as a human was speaking the content. Organizations have adopted NLG enterprise-wide to improve operational efficiency, human productivity and even customer engagement. A computer processes extraordinary amount of data with accuracy and NLG systems is able to determine how best to communicate the findings or analysis of the data. It's already used for a variety of content generation needs in our world including business intelligence dashboards, business data reports, personalized email, and in-app messaging communication, client financial portfolio updates and the like. As the technology for natural language generation improves, this will result in more applications where machines produce easy-to-consume natural narratives that are on par or possibly even better than human-generated content.

NLG Automates Local News – Data Journalism

Except in India, local news is an industry that has been declining around the world for the past decade. Audiences have shrunk as readers head online for news has had a twin effect—advertisers curtailing their budgets and the local news journalists losing their jobs. Without local news, critical local issues go unreported! Leading UK news agency Press Association (PA) came up with a solution of using NLG to plug the gap left by redundant journalists and closed newspaper offices. In this new initiative, PA partnered with news automation specialists Urbs Media to have robots write as many as 30,000 local news stories each month.

RADAR – the first automated news agency

In September 2018 this project called RADAR – Reporters and Data and Robots – successfully completed its first year of automated news agency and was built on natural language generation (NLG) technology, the technology behind Apple's Siri and Amazon's Alexa, as well as the "chatbots" that consumers interact with. In RADAR, the bot wrote local news stories, based on open datasets from government, public services and local authorities. In just over three months URBS published more than 40,000 individual local stories and distributed to nearly all the local news publishers across the UK for use in print and digital products.

RADAR grew out of the idea that a large amount of open data was being made available by Government departments and other public bodies, such as the NHS. This open data contained news stories but was not reaching across the country. Since much of the data was segmented down to local level, each sheet might contain hundreds of individual local stories that would require an army of journalists to vet and write these stories. RADAR could achieve this by combining human journalism skills with Natural Language Generation, a technology that basically allows a sheet of numbers to be translated into a page of words. The principle behind NLG is that computers and humans can work together better when they speak the same language. It was found that teaching computers to understand and communicate with humans in our languages is much quicker and easier than teaching humans to communicate with machines through computer code.

Chef Watson to Bring Creativity And Innovation To Cooking

We thought IBM's Watson defeats Grand masters! Its Chef Watson gives us a glimpse of the creative potential for artificial intelligence through recipes with ingredient combinations and styles of dishes humans would never have considered that has been possible. Its ability to analyze data and overlay scientific information, makes working in the kitchen alongside human chefs effective. It has shown that home chefs in a pantry with only a few ingredients that "couldn't possibly go together" can indeed produce a menu with seasonal ingredients. It could also be an inspiration to professional chefs who want to evolve their menu through "cognitive cooking" and take advantage of global ingredients. For Chef Watson to create a recipe is to pick any ingredient/s between one and four, the dish and the meal that is to be made and entered. A theme such as Oriental, Chinese, Indian or Continental can also be chosen. Watson takes these inputs, compares it with its data base and churns out hundreds of recipe options to choose from besides providing instructions as to how to prepare the dish.

Ideas and Insights

NLG and its applications such as RADAR and Chef Watson helps us understand the types of "creative thinking" artificial intelligence machines can support. These provide the spark to allow our creative endeavours in these activities – may it be cooking or news gathering to go beyond the restrictions of our minds and to discover new possibilities. However, in the foreseeable future, these AI initiatives will need human intervention and its algorithms to help humans embrace the art of the possible.

Case Questions

1. What is NLG?
2. From the case-let describe some applications of NLG.

INTRODUCTION

This book began with highlighting some key factors differentiating digital marketing from a traditional one, pursuing social media and digital media as independent of each other and explained when and how they can work inclusively and when otherwise. A 3D model, "Develop, Design and Deliver" was outlined for integrating digital activities across platforms for customer experience (CX) and use of digital tools including analytics in optimizing and integrating digital platforms for a sustainable RoI was discussed. The immediate previous chapter discussed Marketing 4.0 and Industry 4.0 that were about marketing migrating from traditional to digital and about industry being smart and connected. All these have been possible mainly on account of convergence of technologies and digital transformation. In this chapter, the impact of some of the advances in technologies that are disruptive are discussed.

A news item published on January 3, 2019 indicated that CBSE has decided to introduce Artificial Intelligence (AI) as a skills (elective) subject in Classes 8, 9, 10 (https://digitallearning.eletsonline.com/2019/01/cbse-to-introduce-ai-as-a-skill-subject-in-classes-8910/), to make students well-versed in technologies of future. The news item citing a member of the board's governing body said, "The decision to introduce artificial intelligence as a skill subject was taken at a recent meeting of the board's governing body." The governing body member added, "It is important for the board to modernise the school curriculum to stay abreast of the latest developments as technologies like AI, data analytics and big data are making a huge impact globally." This aptly captures the impact and importance of (disruptive) technologies such as artificial intelligence, machine learning and analytics that are reshaping employment and the future of work, enabling the emergence of new business innovations and competition (http://www.forbesindia.com/article/great-lakes-institute-of-management/aimla-the-new-mantra-for-technology/50467/1).

DEMYSTIFYING MARTECH A.K.A MARKETING TECHNOLOGY

A logical place to begin technological advances and disruptive technologies is with "MarTech". Of late, conversations with marketers/service providers invariably tend towards MarTech with terms such as Hootsuite, Lumascape, consumer journey and that MarTech is going to be the hottest current trend. In the very same sentence, one might encounter both "holistic consumer experience" (Chapters 1 and 4) and "tag management system." Therefore, in this section, an attempt has been made to demystify "MarTech" that is a jargon, a miasma of buzzwords and phrases and present the concept of MarTech in simple terms.

The idea behind MarTech is simple. Today, consumers are empowered and they demand more from the brands they engage with. To meet these expectations, marketers require an understanding or rather a one-to-one

Customer experience (CX): Refers to a customer's experience with a company or brand, at all touchpoints.
ROI: Return of Investment is a performance measure used to evaluate the efficiency of an investment or compare the efficiency of a number of different investments.
CBSE: Central Board of Secondary Education

relationship with the consumers. Marketers should know who the consumers are and how they engage with the brand. These require a lot of data. Marketing technology provides the plumbing tools to gather such data and interpret the same.

What is MarTech?

According to John Koetsier (http://johnkoetsier.com), a mobile economist at Tune and a former journalist who covered the subject for years at publications including VentureBeat, MarTech is everything from an email marketing system like Mailchimp to social media marketing platform like Hootsuite. MarTech gives marketers a one-to-one relationship with their customers. While brands like Uber and Airbnb already have that setup, traditional brands, however, still lag behind. Therefore, many turn towards digital marketing hubs or marketing clouds. Gartner describes a marketing cloud as "giving marketers standardized access to audience data, content, event triggers and analysis so that they can automate complex campaigns, sales and data collection both online and off". MarTech companies usually operate on a SaaS (Services as a Software) model. That is, brands pay vendors based on their usage that could be a yearly fee. Some leading companies which provide digital marketing hub are Adobe Cloud, Salesforce, Oracle and Marketo, who have introduced the latest features in "MarTech" mapping out two categories of software offerings: sales and marketing and website technologies. While the sales and marketing part capture the main categories that marketing departments utilize to plan, execute and analyze marketing campaigns, the website part includes the technologies to create, manage and optimize websites.

MARTECH AND ARTIFICIAL INTELLIGENCE

One of the biggest trends coming out of MarTech is artificial intelligence (AI). Einstein from Salesforce, Sensei from Adobe, Adaptive Intelligent Apps from Oracle and Watson from IBM are some of the solutions developed by these global corporations. The rise of AI is aimed at helping marketers make sense of all their data. Today, companies have access to humongous data about their product/service from sources such as digital ad campaigns, web and social media analytics and mobile apps. The biggest challenge for a marketer is to make sense of all these available information and create a competitive "customer delight" experience. This, according to Koetsier is "being able to integrate all data into a comprehensive picture of a person who wants something or needs something is really, really challenging. Although marketers are likely to see a number of exciting announcements of what AI can deliver, (currently), we are on step two of 100. We are able to use some AI today to make things smarter for marketers, but it is nothing compared to what we will see in five years." The integration of MarTech and AI is the interesting area and the new learning experience for young and seasoned marketers alike...

> **MarTech:** The blending of marketing and technology. Virtually anyone involved with digital marketing is dealing with MarTech, since digital by its very nature is technologically-based. The term "MarTech" especially applies to major initiatives, efforts and tools that harness technology to achieve marketing goals and objectives.
>
> **SaaS (Software as a service):** A method of software delivery and licensing in which software is accessed online via a subscription, rather than bought and installed on individual computers.

AIMLA (Artificial Intelligence, Machine Learning and Analytics) The New Mantra for Technology

AIMLA is a neology for artificial intelligence, machine learning and analytics to become a regular entry in the vocabulary of digitization. AI and ML were already buzzwords and with analytics added, we have AIMLA. Disruptive innovations in digitization, analytics, artificial intelligence, and automation are helping businesses, irrespective of their size, to improve their business decisions, increase productivity, deliver faster, respond sooner to the customer, thereby creating performance and productivity opportunities for business and the economy. Continuing this trend, AIMLA is today, reshaping employment and the future of work, enabling the emergence of new business innovations and competition. Together these technological capabilities will have profound implications for business, the economy, and, more broadly, for society.

In any discussion on disruptive technologies, artificial intelligence (AI) and machine learning (ML) often crop up. Many times, both the terms are used interchangeably though they are not quite the same thing. According to Bernard Marr, " Artificial Intelligence is the broader concept of machines being able to carry out tasks in a way that we would consider "smart". On the other hand, machine learning is a subfield of artificial intelligence which evolved from pattern recognition and computational learning theory that gives computers the ability to learn without being explicitly programmed. To that extent, ML is a necessary condition for AI to flourish ".

Driving Accelerators of AI

Progress in technology enables its use to uncover how human mind works and apply AI to mimic human decision-making process and carry out tasks in more and better ways.

According to McKinsey, three factors driving this process are:

1. Progress in machine-learning algorithms leading to development of deep learning and reinforcement-learning techniques based on neural networks.
2. Availability of hyper scalable computing capacity accessible to users through the Cloud.
3. Generation of massive amounts of data that can be used to train machine learning models using Algorithms and IoT.

The driving factors have led to developments of programs like AlphaGo, that defeated a human champion of the complex board game Go and a lip-reading system that is more accurate than a professional lip reader.

Artificial Intelligence (AI), Machine Learning (ML) and Neural Network

Artificial intelligence devices that are designed to act intelligently can be applied AI or generalized AI.

- Applied AI is more common, e.g. algorithmic trading and manoeuvring autonomous vehicles.
- Generalized AIs – this subset of AI are the current state-of-the-art systems or devices with the ability to handle any task, theoretically! Machine learning has developed from these algorithms and where some of the most exciting advancements take place.
- **Driverless cars – Applied AI**

Computational Language Theory: A subfield of artificial intelligence devoted to studying the design and analysis of machine learning algorithms.

A self-driving car by Google is displayed at the Viva Technology event in Paris, France, June 30, 2016.
Image: Benoit Tessier / Reuters

Exhibit 11.1 Drivers of Artificial Intelligence

The world's first competitive motoring event took place in 1894 from Paris to Rouen in France, over a distance of 126 km that was organized by renowned French journalist turned politician, Pierre Giffard to publicize his newspaper, Le Petite Journal. The paper promoted the event as a Competition for Horseless Carriages that were not dangerous, were easy to drive, and cheap during the journey. The 'easy to drive' clause precluded the use of a travelling mechanic or technical assistant, thereby making steam-powered vehicles ineligible for the main prize.

Albert Lemaître, famous French sporting motorist during that era, drove his Peugeot Type 7 from Paris to Rouen in 6 hours and 51 minutes at an average of 19 km/h (12 mph). The vehicle was powered by an engine built by a little known company called 'Daimler' and bicycle and tyre manufacturer Adolphe Clément-Bayard was the front passenger. However, the winner of the event was the internal combustion engine that had arrived and which over the next century would go on to power industry and change the world.

Fast forward 120 years, in 2015, Daimler's website (https://www.daimler.com/innovation/next/a-city-that-drives-autonomously.html) reports that in Singapore's One-North district, a small electric self-driving car whizzing along with a camera system on its roof, weaves through the on-coming traffic (in Singapore they drive on the left like in India) immediately swerves around an illegally parked motorcycle to park itself. But what is special about it? The car does it all on its own, without the intervention of a human driver. The small white car is driving autonomously and is operated by the Future Urban Mobility initiative of the Singapore MIT Alliance for Research and Development (SMART), a partnership between the city state and the Massachusetts Institute of Technology (MIT) from the US.

THE TECTONIC SHIFT AND IMPACT

Benedict Evans in his outstanding article in 2015 points out three shifts – Mechanical to Electric, Owner to Shared and Driven to Autonomous that feed into each other.

Mechanical to Electrical

The internal combustion engine was a combination of pistons, gears, rods and other parts numbering approximately 2,000. These parts, over time, need replacement on account of wear and tear that has created meta-markets and an industry of ancillaries and servicing cars. None of these failures are expected in an electric vehicle drivetrain that contains just about 20 parts. This means, one can safely assume that a system with 100 times fewer moving parts will be more reliable. We now live in a world where Tesla claims its cars have lasted a million miles while most cars with internal combustion engines last only 150,000 miles. This, of course, is just the beginning. Volvo has already become the first major car manufacturer to commit to start phasing out its combustion engines and gas-powered vehicles from 2019 and targets to sell one million electric and hybrid cars by 2025. The loud and clear message at the 67th edition of the Frankfurt Motor Show (September 2017) was "Electric is the future" and that autonomous cars driven by artificial intelligence are closer to reality than ever before. Anand Mahindra, chairman of Mahindra & Mahindra (M&M), the only manufacturer of electric vehicles in India, recently said at the Bloomberg Global Business Forum in New York that "This (electric vehicles sector) is not a trade-off. This is the single biggest business opportunity for the next couple of decades. Anyone not looking at these opportunities is going to miss out on growth." We are already familiar with the success of Tesla.

Owned to Shared Vehicles

On-demand availability changes car ownership, and also changes which cars are bought. Uber and OLA in Indian cities have already made significant inroads in consumer attitudes and preferences of commuting!

Driven to Driverless

Now the attention is shifting to self-driving cars. For a long time, Google's self-driving car project was in news. The list now includes Volvo, Cadillac, Jaguar, Bosch among other manufacturers. These self-driving cars, when they happen, can potentially change the adoption of on-demand, and transform who buys cars. Driverless cars in on-demand car service cuts the cost, since there are no drivers to pay, lower maintenance costs and lower accident rates which can mean cheaper insurance. In addition, autonomous cars expand supply for on-demand services, and make available more cars to be used for on-demand when their owners are not using them and create a second-order effect of asset utilization as a business model.

Some of the other implications of this paradigm shift will be

- Drivers, mechanics and garages will need to reskill or reinvent themselves
- The cost to commute will become the 'next telecom' (virtually free, that is)
- Most cars will be made from recycled steel, as a result of which, more companies and alloy makers will be impacted
- Fossil fuel/oil-based countries and economies are likely to face crisis – the silver lining being terror funding will considerably reduce
- Cash-rich automotive lubricant companies will discover that there is nothing much to lubricate

From driverless cars to pilotless aircrafts

An UBS research indicates that "new technology is being developed that would make remotely flying an aircraft feasible in the near future." Can new technologies take it to the next level from driverless cars and military drones to aircrafts flying themselves?

A news item published by The Guardian in 2017 quotes UBS (a Swiss Investment Bank) report that pilotless passenger aircraft could save the industry, and airline passengers, \$35bn (£27bn) a year. Independent also quoting the UBS research adds that "new technology is being developed that would make remotely flying an aircraft feasible in the near future. Pilotless planes could, besides cost savings, slash fares for passengers who could see prices drop by over 10 per cent. The average percentage of total cost and average benefit that could be passed onto passengers in price reduction for the US airlines is 11 per cent." Savings on European flights would be less at an average of 4 percent. The biggest savings will come from reducing the cost of employing pilots". UBS estimated that pilots cost the industry £24 billion a year. The study also predicted flights will be safer as the potential for pilot error will be done away with.

A Reuters report in The Straits Times in June 2017 quotes Mike Sinnett, Boeing's vice president of product development, "We're going to need something like six hundred and seventeen thousand more pilots. One of the ways that may be solved is by having some type of autonomous behaviour and that could be anything from taking instead of five pilots on a long-haul flight down to three or two, taking two pilots down to one in a freight situation, or in some cases going from one to none. The basic building blocks of the technology clearly are available." Boeing plans to test self-flying technology in a cockpit simulator this summer, before using it on a real plane next year.

The questions that arise on commercializing this technology are –

- **Feasibility** - The use of commercial, military drones and Mike Sinnet's statement show that the technology exists and is in use. Besides, most commercial aircrafts rely quite heavily on computer controls or "fly by wire" technology and therefore technologically this will only be an extension.
- **Safety** - According to the International Air Transport Association, the airline industry trade body, there were only 1.25 accidents per million jet flights last year – lower than the five-year average, but the interaction between an automated system and a human intervention can cause fatalities when it goes wrong, for example, Air France Flight 447.

UBS: UBS is a global wealth management firm that provides comprehensive advice, solutions and services to wealthy families and individuals around the world.

- **Potential threats -** unmanned cockpit is likely to pose Intervention issues in case of
  - Cyber attacks
  - Computer glitches
  - Terrorists on board
- **Regulatory and ompliances issues –** Globally there seems to be no regulations in place for pilotless passenger planes because they do not exist as yet.
- **Stakeholders views –**
  - Pilots – Concerns on potential threats as mentioned earlier
  - Passengers – UBS research indicated 54 percent of 8,000 people surveyed indicated they would refuse to fly in a plane with no pilot, even if the flight cost less. Whereas millennials and those who had a university degree were more willing to fly without a pilot.
  - Governments - GE reports "a U.S. government and industry collaboration project called Aircrew Labor In-Cockpit Automation System (ALIAS), which aims to replace human co-pilots in two-person aircrews with a robotic system—a "genius" pilot—that never tires, grows fatigued, gets stressed or loses concentration—thanks to its ability to extract vital information from the hundreds of thousands of hours that their human counterparts have logged on any one particular plane". Similar work is also reported by other industry government collaborations across Europe.

It is a long haul with pilotless aircrafts considering that not everybody is on board and customer perception remaining a big barrier to success and the pilots' apprehension. In the Indian context, pilotless aircrafts could be a long-term answer to bail out bleeding Air India and other carriers.

DEMYSTIFYING MACHINE LEARNING

Having looked at AI, we move on to examine a sub-set of AI *viz.* Machine Learning (ML). ML is a subfield of artificial intelligence which evolved from Pattern Recognition and Computational Learning theory. The word machine learning was coined by Arthur Samuel, an American Pioneer in the field of computer gaming and AI in 1959 and postulated that it might be possible to program computers the ability to learn for themselves with very little human intervention. Based on this postulate, technologists realized that it would be possible to code computers to think like human beings if connected to the Internet, access to information given and the information could then be further classified through neural network, the same way as human brain does! Neural network is a system designed to recognize each information and label them according to elements they contain. Essentially, this works on probability, based on data fed, to make decisions, predictions or statements with a degree of certainty. The addition of a feedback loop enables "learning" that is by sensing or being told whether its decisions are right or wrong. These feedback loops facilitate modifying the approach taken, going forward.

Today, more and more companies are using machine learning to improve their business decisions, increase productivity, deliver faster, respond sooner to the customer and do many more things. Every time a prospective customer visits Amazon, product recommendations pop up, either what was searched online or bought the last time or what was bought by others. That is a Machine Learning Algorithm (/s) called "Recommender Systems" working in the backdrop. It learns every user's personal preferences and makes recommendations basis repeated set of activities. That is how Amazon or other ecommerce sites always have recommendation that tempts the prospective customer. Almost every exciting new development in the field of Computer

> **GE Reports:** GE (General Electric) Reports is a daily news, video and social media hub covering GE's transformation into the world's largest digital industrial company.
> **Pattern Recognition:** The process of recognizing patterns by using machine learning algorithm.

Science and Software Development has something related to machine learning behind the veils. Microsoft's Cortana is machine learning. Object and Face Recognitions in Computers is machine learning. These are similar to product recommendation mentioned earlier, that was nothing but data crunching effort of some machine learning algorithm. Machine learning basically is the field of Computer Science that "learns" from data without human intervention. Therefore, whenever machine learning is mentioned, people usually think of "AI" and "Neural Networks that can mimic human brains, such as Self Driving Cars and the like.

Another subset and an extension of machine learning that is deep learning and machine learning is a sub-field of artificial intelligence. AlphaGo that was mentioned earlier in the chapter and often given as an example for deep learning, is actually a combination of ideas from several different fields of AI and machine learning. The relationship between AI, ML & DL can be schematically shown as represented in Figure 11.1:

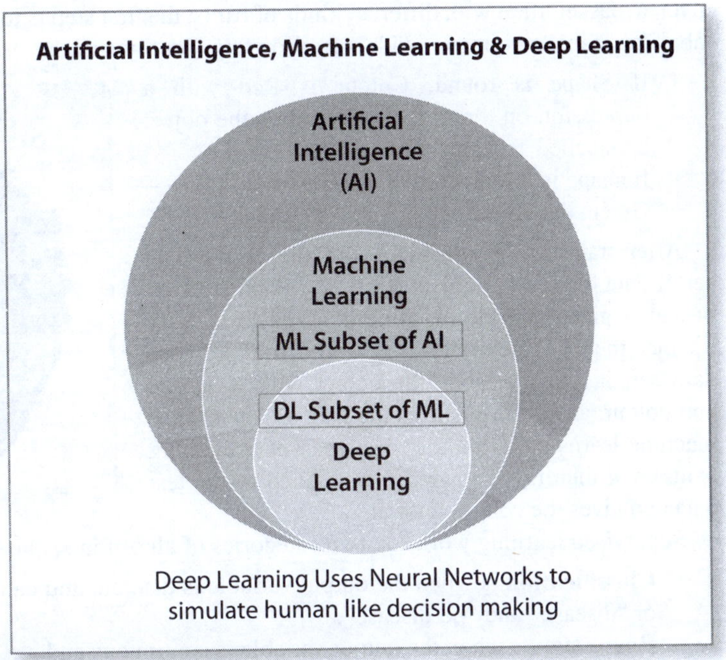

Figure 11.1 Articial Intelligence, Machine Learning & Deep Learning

What is Deep Learning?

As mentioned earlier, machine learning is the subset of AI which is the current state-of-the-art systems or devices with the ability to handle any task-theoretically! Machine learning has developed from these algorithms and where some of the most exciting advancements are taking place. These deep learning algorithms, like the human brain that learns from experience, learn while a repeated task/activity is performed. They also improve the outcomes progressively with each iteration.

It is referred to as 'deep learning' because the neural networks have various (deep) layers that enable learning. Like the human mind, any problem that requires "a thought process " is a problem deep learning can learn to solve but needs humongous amount of data that are hidden in these layers. Thanks to staggering amount of data that is generated every day and improved computing capabilities, deep learning capabilities have grown in recent years. In addition, the proliferation of artificial intelligence (AI) as a service has fuelled advances in deep learning and helped smaller organizations access to artificial intelligence technology and specifically the AI algorithms required for deep learning without a large initial investment. Deep learning allows machines to solve complex problems even when using a data set that is very diverse, unstructured and inter-connected. The more deep learning algorithms learn, the better they perform.

Supervised and Unsupervised Learning

Supervised learning is when a machine is taught or trained to use data that are labelled some of which are tagged with a correct answer. Supervised learning algorithms analyze the given data sets (training or examples) to produce the correct outcome when these machines are provided with a new data set. That is, given a basket filled with different kinds of fruits, the first step is to train the machine on different fruits with labels of shape, colour, etc. with corresponding identity such as

- If Shape is round, Colour is Red with a depression on top of the object, then the object be labelled as Apple.
- If shape is a long curved cylinder and Yellow – Green, the object be labelled as Banana .

After training the machine with the above data set, if data for another object (fruit, say Banana) from basket is given and the machine is asked to identify it, since the machine has already learnt from previous data set, it first classifies the object with its shape and colour, and confirms it as the fruit Banana. Thus machine learns from training data (basket containing fruits) and then this knowledge is applied to the test data and gives the correct answer.

Supervised learning works on two categories of algorithms, classification and regression.

- **Classification** is when the output variable is discrete and can be a category, such as "Red" or "Blue" or "disease" and "no disease".
- **Regression** is when the output variable is continuous and a real value, such as "dollars" or "weight.

In the above example, it was classification at work.

Unsupervised learning

Unsupervised learning, on the other hand, is when machine is trained without guidance. Here, information is not classified or labelled and hence the algorithm needs to provide output without guidance. Therefore, unsupervised learning algorithms work on principles of clustering and association.

- **Clustering** (cluster analysis) discovers inherent groupings, if any, in the data, e.g. grouping customers by purchasing behaviour.
- **Association** is rule based and is to elicit rules that apply or describe large portions of the data. For example, people who buy X also tend to buy Y.

Table 11.1 Difference between Supervised and Unsupervised Learning

	Supervised Learning	Unsupervised Learning
Input Data	Uses Known and Labelled Data as Input	Uses Unknown Data as Input
Computational Complexity	Very Complex	Less Computational Complexity
Real Time	Uses Off-line Analysis	Uses Real Time Analysis of Data
Number of Classes	Number of Classes are Known	Number of Classes are not Known
Accuracy of Results	Accurate and Reliable Results	Moderate Accurate and Reliable Results
Input Data	Uses Known and Labelled Data as Input	Uses Unknown Data as Input
Computational Complexity	Very Complex	Less Computational Complexity
Real Time	Uses Off-line Analysis	Uses Real Time Analysis of Data
Number of Classes	Number of Classes are Known	Number of Classes are not Known
Accuracy of Results	Accurate and Reliable Results	Moderate Accurate and Reliable Results

Machine Learning and Deep Learning – Applications

As suggested by their names, these programs give the computers powers similar to humans—the ability to learn. ML & DL are actively being used today, perhaps in many places and we are probably exposed to these learning algorithm dozens of time without even knowing they are. Some example are—

Web Search Engine – Chapter 5 discussed in SEO & SERP the role of algorithms in ranking pages effectively. All search engines use ML algorithms that have learnt to rank pages through a complex process.

Translations – Today, we automatically go to the Google translator page for translating letters or documents or even signboards when travelling. Deep Learning algorithms help automatically translate between languages. This is a powerful tool in government to government transactions.

Spam Detector – In Chapter 7, in the context of email marketing, we had discussed about taking care to ensure by passing spam detectors. All mail clients are inherently built to detect and classify mails into non-spam and spam. This is achieved by a spam classifier running in the back end of mail application.

Photo Tagging Applications – Deep learning algorithms are commonly used by social media and run quietly behind applications, making it possible to provide the ability to recognize faces. In the anvil are store check outs and overcoming challenges for facial recognition of the same person even when they have changed hairstyles, grown or shaved off a beard or a poor image.

Image Colourization – Now, as soon as we shoot a picture using your smartphone camera, we are able to edit them to black and white or sepia on the handset itself before sharing. Similarly, if we wished to colour an old black and white family photograph, we had to go to a professional. Today, we are able to do so on our own computers and this is again possible with the help of deep learning algorithms.

Virtual Assistants – Kids, children and first time users of smartphones get enamoured with Alexa or Siri that are nothing but deep learning applications that recognize language when humans interact with them.

Chatbots and Service Bots – Today in almost every website, chatbots and service bots that provide customer service are built-in features. Like virtual assistants they respond to an increasing amount of auditory and text questions in more than one language. This once again is on account of deep learning algorithms running in the background.

Vision – All autonomous vehicles have inbuilt deep learning algorithms that converts the sensor data to understand road conditions, rain or shine. It facilitates reading road signs, other vehicles and objects human or otherwise.

Impact and Beyond

Fuelled by science fictions, that we can communicate and interact with electronic devices and digital information, as naturally as we would with another human being, another field of AI*viz.,* Natural Language Processing (NLP) – has become a source of exciting innovation in recent years. NLP applications attempt to understand natural human communication, either written or spoken and communicate in return with us using similar, natural language. ML is used in these instances to help machines understand the vast nuances of human language and to learn to respond in a way that a particular audience is likely to comprehend. Machine learning/Deep learning applications can read, text and figure out whether the person who wrote it is making a complaint or offering congratulations. They can also listen to, say, a piece of music, decide whether it is likely to make someone happy or sad, and find other pieces of music to match the mood. In some cases, they can even compose their own music expressing the same themes, or which they know is likely to be appreciated by the admirers of the original piece. These are all possibilities offered by systems based around ML and neural networks.

Today, more and more companies are using machine learning to improve their business decisions, increase productivity, deliver faster, respond sooner to the customer and do many more things. This is irrespective of the size of the company, small, medium or super large! With the exponential growth of technology, we not only need better tools to understand the data we currently have, but we also need to prepare ourselves for the data we will have in the near future. Going forward, it is likely that human-like AI will be eventually developed.

TECHNOLOGY TRANSFORMING SPORTS

Going beyond enterprises, gizmos and sensors are changing the way sports is played and players being trained. 2014 Cricket Twenty20 World Cup held in Bangladesh brought us a new technological innovation—of the stumps lighting up each time the bails were knocked off, either by the wicket-keeper or otherwise. With conventional bails, it was difficult for the umpire to decide when the bail was 'completely dislodged' from the wicket. But now, with the aid of sensors combined with LED technology, the umpire can take a decision without a shadow of doubt.

Another example of technology is Babolat's Play Pure Drive Racquet System in Tennis—a smart product that looks like a regular racquet on the outside; however, sensors integrated into the handle allow players access to a lot of information and analysis through a smartphone application, such as power, impact locator, type and number of strokes. The connected racquet shares the data recorded with a smartphone or tablet running the Babolat Play app via Bluetooth or USB. Players can review performance history, upload, share and compare stats with other Play Pure Drive users.

It won't be long before similar connected cricket bats and sport shoes are available. They will share performance data and record every stroke, whether the player middled the ball, the angle of his stroke, the movement of his foot, the point of impact, angle, productivity and even defence. These technologies besides facilitating performance also significantly improve real time spectator experience.

Impact on Supply Chain Industry

Technology has always been the backbone of supply chain (SC) since long and the industry has also been evolving over time with advances in technology. The emergence of ecommerce and ebusiness, leveraging advances in information technology are examples. Currently, there is a high expectation that the SC industry is in for further revolution through the adoption of emerging and disruptive technologies like artificial intelligence, machine learning and blockchain.

The emergence of ecommerce spawned the growth of online retailers such as Amazon, eBay, Rakuten (previously buy.com) and Alibaba. These eretailers, by reducing the overhead costs associated with traditional brick-and-mortar retailers, were in a position to offer products at lower prices than their traditional counterparts. In addition, newer platforms such as online payment gateways (PayPal and SecurePay) and online digital wallets (Paytm and MobiKwik) made payments faster, easier and cost effective. In today's economy, this offered an affordable and viable alternative for customers resulting in an online shopping boom.

Technology has aided Rehrig Pacific Company (leading manufacturer of reusable transport packaging system and transportation service provider) in tagging pallets and crates with passive RFID tags for clients like Pepsi to reduce their costs. It has also facilitated novel strategies that can result in effective inventory management in the SC. Virtual pooling is one such strategy where companies manage their inventory as if it is in one location even if they are actually in different locations. This allows them to reduce their stock-out risks as well as shipping costs. An example of virtual pooling is Netflix, which offered movie DVD's to customers. When customers order for a particular movie, they have information only about the availability of the DVD, but no idea about the whereabouts of the DVD.

> **Natural Language Processing:** Natural language processing (NLP) is the ability of a computer program to understand human language as it is spoken. NLP is a component of artificial intelligence (AI).

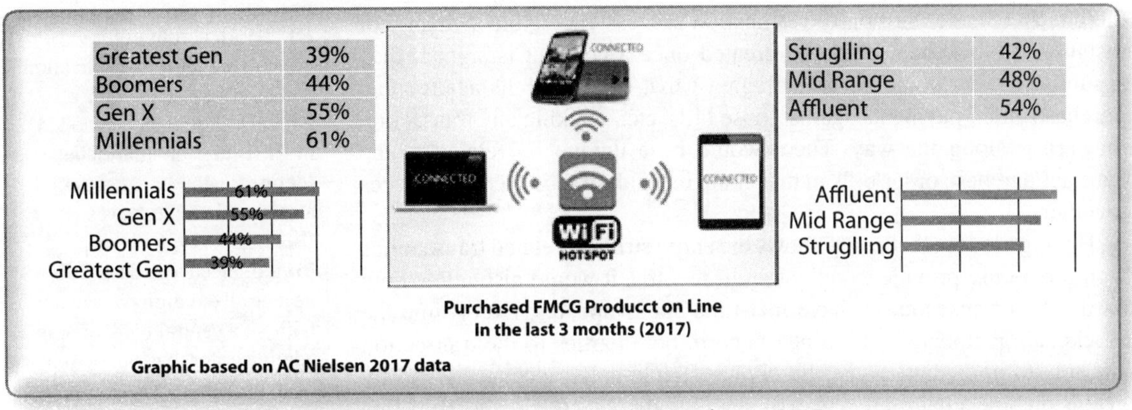

Exhibit 11.2 Online Purchase FMCG Products - 2017

A company in Chicago, Eazystock, has taken virtual inventory pooling to a new level, where local warehouses in a given region act together as a single "virtual warehouse". This warehouse is used to satisfy the aggregate demand over the entire region, resulting in effective inventory management in the SC.

AIMLA (Artificial Intelligence Machine Learning & Analytics) can be potentially useful in SC planning and logistics. Given the enormity of data that is available throughout the Supply Chain, ML has applications in forecasting demand and supply. This data can then be used in optimizing the inventory levels and delivery of goods so as to balance supply and demand. Alternatively, the demand data can also be used in varying the prices (revenue management). OYO rooms, an Indian start-up, has employed AI in boosting occupancy rates and adjusting prices.

Given the current focus of automobile companies on producing autonomous vehicles, there is also a scope for using these vehicles for shipping and logistics activities and reducing transportation lead times (as an autonomous vehicle can run without halting for a longer time than a human driver). Go-Jek, an Indonesian company that revolutionized the informal transport and logistics business, has collaborations with Google regarding AI and ML. The company currently uses GPS to identify drivers close to the customers.

The blockchain is a distributed database that records and stores every transaction that occurs. The key advantage is that new records can be added, but existing records can never be deleted. This can be very useful in ensuring Supply Chain Visibility (SCV) as all information regarding various activities in the supply chain can be securely stored and made available to partners. This technology can potentially help in avoiding bullwhip effect. Companies that have adopted this technology include Bajaj Allianz General Insurance (to reduce the settlement turnaround time) and Bajaj Electricals (to reduce the process cycle for bill discounting).

TECHNOLOGY, VIRTUAL CURRENCY AND BLOCKCHAIN

In 2008, in the name of Satoshi Nakamoto, unknown person or group of people invented a decentralized digital currency without a central bank or a central administrator. It was called bitcoin and created its original reference implementation. As part of the implementation, they also devised the first blockchain database. In the process, they were the first to solve the double-spending problem for digital currency. It was also the first working example of triple-entry accounting.

With the introduction of triple entry accounting and blockchain, traditional accounts will become obsolete, substantive testing on external audits will be reduced and a more control based approach will be adopted as there is an outside third party verification process via the blockchain. For instance, a blockchain could be created once a contract is signed, then a purchase order could be issued against that contract, bills against that purchase order, payments against those bills, etc., tracking any transaction that arises along the way. There would be a unique ID related to the contract/purchase order/bills in that chain to tie all of those separate pieces together.

Having a ledger that easily shows the entire string of related transactions would not only provide excellent audit records, it would also allow both parties to a transaction to have real-time status updates. Every time the blockchain is updated with a new record, both parties to the transaction are able to immediately see the update. Triple-entry accounting and by extension blockchains are a way of agreeing on objective reality. It is two parties agreeing on a version of past events. The third entry in the system, entered into the blockchain, is both a receipt and a transaction. While these entries may look familiar in isolation for each entity but, the big difference is the following:

- These self executing entries are on third party platforms and secured.
- Transactions cannot be altered for any reason whatsoever. Once recorded, these are permanent on the blockchain.
- Every transaction is verifiable (which will allow for an easier audit trail).
- The blockchain is not maintained internally within one company's server, it is decentralized which reduces security threats.
- All transactions use the highest level of encryption technology.

RFID: An acronym for "radio-frequency identification" and refers to a technology whereby digital data encoded in RFID tags or smart labels (defined below) are captured by a reader via radio waves.
Bitcoin: A cryptocurrency, a form of electronic cash. It is a decentralized digital currency without a central bank or single administrator that can be sent from user-to-user on the peer-to-peer bitcoin network without the need for intermediaries.
Blockchain: A blockchain, originally block chain, is a growing list of records, called blocks, which are linked using cryptography. Each block contains a cryptographic hash of the previous block, a timestamp, and transaction data. By design, a blockchain is resistant to modification of the data.

MACHINE LEARNING - JOB LOSS OR NOT?

Any automation, by definition will affect portions of almost all jobs to a greater or lesser degree, depending on the type of work they entail. In this section, having explained AI/Machine/Deep Learning as the field of Computer Science that "learns" from data without human intervention leads therefore to a logical question that is really a guessing game, which jobs will or won't be replaced by machines. We now look at some aspects of job impact on account of machine learning/AI.

In 70s, when LIC of India automated and created in what was then called EDP (Electronic Data Processing) Department, the employees declared a National strike! The reason for the strike was that the machines will adversely impact current employees and future recruits. Many of those employees who are happily retired now, thank LIC for the creation of EDP department that in fact created additional jobs. Earlier in 2017 media reported WIPRO setting up of bots and cutting jobs. Also reported was Tata Motors cutting jobs but not that of blue collar.

EDP (Electronic Data Processing): Refers to the use of automated methods to process commercial data. Typically, this uses relatively simple, repetitive activities to process large volumes of similar information.
LIC: Life Insurance Corporation, popularly known as LIC is Indian state-owned insurance group and investment company.

Though automations will impact jobs, it is unlikely to eliminate occupations/jobs entirely in the foreseeable future, at least in India. A McKinsey study (McKinsey Quarterly, July 2016) in USA indicated that technologies available today, could automate 45 percent of the activities for which people are paid to perform and that about 60 percent of all occupations could see 30 percent or more of their activities automated in the next few years.

In industry many types of activities have the technical potential to be automated, but that potential varies significantly based on % of time spent on predictability and repetitiveness of the job performed. The hardest activities to automate with currently available technologies are those that involve managing and developing people or that apply expertise to decision making, planning, or creative work. These activities, often characterized as knowledge work, can be varied, spontaneous, where automation can provide an excellent support job but humans are still needed to provide proper goals, interpret results, or provide checks and balances. Thus in managing others (HR), applying expertise (doctors, chefs, sportsmen), stakeholder interactions (P.R., waiters and nurses), unpredictable physical work (forestry, projects) that are essentially non repetitive/unpredictable, automation could only be a support and not an eliminator of a job.

Besides technical potential, technical feasibility needs to be considered since each whole occupation/job is made up of multiple types of activities, each with varying degrees of technical feasibility! For example, though a salesman's job may seem repetitive and admin and reports part of it can be automated, it is unlikely a salesman will be eliminated. Similarly, the importance of human interaction is clearly evident in two sectors that, so far, have a relatively low technical potential for automation: Healthcare and Education!

Therefore, in practice, automation will depend on more than just technical feasibility, four other factors are involved, *viz*.

1) costs to automate;
2) the relative scarcity, skills, and cost of workers who might otherwise do the activity;
3) benefits (e.g., superior performance) of automation beyond labour-cost substitution; and
4) regulatory and social-acceptance considerations.

The above considerations were the primary reasons for India to become major ITES outsourcing destinations essentially on account of cost arbitrage versus skills and automation. Now Indian IT/ITES is also slowly gearing up to the fact that in some sectors machine learning and AI will impact their revenues thus making significant realignment to their portfolios and jobs.

TECHNOLOGY IN MARKETING COMMUNICATION – IS IT RIP FOR TRADITIONAL MEDIA

Considering this book is titled " Digital Marketing – From Fundamental to Future", it is imperative that we examine how digital marketing has impacted other marketing communication channels.

It was in 1440s that the printing press was invented by Johannes Gutenberg. However, it took nearly 300 years for the first print publication to appear and one more century to leverage this technology as a source revenue through advertising. The first print advertisement in a newspaper came out in France in 1836. In the next hundred years, since 1940, we have had other advertising media such as radio, television, POP, outdoor. It was around this time that the earliest computer was also invented. None of these technological advancements superseded advancement prior to them. Magazines were still popular when radio advertisements started catching up. Radio was still popular when TV advertisement was the in thing. The earlier and older sources of marketing communication were still used. Similarly, today the buzz is digital marketing that has shadowed other marketing communication channels. Now most marketers spend a lot of time in understanding the digital tools and various digital marketing techniques that are seen as an ocean of opportunities.

Looking at the media evolution in India, it was in 1927 that the Indian Broadcasting Company (IBC), was established in Bombay. This later became the All India Radio (AIR) in 1936. Between this period till the 1970s, radio, print and outdoor were the available media. TV transmission by Doordarshan (DD) started in 1972 in Bombay and Amritsar and slowly extended to 5 other cities by 1975. Transmission then used to be twice a day. When the colour television transmission through LPTs (Low Power Transmitters) started in 1982, TV became a rage and every Indian house-hold, eagerly awaited some popular programs like the first

Hindi Soap Opera – Hum Log, Chaaya Geet and weekend movies, besides playing host to neighbours. Radio nevertheless was still considered as a popular medium of advertising given the rural reach and the ubiquitous and unique Indian Tea stalls.

Internet and mobile phones appeared only in 1995 but the Indian infrastructure did not support the bandwidth then. However, considering that the first web page globally went online in 1991, India was not far behind. While India was still getting used to the dial-up connection, the early 90s saw the introduction of cable TV in major metros that was a huge wave. People were glued to the televisions and at the beginning of this millennium, TV shows like "Kyonki Saas bi Kabhi Bahu Thi" and "Kaun Banega Crorepati (KBC)" became popular. Advertising budgets in favour of TV advertising catapulted and witnessed a robust growth since 1982 despite high tariffs. Companies competed for the advertising slots of popular programs to maximize their marketing efforts.

Though television advertising is still popular, this decade has brought in significant changes in marketing. While for several decades, television, print, radio advertising and outdoor ruled the advertising space, social media marketing brought in a huge change in a short span. Suddenly marketers started focusing more on planning their campaigns on social media, many of them assuming social media marketing and digital marketing as one and the same. In as much as digital marketing includes all forms of electronic medium both internet and non-internet based, a lot of focus was kept on social media channels and web, because of the sharing capability of social media and its ability to multiply its reach among the micro-communities.

POP (Advertising): Point-of-purchase (POP) advertising is in-store advertising that is meant to catch the attention of shoppers while they are in an establishment.
All India Radio (AIR): National public radio broadcaster of India
OTT: Over the top (OTT) is a term used to refer to content providers that distribute streaming media as a standalone product directly to viewers over the Internet, bypassing telecommunications, multichannel television, and broadcast television platforms that traditionally act as a controller or distributor of such content.
WPP: WPP Plc is a British multinational advertising and public relations company.

With the introduction of cell phones, especially the smartphones, the popularity of social media has grown exponentially. With 2.2 billion users in 2017, if it were a country, Facebook will be the largest country on earth. Several networking apps have mushroomed in no time and most of these apps target the millennials, thereby making these platforms hot for marketers to sell their products and services. This has led to a paradigm shift

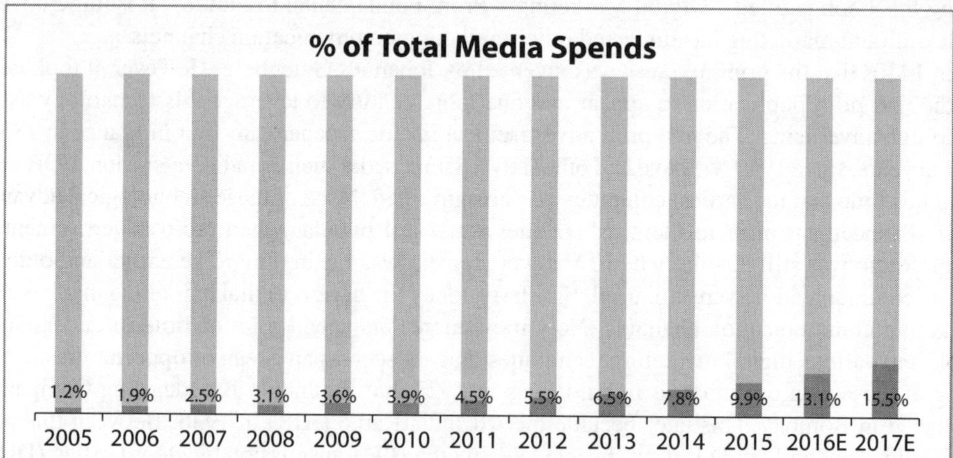

Figure 11.2 Digital Advertising in India – 2005 - 2017

from marketplace to a concept called "marketspace" (Chapter 2). Marketspace concept is one which involves information and communication-based electronic exchange environment, where goods and services instead of being sold only physically are marketed through an online space that facilitates bi-directional commerce.

According to a report released by WPP-owned company Group M, digital will remain the fastest growing medium seen expanding at 30 percent as OTT (over-the –top) platforms gain popularity and gain better Ad rates. Group M had indicated that in 2017, India's digital advertising was expected to touch INR 9500 crores or $1.5 bn. - a growth of 47 percent over 2016 and approximately 15.5 percent of total advertising spending. While the overall digital ad spending has grown by 47 percent in 2017, mobile ads have shown a robust growth of 110 percent. The report also indicates that an average of 1.13 hours is spent by an average Indian on digital media, which has given a boost to online advertising, online shopping and ecommerce.

Given that in India 91 percent is still traditional retailing and 84 percent is non-digital advertising, the moot question is, is it RIP for traditional media or traditional brick and mortar models being replaced by digital marketing and brick and click model respectively? Unlikely! Since notwithstanding all the above, recorded history from Ca 1400 AD indicates none of the technological advancements superseded advancement prior to them; on the contrary, they co-existed.

CAREER IN MARKETING: GOING DIGITAL TRADITIONALLY

In conclusion it is only fair to examine careers in marketing. Marketing jobs were considered as dream jobs in 70s and 80s. Invariably, the incumbent had to begin in field sales before moving to market and then take up higher responsibilities. Thanks to ITC, Lever and other MNCs, over the years, the marketing field has only been emerging and attracting creative and driven individuals to choose this as a major career path. Marketing, on the whole, is undergoing a sea change with every industry metamorphosing and offering various opportunities. And, with the advancement of technologies, evolving new fields including digital and social media, businesses are constantly transforming their functioning methods and deliverables, inviting more and more millennials to be part of this rapidly growing landscape. Be it an aspiring or a freshly minted MBA or a professional planning for a transition, marketing continues to be a popular career choice even today.

Though marketing has a high rate of interest with multiple prospects, it is also laden with risks while making managerial decisions, especially to those who skip the basics and begin with digital marketing directly. The millennials seem to be overwhelmed with the term 'Digital Marketing'. True that the buzzword in organizations is going digital, but as an aspiring marketer, one needs to have a strong knowledge about the fundamentals before jumping into digital techniques.

MARKETING: TRADITION VS DIGITAL

Marketing is a process of 'CCDVTP' - Create, Communicate, and Deliver Value to a Target customer at a Profit" (Kotler, 2014). To achieve this and ensure profitability, businesses work in two ways – (i) Traditional Marketing - refers to the conventional methods of marketing using promotion or advertising of any product through print advertisement, newsletters, billboards, etc. (ii) Digital Marketing – refers to methods using digital medium, mainly on the Internet, and technologies including mobile phones, apps, etc.

Historically, in India, traditional marketing has been successful through offline promotional methods, face to face selling, cold calling, allowing direct connection with a consumer. Traditional practices also mould you with skills required for marketing—how to structure and value a product, how to interact with a consumer and improvise verbal communication skills.

Whereas the digital method completely deals in a virtual world, lacks physical connect, and every communication and process occurs online. A significant growth in recent years and new skill sets such as analytics, artificial intelligence, machine learning and well-paid secured jobs have been some of the benefits of digital marketing.

Integrating Traditional Marketing (TM) and Digital Marketing (DM)

Although the growth in online marketing has been phenomenal in recent years, tech companies and researchers are constantly looking at ways to offer digital services that surpass TV and offline space. With Netflix and Amazon expanding their market presence, TV is being consumed digitally these days. However, to sell these products and cater to the needs of consumers, a marketer should immerse and understand Language of Things (value, consumer behaviour, pricing) as well as the Internet of Things. And, this can be achieved only with a strong base of traditional method.

According to the Audit Bureau of Circulation (ABC) report (May 2017), consumers rated that they still prefer print and TV over digital media. Given that in India 91 percent is still traditional retailing and 84 percent is non-digital advertising, professionals, as well as millennials, should look at these advantages and understand the strategic side of going for basics.

Merging of technologies, cost factor, real-time engagement can be interesting, enticing millennials toward DM as a career. But, on the flip side, one must be aware of the fact that these are also leading to tech disruptions, exposing personal information, examples being the recent Facebook data breach, Cambridge Analytica scandal, and resulting in job loss and other exploitable vulnerabilities.

Therefore, an aspiring marketer should look at integrating traditional marketing with digital marketing support. Balancing the right mix of both is one of the best ways to specialize in marketing. And, doing that in a classroom environment enriches one with more conversations, debates and live demonstrations of marketing techniques. It further encourages confidence level, creative marketing and communication skills and nurtures the individual as an industry ready professional.

One must understand, be it any industry, digital marketing skills are often looked at as an additional skill set. The emergence of new tech skills is going to be a never-ending cycle. But, as a marketer, on a long run, bringing more skill sets on to the table with basics in core marketing values (CCDVTP), enables to strengthen career prospects of an individual and his/her role in an organization.

CAREER CHOICES

There are plenty of career opportunities for an individual planning to opt for marketing, as the field itself is diverse. Some of the trending jobs in the market are marketing and sales specialist, brand manager, advertising specialist, research analyst, sales and business development, and if you are planning to shift into communications team in an organization, with digital skill set you be able to land up in as a social media manager or an SEO specialist. With automation technologies such as machine learning playing an increasingly great role in everyday life, their potential effect on the workplace has also become a major focus of research and public concern. The discussion tends toward a guessing game: which jobs will or won't be replaced by machines! The implication is also that students and workforce would need to re-skill themselves, re-learning current tools and applications. To this end, we are sure this book will be a helpful tool!

CHAPTER SUMMARY

- CBSE has decided to introduce artificial intelligence (AI) as a skill (elective) subject in classes 8, 9, 10, to make students well-versed in technologies of future. This aptly captures the impact and importance of (disruptive) technologies such as artificial intelligence, machine learning and analytics that are reshaping employment and the future of work, enabling the emergence of new business innovations and competition.
- According to John Koetsier, MarTech is everything from an email marketing system like Mailchimp to social media marketing platform like Hootsuite.

MarTech gives marketers a one-to-one relationship with their customers.

- MarTech companies usually operate on a SaaS (Services as a Software) model. That is, brands pay vendors based on their usage that could be a yearly fee.
- MarTech has 2 components, the sales and marketing part captures the main categories that marketing departments utilize to plan, execute and analyze marketing campaigns, the Website part includes the technologies to create, manage and optimize websites.
- One of the biggest trends coming out of MarTech is artificial intelligence (AI). Einstein from Salesforce, Sensei from Adobe, Adaptive Intelligent Apps from Oracle and Watson from IBM are some of the solutions developed by these global corporations.
- AIMLA is a neology for Artificial Intelligence Machine Learning and Analytics to become a regular entry in the vocabulary of digitization. AI & ML were already buzzwords and with analytics added, we have AIMLA.
- AIMLA is today reshaping employment and the future of work, enabling the emergence of new business innovations and competition. Together these technological capabilities will have profound implications for business, the economy, and, more broadly, for society.
- According to Bernard Marr – "Artificial Intelligence is the broader concept of machines being able to carry out tasks in a way that we would consider "smart". On the other hand, machine learning is a subfield of artificial intelligence which evolved from Pattern Recognition and Computational Learning theory that gives computers the ability to learn without being explicitly programmed. To that extent, ML is a necessary condition for AI.
- Artificial intelligence devices that are designed to act intelligently can be Applied AI or Generalized AI. Applied AI is more common, e.g. algorithmic trading and manoeuvring an autonomous vehicle and generalized AIs are systems or devices that can theoretically handle any task and where some of the most exciting advancements are taking place. It is also the area that has led to the development of machine learning. This subset of AI can be termed as the current and state-of-the-art.
- In 2015, Daimler's website reports that in Singapore a small white car was driving autonomously and was operated by the Future Urban Mobility initiative of the Singapore MIT Alliance for Research and Development (SMART), a partnership between the city state and the Massachusetts Institute of Technology (MIT) from the US.
- Benedict Evans in 2015 pointed out three tectonic shifts in driverless cars – Mechanical to Electric (from 2000 to 20 parts), Owner to Shared e.g. Uber) and Driven to Autonomous that feed into each other.
- Some of the other implications of this paradigm shift were
    - Drivers, mechanics and garages will need to reskill or reinvent themselves.
    - The cost to commute will become the 'next telecom' (virtually free, that is).
    - Most cars will be made from recycled steel, as a result of which, ore companies and alloy makers will be impacted.
    - Fossil fuel/oil-based countries and economies are likely to face crisis – the silver lining being, terror funding will considerably reduce.
    - Cash-rich automotive lubricant companies will discover there there is nothing much to lubricate.
- UBS research in 2017 indicates that "new technology is being developed that would make remotely flying an aircraft feasible in the near future." The questions that arise on commercializing this technology are feasibility, safety, cyber-attacks, terrorists on board and regulatory and compliance issues.
- The word "machine learning" was coined by Arthur Samuel, an American Pioneer in the field of Computer gaming and AI, in 1959 postulated that it might be possible to program computers an ability to learn for themselves with very little human intervention. Essentially, this works on probability, based on data fed, to make decisions, predictions or statements with a degree of certainty.
- Every time a prospective customer visits Amazon, product recommendations pop up either what was searched online or bought the last time or what was bought by others. That is a machine learning algorithm (/s) called "Recommender Systems" working in the backdrop. It learns every user's personal preferences and makes recommendations basis repeated set of activities.
- Another subset and an extension of machine learning that is deep learning and machine learning is a sub-field of artificial intelligence. AlphaGo, often given as an example for deep learning, is actually a combination of ideas from several different fields of AI and machine learning.

- Deep learning is a subset of machine learning where artificial neural networks, algorithms inspired by the human brain, learn from large amounts of data and do tasks that typically require human intelligence.
- Proliferation of AI as a service has fuelled advances in deep learning and helped smaller organizations access to artificial intelligence technology and specifically the AI algorithms required for deep learning without a large initial investment.
- Supervised learning is a learning in which the machine using data is taught or trained using data that is well labelled with some data tagged with correct answer. Supervised learning algorithms are classified into two categories: classification and regression.
- Unsupervised learning is when machine is trained using information that is not classified or labelled, thereby allowing the algorithm to act on that information without guidance. Here the task of machine is to group unsorted information according to similarities, patterns and differences without any prior training of data.
- Unsupervised learning algorithms are classified into two categories, clustering and association.
- Machine learning and deep learning applications are web search engine, photo tagging applications, spam detectors, virtual assistants, translations, vision for driverless vehicles, chatbots and service bots, image colourization, etc.
- Impact of ML & DL is that today, more and more companies are using machine learning to improve their business decisions, increase productivity, deliver faster, respond sooner to the customer and do many more things irrespective of the size of the company—small, medium or super large!
- Technology in sports are LED stumps, Babolat's Play Pure Drive Racquet System in Tennis. These technologies, besides facilitating performance also, significantly improve real time spectator experience.
- Technology has always been the backbone of supply chain (SC) since long and the industry has also been evolving over time with advances in technology. The emergence of e-commerce and e-business, leveraging advances in information technology are examples.
- Technology has aided Rehrig Pacific Company (leading manufacturer of reusable transport packaging system and transportation service provider) in tagging pallets and crates with passive RFID tags for clients like Pepsi to reduce their costs.
- Virtual pooling is one such strategy where companies manage their inventory as if it is in one location even if they are actually in different locations. This allows them to reduce their stock-out risks as well as shipping costs. An example of virtual pooling is Netflix, which offered movie DVDs to customers.
- OYO Rooms, an Indian startup, has employed AI in boosting occupancy rates and adjusting prices.
- The blockchain is a distributed database that records and stores every transaction that occurs.
- Technology, virtual currency and blockchain in 2008, unknown person or group of people invented a decentralized digital currency without a central bank or a central administrator called bitcoin. In the process, they were the first to solve the double-spending problem for digital currency. It was also the first working example of triple-entry accounting.
- With the introduction of triple entry accounting and blockchain, traditional accounts will become obsolete. Blockchains are a way of agreeing on objective reality. It is two parties agreeing on a version of past events. The third entry in the system, entered into the blockchain, is both a receipt and a transaction.
- Every transaction is verifiable (which will allow for an easier audit trail). The blockchain is not maintained internally within one company's server, it is decentralized which reduces security threats. All transactions use the highest level of encryption technology.
- Any automation, by definition will affect portions of almost all jobs to a greater or lesser degree, depending on the type of work they entail. Though automations will impact jobs, it is unlikely to eliminate occupations/jobs entirely in the foreseeable future, at least in India. A McKinsey study (McKinsey Quarterly, July 2016) in USA indicated that technologies available today, could automate 45 percent of the activities for which people are paid to perform and that about 60 percent of all occupations could see 30 percent or more of their activities automated in the next few years.
- Though a salesman's job may seem repetitive and admin and reports part of it can be automated, it is unlikely a salesman will be eliminated. Similarly, the importance of human interaction is clearly evident in two sectors that, so far, have a relatively low

technical potential for automation: Healthcare and Education!

- Given that in India 91 percent is still traditional retailing and 84 percent is non-digital advertising, will traditional media or traditional brick and mortar models be replaced by digital marketing and brick and click model respectively? Unlikely since notwithstanding all the above, recorded history from Ca 1400 AD indicates none of the technological advancements superseded advancement prior to them; on the contrary, they co-existed.
- Though marketing has a high rate of interest with multiple prospects, it is also laden with risks while making managerial decisions, especially to those who skip the basics and begin with digital marketing directly.
- Historically, in India traditional marketing has been successful through offline promotional methods, face to face selling, cold calling, allowing direct connection with a consumer. Traditional practices also mould you with skills required for marketing—how to structure and value a product, how to interact with a consumer and improvise verbal communication skills.
- Digital methods completely deals in a virtual world, lacks physical connect, and every communication and process occurs online. A significant growth in recent years and new skill sets such as analytics, artificial intelligence, machine learning and well paid secured jobs have been some of the benefits of digital marketing.
- An aspiring marketer should look at integrating traditional marketing with digital marketing support. Balancing the right mix of both is one of the best ways to specialize in marketing since in any industry, digital marketing skills are often looked at as an additional skill set.
- There are plenty of career opportunities for an individual planning to opt for marketing, as the field itself is diverse but students and workforce would need to re-skill themselves re-learning current tools and applications.

CLOSING CASE

CASE LET

SPACE TREK BOTIFIED

Since December 2018, various popular channels in India such as Star, Sony, TV 18, Zee have been flashing in their channels that pursuant to TRAI guidelines, the subscription rates as being significantly lowered. These channels also ran TV commercials emphasizing reduction in monthly subscription charges. On January 10, 2019, TRAI in a press release clarified that consumers have full freedom to choose their desired 100 standard definition channels within network capacity free. The desired channels could be in a-la-carte, Free to Air channels, or Pay channels or bouquet of pay channels or any combination thereof and that the choice completely rests with the consumers. However, none of the DTH service providers or cable operators had migrated to the new tariff.

Sachin was a marketing intern in Space Trek, a service provider with presence in multiple locations across Chennai. Considering the growing subscriber base in multiple locations and operational costs, they decided to shift most of the customer query handling online. One office with multiple channels of social media and digital properties helped them to interact and service the customers easily without having to establish offices in every area. Sachin was hired as a social media intern to promote their brand and handle social media properties in line with their ambitious growth plans. The plan worked out and all consumers engaged with Space Trek through social media. The engagement peaked in the beginning or at the end of a month and was low in rest of the days. Space Trek had a weak website and relied heavily on social media. This was one of the reasons why Space Trek's email marketing campaign to reach out to their customers did not yield great results. With inconsistent traffic, Space Trek was contemplating the idea of hiring more social media executives to run the operations. However, due to varying volumes of engagement, hiring more executives proved to be costly. Sachin was given the task to identify the solution for this challenge, for, Space Trek planned to expand their base further in more areas in and out of Chennai.

Around the same time came the press statement of TRAI that consumers' freedom of choosing channels, coupled with channels advertising revised tariff and service providers not migrating to the new tariff regime, raised doubts in the minds of customers on what exactly needs to be done. Sachin suddenly found the company's generic query inbox was inundated with emails and social media notifications. The number of messages was growing exponentially with time.

To cope with additional traffic and queries, Sachin proposed the idea of using bots as a solution to this challenge. Assisted by a developer and using tools from the web, Sachin employed bots in social media networks. He programmed the bots to provide automated customers service, such as answering important questions, providing important content and personalized offers on demand, while inspiring engagement from social media users. The bots were built and deployed along with a website and other social media applications. Soon, the bots were able to take 50% to 80% of all incoming requests. Bots were able to distinguish between informational and transactional requests. Bots developed to understand complicated requests and carefully transfer to the live operators in the respective offices.

The bots recognized the intent and built a dialogue tree to suggest course of action and solve consumer requests. It increased the efficiency in customer service and overall brand perception. Space Trek became a pioneer in this business to use to such technology to reach out to the customer in a field that is highly fragmented with small players. Messenger marketing continually saw over 70% open rates and 50% click through rates compared to the traditional email marketing resulting in better ROI.

Bots were able to handle requests 24/7 round the year resonating with better consumer satisfaction and surpassed the average engagement rate of conventional social media. With cost saving of more than Rs. 80,000/month using bots, Space Trek was ready to move on for further expansion and diversification in its portfolio. With 42% of consumers already using digital assistants worldwide, bots really helped Space Trek to make its mark in the industry.

Case Questions

1. What are the challenges faced by the company that led to the decision of using bots?
2. What were the areas impacted by using bots in marketing automation?

REVIEW QUESTIONS

1. Why has CBSE in India decided to introduce artificial intelligence in the syllabus for classes 8, 9 and 10?
2. What is MarTech? Explain with appropriate examples.
3. Explain AIMLA, its significance and impact with appropriate examples.
4. What are the drivers and accelerators of AI as in ML and DL?
5. Explain some applications of AI,ML and DL.
6. What are supervised and unsupervised learning?
7. Explain your understanding of the impact of technology in sports and supply chain.
8. What are blockchain and cryptocurrency?
9. Would technology in marketing communication replace traditional media?
10. How do you interpret going digital traditionally?

ACTIVITY QUESTIONS

1. Try Alexa or Cortina with a difficult question such as the meaning of "supercalifragilisticexpialidioucious" and explain the learning from the same.
2. Do a Google search and get some real life examples of supervised and unsupervised learning.

KEY TERMS

All India Radio (AIR)
Bitcoin
Blockchain
CBSE
Computational Language Theory
Customer experience (CX)
EDP (Electronic Data Processing)
GE Reports
LIC
MarTech
Natural Language Processing
OTT
Pattern Recognition
POP (Advertising)
RFID
ROI
SaaS (Software as a service)
UBS
WPP

REFERENCES

1. http://businessworld.in/article/Technology-In-Marketing-Communication-Is-It-RIP-For-Traditional-Media-/14-04-2018-146341/.
2. http://johnkoetsier.com.
3. http://techstory.in/demystifying-marketing-technology/.
4. http://www.bloncampus.com/news-wrap/how-technology-is-transforming-sports/article8960295.
5. http://www.businessworld.in/article/Impact-Of-New-Smart-Technologies-On-Supply-Chain-Industry-Boon-Or-Bane-/30-10-2018-163200/.
6. http://www.forbesindia.com/article/great-lakes-institute-of-management/aimla-the-new-mantra-for-technology/50467/1.
7. http://www.forbesindia.com/article/great-lakes-institute-of-management/from-horseless-to-driverless-next-big-opportunity-for-tech/48311/1.
8. http://www.forbesindia.com/article/great-lakes-institute-of-management/triple-entry-accounting-block-chain-are-they-vaccines-for-financial-scams-/49945/1.
9. https://digitallearning.eletsonline.com/2019/01/cbse-to-introduce-ai-as-a-skill-subject-in-classes-8910/.
10. https://techstory.in/?s=ibm+watson.
11. https://www.ben-evans.com/benedictevans/2015/7/27/ways-to-think-about-cars.
12. https://www.daimler.com/innovation/next/a-city-that-drives-autonomously.html.
13. https://www.forbes.com/sites/bernardmarr/2018/10/01/what-is-deep-learning-ai-a-simple-guide-with-8-practical-examples/#5a8972918d4b.
14. https://www.ge.com/reports/ghosts-cockpit-pilotless-flight-takes-off/.
15. https://www.independent.co.uk/travel/news-and-advice/pilotless-plane-remote-controlled-flight-drone-aircraft-2025-aviation-technology-a7884911.html.
16. https://www.mckinsey.com/business-functions/digital-mckinsey/our-insights/where-machines-could-replace-humans-and-where-they-cant-yet.
17. https://www.straitstimes.com/world/united-states/boeing-to-test-self-flying-planes.
18. https://www.theguardian.com/business/2017/aug/07/pilotless-planes-what-you-need-to-know.

INDEX

F

G

H

I

N

O

P